SCIENTIFIC METHOD

SCIENTIFIC
optimizing applied

METHOD
research decisions

RUSSELL L. ACKOFF

Professor and Director

with the collaboration of **SHIV K. GUPTA**

Assistant Professor

and **J. SAYER MINAS**

Assistant Professor

Operations Research Group
Case Institute of Technology

New York and London, **JOHN WILEY & SONS, INC.**

To my parents, Fannie and Jack,
to my wife, Alec,
and to our children, Alan, Karen, and Karla,
who are responsible for whatever method
there is in my madness, and for some
of my madness as well.

PREFACE

One argument that appears at the end of this book is that the various scientific disciplines provide different ways of looking at the same phenomenon. Science itself is a phenomenon that may be looked at in many different ways. In this connection my friend Anatol Rapoport observed, after reading the manuscript of this book, that it is

. . . definitely slanted to the decision maker, the man of affairs, the manipulator of men, machines, and resources. The Epilogue [Chapter 15] puts science into a broader social context, and, of course, it should do so. The "decision maker" (businessman, administrator, even the military man . . .) is after all a human being, and there is no reason why this should not be pointed out to him together with some remarks on what it means to be human. However, the bulk of this book is not written from the point of view of the "humanities." The title does not say this. Therefore the preface should say it in no uncertain terms, namely, that scientific method is treated here from a certain point of view, where the point of departure is a "problem" defined in "what to do" terms. It is also advisable to let the reader know that there are other points of departure. Science emerged not only from technology and administration; it emerged from art and religion as well. There the points of departure were not at all "problems" faced by "decision makers." Even though every intellectual itch can be interpreted as a problem, if definitions are stretched far enough, the motivations of Kepler, Newton, Darwin, Mendel, von Humboldt, Mendeleyev, Helmholtz, and Einstein were for the most part not the *kinds* of motivations which are here taken as points of departure of scientific investigation.

As you point out, the distinction is not so much between "pure science" and "applied science." Pure science can certainly also be harnessed to problem-oriented motivations. If this is done, the distinction becomes only one between echelons in an organized enterprise. There is, however, a deeper psychological distinction which puts science into a dual role, namely, as a branch of the humanities and as an adjunct to technology. The tone, examples, the orientation of the volume are so definitely toward the latter aspect of science that it seems advisable to make an explicit acknowledgment of this slant. The frequently emphasized implications that science is power should be coupled with equally important reminders that science is also wisdom; i.e., avoidance of self-deception rather than a gain of control. I know the two are closely related, but there are also psychological distinctions between the two orientations which deserve bringing out.

I agree so thoroughly with these observations and so admire the way they are stated that I obtained Rapoport's permission to quote them here.

This is essentially a "how to do it" book rather than a "what to do it for" book. Furthermore it is a "how it *ought* to be done" book rather than a "how it is done" book. It is a book on planning or designing the use of science in the pursuit of objectives. It leaves open the questions of what objectives ought to be pursued, what problems should be solved, and what questions should be answered. I recognize, of course, that the progress of science, in particular, and of civilization, in general, may depend more on what questions are asked than on how they are answered. But certainly one cannot minimize the importance of answering questions and solving problems efficiently.

Since the emphasis in this book is on rational planning, little space is devoted to the role of hunch and intuition. This is not meant to imply that this role is minor. To the contrary, it may be the principal distinguishing factor between great scientific inquiry and that which is mediocre or poor. But brilliant and critical insights and hunches cannot be planned. Their role in science is much like that of the wildcat explorer for oil. Although the odds are against him, he occasionally strikes oil and opens for exploration other regions which were previously ignored. Nevertheless, the health and progress of the oil industry depend more on systematic exploration and playing of averages than on the pursuit of the unique long shot. These extraordinary strikes will come no matter what we do; we cannot plan for them but we can expect and exploit them when they come.

In brief, this book is intended to improve the skill of the scientist in the conduct of inquiry. Although the philosophers have worked in this area and have produced some important overall strategies of research, these have seldom been translated into procedures that are usable by the scientist or into a language that can be understood by him. The approach to scientific inquiry here is much more scientific than philosophical. It attempts to turn science in on itself to investigate its own procedures.

Because this type of effort has not been made frequently in the past, this book raises more questions about scientific inquiry than it answers. I have seldom, if ever, been able to find best answers, but I have consistently tried to find better ones than are commonly accepted. My objectives will have been accomplished if I succeed in attracting a few scientists to the study of scientific inquiry in its own right and if a few more find ways of improving their research procedures.

Although this book depends more on analysis than it does on research experience, the examples throughout are drawn from my own experience. This experience has been primarily involved with study of the operations of complex and purposeful man-machine systems. I hope that the reader will be able to find analogous examples from his own experience. Since my research experience has been interdisciplinary in character, I hope that the examples will emphasize the fact that the principles discussed are meant to be applicable in all branches of science.

My debts to others are many. First there are those to my teachers and friends, E. A. Singer, Jr. (now deceased), Thomas A. Cowan, and C. West Churchman, who plowed the ground, planted the seeds, and provided the sun and the water. I can claim only to have provided some of the ground on which they could work.

Secondly, I am very grateful to my collaborators, J. Sayer Minas and Shiv K. Gupta. Let me make it clear that they cannot be held responsible for any of the content or the style of the book. The selection of the material and the writing are mine, but I have so exploited their thoughts, creative and critical, that an acknowledgment in a preface alone would not reflect the extent of their contribution to this work.

Criticism of the manuscript from C. West Churchman, Anatol Rapoport, D. V. Lindley, and Leon Pritzker made it possible for me to reduce the number of errors it contained and to improve the exposition in many places.

I am also indebted to my best teachers, my students, who have struggled through several versions of this book and whose reactions have made many improvements possible. I have used not only their criticisms but also some of their output. In particular, I should like to thank Halim Dogrusoz, Rudolph Reinitz, and Peter C. Fishburn for permission to use their work and ideas. I am similarly indebted to my former colleague, Fred Hanssmann.

I am grateful to Grace White and Betty Keck for their devotion beyond the call of duty in the preparation of this manuscript, and frequently for preparing me for work on it.

I would like to thank the following for permission to use material from their publications: The Macmillan Company; American Association for the Advancement of Science (*Science*); Cambridge University Press; Holt, Rinehart and Winston, Inc.; Methuen and Co., Ltd.; The American Sociological Association (*The American Sociological Review*); George Allen and Unwin Ltd; G. P. Putnam's Sons; Princeton University Press; *The Journal of Philosophy;* Penguin Books Ltd.; The University of North Carolina Press; *Econometrica;* Macmillan and Co., Ltd.; Prentice-Hall, Inc.; Operations Research Society of America (*Operations Research*); The Royal Society of London (*Proceedings of the Royal Society of London*); Dover Publications Inc.; J. B. Lippincott Company; *Psychometrika; Psychological Review;* The RAND Corporation; *American Journal of Psychology;* The Institute of Management Sciences (*Management Science*); and John Wiley & Sons.

Finally, I am particularly grateful to the University of Chicago Press for permission to base part of the chapter on sampling on some of my earlier writing on the same subject which appeared in Chapter IV of *The Design of Social Research* (1953).

RUSSELL L. ACKOFF

Birmingham, England
January, 1962

CONTENTS

xi

1

THE NATURE OF SCIENCE AND METHODOLOGY

THE MEANING OF "SCIENCE"

Since this is a book about science, we should begin by seeking some common agreement as to what science is. The extensive literature addressed to the definition or characterization of science is filled with inconsistent points of view and demonstrates that an adequate definition is not easy to attain. Part of the difficulty arises from the fact that the meaning of science is not fixed, but is dynamic. As science has evolved, so has its meaning. It takes on new meaning and significance with successive ages. This evolution is not to be stopped by the act of defining. Although we cannot expect to attain an ultimate definition of science, it is desirable to reach some common understanding of the concept in order to proceed. For our purposes it is only necessary to agree on a few of its essential characteristics.

First, we shall consider science as a process of inquiry; that is, as a procedure for (a) answering questions, (b) solving problems, and (c) developing more effective procedures for answering questions and solving problems. We will consider the distinction between questions and problems later.

Science is also frequently taken to be a body of knowledge. We shall concentrate, however, on the process which generates this knowledge rather than on the knowledge itself.

Not all inquiry is scientific. There is a large class of nonscientific inquiry, including what we call "common-sense" inquiry. The differ-

1

ence between these types of inquiry is important. This difference must lie either in subject matter or in method, or both. It has been proposed in the past that common-sense (and other kinds of non-scientific) inquiry is concerned with more immediate and practical problems than is science. It has become increasingly clear, however, that science, particularly "applied science," does deal with immediate and pressing problems. On the other hand, philosophic inquiry, for example, is frequently directed toward problems which are neither immediate nor pressing.

Some have argued that common-sense inquiry is qualitatively oriented, whereas scientific inquiry is quantitatively oriented. For example, John Dewey (1938, p. 65) observed:

> The problem of the relation of the domain of common sense to that of science has notoriously taken the form of opposition of the qualitative to the non-qualitative; largely, but not exclusively, the quantitative.

That this distinction breaks down is clear from Herbert Dingle's (1953) observation that the outstanding scientific achievement of the nineteenth century was the theory of evolution. This theory, he notes (p. 6), "has nothing whatever to do with measurement. It is concerned with qualitative changes, and treats them qualitatively." Even if one disagrees with Dingle's characterization of the theory of evolution, the point is not removed: an eminent historian of science is willing to include in science a theory that he considers to be completely qualitative. Furthermore, there are obvious instances of common-sense inquiry which are quantitatively oriented. For example, a motorist who, with the aid of road maps, seeks the shortest route between two cities is engaged in a quantitative common-sense inquiry.

It seems clear that there is a considerable overlap in the questions and problems investigated scientifically and nonscientifically. It is also clear, however, that at the present time there are a considerable number of questions and problems (e.g., ones involving ethics) which cannot be fruitfully investigated by science. This has led some to assert that at least some questions and problems are, by their very nature, incapable of being answered or solved scientifically. Consequently, such expressions as "the limitations of science" are quite common in discussions of science. But as yet the limits of science have not been adequately defined, for there is hardly a type of question or problem to which science successfully addresses itself today that, at some time in the past, someone did not claim was not susceptible to scientific inquiry. We need not concern ourselves with whether or not such a limit exists, since it is clear that, until it is well defined and generally accepted, it cannot be used to distinguish between scientific and nonscientific inquiry.

It is generally recognized that through the use of science (as contrasted with common sense) we are more likely to obtain the correct answers to questions and better solutions to problems. This is to assert *not* that better results are always obtained by science, but that such results are *more likely* to be obtained by its use. This follows from the superiority of the scientific process of inquiry. This superiority of scientific inquiry derives from the fact that it is *controlled*. *A process is controlled to the extent that it is efficiently directed toward the attainment of desired objectives.* Thomas Huxley [in Wiener (1953, p. 130)] made essentially the same observation when he wrote:

> Science is, I believe, nothing but trained and organized common sense, differing from the latter only as a veteran may differ from a raw recruit: and its methods differ from those of common sense only so far as the guardsman's cut and thrust differ from the manner in which a savage wields his club.

Control of research is exercised in various degrees. Perfect control is an ideal which is approximated more and more closely with the advance of science, but it is never attained. Every inquiry has some controlled and some uncontrolled aspects. Consequently, there are many gradations of inquiry rather than the simple dichotomy: scientific and nonscientific.

It should be noted that, even where scientific inquiry can do a "better" job than common-sense inquiry, it is not always to be preferred. If the cost of the inquiry and the value of the outcome are taken into account, there are many situations in which scientific inquiry is not justified. Also there are many situations where an answer or solution is needed very quickly (e.g., in emergencies). Here, less than the best answer, but an adequate one obtained "in time," is to be preferred to one that is better but late. Most of the prosaic decisions that each of us makes daily about such things as the way to get to work, where to eat, and what clothes to wear do not presently justify scientific inquiry. Science not only reaps the benefits of self-consciousness and control, but must also pay the associated cost. It should be realized, however, that much of the common knowledge and common sense that provide the basis on which today's prosaic decisions are based is itself based on the products of yesterday's science.

Control, though necessary, is not sufficient to distinguish between scientific and nonscientific inquiry. Science is also characterized by the goals of self-perpetuation and self-improvement. It is an ongoing institution which pursues an ideal: to increase without limit our knowledge and our ability to answer questions and solve problems. This imposes the requirement on scientific research that it be conducted in such a way as to increase the efficiency of future research. That is, research must be designed to inform and instruct us on how to improve the conduct of research itself. It is for this reason that many reports on scientific research include discussion of how the research ought to have been done in light of the experience gained in having done it the first time. In science, then, every research effort not only has the purpose of answering a question or solving a problem, but also has the aim of testing, evaluating, and improving the research procedures employed.

EXPERIMENTATION AND RESEARCH

Experimentation is sometimes taken to be identical with scientific research. Not all scientific research, however, involves experimentation. Experimentation, as conceived in the nineteenth century, involved the physical manipulation of objects, events, and their properties. Physical manipulation was taken to be identical with control. This is reflected in the writings of F. H. Giddings (1924, p. 55):

> In scientific experimentation we control everything that happens. We determine when it shall occur and where. We arrange circumstances and surroundings, atmospheres and temperatures; possible ways of getting in and possible ways of getting out. We take out something that has been in, or put in something that has been out, and see what happens.

But our enthusiasm for experimentation may blind us to the fact that controlled inquiry can be conducted without physical manipulation. For example, consider astronomy. Although the situation may change in the future, up to now the astronomer has not been able to manipulate physically the objects of his study. Control can also be obtained by the conceptual manipulation of symbolic representations (models) of the phenomena under study. (We shall consider the use of models for this purpose in Chapter 4.)

Though control is not synonymous with physical manipulation, some scientists consider it useful to distinguish between inquiries in which control is obtained in this way (as in a laboratory) and those in which it is not (as in a field survey). They tend to restrict the use of the term *experimentation* to research involving physical manipulation and to employ the term *research* to cover experimentation and any other type of controlled inquiry.

With the development in recent years of the techniques of *designed experimentation* (to be discussed in Chapter 10) it has become clear that physical manipulation is not as necessary for experimentation as it was once thought to be; it can be replaced effectively by techniques of classification and randomization. Nevertheless, some physical manipulation does seem to be involved in most experimentation. It is less likely to be so involved in the future.

SCIENTIFIC TOOLS, TECHNIQUES, AND METHODS

Scientific progress has been two dimensional. First, the range of questions and problems to which science has been applied has been continuously extended. Second, science has continuously increased the efficiency with which inquiry can be conducted. The products of scientific inquiry then are (1) a body of information and knowledge which enables us better to control the environment in which we live, and (2) a body of procedures which enables us better to add to this body of information and knowledge.

Science both informs and instructs. The body of information generated by science and the knowledge of how to use it are two products of science. As already indicated, we will not be concerned here with the body of information and knowledge which it has generated; that is, not with the specific theories, laws, and facts that have been developed in the various physical, life, and behavioral sciences. Instead we will be concerned with the procedures by which science generates this body of knowledge, the process of inquiry.

The procedures which characterize science are generally referred to as *tools, techniques,* and *methods.* The common inclination to use these three terms interchangeably conceals some distinctions which are important to understand in discussing scientific procedures.

By a scientific *tool* we mean a physical or conceptual *instrument* that is used in scientific inquiry. Examples of such tools are mathematical symbols, electronic computers, microscopes, tables of logarithms and random numbers, thermometers, and cyclotrons.

By a scientific *technique* we refer to a way of accomplishing a scientific objective, a scientific *course of action.* Techniques, therefore, are ways of using scientific tools. For example, the various sampling procedures discussed in Chapter 7 are scientific techniques which employ a table of random numbers, a scientific tool. The use of the calculus and graphic analysis are different techniques for finding the minimum or maximum value of a function.

By a scientific *method* we refer to the way techniques are selected in science; that is, to the evaluation of alternative courses of scientific action. Thus, whereas the techniques used by a scientist are results of his *decisions,* the way these decisions are made is the result of his *decision rules.* Methods are rules of choice; techniques are the choices themselves. For example, a procedure for selecting the best of a set of possible sampling designs is a scientific method; and the selection of the most suitable of a set of alternative ways of measuring a property, such as length, hardness, intelligence, or cooperation, involves the use of a method.

The study of scientific methods is frequently referred to as *methodology.* The objective of methodology is the improvement of the procedures and criteria employed in the conduct of scientific research. For this reason, methodology is often referred to as the logic of *science.*

In this book our concern will be primarily with the methods of science rather than with its techniques and tools. First, the various phases of research activity will be identified, phases which are involved either implicitly or explicitly in every research project. Then the methodology of each phase will be considered.

The discussion of methodology is designed to establish the highest possible standards of control in scientific research. It is as important to have methodological standards in science as it is to have standards of measurement. These not only set goals to be sought in scientific performance, but they also provide a basis for adjusting results obtained under less than the best possible conditions. In the measurement of length, for example, no scientist can ever meet all the environmental, instrumental, and operational specifications of the standard of measurement which has been established. But if a scientist knows how the actual environment, instruments, and operations differ from the ideal ones, then—if equipped with adequate theory—he can adjust his results for these deviations. For example, if he cannot measure the length of a metal bar at the specified standard temperature, he can adjust for the effect of temperature by use of the linear coefficient of expansion of that metal. The existence of a standard informs the scientist as to what kind of knowledge is necessary in order to make such adjustments (e.g., the coefficient of expansion). The ability to adjust data to standard conditions makes possible the comparison of results of research conducted under different conditions and the efficient accumulation of the results of scientific research.

As indicated, the role of a methodological standard in science is much like that of a standard of measurement. It performs the following functions:

(1) It provides a basis for determining the extent to which any research is controlled and, hence, scientific. In this way it provides a procedural goal for scientists. The standard at any moment of time represents the best we know at *that* time, not for all time. Standards are themselves subject to continuous modification by what we learn in trying to use them. By making explicit our conception of the best research procedure we facilitate future improvements in both the standard and our efforts to approximate it.

(2) Together with the appropriate theory it provides a basis for adjusting results obtained by use of less than the best known techniques so as better to approximate results that would have been obtained by use of the best known techniques.

(3) It makes explicit the kind of knowledge required to effectively adjust to the standard.

PURE AND APPLIED SCIENCE

The distinction between pure and applied science plays a central role in most contemporary discussions of science. It is generally acknowledged that the distinction is difficult—if not impossible—to make precise. Such a state of affairs is generally a sign that we are trying to treat qualitatively a distinction that is fundamentally quantitative. In other words, it is likely that pure science and applied science represent ranges on a scale and that a point of separation is difficult to specify. What is the nature of this underlying scale?

Pure research is frequently characterized as that which is conducted "for its own sake." For example, according to Norman Campbell (1952, p. 1):

First, science is a body of useful and practical knowledge and a method of obtaining it. It is science of this form which played so large a part in the destruction of war, and, it is claimed, should play an equally large part in the beneficient restoration of peace. . . . In its second form or aspect, science has nothing to do with practical life, and cannot affect it, except in the most indirect manner, for good or for ill. Science of this form is a pure intellectual study . . . its aim is to satisfy the needs of the mind and not those of the body; it appeals to nothing but the disinterested curiosity of mankind.

It should be observed that the results of pure research are published in one form or another, and hence such research is conducted at least for the sake of those to whom the results are disseminated. "For its own sake," then, means "for science's sake." That is, the research is not expected to yield results which are immediately useful outside the domain of science, but they are intended to be useful within this domain.   Hence, an operationally meaningful distinction between pure and applied research depends on the nature of the intended consumers of the research results.   Therefore, pure research is research which does not consider uses of its results outside the domain of science.   It is relatively rare, however, that the results of "pure" research do not eventually become useful outside the domain of science. Whether or not they are applied depends on others.

If one bases the distinction between pure and applied research on the researcher's intention, we are left with the possibility of two research projects which are alike in all respects except for the intentions of the researchers involved, one pure and one applied.   That is, the distinction is based not on a difference in the kind of research conducted, but on a property of the researcher.   Furthermore, since the researcher's interest in application of his results outside the domain of science may vary in intensity and degree, this distinction seems ultimately to be quantitative rather than qualitative.   This would explain in part the fuzziness of the distinction.

Much of what is thought to be pure research at one time eventually is applied to practical problems outside the domain of science.   On the other hand, it is clear that many of the questions to which pure science has addressed itself have been generated out of difficulties encountered in applied research.   For example, in trying to estimate the future demand for a specified commodity it becomes apparent that the cost of an error of any given magnitude depends on the sign (positive or negative) of the error.   Commonly used estimating procedures assume that such cost of error is independent of whether the error is the result of overestimation or underestimation.   Therefore, an inquiry may be started to develop an estimating procedure which can be used effectively where the cost of error depends on both the magnitude and the sign (i.e., direction) of the error.   Although the original inquiry may have been "applied," the search for better estimating procedures would normally be thought of as "pure" research.

A related way of distinguishing between pure and applied research lies in the distinction between trying "to answer a question" and "to solve a problem."   This distinction will receive further attention in Chapter 2.   For the present it is enough to observe that an individual has a problem if he wants something he does not have, has unequally effective alternative ways of trying to get it, and is in doubt as to which alternative is "best." Therefore, in attempting to solve a problem we may engage in research to attain information and instruction in order to decide how best to pursue the objective(s) that define the problem. Put another way, in solving problems we may try to answer questions for the sake of better pursuing a specified set of objectives. If, on the other hand, our concern with a question does not involve use of its answer in pursuit of any specific objective, then we do not have a problem.

When questions, in the sense in which we have just discussed them, are answered by scientific methods, this activity would, then, normally be thought of as pure research. Where problems are solved by scientific research, if any of the objectives involved are nonscientific in character, the research is thought of as applied. This does not mean that all problems fall into the domain of applied research. Methodological problems, for example, belong in the domain of pure science, since the objectives involved are scientific in character.

Having tried to make the distinction between pure and applied research meaningful, it should again be observed that to maintain it is very difficult. This is not as serious as it was once thought to be. To a large extent the distinction was made in order to provide status to scientists who considered themselves "pure" at a time when it was thought that pure scientific problems required a greater knowledge and ability for their solution than did applied problems. This type of scientific snobbery has diminished with the growth of the realization that difficulty in science is not related to applicability of results.

TYPES OF QUESTIONS AND ANSWERS

The types of questions which science can answer, and their answers, can be classified in many ways. Our concern here, however, is with a type of classification which sets the stage for the methodological discussions to follow.

Answers to questions are *statements* whose parts are *expressions*. It is useful to classify statements in terms of their form and scope and the form of the expressions that they contain. The scheme we will use is the following:

(1) Form of statements
  (*a*) Predication—classification
  (*b*) Comparative
  (*c*) Functional

(2) Form of expressions
    (*a*) Qualitative
    (*b*) Quantitative
(3) Scope of statements
    (*a*) Particular
    (*b*) General

Form of Statements

A statement may be represented abstractly by the following form:

$$F(x_1, x_2, \cdots, x_n),$$

where $x_1, x_2, \cdots, x_n$ represent the subjects or nouns of the statement, and F represents the relationship among them that the statement asserts. The subjects are referred to as *arguments*, F is referred to as the *predicate*, and n is the *degree of the predicate*. For $n = 1$ (i.e., a predicate of degree 1), we have the subject-predicate type of statement. For example, the statement

Charles is a male

has the form

$$F(x),$$

where x denotes the subject "Charles," and F denotes the (monadic) predicate "is a male." For $n > 1$, we have a relational sentence. For example,

New York is east of Chicago

has the form

$$F(x_1, x_2),$$

where x_1 and x_2 denote "New York" and "Chicago" and F denotes the predicate "is east of." An example of a statement containing a triadic predicate (i.e., a predicate of degree 3) is

Chicago lies between New York and Denver,

which has the form

$$F(x_1, x_2, x_3).$$

It should be noted that the statement

Charles and Tom are males

may be intended as an abbreviation of

Charles is a male and Tom is a male,

which has the form

$$F(x_1) \ and \ F(x_2)$$

rather than

$$F(x_1, x_2).$$

Predication and classification

As indicated above, a *simple* subject-predicate type of statement is one which has the form $F(x)$; for example,

Charles is a male.

Such a statement attributes a property to an object, event, or state. A *compound* predicational statement combines two or more simple ones. For example,

Charles is a male $[F_1(x)]$

and

Charles is an adult $[F_2(x)]$

can be combined into

Charles is an adult male.

This statement can be represented by $F_1(x)$ and $F_2(x)$. Similarly, the statement

Charles and Tom are adult males

combines two compound predicational statements and can be represented by $F_1(x_1)$, $F_1(x_2)$, $F_2(x_1)$, and $F_2(x)_2$. This symbolism makes explicit the fact that confirmation of the statement requires four attributions.

In order to confirm simple predicational statements, it is necessary to (*a*) identify the subject and (*b*) define the attributed property. Identification involves specifying a set of properties which are sufficient to differentiate the subject from any other possible subjects. Hence, identification involves a compound predicational statement, $[F_1(x), F_2(x), \cdots, F_m(x)]$, where $F_1, F_2, \cdots, F_m$ are sufficient to identify x. We will discuss the form of scientific definitions in detail in Chapter 5.

It will be noted that the statement

Charles is a male

is equivalent to

Charles is a member of the set of males.

That is, every predicational statement *classifies* its subject. Therefore, corresponding to each (monadic) predicate, F, defined over a set, S, there is a subset of S consisting of all those members of S having the predicate F. A simple predicate applied to a set, then, creates two classes. If there are m predicates, 2^m classes can be constructed. (Classification will be discussed in detail in Chapter 6.)

Relations and comparisons

As already indicated, a statement with a predicate of degree greater than 1 is called a *relational statement*. In $F(x_1, x_2)$ a property is attributed to x_1 and x_2 taken collectively. For example, in the statement

Charles is the brother of Horace

"is a brother of," the predicate, cannot be attributed to either subject taken separately, as "are male" can. It will be noted that in this statement we can revise the order of the subjects, Charles (x_1) and Horace (x_2); that is,

$$F(x_1, x_2) \text{ implies } F(x_2, x_1).$$

Where this condition holds for every pair of subjects, the predicate is said to be a *symmetric* relation. Such a relation *does not order* the subjects, but a relation which is not symmetric may; for example,

Charles is younger than Horace.

Here $F(x_1, x_2)$ does not imply $F(x_2, x_1)$. Charles and Horace are said to be an ordered pair.

For a relation to order more than two subjects it must be *transitive*, in addition to not being symmetric. A (dyadic) predicate is said to be transitive if and only if, for any triplet of arguments, x, y, and z, $F(x, y)$ and $F(y, z)$ together imply $F(x, z)$. A *comparative statement* is any statement the principal predicate of which is an ordering relation. For example, the predicate "is less than" defined over the real numbers provides an ordering of the real numbers.

Ordering relations are of two types, quasi and strict, depending upon whether the relation is *reflexive* or *irreflexive*. A (dyadic) relation F defined over a set S is said to be reflexive if and only if $F(x, x)$ is true for every x in S. It is said to be irreflexive if and only if $F(x, x)$ is false for every x in S.

Examples of quasi-ordering relations are "less than or equal to" in the domain of real numbers, "is at least as tall as" in the domain of human beings, and "implies" in the domain of statements. Examples of strict ordering relations are "is less than" in the domain of real numbers, "is the ancestor of" in the domain of human beings, and "is a proper subset of" in the domain of sets.

There are many different types of ordering relations, some of which will be discussed in detail in Chapter 6.

Functions

A particularly important class of relational statements consists of ones involving a *functional* relation. In a statement of the form $F(x_1, x_2 \cdots, x_n)$, where $n > 1$, if when F and all but one of the x's are specified, the value of the remaining x is completely determined, then F is a *strong* functional relation. For example, consider the (dyadic) statement

Gloria is the spouse of Charles,

which can be represented as $F(x_1, x_2)$. Once F is specified as "is the spouse of" and either x_1 or x_2 is specified (Gloria or Charles), then the value of the other is completely determined. This statement may be rewritten as either

$$x_1 = f_1(x_2)$$

or

$$x_2 = f_2(x_1),$$

which are in the usual functional notation.

Consider the triadic predicate F defined over the real numbers such that $F(x_1, x_2, x_3)$ means "x_1 is the sum of x_2 and x_3." Such a predicate yields a function for all its arguments, and we may write

$$x_1 = f_1(x_2, x_3)$$
$$x_2 = f_2(x_1, x_3)$$
$$x_3 = f_3(x_2, x_3).$$

In this case,

$$f_1(x_2, x_3) = x_2 + x_3$$
$$f_2(x_1, x_3) = x_3 - x_1$$
$$f_3(x_1, x_2) = x_2 - x_1.$$

Note the important property of statements involving strong functional relations: if the value of any (independent) argument inside the functional bracket is changed, the value of the (dependent) argument on the left side of the equation must be changed.

Now let us consider a *weak* functional relation; for example, the dyadic predicate "is the father of" in the domain of human beings. $F(x_1, x_2)$ means "x_1 is the father of x_2." For any given value of x_2, there is only one value of x_1 such that $F(x_1, x_2)$ is true. In this case, however, specifying x_1 does not determine x_2, since x_1 may be the father of several persons. In general, a predicate is a weak functional relation for its kth argument if and only if, (*a*) when the values of all arguments except the kth are fixed, precisely one value for the kth argument is determined, and (*b*) a change in an x other than x_k may not necessitate a change in x_k. For example, in the statement

F. D. R. was the father of James Roosevelt

if "F. D. R." is changed, "James Roosevelt" must be also; but, if "James Roosevelt" is changed, "F. D. R." need not be (if one of his other offspring is substituted for James). In the earlier example in which F denotes "is the spouse of," both x_1 and x_2 were *sufficient* to completely determine the other. In this example, x_2 is sufficient (relative to the predicate "was the father of") to determine x_1, but x_1 is not sufficient to determine x_2. However, x_1 is sufficient to specify a class of subjects any one of which substituted for x_2 makes the statement true; therefore, x_1 *bounds* the values of x_2.

When we examine the type of statements yielded by scientific research which take the form

$$x_1 = f(x_2, x_3, \cdots)$$

we observe three different types which are characterized by the property of the function. Consider first the familiar law of freely falling bodies:

$$s = \tfrac{1}{2}gt^2,$$

in which s is the distance traveled, g is the gravitational constant, and t is the time from release. We note that (for nonnegative s, g, and t)

$$s = f_1(g, t), \quad \text{where } f_1(g, t) = \tfrac{1}{2}gt^2$$

$$g = f_2(s, t), \quad \text{where } f_2(s, t) = 2s/t^2$$

$$t = f_3(s, g), \quad \text{where } f_3(s, g) = \sqrt{2s/g}.$$

Clearly, the functional relation involved in this law is *strong*, since the value of each argument is completely determined by the other two.

Now consider a statement of the form

$$x_1 = f(x_2, x_3, \cdots, x_k),$$

where $x_2, x_3, \cdots, x_k$ is a subset of a set of arguments which is sufficient to completely determine the value of x_1. The subset, then, only partially determines (i.e., bounds) the value of x_1. For example, suppose that in fact

$$x_1 = x_2 + x_3,$$

that x_2 and x_3 are independent, and that x_3 can assume three different values: $-1, 0$, and 1. Suppose further that we do not know about x_3 but we do know that the value of x_1 depends on the value of x_2 and something else. Then, from observation we could determine that either

$$(a) \qquad x_1 = x_2 - 1$$

$$(b) \qquad x_1 = x_2$$

or

$$(c) \qquad x_1 = x_2 + 1.$$

Suppose also that the probabilities of observing each were $p(a) = 0.25$, $p(b) = 0.25$, and $p(c) = 0.50$. We could now compute $E(x_1)$, the expected value of x_1:

$$E(x_1) = 0.25(x_2 - 1) + 0.25(x_2) + 0.50(x_2 + 1)$$

$$= 0.25x_2 - 0.25 + 0.25x_2 + 0.50x_2 + 0.50$$

$$= x_2 + 0.25.$$

Now, although the expected value of x_1, $E(x_1)$, is completely determined the value of x_1 is not. We know that a change in x_2 is *not* sufficient to result in a change in x_1, since a change in x_3 may compensate for it. But we do know that knowledge of the value of x_2 is necessary for determining the value of x_1. Then x_2 is not a deterministic cause of x_1, but it is a *probabilistic* cause or *producer* of x_1.

Suppose that we do not know whether the value of x_1 depends on the value of x_2; that is, we know of no necessary connection between x_1 and x_2, but we have observed that x_1 tends to increase as x_2 does. Once again we may express x_1 as a function of x_2, but this is a *pseudo* function, since x_2 is not sufficient for, and we do not know that is necessary for, determining the value of x_1. We cannot say that x_2 is either the cause or the producer of x_1, but we may be able to say that they are *correlated*.

We have noted three types of functions:

(1) Cause-effect (deterministic causality).
(2) Producer-product (probabilistic causality).
(3) Correlation.

Unfortunately, cause-effect has frequently been treated ambiguously in science, and hence the important distinction between cause-effect and producer-product relationships is seldom made. We will consider these relations in detail in Chapter 10, but in the meantime they may be distinguished as follows.

When one phenomenon, X, is said to cause another, Y, several different things may be meant:

(1) X is necessary and sufficient for Y.
(2) X is necessary but not sufficient for Y.
(3) X is not known to be either necessary or sufficient for Y, but they tend to be present or absent together.

The first of these is *deterministic* causality, the second is *probabilistic* or nondeterministic, and the third is *correlation* and may not involve causality at all.

Now let us make the meaning of these three types of function more precise. Let E_1 and E_2 represent the environments of X and Y, respectively. They may or may not be the same. Let the symbol "$\rightarrow$" represent "is always followed by"; and "X in E_1" and "Y in E_2" represent X and Y in their respective environments.

Suppose that a phenomenon of type X in an environment of type E_1 is always followed by a phenomenon of type Y in an environment of type E_2; that is,

$$X \text{ in } E_1 \rightarrow Y \text{ in } E_2.$$

Then X in E_1 is *sufficient* for Y in E_2: whenever X occurs in E_1, Y later occurs in E_2. Consider the role of X, given its environment. Let X' and Y' represent the nonoccurrence of phenomena of type X and Y. If both

$$X \text{ in } E_1 \rightarrow Y \text{ in } E_2$$

and

$$X' \text{ in } E_1 \rightarrow Y' \text{ in } E_2$$

are true, then (given E_1) X is both necessary and sufficient for Y, since Y occurs only if X does, and Y always occurs if X does. Within the environment E_1, X completely determines the occurrence of Y in

E_2 and hence can be said to be the deterministic cause of Y. For example, if we can define an environment, E_1, within which striking a bell, X, is always followed by a ringing of the bell, Y, then in the environment E_1 striking the bell is the deterministic cause of its ringing.

Now suppose that two phenomena, X_1 and X_2, are jointly necessary and sufficient in E_1 for the subsequent occurrence of Y in E_2; that is,

$$X_1 \text{ and } X_2 \text{ in } E_1 \rightarrow Y \text{ in } E_2$$

$$X_1' \text{ and } X_2 \text{ in } E_1 \rightarrow Y' \text{ in } E_2$$

$$X_1 \text{ and } X_2' \text{ in } E_1 \rightarrow Y' \text{ in } E_2.$$

Phenomena of the type X_1 are necessary but not sufficient for Y. If X_1 occurs, Y occurs or not, depending on whether X_2 occurs. Hence, the probability that Y will occur given X_1 in E_1 depends on the probability that X_2 will occur in E_1. Consequently, X_1 (and X_2) are probabilistic (nondeterministic) causes of Y. We will call X_1 and X_2 *producers* of Y, and Y the *product* of X_1 and X_2. If, in addition to the three conditions given above, the following two also hold:

$$X_1 \text{ and } X_2 \text{ in } E_1' \rightarrow Y' \text{ in } E_2$$

$$X_1' \text{ and } X_2' \text{ in } E_1 \rightarrow Y' \text{ in } E_2,$$

then the environment E_1 is also necessary but not sufficient for Y, and it too is a producer (a coproducer) of Y.

In general, anything which is necessary but not sufficient for the subsequent occurrence of another thing is the producer of the second thing. For example, a seed does or does not produce a plant in some plots of ground, depending on whether there is enough sun and water; or a bell in a jar rings if struck, providing enough air is present.

Now suppose that the following conditions hold:

$$X_1 \text{ and } X_2' \text{ in } E_1 \rightarrow Y \text{ in } E_2$$

$$X_1' \text{ and } X_2 \text{ in } E_1 \rightarrow Y \text{ in } E_2$$

$$X_1' \text{ and } X_2' \text{ in } E_1 \rightarrow Y' \text{ in } E_2.$$

Then, given E_1, X_1 and X_2 are separately sufficient for Y, but neither is necessary. Neither X_1 nor X_2 can be said to be the cause of Y, since a cause (deterministic or probabilistic) must be necessary for its effect. In all likelihood, however, in such cases X_1 and X_2 have a common property which is necessary for Y and hence is a cause of it. For example, a person may be allergic to both bread and cake. Either one leads to an allergic reaction. The person may be reacting to the wheat flour which they have in common. The flour, not the bread or cake, produces the reaction. In speaking loosely we may refer to the bread or cake as producing the reaction, but in science such inexactness is to be avoided if possible.

Finally, there is the situation in which X in E_1 may sometimes be followed by Y, and sometimes not. Furthermore, X' in E_1 may sometimes be followed by Y and sometimes not. But suppose that Y is more likely than not to occur when X has preceded it. Then we say that the occurrence of X and Y is positively *correlated*.

Consider, for example, a person who usually brushes his teeth once a day, just before going to sleep at night. Brushing his teeth is neither necessary nor sufficient for his going to sleep and hence is neither the cause nor the producer of his retiring for the night. And yet the two events usually occur together. To take another example, in one large city it was discovered that people who live in neighborhoods in which there is a heavy soot-fall are more likely to get tuberculosis than people who live in neighborhoods with less soot-fall. Yet medical research has shown that soot-fall is neither necessary nor sufficient for the occurrence of tuberculosis. Hence, the values of two variables may tend to change together, and yet the variables may not be causally connected. Such variables are said to be correlated.

The knowledge that two things tend or do not tend to change together can, nevertheless, be very useful. For example, when we see the person in the above illustration brush his teeth at night, we can predict with some assurance that he is about to retire. That is, we can use our knowledge of the value of one variable to predict the value of another.

Correlation analysis enables us to measure the tendency of variables to change or not to change their values together. We shall discuss the technical aspects of such analysis in Chapter 10. But it is important to post a warning here—a warning which shall be posted again, since failure to heed it leads to one of the most prevalent errors in the social sciences. To establish that two things tend to change or occur together is not to establish that they are related directly or even indirectly by a producer-product or cause-effect relationship. We cannot infer production or causation from correlation alone. On the basis of the correlation between soot-fall and tuberculosis mentioned above, one researcher concluded that soot-fall was a producer of tuberculosis. But subsequent research showed that dietary deficiencies are in fact producers of tuberculosis. Further, dietary deficiencies are likely to occur most frequently among low-income groups. Low-income groups are likely to live in low-rent districts. Districts have low rent, among other things, because of heavy soot-fall. Thus soot-fall and tuberculosis are accidentally, not essentially, connected.

Form of Expressions in Statements: Quality and Quantity

Compare the following two statements:

John is heavy

and

John weighs 150 pounds.

Both appear to be simple predicational statements of the form $F(x_1)$, where x_1 denotes "is heavy" in the former and "weighs 150 pounds" in the latter. The obvious difference between these two statements is that the second contains a *number*. What is not so obvious is that, because the second statement contains a number in what appears to be its predicate, it should be represented as a functional statement of the form $F(x_1, x_2)$, where F denotes "is equal to," x_1 denotes "John's weight," and x_2 denotes "150 pounds." This is a *weak* function, since specification of F and x_1 completely determines x_2, but F and x_2 do not determine x_1.

A transformation similar to changing

John weighs 150 pounds

into

John's weight is equal to 150 pounds

cannot be performed on

John is heavy.

We can transform this statement into

John's weight is greater than W *pounds*

or

John's weight is greater than W$_1$ *pounds and less than* W$_2$ *pounds.*

There is, however, no reasonable transformation of "John is heavy" into a statement containing the relationship of strict equality.

Numbers may be used in statements for a variety of purposes:

(*a*) To identify (or name) the subject; for example,

This is cab number 432.

(*b*) To identify the class in which the subject is placed; for example,

He is a registered voter in the Fourteenth Ward.

(*c*) To identify the number of subjects in a class; for example,

There are 5320 voters in the Fourteenth Ward.

(*d*) To identify the rank order of a subject in a class; for example,

The Fourteenth Ward is the third largest in the city.

(*e*) To identify the number of units on a scale which corresponds to the subject's property; for example,

John weighs 150 pounds.

Each of these statements can be put into a weak function form, but only the last is an example of what we normally think of as measurement. We will consider all these types of number assignment in Chapter 6, but here some observations on properties which are treated qualitatively and ones which are measured (i.e., treated quantitatively) are in order.

It is important to observe that qualitative predication may involve quantification. For example, in order to determine the color of an object it may be necessary to measure the wave length of light reflected from it under certain specified conditions.

Any property which can be quantified can also be treated qualitatively. A quality can be thought of as a range along a scale in terms of which the property can be measured. For example, a person can be said to be "tall" if he is over 5 feet 10 inches, "medium" if he is between 5 feet 6 inches and 5 feet 10 inches, and "short" if he is under 5 feet 6 inches.

It is also true that any qualified property is potentially capable of being expressed quantitatively in terms of such a range along a scale. We may never be able to translate all qualities to such measures, but, as science progresses, it converts more and more qualities into equivalent quantitative expressions. But this is not a one-sided development. As science develops more measures, it also requires new kinds of qualitative judgments. For example, height can be measured as a vertical distance; but to do so requires our ability to determine verticality. We can convert verticality into a measure of the angle between a straight line and a radius projected from the earth's center of gravity. This requires our ability to determine straightness, and so on. Quantification at any stage depends on qualification. What is qualified at one stage may be quantified at another, but at any stage some qualitative judgments are required. Consequently, progress in science not only is a function of an increased capacity to quantify efficiently (i.e., to measure) but also depends on an increased capacity to qualify efficiently.

The Scope of Statements: The Particular and the General

One statement can be said to be more general than another if it *implies* and *is not implied by* the other; that is, if the truth of the second necessarily follows from the truth of the first and not conversely. Scientific statements are about things under certain conditions. The larger the class of things to which reference is made, and the more inclusive the set of conditions, the more general is the statement. For example, the statement

All X's have the property Y under conditions $(C_1, C_2, \cdots, C_n)$

is more general than the statement

This X has the property Y under conditions $(C_1, C_2, \cdots, C_n)$.

Each statement can also be further generalized by enlarging the range of environments in which it holds.

The less general a statement, the more *fact-like* it is; the more general a statement, the more *law-like* it is. Hence, facts and laws represent ranges along the scale of generality. There is no well-defined point of separation between these ranges.

General statements are of two types. The first type refers to a class of events or conditions each instance of which has been observed. The second type refers to classes of things and/or conditions some of which have not been observed and all of which can never have been observed. If, for example, we observe that each of four pots of water boils at 100° C and make a statement to this effect, then this statement is of the first type. If we infer from these observations that the boiling point of water at standard atmospheric pressure is 100° C, we have made a statement of the second type. The term *law* is normally restricted to general inferential statements of the second type which in addition assert a causal (deterministic or probabilistic) relationship.

A *theory* is a still further generalization.   Wolf (1928, pp. 126–127) pointed this out as follows:

. . . Newton's theory of gravitation (especially in its original causal sense) is an explanation of Kepler's three laws and of Galilei's Law of Falling Bodies; the Kinetic Theory of Gases is an explanation of Boyle's, Avogadro's, and Gay-Lussac's Laws (and of the separate laws which they summarize); and the Undulatory Theory of Light explains Snell's Law of Refraction (and the laws of which this is a summary) by reducing the bending of a ray of light, as it passes from one medium to another of different density, to differences in the velocities of light in the two media.

There is a tendency to distinguish such a more comprehensive law from the less comprehensive laws, which it explains, by calling it a *Theory*.

Perhaps the relationship between theory, law, and fact is best grasped in the context of a deductive system.   In a deductive system there are (1) a set of undefined and defined concepts, (2) a set of assumptions (axioms and postulates, or formation and transformation rules), (3) a set of deduced theorems, and (4) instances of the theorems.   The assumptions constitute the theory, the theorems constitute laws, and the instances of the theorems are the facts.   In the construction of scientific theories the objective is to construct just such a deductive system.

A theory, however, is more than a generalization from which laws can be deduced because, as Campbell (1952, pp. 82–83) observed,

. . . there are an indefinite number of "theories" from which the laws could be deduced; it is a mere logical exercise to find one set of propositions from which another set will follow. . . . For instance, that the two propositions (1) that the pressure of gas increases as the temperature increases (2) that it increases as the volume decreases, can be deduced from a single proposition that the pressure increases with increase of temperature and decrease of volume.   But of course the single proposition does not explain the two others; it merely states them in other words.

A theory must, according to Campbell (1952, p. 89), satisfy two additional conditions:

. . . it must explain those laws in the sense of introducing ideas which are more familiar or, in some other way, more acceptable than those of the laws; [and] it must predict new laws and these laws must turn out to be true.

In the assertion of three levels of generality in facts, laws, and theories it is frequently implied that because of differences in generality facts are simplest to confirm, laws more difficult, and theories most difficult.   Now this is true in one sense: in the sense that at present the methodology of confirming facts is much more highly developed than is the corresponding methodology for dealing with laws and theories. For example, Churchman (1961, pp. 76–77) observes that

> There are an infinite number of hypotheses contained in . . . [a] theory. Which ones should be tested?
>
> One might appeal to common sense and assert that the tests should be "spread out" equitably over the interval.

But what do "equitably" and "the interval" mean? Churchman (1961, p. 77) points out that this is not easy to answer.

> In practice, we need a theory of theory-testing . . . most scientists recognize that the mere accumulation of measurements that "confirm" a theory do not add to one's confidence in the theory, for they may merely over-test one or more hypotheses, and under-test the rest. Thus, on a vague level, one feels that a theory ought to be tested under "widely different" circumstances, but this prescription is difficult to define.

There is another sense in which theories are held to be more difficult to confirm than facts. It is maintained by some that the confirmation of facts does not require use of theory but that confirmation of theories does entail confirmation of fact. This is not true. For example, Churchman (1961, p. 81) notes:

> . . . the practice of science shows that such a proposition [statement] as "An observed object X weighs k pounds" or "An observed object X is blue" are, methodologically interpreted, elliptical for "If X is observed under any of the conditions C_i belonging to the class of conditions C, by any observer O_j belonging to the class of observers O, the recorded observations will all belong to a class of propositions P." The confirmation of this proposition belongs to the last type—the theories. By a similar argument, all other propositions of science are—methodologically interpreted—theories.

In Chapters 5 through 10 we will explore what is involved in "proving" or "finding" facts. It will be clear in this discussion that the concept of confirmation of even "simple" facts by direct and immediate observation is a methodological myth inherited from the past.

It is maintained by some that, although laws and theories are more difficult to confirm than facts, they are less difficult—or at least no more difficult—to disconfirm than facts. In principle, a law or theory can be disconfirmed by just one contradictory fact. But in practice the fact which appears to contradict the law or theory is itself always subject to doubt. Consequently, there have been many historical instances where facts which appear to contradict laws or theories have been rejected in order to maintain a law or theory in which the scientist had more confidence than he did in the fact. Furthermore, as Churchman (1961) and many before him have shown, the confirmation of a fact itself presupposes a theory and hence the validity of a fact always depends on the validation of the assumed theory. For example, it was once assumed (and still is by some) that, if facts and theory do not agree, then the theory must be false. As the history of science shows, however, the scientist is just as likely (if not more so) to question the validity of the facts as he is to question the validity of the theory.

TYPES OF PROBLEMS

Research that is directed toward the solution of problems can also be divided into two major classes: *evaluative* and *developmental*. An evaluative problem is one in which the alternative courses of action are completely specified in advance and the solution consists of selecting the "best" of these. A developmental problem involves the search for (and perhaps construction or synthesis of) instruments which yield a course of action that is better than any available at the time. For example, the selection of the best of two or more existings drugs for curing a specified ailment is an evaluative problem. Developing a better drug than any available is a developmental problem. In discussing the phases of research we shall consider each of the types of research that have been identified and explore their methodological differences and similarities. But the basis of these comparisons will be laid throughout by a detailed consideration of evaluative problem solving because here, as we shall try to show, we are presently capable of attaining our highest degree of methodological self-consciousness and sophistication.

As we shall see in some detail, applied research has the advantage of being able to formulate criteria of its own efficiency in terms of the objectives for which the problem is being investigated. Because of its lack of specific objectives, pure research cannot formulate such criteria as explicitly. Consequently, pure research makes many implicit assumptions about the conditions under which its results will be applied. In applied research these assumptions are frequently found to be unrealistic. To elaborate a previous example, in pure research the seriousness of various errors can seldom be measured. Hence estimates are made in a way that is "best" only if the seriousness of an error is independent of its sign; that is, if the seriousness of an error of $+x$ is equivalent to the seriousness of an error of $-x$. In applied problems, however, there are few cases in which this condition holds. Hence different estimation procedures are required in applied science, and serious questions about the estimating procedure of pure science are raised. (This problem will be discussed in detail in Chapter 8.)

It will be observed, as we go into detailed discussion of scientific method, that in general we have the opportunity of making research-design (methodological) decisions more self consciously in applied science than in pure science. This fact is not generally appreciated; to the contrary, it is commonly believed that pure research tends to be methodologically superior to applied research. Hence the general approach of this book may be contrary to the intuition and beliefs of many.

We shall first discuss the methodological aspects of each phase of research in an applied context, and then consider what we can learn from this presentation that can be used in the pure-research context.

THE PHASES OF RESEARCH

The phases of research have traditionally been identified as

(1) observation,
(2) generalization,
(3) experimentation,

or as some variation of these. For example, D'Abro (1951, p. 3) lists the stages of the scientific method as

(a) the observational stage,
(b) the experimental stage,
(c) the theoretical and mathematical stage (in physics).

He then comments (p. 3) on their sequence as follows:

The order in which these stages have been listed is the order in which they arise in the study of any group of physical phenomena. It is also the chronological order in which they were discovered.

One could take issue with the assertion concerning chronology, for example, on the grounds that atomic theory was apparently formulated in qualitative form by Democritus without his engaging in either of the first two stages. This issue, however, is not as important as the one arising from the implication that the order of the steps is fixed. The position we shall take here is that all stages may and usually do go on simultaneously. Some previous or new theory may suggest and direct new observations. The empirical tradition asserts the primacy of observation in science, but more sophisticated philosophical analysis has shown that observation always presupposes a criterion of relevance, and this criterion, in turn, always involves some theory. This is not to assert the primacy of theory. To the contrary, some modern philosophies of science, such as pragmatism and experimentalism, assert the "cyclic" and interdependent characteristic of these stages of scientific method.*

The various three-stage breakdowns of the research process have been made primarily by scientists preoccupied with pure research. From the point of view of applied research a finer breakdown is necessary. There are almost as many listings of applied-research phases as there are persons who have tried to provide such a classification. Since most such listings are essentially equivalent, it does not make much difference which one is used as long as its meaning is made clear. Here we shall discuss research in six phases:

(1) Formulating the problem.
(2) Constructing the model.
(3) Testing the model.
(4) Deriving a solution from the model.
(5) Testing and controlling the solution.
(6) Implementing the solution.

This book is organized around a discussion of each of these phases of research. These phases are not discrete stages each of which is completed before the next is begun. In general all phases go on simultaneously and are completed together. They frequently are begun, however, in the order in which they are listed.

The research process is usually cyclic. For example, if, when testing a model, it is found to be deficient, the formulation of the problem and the model may be re-examined and modified. This leads to new testing and, in some cases, to further revision in the formulation of the problem and the model.

It will be observed that formulating the (applied-research) problem has much in common with the "observational" phase of pure research; "generalization" with "model construction" and "derivation of the solution," and "experimentation" with "testing the model and solution." The control phase of applied research corresponds with efforts to further generalize the results of pure research, and implementation corresponds with efforts to use the results of one piece of pure

---

* For detailed discussion of the primacy of observation or theory see Churchman (1961), Churchman and Ackoff (1950), Dewey (1929 and 1938), and Singer (1959).

research in another. As indicated, these similarities and differences will be explored in some detail.

THE PHILOSOPHY OF SCIENCE

Before about a century ago most of what we today call science was called *natural philosophy*. Philosophic inquiry and scientific inquiry were not differentiated from each other, at least popularly, until about the middle of the nineteenth century. In the days when all scientists were philosophers and most philosophers were scientists a great deal of attention was given to the way in which knowledge was acquired. Inquiry into this procedure—which was more philosophically than scientifically oriented—was alternately called *epistemology* and the *theory of knowledge*.

With the separation of science from philosophy there came an increased awareness of the superiority of the methods and techniques of science for acquiring knowledge. Consequently, those who were concerned with the theory of knowledge turned more and more to the analysis of scientific method. Since this inquiry was itself largely speculative in character, it remained philosophic and came to be known as the *philosophy of science*.* Scientists as well as philosophers engage in the philosophy of science, which is one of the few remaining grounds on which they meet. But even this ground has been shrinking as the study of scientific method itself has become less and less speculative and more and more scientific. Today the breach between the philosophy of science and the science of methodology is wide enough to make it difficult for all but a few to straddle.

This breach is unfortunate. Although most contemporary professional philosophers have little knowledge of present-day science, they do know the history of epistemology and the theory of knowledge and are interested in methodological problems. Scientists, on the other hand, generally know little of this history and are inclined to take

---

* Although the study of scientific method has been a major part of the philosophy of science, it has by no means been the only part. This branch of philosophy has had at least three other types of interest in science:

(1) Conceptual analysis: the attempt to define concepts or problem areas in such a way as to make them susceptible to scientific study.

(2) Examination of assumptions concerning the nature of reality which "underlie" science.

(3) Synthesis: the attempt to fuse the findings of the various branches of sciences into one consistent view of reality, a *Weltanschauung*.

for granted their own methods of acquiring knowledge. As a consequence, methodology has developed slowly, and the practices of scientists often fail to incorporate the results that earlier methodological inquiries have produced.*

CONCLUSION

Methodology can be considered to be a special type of problem solving, one in which the problems to be solved are research problems. We will see later that any problem situation, and hence research-problem situations, can be represented by the following equation:

$$V = f(X_i, Y_j),$$

where V = the measure of performance or accomplishment that we seek to maximize or minimize.

X_i = the aspects of the situation we can control; the "decision" or "choice" or "control" variables.

Y_j = the aspects of the situation (environment of the problem) over which we have no control.

Then solving a problem consists of finding those values of the *decision* variables, X_i [expressed as a function, $g(Y_j)$], which maximize (or minimize) V. Theoretically it is possible to formulate *problems in research design* in this way and to find "optimizing" solutions. The attainment of such optima is the objective of methodology. At the present time we can formulate only a few research problems in this way, but this achievement is the product of just a few years of such study of research procedures. Even where we cannot find such optima, however, we can learn a great deal about the relative effectiveness of different research procedures by attempting to formulate them in this way. Such an effort is the most efficient way we have of precisely defining problems in methodology and of directing scientific research to their solution.

This book will raise many more questions than it will answer. In methodology, as in the rest of science, the solution of one problem raises several new ones. But, in general, progress in methodology and science is as much a matter of moving from question to question as it is of moving from answer to answer.

---

* There have been many studies of the development of epistemology and philosophy of science. See, for example, Churchman and Ackoff (1950).

BIBLIOGRAPHY

Campbell, N. R., *What Is Science?* New York: Dover Publications, 1952.

———, *Foundations of Science.* New York: Dover Publications, 1957.

Churchman, C. W., *Theory of Experimental Inference.* New York: The Macmillan Co., 1948.

———, *Prediction and Optimal Decision.* Englewood Cliffs, N. J.: Prentice-Hall, 1961.

———, and R. L. Ackoff, *Methods of Inquiry.* St. Louis: Educational Publishers, 1950.

Columbia Associates, *An Introduction to Reflective Thinking.* Boston: Houghton Mifflin Co., 1923.

D'Abro, A., *The Rise of the New Physics.* New York: Dover Publications, 1951.

Dewey, John, *The Quest for Certainty.* New York: Minton, Balch and Co., 1929.

———, *Logic: The Theory of Inquiry.* New York: Henry Holt and Co., 1938.

Dingle, Herbert, *The Scientific Adventure.* New York: Philosophical Library, 1953.

Freeman, Paul, *The Principles of Scientific Research.* London: MacDonald and Co., 1949.

Giddings, F. H., *The Scientific Study of Human Society.* Chapel Hill: University of North Carolina Press, 1924.

Huxley, Thomas H., "Educational Value of Natural History Sciences," in Wiener (1953).

Ritchie, A. D., *Scientific Method.* New York: Harcourt, Brace, and Co., 1923.

Russell, Bertrand, *The Scientific Outlook.* Glencoe, Ill.: Free Press, 1951.

Singer, E. A., Jr., *Experience and Reflection.* Philadelphia: University of Pennsylvania Press, 1959.

Westaway, F. W., *Scientific Method.* New York: Hillman-Curl, 1937.

Wiener, P. P. (ed.), *Readings in Philosophy of Science.* New York: Chas. Scribner's Sons, 1953.

Wilson, E. B., Jr., *An Introduction to Scientific Research.* New York: McGraw-Hill Book Co., 1952.

Wolf, A., *Essentials of Scientific Method.* London: George Allen and Unwin, 1928.

2

THE MEANING OF
"OPTIMAL SOLUTIONS
TO PROBLEMS"

THE NATURE OF PROBLEMS

The minimal necessary and sufficient conditions for the existence of a problem are as follows:

(1) An *individual* who has the problem: the *decision maker*.

(2) An *outcome* that is desired by the decision maker (i.e., an objective). Without the desire to obtain an as-yet-unattained outcome there can be no problem. Therefore, in the state of Nirvana—in which all desire is supposed to be suspended—there can be no problem. An objective, then, is an outcome which has positive value for the decision maker. Every problem situation must involve at least two possible outcomes (O and not-O), but only one outcome may have a positive value.

(3) At least *two unequally efficient courses of action* which have some chance of yielding the desired objective. There must be a "real" difference between the choices available to the decision maker. If he has a choice between equally efficient or completely inefficient alternatives, he may think he has a problem, but the problem has only subjective (not objective) reality.

(4) A *state of doubt* in the decision maker as to which choice is "best." There must be a question in the mind of the decision maker as to which choice to make.

(5) An *environment* or *context* of the problem. The environment

30

consists of all factors which can effect the outcome and which are not under the decision maker's control.

Problems, of course, may be considerably more complex than the minimal one described. Complications may result from such conditions as the following:

(a) A group of individuals, rather than one, must make the decision.

(b) The decision maker(s) make the decision but others carry it out. Such is the case when managers of industrial, military, or governmental activities make policies or plans which others must follow.

(c) The decision may have an effect on others who may react to it in such a way as to affect its efficiency. Reactions which decrease the efficiency of the original action are called *counteractions*. Those in conflict or competition, for example, tend to counteract each other's action.

(d) More than one objective may be involved in a problem, and the objectives may not be consistent. For example, a person may want "to save money" and still "have a good time" in circumstances where fun is not to be had without spending. Furthermore, the objectives may change with time.

(e) The number of possible courses of action may be very large; in fact, infinite.

To *solve* a problem, whether simple or complex, is to make the *best* choice from among the available courses of action.

In order to maximize our chances of attaining or approximating the best or optimal solution to a problem, it is apparent that we must understand what the "best" or "optimal" solution to a problem is. In determining what such a solution is we are concerned with the choices a decision maker *should* make, not necessarily with those he normally makes.

It is not at all obvious what is meant by the "best" solution to a problem. A final definition of "best" in this context has not yet been attained, and it is not likely that it ever will be. With the development of *decision theory* in the last decade this conceptual problem has received more attention than ever before. Decision theory is both descriptive and normative. No attempt will be made here to survey descriptive decision theory.*

* The most intensive survey of normative decision theory is that provided by Churchman (1961). A detailed treatment is also provided by Edwards (1954), Luce and Raiffa (1957), Gore and Silander (1959), Chernoff and Moses (1959), and Miller and Starr (1960).

The analysis of criteria of "best" choice on which we are about to embark is divided into three parts that are based on the distinctions described by Luce and Raiffa (1957, p. 13) as follows:

The field of decision making is commonly partitioned according to whether . . . it is effected under conditions of (*a*) certainty, (*b*) risk, or (*c*) uncertainty. . . .*

(*a*) *Certainty* if each action is known to lead invariably to a specific outcome. . . .

(*b*) *Risk* if each action leads to one of a set of possible outcomes, each outcome occurring with a known probability. These probabilities are assumed to be known to the decision maker. . . .

(*c*) *Uncertainty* if either action or both has as its consequence a set of possible specific outcomes, but where the probabilities of these outcomes are completely unknown or are not even meaningful.

In problems arising under risk conditions our analysis will reveal that an optimal decision can be defined as one which *maximizes the mathematical expectation of value or utility.* The meaning of this criterion, however, depends on whether the objectives are defined *qualitatively* or *quantitatively.* We will consider three types of problem situations: those involving (1) only qualitative objectives, (2) only quantitative objectives, and (3) a combination of these. We will also consider the effect of other participants on the decision maker through counteractions and reactions to the decision maker's choice.

In the discussion of uncertainty problem situations we shall determine what adjustments in previously discussed procedures are required.

Before considering the various types of problems it is necessary to clarify the meaning of such expressions as *qualitative* and *quantitative objectives, courses of action,* and *efficiency.*

QUALITATIVE AND QUANTITATIVE OBJECTIVES

A qualitatively defined outcome is one which, following the choice of a course of action, is either obtained or not. There are no "in betweens." That is, the outcome of an effort to obtain such an objective can be only one of two types: successful or unsuccessful. For example, if a person's objective in going to a bookstore is to obtain a

---

* Luce and Raiffa (1957, p. 13) include a fourth type which we will consider in Chapter 9: "a combination of uncertainty and risk in the light of experimental evidence. This is the province of statistical inference. . . ."

certain book, then "obtaining that book" is a qualitative objective, since either he succeeds or not. Or, to take another case, a person who needs $10 to pay a bill may go out "to obtain at least $10." Although this outcome involves a quantity, it is qualitative in the sense used here because the person either succeeds in obtaining at least $10 or he doesn't.

A quantitatively defined outcome is one which is (or is not) obtained in various degrees. That is, the extent to which such an outcome is obtained is potentially measurable. For example, if a person goes out "to borrow as much as possible," the mount of success can be measured by the amount borrowed. Or, if a person tries "to reach a specified destination in the shortest possible time," his success or lack of it is measurable by the amount of time required. It should be observed that a quantitatively defined outcome is really a set of objectives differentiated from each other by values along a specified scale.

Qualitative objectives can, at least in principle, also be described in terms of a scale. For example, "to borrow at least $10" can be specified by the *range* of the scale of dollars from 10 up. Failure to obtain this objective can be defined as obtaining less than $10. Dollars are treated qualitatively if there are two or more ranges on the dollar scale within which the borrower places an equal value on all quantities: if, for example, he places an equal value on "$10, $11, . . . , $20," then he treats "to obtain from $10 to $20" as a qualitative objective. On the other hand, if he places a different value on each point of the scale measuring the objective, he treats the objective quantitatively. Thus the significance of the distinction between qualitative and quantitative outcomes lies in the measurement of efficiency of the courses of action relative to such outcomes.

COURSES OF ACTION

A course of action is not to be construed as a mechanistically specified pattern of behavior. Variations in the action with respect to certain physical characteristics may not change the course of action. For example, "driving a car" may be designated as a course of action. There are many different ways of driving a car, but it is frequently useful to group these into one class of behavior. Despite the variations within the class, it can be distinguished from such other classes as "taking a bus." A course of action may be specified with varying degrees of rigidity, depending on the purposes of the research. For one purpose it may be desirable, for example, to distinguish between left-hand and right-hand driving. For another purpose it may be desirable to group uses of any self-powered vehicle into one course of action.

This flexibility of defining (or, more precisely, of individuation) also applies to physical objects. For one purpose an automobile may be considered as *one* physical object; for another it is a composite of many other units (e.g., wheels and transmission); and for still another it may be considered to be a part of a unit (e.g., a fleet of cars).

Notice the relativity of *courses of action* and *outcomes*. These are conceptual constructs which can be converted into each other, depending on the interests of the researcher. For example, "sawing a tree" may be considered as a course of action which yields the "falling of a tree" as an outcome. But "felling a tree" may be considered as a course of action which can yield the outcome "clearing a path." Such relativity of concepts is common in all areas investigated by science and hence does not present any unique methodological problem in this context.

There are situations in which the decision maker does not directly select a course of action. Rather he selects a procedure or rule which permits the selection of a course of action in a specific context. This procedure or rule specifies how the course of action to be taken should be derived from information available at the time action must be taken, though this information is not available at the time at which the decision rule is selected. Such a procedure or rule is called a *strategy* and is itself a type of course of action. For this reason we will use the terms *course of action* and *choice* to apply to both simple-choice and strategic-choice situations.

MEASURES OF EFFICIENCY

There are several types of measure of efficiency, the definitions of which require the concepts of *input* and *output*. *Input* refers to the resources which are consumed or expended in taking a course of action. A resource is anything of value; for example, men, money, material, time, or some combination of these. Thus, input refers to the "cost" of a course of action, where cost is used in a very general sense which is not restricted to monetary considerations.

Output may be measured in terms of either the resources which result from taking the course of action or the psychological or sociological characteristics of the resulting state. For example we may talk about the money earned, the material produced, the time saved, or the amount of enjoyment which results from a course of action. Thus, output refers to the "return" or "pay-off" resulting from a course of action.

Outcomes—and hence objectives (i.e., desired outcomes)—may be defined in terms of either inputs or outputs, or both. For example, "to reduce production costs" is an input objective, whereas "to increase the amount produced" is an output objective. In the objective "to increase profit," the *difference* between input and output is critical.

The type of measure of efficiency required depends on whether the amounts of input and/or output are specified in the definition of the relevant outcome. The four possibilities are as follows:

(1) *Specified (or irrelevant) outputs and inputs.* Here the measure of efficiency is simply the probability that the outcome will occur. For example, such an outcome would be "winning this game of chess." This is a qualitative outcome, since it is either obtained or not. Inputs (e.g., time and effort) are not relevant. Therefore the efficiencies of alternative plays or strategies are measurable in terms of "probability of success."

(2) *Specified outputs and variable inputs.* Here alternative courses of action are evaluated with respect to the inputs required to obtain a specified output. For example, if there are two different processes for producing an item, that process which requires least time or cost, or some combination of these, could be considered to be the most efficient. Or the track man who runs a mile (specified output) in the least time (variable input) wins the race and is the most efficient.

(3) *Variable outputs and specified inputs.* Here alternative courses of action with specified fixed inputs are evaluated relative to the amount of output they yield. For example, the production process which yields the most product per unit of cost or time is the most efficient. Or the automobile which, starting from a stationary position, covers the greatest distance in a specified time can be considered to be the most efficient.

(4) *Variable inputs and outputs.* Here neither input nor output is specified, and their difference or ratio is used as a measure of efficiency. The course of action which yields the greatest difference between output and input can be considered to be the most efficient. As already indicated, profit is measured by such a difference. Return on investment, on the other hand, is a ratio of output to input.

The discussion of efficiency could end here were it not for the fact that in most problem environments a course of action will yield dif-

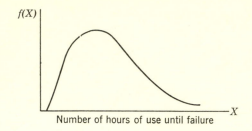

Number of hours of use until failure   FIGURE 2.1.   An efficiency function.

ferent inputs and/or outputs on different trials. For example, a production process does not maintain a constant output per unit of input, or a runner does not always complete a mile in the same time. Inputs and outputs vary, and this variation must be taken into account. In any particular case, if we determine the relative frequency with which the relevant inputs and/or outputs occur, we can formulate a probability-density function of these outcomes which we shall call an *efficiency function*.

For example, a table which shows the percentage of light bulbs that can be expected to fail after various numbers of hours of usage— a so-called "life table"—can be converted into an efficiency function. When plotted graphically, such a function might appear as shown in Figure 2.1. In this function, the area under the curve is set equal to 1 so that the area between any two ordinates represents the probability of failure in the interval represented by the distance between the ordinates. As we shall see, efficiency functions are required to define optimal solutions in risk problem situations involving quantitative outcomes.

RISK PROBLEM SITUATIONS

Qualitative Objectives Only

The simplest type of problem situation is one involving only two possible outcomes, both qualitatively defined, and two courses of action. Let O_1 and O_2 represent the outcomes, C_1 and C_2 the courses of action, and P_{ij} the probability that C_i will produce O_j. An illustrative situation of this type is shown in Table 2.1, which is called an *efficiency matrix*.

Which of the two courses of action shown is the better? On reflection it becomes clear that this question cannot be answered unless we know which of the outcomes is desired. That is, it is necessary to know the *relative values* of these outcomes to the decision maker. If he desires O_1 and not O_2, C_1 is the better action. On the other hand, if O_2 is his objective, C_2 is the better choice.

As much as scientists might like to avoid the necessity of having to deal with measures of even "relative" value, they have no alternative in dealing with problem situations. It should be noted, however, that although relative values must be assigned to the outcomes these are not the scientist's values unless the problem he is trying to solve is his own. The values involved are those of the decision maker. Since, to the scientist, an acceptable solution to the decision maker's problem must be consistent with science's objectives, the scientist's values are involved indirectly. But we do not want to confuse the decision maker's choice of a solution to his problem and the scientist's choice of a decision maker's problem on which to conduct research.

Recognition of the necessity for determining the relative importance of outcomes to decision makers has, in recent years, given rise to a new area of scientific inquiry, *value theory*. In the next chapter we shall consider some of the problems and techniques which have been developed in this area. For the time being, however, we will assume that we have a way of measuring the relative values of the outcomes. These we shall represent by V_j.

In the particular example shown in Table 2.1, let $V_1 = 0.7$ and $V_2 = 0.3$. Then we can compute the sum of the "weighted" efficiencies of each course of action:

$$\sum_{j=1}^{n} P_{ij}V_j,$$

TABLE 2.1.   AN ILLUSTRATIVE EFFICIENCY MATRIX *

Outcomes

		O_1	O_2
Courses of Action	C_1	$P_{11} = 0.6$	$P_{12} = 0.4$
	C_2	$P_{21} = 0.2$	$P_{22} = 0.8$

* If the two outcomes are exhaustive and exclusive, then the sum of the probabilities in each row must equal 1.0, otherwise not. In any case, the sum of the probabilities in a column need not equal 1.0.

where P_{ij} is the probability that the ith course of action will yield the jth outcome, and V_j is the relative value * of that outcome. For C_1:

$$\sum_{j=1}^{2} P_{1j}V_j = 0.6(0.7) + 0.4(0.3) = 0.54.$$

For C_2:

$$\sum_{j=1}^{2} P_{2j}V_j = 0.2(0.7) + 0.8(0.3) = 0.38.$$

The sum of the weighted efficiencies of a course of action is the *expected* (*relative*) *value* associated with that course of action. It seems reasonable to use "maximum expected value" as the criterion of "best" decision. (Then C_1 would be the one to choose in the illustrative problem.) But why should this criterion be used?

Justification for maximizing expected value

The principal argument which has been used to defend the criterion of maximization of expected value is based on its apparent "reasonableness." It seems obvious to many that this *ought* to be the criterion employed by rational beings. In fact, use of this criterion is often cited as a necessary (if not sufficient) condition for rational choice. Despite the widespread acceptance by decision theorists of the superiority of this criterion, science is ultimately obliged to find less intuitive grounds on which to support its selection of a criterion of choice, whatever that criterion may be. Purely intuitive or rational grounds for selecting such a criterion † are ultimately doomed in science. Such grounds must eventually have empirical as well as rational content.

At present we can only suggest how these grounds might eventually be found. In order to develop such a suggestion let us first consider briefly the related question of how science might find grounds to support the "ought" in an assertion such as "X ought to do A in this environment." Churchman (1961) has made the most exhaustive analysis to date of how science might establish grounds for asserting this "ought." In essence, his argument is as follows.

In establishing an assertion of the form "X is k units" science must resort to a set of idealized conditions and operations called a *standard*. (In Chapter 6 we will discuss such standards in detail.) The

---

* We shall use the term *value* to mean "relative value," which is a measure of value assigned to an outcome that depends on the specific alternative outcomes that can occur in a particular context.

† For example, see Chernoff (1954).

assertion "X is k units," then, is equivalent to the assertion, "X would exhibit such-and-such properties and behavior under standard conditions." Churchman (1961, pp. 17–18) then reasons:

> Suppose we could agree on the standard conditions for measuring the values of outcomes. Then we would say that "X values an outcome to degree k" means "X would exhibit such-and-such behavior in the standard environment for value measurements." The present suggestion is to assert that the "ought" in a recommendation can be stated as follows: "X ought to do A in *this* environment" means "X would do A in the standard environment that defines value measurements."
>
> . . . If a scientist states that an executive should follow a certain course of action, he says in effect, "I have measured the values of the executive— or his organization—for the various outcomes that may result from his decisions. These measurements predict what he would do if he were making his decision under the standard condition of value measurements. When I say he ought to exhibit such-and-such behavior, I mean that this is the behavior he would exhibit if these standard conditions held. Of course he may not do what he ought to do; that is, the standard conditions may not hold in this environment." *

Just as science must develop standard conditions for the measurement of value, so must it eventually develop standard conditions for the determination of what criterion of choice a person employs. Once such conditions exist and we can use them experimentally, we can then translate "A decision maker, X, ought to use criterion C in this environment" into "X would use criterion C in the standard conditions that define criterion preference."

The extensive experimentation directed toward determining how people actually do make decisions has, in general, failed either to define or to observe choice under explicitly specified standard conditions. As a consequence, the observations which have been made have many alternative interpretations, and little can be inferred about a general criterion of choice.

At this stage we can only suggest a standard situation that might eventually be used to determine what criteria of choice a person actually uses. Consider a situation in which there are m courses of action available ($C_1, C_2, \cdots, C_i, \cdots, C_m$), only one of which can be selected at a time. Let there be n possible outcomes ($O_1, O_2, \cdots, O_j, \cdots, O_n$), which exhaust the possible consequence of a choice. Let P_{ij}, the probability that the ith course of action will produce the jth outcome, be

---

* In Chapter V of his book Churchman attempts to define these standard conditions. For an earlier effort to establish such a standard see Churchman and Ackoff (1947).

known perfectly by the decision maker. Further, the decision maker must be completely aware of the relative values, V_j, of the possible outcomes. He must have no preference among the alternative courses of action for their own sake. Now there must be an explicitly formulated list of criteria of choice ($CC_1, CC_2, \cdots, CC_m$) such that each course of action is best by one and only one criterion, and for every criterion there is only one best choice (i.e., the C_i and CC_i are uniquely paired). Then the probability that the decision maker will select C_i would be a measure of his degree of preference for the corresponding criterion of choice.

Before such a standard could be used effectively, we would have to know much more than we do now about controlling such variables as knowledge of probabilities, preferences among courses of action, and awareness of value.*

If, in a particular problem situation, choices were always made so as to maximize expected value using this criterion, the average value attained would tend to this expectation and would be greater than if any other criterion were used. But what if we have a set of decision situations in each of which only one choice is to be made? Here too it can be shown that the average value attained will tend to be maximum if this criterion is used.

Other criteria of choice will be considered in subsequent sections of this chapter.

Quantitative Objectives Only

We have already considered how the efficiency of a course of action can be represented relative to a quantitative outcome. The inputs and/or outputs associated with a particular course of action will vary, but not all inputs and/or outputs will occur with the same frequency. Then we should determine the probability associated with each possible input and/or output and thus establish a probability-density function which we have called an *efficiency function*. If the inputs and/or outputs are measured along discrete scales, the function will also be discrete.

Consider first two courses of action relative to one quantitative outcome. Then an efficiency function would be obtained for each course of action: $f_1(X)$ for C_1 and $f_2(X)$ for C_2. Now we need some criterion for selecting that course of action which has the "best"

---

*An effort to construct standards for these concepts can also be found in Churchman and Ackoff (1947) and Churchman (1961).

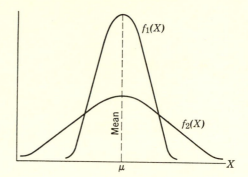

FIGURE 2.2. Two efficiency functions with equal means but unequal dispersions.

efficiency function. Common sense seems to indicate that we should select the course of action which has the highest average efficiency. But on reflection we observe first that two courses of action may have the same average efficiency but have different dispersions or spreads. (See Figure 2.2.) In some situations the possibility of a very large outcome may be relevant to the choice made. For example, a course of action which has some probability (though small) of resulting in bankruptcy for a company may be less desirable than one which has practically no possibility of such an outcome.

More generally, we can say that maximum "average efficiency" is an acceptable criterion of choice in problems involving one quantitative outcome only if the *value* of the outcome is a linear function of the measure of the outcome. Only if this condition holds is the course of action with the maximum average efficiency *necessarily* the one which yields the maximum expected value. A linear value function, however, is not very common. For example, outcome is frequently measured in dollars, and investigations have shown that the value of money is usually *not* a linear function of the amount [see Markowitz (1952)].

Consider the two efficiency functions shown in Figure 2.2. These two functions have the same average. To select the best course of action it is also necessary to know the value function of the X-scale. In Figure 2.3 two possible value functions are shown. It should be noted that a value function need not be monotonically increasing, as in $V_1(X)$. For example, the value of arsenic in a drug may increase as the amount of arsenic increases up to a certain amount, but as it approaches a lethal dose the value decreases.

If $V_1(X)$ holds, then C_1 will yield the maximum expected value. If $V_2(X)$ holds, then C_2 will yield the maximum expected value. In

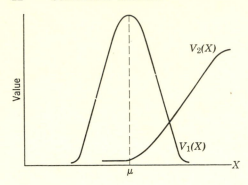

FIGURE 2.3. Two value functions.

these cases the expected value of a course of action, C_i, relative to a single quantitative outcome measured along an X-scale is:

$$\int_{-\infty}^{\infty} V(X) f_i(X)\, dX,$$

the sum of the weighted efficiencies. (In the next chapter we will consider how the values $V(X)$ can be estimated.)

Two or more quantitative objectives

If we have a problem involving two courses of action and two quantitative outcomes, the efficiency matrix will appear as it did in Table 2.1, but the insertions in the cells will be efficiency functions rather than single measures. Suppose, for example, that O_1 involves costs with the associated objective "to minimize costs," and O_2 involves time with the associated objective "to minimize delay to (say) customers." In most industrial contexts these two objectives, it will be noted, cannot be pursued simultaneously. The consequences of this fact will become clear as we proceed. Now in each cell we will have an efficiency function which gives the probability of expending various inputs expressed along a cost scale for O_1 and a time scale for O_2. We cannot "add" the efficiency functions for each course of action because the output scales are expressed in different units. Since addition is necessary if we are to evaluate the courses of action relative to *all* the relevant outcomes, we must find some way of either transforming one scale into the other or transforming both into some other scale. Such a transformation consists of equating various quantities on one scale with quantities on the other, or converting both to an absolute scale of value. Since we do not yet have scales of absolute value, it is necessary first to transform the outcome scales (X_1 and X_2) into each other and then to find the

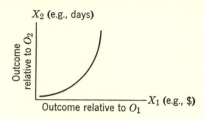

FIGURE 2.4. A transformation function.

relative values of units along one of these scales. In transforming the scales we must weight the relative importance of units of the different scales. Successive units on one scale may not be equally valuable relative to units on the other. For example, a two-day delay to a customer may cost (in dollars) more than two one-day delays. Such transformation (or trade-off) functions are seldom linear. Figure 2.4 shows such a function.

It may be wondered why the two efficiency scales cannot be transformed into value scales and then added, thereby eliminating the need of transforming one efficiency scale into the other. The reason is that current methods can establish only the *relative* values of units on an efficiency scale, not the absolute values. Therefore, a specified relative value on one efficiency scale is not necessarily equal to the same relative value on another efficiency scale. In order to make the relative values comparable a transformation of at least some points on the efficiency scales is required.

Once such a transformation function is obtained, it is possible to express both efficiency functions in terms of either scale and then to combine them by "addition" into an *effectiveness* function. For example, if $f_{11}(X_1)$ and $f_{12}(X_2)$ represent the efficiency functions of C_1 for O_1 and O_2, respectively, where X_1 and X_2 are values on the corresponding outcome scales, and if we obtain a transformation function $[X_2 = g(X_1)]$, then the effectiveness function of C_1 could be expressed as a function of X_1, $h(X_1)$, where

$$h(X_1) = \int_{a=0}^{a=X_1} f_1(a)f_2[g(X_1 - a)] \, da.*$$ (1)

The effectiveness function could equally well be expressed in terms of X_2.

* It is assumed here that outcomes on X_1 and X_2 are independent. If this is not the case,

$$h(X_1) = \int_{a=0}^{X_1} f_1(a)f_2[g(X_1 - a)/a] \, da.$$

Now, if a value function, $V(X_1)$, is obtained, the expected value of C_1 is $EV(C_1)$, where

$$EV(C_1) = \int_{-\infty}^{\infty} V(X_1)h(X_1)\,dX_1.$$

It should be noted that this measure, expected value, incorporates within it a weighting of the dispersion (variance) of the efficiency and effectiveness functions. That is, the expected values derived from (a) two efficiency functions with the same average but different dispersions and (b) a nonlinear value function, will differ. The variance of the value of the outcome, therefore, has no significance. (The variance of the *estimate* of expected value, however, is significant.) Hence, one of the advantages of this measure is that it can stand alone; unlike expected efficiency and expected effectiveness, it need not be considered in connection with a measure of variability.

Mixed Outcomes: Qualitative and Quantitative

Consider a situation involving two objectives, one qualitatively defined and one quantitatively defined. For example, in a business situation management may wish "to have the largest share of the market" and to "maximize annual net profit." The first objective involves two qualitative outcomes:

O_1: to have a larger share of the market than any competitor.
O_2: not to have a larger share of the market than any competitor.

The profit objective involves an outcome defined along a dollar scale (X). It is first necessary to find what amount of net profit is equivalent in value to attainment of O_1. This may be done by techniques to be considered in the next chapter. Let X_a represent the amount of profit so determined. Then, for a course of action C_i, the expected value is given by

$$EV(C_i) = P_{i1}V(X_a) + P_{i2}[1 - V(X_a)] + \int_{-\infty}^{\infty} V(X)f_i(X)\,dX, \quad (2)$$

where $f_i(X)$ is the efficiency function of C_i relative to the profit outcome, and $V(X)$ is the value function of the X-scale.

In general, then, the qualitative objective is transformed to a value on the scale used to measure either efficiency (in the case involving one quantitative outcome) or effectiveness (in the case involving more than one such objective). The value of this transformed quantity is obtained from the value function of the scale employed. Then for a specific course of action the expected values for the qualitative and quantitative objectives are added.

Counteractions and Reactions

In some problem situations a choice of a course of action (C_i) by one decision maker will produce a responsive action (R_k) by another decision maker. Such is the case in competitive situations; for example, in auction bidding, in pricing of products, in most athletic games, and in wars. The responsive action may increase or decrease the efficiency of the first choice: cooperate or conflict with it.

Suppose that the first decision maker, A, has two choices, C_1 and C_2; and the second decision maker, B, has two responses, R_1 and R_2: two possible qualitative outcomes are involved, O_1 and O_2, which have relative values V_1 and V_2 to A.

If B makes his choice independently of A's and a fixed probability can be assigned to each of B's choices, then the expected value of A's choice of C_i would be

$$EV(C_i) = P(R_1)[P(O_1|C_i, R_1)V_1 + P(O_2|C_i, R_1)V_2]$$
$$+ P(R_2)[P(O_1|C_i, R_2)V_1 + P(O_2|C_i, R_2)V_2], \quad (3)$$

where $P(O_j|C_i, R_k)$ is the probability that O_j will occur if A selects C_i and B selects R_k. If B's choice is conditioned by A's choice, we would substitute $P(R_1|C_i)$ and $P(R_2|C_i)$ for $P(R_1)$ and $P(R_2)$ in this equation.

If the outcomes O_1 and O_2 are quantitatively defined along scales X_1 and X_2, the efficiency function for each course of action (C_i) would have to be determined for each possible counteraction (R_k). Let $f_{ik}(X_j)$ represent the efficiency function of C_i for O_j if R_k is selected. Then the composite efficiency function of C_1 for O_1 would be

$$f_1(X_1) = P(R_1|C_1)f_{11}(X_1) + P(R_2|C_1)f_{12}(X_1). \quad (4)$$

Using these composite functions, expected values can be determined in the manner discussed above. If the probabilities associated with the responses, $P(R_k)$, are not known but the efficiency functions, $f_{ik}(X_j)$, are known, we have a problem which combines risk and uncertainty. This type of problem will be considered below.

If the probabilities, $P(R_k)$, and the efficiency functions, $f_{ik}(X_j)$, are unknown to decision maker A, he must make a decision under complete uncertainty. In such a situation he has no basis for choice, and hence the choice must be arbitrary. If, on the other hand, A knows exactly what choice B will make, and what outcome will occur for any combination of his action and B's, A will make his decision under certainty.

DECISIONS UNDER CERTAINTY

If a decision maker has a well-specified set of alternative courses of action for each of which there is one and only one outcome, then— if he can determine the value of each outcome—he should simply select that course of action whose outcome has maximum value. Although in specific problems of this type it may be quite difficult to formulate the alternative courses of action, to identify the outcome associated with each, and to determine their relative values, the principle of choice involved is quite simple.

Now suppose that a second decision maker, B, is involved and that his interests are in conflict with those of the first decision maker, A. This is the type of decision situation which has been the subject of study in game theory.

Intuitively, the problem of conflict of interest is, for each participant, a problem of individual decision making under a mixture of risk and uncertainty, the uncertainty arising from his ignorance as to what others will do [Luce and Raiffa (1957, p. 14)].

In game theory this type of problem situation is idealized in such a way as to transform it into a decision under certainty or risk. This is not accomplished directly by assuming knowledge of what the opponent will do, but indirectly by assuming that the opponent has certain information and that he is motivated in certain ways; that is; that he behaves "rationally."

In point of fact, assumptions about the motivations of players are not sufficient to eliminate completely the uncertainty aspects of the problem [Luce and Raiffa (1957, p. 14)].

Put another way, the central problem of game theory does not turn out to be what choice to make given certain or probabilistic knowledge of the opponent's choices, but rather what choices can the opponent be assumed to make, given certain assumptions about his state of knowledge and motivations. Let us be more specific.

A "game" is a decision situation involving conflict of interest between two or more interacting decision makers in which the following conditions hold:

(1) Each decision maker has available to him a set of two or more well-specified choices or sequences of choices called "plays."

(2) Every possible combination of plays available to the players leads to a well-defined end-state (e.g., win, lose, or draw) which terminates the game.

(3) A specified pay-off for each player is associated with each end-state.

These conditions can be represented in a pay-off matrix in which the pay-off associated with each possible combination of choices is shown, as is done in Table 2.2. Inferences as to what the other player is going to do are derived from the conditions of the game, (1)–(3) above, and from the following two assumptions:

(4) Each decision maker has perfect knowledge of the game and his opposition; that is, he knows the rules of the game in full detail and the pay-off functions of all other players.

(5) All decision makers are "rational"; that is, each player, given two alternatives, will select the one he prefers: the one which yields the greater value to him.

TABLE 2.2.   A PAY-OFF MATRIX

(Relative Values of All Possible Outcomes)

Player B's Possible Plays

		b_1	b_2	$\cdots$	b_j	$\cdots$	b_n
	a_1	V_{11}	V_{12}	$\cdots$	V_{1j}	$\cdots$	V_{1n}
	a_2	V_{21}	V_{22}	$\cdots$	V_{2j}	$\cdots$	V_{2n}
	.	.	.		.		.
	.	.	.		.		.
Player A's	.	.	.		.		.
Possible Plays	a_i	V_{i1}	V_{i2}	$\cdots$	V_{ij}	$\cdots$	V_{in}
	.	.	.		.		.
	.	.	.		.		.
	a_m	V_{m1}	V_{m2}	$\cdots$	V_{mj}	$\cdots$	V_{mn}

In some games these two assumptions do seem to reduce the situation to one of decision under certainty. For example, consider a two-person game in which whatever one loses the other gains (i.e., the sum of the gains and losses from any play are equal to zero). This is called a *two-person zero-sum game*. Now suppose that the following pay-offs apply to A, the pay-offs to B being the negatives of those to A:

	Player B		
	Choices	b_1	b_2
	a_1	1	4
Player A			
	a_2	2	3

Clearly, if A knows that B will select b_1, A should select a_2; if B selects b_2, A should select a_1. Which choice will B make? Given assumptions (4) and (5) above, A may reason as follows:

> B observes that if he selects b_1 the most I can gain and he can lose is 2, but if he selects b_2 I can gain and he can lose as much as 4. Therefore he will select b_1 and I should select a_2.

In this reasoning B is assumed to act so as to minimize his maximum possible loss, and hence to minimize A's maximum possible gain. A, on the other hand, acts so as to maximize his minimum possible gain. These principles of choice are called the *minimax* and *maximin*, respectively.

Now let us look at B's reasoning about A:

> A observes that if he selects a_1 the least he can gain is 1, but if he selects a_2 the least he can gain is 2. Therefore he will select a_2 and I should select b_1.

Note that the conclusions reached by A and B are identical. Note also that neither player can improve his pay-off by changing his choice if the other player does not change his choice. Hence these choices are said to maximize the "security level" of each player, and the combination of choices, a_2 and b_1, is said to be an *equilibrium* pair. Such a pair is called the *solution* to the game.

Not all two-person zero-sum games have such a solution. This solution can be shown to exist only if the pay-off matrix has an entry which is the highest in its column and the lowest in its row. An entry of this type is called a *saddle point*. Several or no such entries may exist. For example, consider the following case, in which a saddle point does not exist:

Player B

	Choices	b_1	b_2
	a_1	2	4
Player A			
	a_2	3	1

Again these are pay-offs to A.

Now suppose that A reasons about B as he did in the previous case:

B observes that if he selects b_1 the most he can lose is 3, but if he selects b_2 the most he can lose is 4. Therefore he will select b_1 and I should select a_2.

If B were to reason about A as he did before the result would be:

A observes that if he selects a_1 the least he can gain is 2, but if he selects a_2 the least he can gain is 1. Therefore he will select a_1 and I should select b_1.

Note now that the conclusions reached by the two players are not the same. Furthermore, if the choice pair a_2 and b_1 is made, B could improve his pay-off by changing to b_2, in which case A could improve his pay-off by changing to a_1, in which case B could improve his pay-off by changing to b_1, and so on without end. There is no equilibrium point, a point at which this reasoning can come to rest.

This last case shows that some games cannot be reduced to decisions under certainty even with assumptions (4) and (5). However, game theory has shown how this last situation can be reduced to one of risk. The details of this reduction need not concern us here. The important point for this discussion is that the ability of game theory to convert a decision situation involving conflict of interests into a decision under certainty, however limited that ability may be, depends on the assumption of complete knowledge on the part of all decision makers involved. It is sufficient for our purposes to observe that the assumption of perfect knowledge is seldom, if ever, justified in real problem situations.

In most real conflict decision situations the choices available to the players seldom completely determine the outcome. The choices and the environment cannot be defined so as to be sufficient for any specified outcome. Consequently, even if all the choices are known, the outcome is known only probabilistically at best. Furthermore, even if the outcomes were known with certainty, the values placed on them by the opposing players are seldom, if ever, known with certainty. For one or both of these reasons the pay-offs in real situations are almost always known with less than certainty.

It is for these reasons, more than any other, that game theory has found so little application. It has even been extremely difficult to apply in contrived laboratory situations because of the inability of experimenters to control the values which subjects place on outcomes. To say that the theory has little value in problem solving is not to say that it has little value. To the contrary, it is a very important scientific achievement for reasons which have been well stated by Rapoport (1959).

What happens to the concept of a game if the assumption of perfect knowledge is dropped? Is it then a suitable model of decision under uncertainty? We turn to these questions in the next section.

DECISIONS UNDER UNCERTAINTY

If the assumption of perfect knowledge in game theory is replaced with an assumption of complete ignorance, the result is a model of an uncertainty problem situation. We argued in the last section that to assume perfect knowledge of the players is to assume too much. In this section we will argue that to assume complete ignorance is to assume too little. The argument is based on the observations that in order to formulate a pay-off matrix for a problem situation some knowledge of the opposition (be it a decision maker or nature) is necessary and that this knowledge can and should be used in the decision process.

In the uncertainty game it is assumed that neither player can assign probabilities to the possible plays of his opponent. It is apparent that, if a player could assign such probabilities and could construct a pay-off matrix, he could try to maximize expected value; or if, as the principle of insufficient reason states, he is justified on the basis of his ignorance in assuming that his opponent is equally likely to select each possibility, he could still employ this criterion of best choice. Otherwise he must employ some other criterion. The three criteria which have been most seriously considered for this state of ignorance are the *maximin utility, minimax regret,* and *Hurwicz α.*

Criteria of Choice under Uncertainty

The most widely cited criterion is the *maximin* utility principle. Here the worst possible outcome (minimum gain) that is associated with each possible course of action is identified. Then that course of action is considered best whose associated minimum possible gain is maximum. More precisely, let a_i represent the strategies or courses of action available to the decision maker A, and let b_j represent the choices available to an opposing decision maker or "nature," B. Then, according to the maximin criterion that decision is best for which

$$\max_{a_i} \min_{b_j} [V(a_i, b_j)], \tag{5}$$

where V is the value of the outcome that follows the joint selection of a_i and b_j.

The most common criticism of this criterion is that it is conservative if not "pessimistic." That is, the criterion is criticized for being based on an "expectation of the worst." How can expectations be relevant in a situation in which probabilities are unknowable or meaningless? If this criticism is valid, then the possibility of prediction is implicitly assumed.

Hurwicz (1951) attempted a generalization of the maximin criterion to make it less pessimistic. His generalized criterion is as follows:

$$\max_{a_i} [\alpha \max_{b_j} V(a_i, b_j) + (1 - \alpha) \min_{b_j} V(a_i, b_j)], \tag{6}$$

where α is some preselected number between 0 and 1. It is what might be called the *index of optimism*. If α is set equal to zero, the Hurwicz criterion reduces to the simpler form of the maximin criterion given above. If α is set equal to 1, the criterion becomes maximization of maximum gain. The decision maker is supposed to select the value of α.

This criterion has some undesirable characteristics even from the point of view of those who accept the meaningfulness of the assumption of complete ignorance in a game against nature.* But these need not concern us here. It should be noted, however, that α can be interpreted as an estimate of the probability that the opponent will select a course of action which maximizes the decision maker's losses. Thus, the index of optimism can be taken to be a subjective probability estimate.

A third choice criterion, *minimax regret* (or *minimax risk*), was proposed by Savage (1951).

Let the pay-offs to decision maker A be the following:

	S_1	S_2
a_1	0	50
a_2	10	5

* See, for example, Radner and Marshak in Thrall, Coombs, and Davis (1954, pp. 61–68).

For each state of nature, S_1 and S_2, we can determine which course of action, a_1 or a_2, would yield the maximum gain and then prepare a regret matrix in which we enter the difference between the pay-off obtained and that which would have been obtained if the best a had been selected. For example, the matrix given above can be transformed into the following regret matrix:

	S_1	S_2
a_1	10	0
a_2	0	45

According to this criterion, A should select that a for which the maximum regret is minimum, in this case a_1. More precisely, he should

$$\min_{a_i} \max_{b_j} R[a_i, b_j] = \min_{a_i} [\max_{b_j} \max_{a_{i'}} V(a_i', b_j) - V(a_i, b_j)], \qquad (7)$$

where a_i' represents the choice that one would have made if he had known the choice b_j in advance. Then, the regret function, R, is the difference between the value received from a given course of action and the value that would have been obtained had one known beforehand what choice opposition or nature would make.

Selection of a Criterion of Choice

The availability of the three criteria we have just considered presents the problem of determining which one is most suitable in a specific situation. On this point Arrow (1958, p. 12) remarks:

> It is clear that we do not really have a universally valid criterion for rational behavior [best choice] under uncertainty. Probably the best thing to be said is that different criteria are valid under different circumstances.

How can we determine which criterion is valid under any specific set of circumstances? What is lacking at present is a meta-criterion which would enable us to determine which of the available criteria of best choice is the best criterion. One can direct his efforts either to finding such a meta-criterion or to showing that the assumption of complete ignorance, which has led to the multiplicity of criteria, is—in some sense—invalid. We shall take this latter course.

The Assumption of Complete Ignorance

Others have called into question the *desirability* of assuming complete ignorance of the probabilities of the opponent's choices. For example, Luce and Raiffa (1957, p. 299), commenting on the situation in which the "opponent" is nature, observe:

A common criticism of such criteria as the maximin utility, minimax regret, Hurwicz α, and that based on the principle of insufficient reason is that they are rationalized on some notion of *complete* ignorance. In practice, however, the decision maker usually has some partial information concerning the true state. No matter how vague it is, he may not wish to endorse any characterization of complete ignorance, and so the heart is cut out of criteria based on this notion.

The point to be made, however, is neither that the assumption of complete ignorance is empirically false nor that it is undesirable. It is a much stronger point that must be made: the assumption of complete ignorance is *inconsistent* with the knowledge required to represent a problem in a pay-off matrix.

Let us restate the misconception from which this inconsistency arises. In a real problem-solving situation the decision maker is not given the pay-off matrix; he must extract it out of the problem situation itself. A preformulated problem, such as is used in a laboratory game, is a contrived exercise in which the decision maker is presented with the pay-off matrix but not the information from which it was derived. The procedure by which he does or should solve this *exercise*—it is not a problem—is not necessarily the same as what he does or should do in a real problem situation that can be represented by a pay-off matrix.

This can be seen by reference to a hypothetical advertising problem drawn up by Shubik (1955, p. 47):

Two firms, A and B, each have a million dollars to spend on advertising their products in a certain market area. They can use the media of radio, television, newspapers, magazines, and billboards. For simplicity, we will group these five alternatives into radio, television, and printed media. The marketing research sections of each firm work out the expected effect of any contingency. We will discuss the decision-making at firm A only. A pay-off matrix of 4×4 is drawn up. This contains information on the 16 contingencies that might arise if either firm spent all its money advertising solely by means of radio, television, or printed media, or decided to save the million dollars and not advertise at all. Each entry in the payoff matrix represents the amount of extra revenue above cost estimated under these circumstances (in millions of dollars).

First we observe that there are many possible advertising media which are not included in this game. For example, the firms could advertise by use of skywriting, point-of-sale displays, and traveling exhibitions. In practice these could be excluded for only one reason: their choice by competition is extremely unlikely. To exclude them, then, presupposes some knowledge of the probabilities of competitive choices. Now one might reply that this is doing injustice to an example and that the alternatives could be formulated so as to be exclusive and exhaustive. For example, one might formulate the alternatives as:

- (*a*) Visual but not auditory.
- (*b*) Auditory but not visual.
- (*c*) Visual and auditory.
- (*d*) Neither.

Now it will be observed that there are different types of advertising that can occur in any of these categories. For example, "visual but not auditory" includes newspapers, magazines, billboards, skywriting, and so on. To associate a pay-off with such an alternative defined as "visual but not auditory," then, presupposes some knowledge of the probabilities of choice associated with these subalternatives. No matter how fine the classification, this problem remains. Prediction of the outcome of any class of actions presupposes some knowledge of the likelihood of selection of the alternatives within the class.

Even in Shubik's original classification many subalternatives are possible in each category. For example, "radio" may mean spot announcements or sponsored programs, day or night programs, many short commercials or a few long ones. To associate a pay-off with "radio," then, also *necessarily assumes* some knowledge of the distribution of probabilities associated with these subalternatives.

These observations raise the question as to whether it is ever possible to define a choice so that no variations of action are possible. Our earlier discussion of the nature of courses of action showed that a course of action is always a class of courses of action. Since no two different things can be identical in every respect, it follows that variations within the class are unavoidable. But one might still argue that, although there are differences among the elements of the class, these differences may not affect the probabilities associated with possible outcomes, and hence these outcomes can be determined without any knowledge of the opponent. For example, it might be argued that the effects of all different kinds of "visual but not auditory" advertising are the same; that the outcome is independent of the "copy" (content of the ad), its geographic distribution, and who the advertiser is. Obviously we can construct games (e.g., tic-tac-toe) in which the outcome depends only on the play. That is, we can *contrive* situations where an outcome is mechanistically or logically (i.e., deterministically) linked to a course of action. The question before us, then, can be reformulated as follows: can a problem situation as it arises in "reality" be adequately represented by a model in which choices are deterministically linked to outcomes? Anyone familiar with the behavioral sciences is aware of the fact that we are a long way from being able to define courses of actions and outcomes in a specified environment so that the connection between them is completely deterministic and (therefore) so that they are independent of such factors as who makes the selection. As long as outcomes, as we now define them, depend on variations among the elements in a class of courses of action or on outside factors, we cannot specify an outcome without having some knowledge of the effect of these variations. And this type of knowledge cannot be obtained without some knowledge of the likelihood associated with various possible values of the action variables affecting the outcome.

Nature as an opponent

One might agree that we cannot know an opponent's choices and the pay-offs associated with joint choices unless we also know something about the probabilities of the opponent's choices. One may still argue, however, that when nature is the opponent such knowledge may not exist. To examine this argument let us first recast the problem into a pay-off matrix which shows nature as the opponent. Let C_1, C_2, $\cdots$, C_i $\cdots$, C_m represent the choices or plays available to the decision maker. Let O_1, O_2, $\cdots$, O_j, $\cdots O_n$ represent the possible outcomes of these choices. These outcomes are produced not only by the decision maker's choice but also by the value of variables which he does not control. These can be called *nature's choices*. Let the states resulting from nature's choices be represented by S_1, S_2, $\cdots$, S_k, $\cdots$. Then for each pair of choices (C_i, S_k) a certain outcome or state, O_j, occurs which has an associated value to the decision maker, V_j. If the decision maker can determine the probability associated with each of nature's choices, $P(S_k)$, then he can attempt to maximize expected value. The question we want to consider first is: can the decision maker ever know what the S_k are and not have some knowledge of these probabilities?

In order to explain this kind of problem situation the following very simple analogy is sometimes used. Suppose that nature consists of an urn filled with black and white balls and its choices consist of random draws of a ball from the urn. Suppose that this is all we know about nature's choices; then, "obviously" we do not know the probabilities associated with these choices. But is this last supposition consistent? This model of a choice situation is *not* a model of a problem situation. It fails to model reality for exactly the same reasons as the previously discussed competitive game does: it fails to provide the decision maker with the information required to formulate the problem. Specifically, it does not tell him how it was determined that there are only black and white balls or even only balls in the bowl, and how it is known that the draws are made at random. Consideration of how such assertions or assumptions could be justified in practice reveals that information would be required which could be used to formulate a reasonable assumption concerning the distribution of colors of the balls in the bowl.

Recently a defender of the bowl analogy suggested the following modification of the model. "The bowl is filled as follows: A biased coin is used. Each time it comes up heads a black ball is put in the bowl; otherwise a white one is inserted." The situation is not changed by this modification. The information required to establish the fact that the coin is biased is sufficient to provide an estimate of the probabilities of white and black draws.

In general terms, this argument has been to the effect that one cannot know what uncontrolled variables affect an outcome without having some knowledge of the likelihood of various values of these variables occurring.

A number of decision theorists have objected to the argument just given with the observation that in many "real-life" situations certain information cannot be gotten directly but can only be inferred. The argument here, however, is not based on the insistence of access to direct observation involving no inferences. To the contrary, in other places [e.g., Churchman and Ackoff (1950)], I have maintained that all data are the result of inferential processes.* The argument is based on the observation that in such games as have been described the information used to match the characteristics of the game to the problem situation must be made available to the decision maker who must solve it before the game can become an adequate model of the problem situation. The argument thus far against the validity of the assumption of complete ignorance can be restated as follows: a problem situation cannot be formulated without some knowledge of the probabilities associated with possible outcomes. But up to this point we have considered only situations in which possible outcomes are known. They may not be known initially, in which case research must be used to uncover them so that a complete formulation of the problem can be made. Let us consider a situation of this type.

* See also Churchman (1961).

Objective and subjective probabilities

Consider the following type of problem situation. In the development of a new military weapon and policies for its use we may not know who the enemy will be, or where, when, and under what circumstances the weapon will be used. Here we *seem* to be in a state of complete ignorance. In military projects of this type there are two fairly standard practices. First, a *countermeasures group* is usually established which tries to develop instruments and tactics to combat the new weapon. The enemy is assumed to establish such a group. On the basis of the countermeasure studies estimates are made as to what the enemy is likely to do. Second, the weapon and its use are usually tried in "map problems" which are simulated military engagements. These are designed to involve the most likely enemies, the most likely locations, times, and so on. For example, Britain or Canada is seldom, if ever, used in the United States as the hypothetical enemy in such problems. Once a likely enemy is designated, extensive studies of its present and future capabilities are used to estimate the likelihood that it will employ certain specified tactics.

It can be argued that the estimates of probability obtained in this way are not based on observed relative frequencies, and hence are not *objective* probabilities. This may be true, but so-called *subjective* probabilities should not be discarded lightly. Savage (1954) has developed a theory of subjective probability which must be taken seriously. According to Luce and Raiffa (1957, p. 300), the school led by Savage

. . . holds the view that by processing one's partial information (as evidenced by one's responses to a series of simple hypothetical questions of the yes-no variety) one can generate an *a priori* probability distribution over the states of nature which is appropriate for making decisions. This reduces the decision problem from one of uncertainty to one of risk.

Churchman (1961, Chapter VI) puts both the traditional concepts of objective probability and the newer concepts of subjective probability to an exhaustive analysis. He summarizes (pp. 168–169) his analysis as follows:

We began with the hope that an objective measure of probability could be found in the operations of counting membership in classes. We conclude that no matter what major aspect of this definition we choose to analyze, we are always driven to the necessity of introducing judgment; the operation of verifying class membership is based on judgment; the operation of verifying the theory of sampling is based on judgment; the verification of a theory of the generation of events is based on judgment.

Should we conclude that ultimately what probability really means is the measure of the breadth and tenacity of expert opinion? We could certainly say this, and argue that in many—but by no means all—cases this measure depends on relative frequencies, because expert judgment is highly influenced by relative frequencies. We could thus be led to consider the definition of probability in terms of frequencies to be a special case of the more general definition in terms of judgment.

The crucial question is whether we could do the opposite . . . and define good judgment in terms of relative frequencies. . . . Can the frequency concept of probability be used to express the degree of validity of a theory? It would certainly be naïve to suggest that we "count" the instances where the theory has held and the instances where it has failed—because our data are never of the form that clearly does one or the other. But we could count instances that are judged to confirm and instances that are not judged to do so. We could also count favorable expert opinions and unfavorable ones. Indeed, the whole idea of well-substantiated judgment seems to rest on such a counting procedure.

Hence we conclude that either definition of probability is feasible. . . . In effect, we want to know which is the better standard for probability measures: relative frequency or well-substantiated judgment? Relative frequency standards have been much more carefully studied and developed; the judgment standard is often much easier to apply. . . . Whichever standard is chosen it is essential that data collected under the other standard be adjustable; this means, simply, that relative frequencies must agree, by some acceptable method, with judgment probabilities and that judgment probabilities must agree with relative frequencies, in those cases where both methods are applicable.

Summarizing our argument up to this point, then, we have observed that, in problem situations where probabilities can be assigned to possible outcomes, maximizing expected value can be used as a criterion of best choice. We have also observed that in models of problem situations in which the decision maker cannot estimate such probabilities it is because he is deprived of information that is necessary for formulating the problem. Even if sufficient information is not available for estimating probabilities on an objective (relative-frequency) basis, judgment can be used to obtain subjective probabilities. Although there are methodological problems associated with both types of measure of probability, neither can be discarded as invalid relative to the present state of the theory of probability. Finally, the possibility of conducting research to obtain estimates of the probabilities associated with possible outcomes should be kept in mind. One of the principal reasons for using research to assist in problem solving is that it can provide such data as are required for making a better decision than would otherwise be made.

Now we want to consider just what kind of probability estimates are required in problem situations.

Required Estimates of Probability

Let us consider a decision involving opposition or nature from the point of view of maximizing expected value. Suppose that the pay-off to A is as follows:

	b_1	b_2
a_1	-2	2
a_2	1	3

According to the maximin criterion, the best choice for A is a_2 and for B it is b_1.

Closer examination of this decision situation from the point of view of decision maker A reveals that it is a waste of his time to find the maximin choice because no matter what B does A is better off if he selects a_2; hence, a_2 is called the *dominant* choice. In such a case it is not worth considering any other choice.

The choice b_1 is also dominant for B.

Now consider the following pay-offs to A:

	b_1	b_2
a_1	-2	4
a_2	1	3

A no longer has a dominant choice. Suppose that B were to select b_1 with probability P and b_2 with probability $(1 - P)$. Then, if A selects a_2, his expected value is

$$P(1) + (1 - P)3$$

and, if A were to select a_1, his expected return would be

$$P(-2) + (1 - P)4.$$

The choice a_2 would give A a larger expected return if

$$P(1) + (1 - P)3 > P(-2) + (1 - P)4.$$

Solving, we obtain $P > 0.25$. Therefore, as long as the probability that B will select b_1 is greater than 0.25, A should select a_2. If, however, P were less than 0.25, A should select a_1. For example, if $P = 0.1$, then the expected value of a_1 is

$$0.1(-2) + 0.9(4) = -0.2 + 3.6 = 3.4$$

and the expected value of a_2 is

$$0.1(1) + 0.9(3) = 0.1 + 2.7 = 2.8.$$

In this case the exact value of P need not be known; A need only know if it exceeds 0.25.

It can be shown that in many, if not most, problem situations the probability associated with each possible outcome need not be known exactly to select a course of action which maximizes expected value. In some cases only a ranking of probabilities is sufficient, and in other cases knowledge that the probabilities do or do not exceed some specifiable value is sufficient.

Errors in estimating probabilities

We have argued that wherever one can define possible choices of nature or an opponent it is possible to estimate the probability associated with each choice. This does not mean that we can always obtain estimates in which we have confidence. The decision maker and the researcher may be very concerned about the possibility of serious consequences following from errors of estimation. There are two ways of approaching this uncertainty of estimation:

(1) If the decision maker must act—that is, he cannot delay the problem—then the estimates of probability should be made in such a way as to take into account the serious outcomes of which he is apprehensive. A procedure for so doing will be described in Chapter 8.

(2) If the problem can be delayed, then either research should be conducted so as to obtain better estimates of these probabilities, or consideration should be given to the question as to whether the right problem is being studied. In such cases the right problem may very well be, "How can the problem situation be changed so that expected values can be maximized?" Consider the following case. A company was trying to determine through research by how much it should increase its overloaded production facilities. The company produced equipment that is consumed in quantity only when general economic conditions are good. It had developed an effective forecast of future sales assuming the continuation of prosperity. But since even a mild recession could have serious consequences to the business (particularly with expanded facilities), it was also necessary for the company to forecast general economic conditions. It did not feel that it could do this with sufficient accuracy, and it was pessimistic about the possibility that research would improve this situation. This led the company's management to ask the question, "What can we do to prevent a recession or depression from having such serious consequences on our business?" The answer management came up with was to find a new product which could be made with existing facilities but which had a reaction to general economic conditions opposite to that of their

current product. Management directed research to be conducted to find such a product, and it was found. This reduced the seriousness of large errors in forecasting the probability of a receding market for the original product. Once this was accomplished, the question of expanding facilities was reopened and solved with confidence.

It is quite common in the military, when it becomes clear that the outcome of a battle depends on what an enemy does and where what the enemy does cannot be accurately predicted, to attempt to develop equipment and tactics which are less sensitive to what he does. The principle involved here is the same as that employed in the industrial example given above.

BEST ANSWERS TO QUESTIONS

In order to apply the concept of "best decision" (as we have developed it) to pure research, it is necessary to evaluate the losses (and gains) from falsely (or correctly) rejecting or accepting a "pure" research hypothesis or to evaluate the losses due to error in estimating the value of a parameter when this estimate may be used for many purposes of which the researcher cannot be aware. Since these evaluations do not seem possible—or at least feasible—it appears that the pure researcher requires a criterion of "best answers to questions" which has no reference to outcomes of decisions and their values.

Most pure researchers in the classical tradition feel that they have had such a criterion for some time: minimization of error. They believe, further, that error can be defined and measured without consideration of consequences and their values.

We are going to argue to the contrary: that every concept of error contains an implicit set of assumptions concerning the value of consequences. From this we will *not* conclude that the pure researcher must explicitly formulate consequences and their values—for this he clearly cannot do in many circumstances—but that *he must measure and report errors in such a way that they can be adjusted to suit circumstances in which the values of consequences differ from those implicit in his measure of error.*

Since later chapters will consider in detail each type of question asked in pure science, here we will consider only one type of question, that involving the estimate of a parameter. We will consider only those aspects of estimation which are relevant to the argument. Estimation will be considered in detail in Chapter 8.

Suppose that we are trying to estimate a parameter the true value of which is Y. Let y_i represent estimates of this parameter. The error of a particular estimate, y, clearly seems to be the difference between Y and y. Such a measure of error, however, has no operational meaning because it would require a knowledge of the true value of the parameter. Consequently error must be measured in a way which does not presuppose knowledge of the true value of the parameter being estimated. This is done by measuring properties of the set of estimates yielded by an estimating procedure, rather than by measuring the properties of any one specific estimate.

Such a procedure, however, involves two kinds of error, *bias* and *variability*. The bias of an estimating procedure is defined as the difference between the expected value of estimates yielded by the procedure and the true value. Bias in this sense can be calculated without knowledge of the true value of the parameter. There is a variety of ways to measure variability; the most commonly used is the *variance,* which is the mean squared deviations of the estimates from the true value. This measure can itself be estimated from observed data but cannot be known without error unless the true value is also known. For the purposes of this discussion we need consider only the first type of estimating error, bias. Note now that we cannot determine which of a set of estimates of a parameter's value is "best." We must settle for trying to define a best estimating procedure. Such a procedure may not yield the best possible estimate in any specific situation, but in some sense it yields estimates which are best "in the long run."

The naïve researcher might assert that the best estimating procedure is one that minimizes bias and variability. There are problem situations, however, in which such an estimate is obviously not the best. For example, consider a situation in which for every unit of overestimation there is a loss of $1 and for every unit of underestimation there is a loss of $1,000,000. Common sense says *we should deliberately bias* our estimating procedure toward overestimation *so as to reduce the expected loss* due to errors. Of course, it is just as likely that in another situation these penalties are reversed so that the bias should be in the other direction.

The pure researcher cannot produce an estimate which will minimize losses due to estimating errors in all possible situations in which it might be used. He can, however, make and report his estimate in such a way that it can be appropriately adjusted (in a way to be considered in Chapter 8). Therefore, from the point of view of future application of the estimate in problem situations it does not matter what the magnitude of the bias is, providing that it is made explicit.

But what of using the estimate in answering another question (as in pure research) the consequences of which are not known? The pure scientist will ordinarily use an unbiased estimate which can be shown to be best (in the sense of minimizing expected losses due to error) only if the cost of error is independent of its sign (plus or minus). Wherever a pure scientist uses such an estimate, he implicitly assumes that this condition holds. The assumption is convenient in the sense that it simplifies estimating procedures. But it is important that convenience not be confused with the quality of the estimate.

What we have shown, then, is that an estimating procedure which yields estimates that can be said to have no bias (and hence no error of this type) is not the best estimate in all situations in the sense that it will not always minimize the expected cost due to estimating errors.

The costs due to estimating errors vary from situation to situation: the function which relates cost of error to magnitude of error varies widely from one problem situation to another. Consequently, it is not possible to develop a criterion of best estimates in terms of error alone which will best serve our purposes in every situation.

The discussion in Chapter 1 indicated that science seeks generality of its results, applicability over the widest possible range of conditions. This objective is not met by any single estimated value of a parameter. Different estimates derived from the same data are required for different circumstances. Consequently, the objective of an estimating procedure should be to provide the information necessary for preparing that estimate in any specific situation which minimizes the expected cost of errors due to estimation. Ultimately, then, the best answer to a question is one which can be used in any problem situation to obtain a best solution. Truth and error of information have no meaning independently of the way in which the information is applied. "Correspondence with reality" cannot be used to measure error, since reality is not known in a way which permits such computation. Information corresponds to reality in any specific situation to the extent that it can be used to accomplish our objectives in that situation; that is, to obtain best solutions to problems.

It may seem heretical to assert that the quality of an answer to a pure research question depends on how well that answer can be used in applied research. This is to assert that the ultimate consummation of science comes in the real world of problems and not in the abstract world of pure questions.

SUMMARY

A problem was shown to consist of a decision maker, one or more objectives, two or more unequally efficient courses of action, a state of doubt, and an environment. Problems were divided into three classes: *certainty*, in which the outcome of any course of action is known; *risk*, in which the probabilities associated with possible outcomes are known or can be estimated; and *uncertainty*, in which these probabilities are unknown. In order to measure the expected value of a course of action we found that it was necessary (1) to measure the efficiency of a course of action for each outcome in terms of probability of success, and (for quantitative outcomes) inputs and/or outputs, (2) to transform various scales used to measure efficiency into a single standard scale, and (3) to evaluate units along this scale. Combining these measures, it is possible to measure the expected value of a course of action. We took maximization of this value to be the criterion of a best solution to a problem.

Justification of this criterion is largely intuitive at present. We did, however, outline a procedure for determining what criterion should be used. It consists essentially of determining what criterion would be preferred under idealized conditions in which the decision maker has perfect knowledge. It is to be expected that experimental work will move in this direction in the near future.

We then considered a game as a model of a problem situation involving two or more decision makers with conflicting interests. Some such situations are transformed by game theory into decisions under certainty by assuming perfect knowledge and rationality of the decision makers involved. The assumption of perfect knowledge was criticized as being unrealistic. If it is dropped and we assume complete ignorance of opposition's or nature's choices, we have an "uncertainty" game. We found this model to be inconsistent. It denies the decision maker access to information he would require to formulate his problem as such a game, specifically information about the probabilities of the possible outcomes. We argued that the formulation of a problem (e.g., identification of courses of action and possible outcomes) already uses estimates of probabilities of outcomes. These probabilities may be either objective (i.e., based on observed relative frequencies) or subjective (i.e., based on judgment). We considered the relationship between these types of probability and found both to be useful in science.

In effect, then, we removed the necessity of dealing separately with uncertainty problem situations, because the uncertainty is contrived and not a characteristic of the problem situation itself. Analysis of various decision models showed that the probability estimates required to maximize expected return may not need to be "point" estimates; rankings or ranges may be sufficient.

Finally, we considered the criterion of best answers to questions. We examined the assertion that minimization of error provides such a criterion. We found that for one type of estimating error, bias, minimization is not always desirable, since it may not minimize the expected costs due to estimating errors. Error cannot be so defined that its minimization will always result in minimization of these costs. Consequently, the pure researcher cannot produce any one answer that is best as long as his criterion for so doing depends only on error. But since he cannot anticipate all the problem situations in which his answers may be used, he should give his answers in such a way that they can be adjusted to minimize the relevant costs in any particular situation.

BIBLIOGRAPHY

Arrow, K. J., "Utilities, Attitudes, Choices: A Review Note," *Econometrica,* **26** (1958), 1–23.

Chernoff, H., "Rational Selection of Decision Functions," *Econometrica,* **22** (1954), 422–443.

———, and L. E. Moses, *Elementary Decision Theory.* New York: John Wiley and Sons, 1959.

Churchman, C. W., "Problems of Value Measurement for a Theory of Induction and Decisions," *Proceedings of the Third Berkeley Symposium on Mathematical Statistics and Probability.* Berkeley: University of California Press, 1955, pp. 53–59.

———, *Prediction and Optimal Decision.* Englewood Cliffs, N. J.: Prentice-Hall, 1961.

———, "Decision and Value Theory," in *Progress in Operations Research: I,* ed. by R. L. Ackoff. New York: John Wiley and Sons, 1961, pp. 35–64.

———, and R. L. Ackoff, *Psychologistics.* Philadelphia: University of Pennsylvania Faculty Research Fund, 1947. (Mimeographed)

———, and ———, *Methods of Inquiry.* St. Louis: Educational Publishers, 1950.

Davidson, D., P. Suppes, and S. Siegel, *Decision-Making: An Experimental Approach.* Stanford: Stanford University Press, 1957.

Edwards, W., "The Theory of Decision-Making," *Psychological Bulletin,* **51** (1954), 380–417.

Gore, W. S., and F. S. Silander, "A Bibliographical Essay on Decision-Making," *Administrative Science Quarterly,* **4** (1959), 97–121.

Hurwicz, L., "Optimality Criteria for Decision Making under Ignorance," *Cowles Commission Discussion Paper, Statistics,* No. 370, 1951. (Mimeographed)

Luce, R. D., *Individual Choice Behavior.* New York: John Wiley and Sons, 1959.

———, and H. Raiffa, *Games and Decisions.* New York: John Wiley and Sons, 1957.

Markowitz, H., "The Utility of Wealth," *Journal of Political Economy,* **60** (1952), 151–158.

Miller, D. W., and M. K. Starr, *Executive Decisions and Operations Research.* Englewood Cliffs, N. J.: Prentice-Hall, 1960.

Radner, R., and J. Marschak, "Note on Some Proposed Decision Criteria," in Thrall, Coombs, and Davis (1954).

Rapoport, A., "Critiques of Game Theory," *Behavioral Science,* **4** (1959), 49–66.

Savage, L. J., "The Theory of Statistical Decisions," *Journal of the American Statistical Association,* **46** (1951), 55–67.

———, *The Foundations of Statistics.* New York: John Wiley and Sons, 1954.

Shubik, M., "The Use of Game Theory in Management Science," *Management Science,* **2** (1955), 40–54.

Simon, H. A., *Models of Man.* New York: John Wiley and Sons, 1957.

Thrall, R. M., C. H. Coombs, and R. L. Davis (eds.), *Decision Processes.* New York: John Wiley and Sons, 1954.

von Neumann, J., and O. Morgenstern, *Theory of Games and Economic Behavior.* Princeton, N. J.: Princeton University Press, 3rd ed., 1953.

Wasserman, P., and F. S. Silander, *Decision-Making: An Annotated Bibliography.* Ithaca, N. Y.: Graduate School of Business and Public Administration, Cornell University, 1958.

3

FORMULATING THE PROBLEM

INTRODUCTION

In applied research it is necessary to translate the decision maker's problem into a research problem. This requires a complete identification of the components of the decision maker's problem, which are

(1) the decision maker(s),
(2) his (or their) relevant objectives,
(3) the possible courses of action,
(4) the context: those aspects of the problem environment which, though not subject to the decision maker's control, may affect the outcome of his choice of action. These may be

    (*a*) "acts of nature," or
    (*b*) acts of other decision makers: reactions or counteractions.

Such identifications as are required may be very simple or quite complex, depending primarily on the problem context. If, for example, the decision maker controls a large organization within (or to) which others may react and which may be sensitive to general social or economic conditions, the mere formulation of the decision maker's problem may itself require considerable research and consume a significant portion of the total research time available.

Since our concern is not with specific techniques of research, we shall not treat in detail the actual operations involved in problem formulation. But it will be necessary at least to sketch these in order to have a background for discussion of the methodological problems involved in formulating the research problem.

In this discussion of the aspects of problem formulation we will concentrate on problem situations involving the operations of complex (i.e., organized man-machine) systems because the development of a simplified representation of a complex situation is a part of problem formulation. Hence, to use a simple example would be to ignore this essential feature of problem formulation.

Let us consider a decision maker whose choice will affect the operation of a complex man-machine system operating in a social context; for example, a government agency, a military arm, or an industrial organization. The decision maker may be a government official attempting to establish a public policy, a military leader seeking the best way to regulate purchasing of supplies, or a factory manager trying to determine how much of each of a set of products should be produced in the next month. In each of these cases the environment of the problem contains many forces which affect the kinds of choice which can be made and the kinds of outcome they will yield. It is generally necessary, therefore, to determine first how the environment and the context are related to the problem under consideration. By so doing, the various components of the problem can be identified and a foundation can be laid for subsequently establishing the relationship between these components.

ANALYSIS OF THE CONTEXT OF THE PROBLEM

Systems (and most problem contexts) consist of a set of needs or desires and interrelated activities connected by the flow of information which leads to decisions bringing about actions designed to yield some outcome that will satisfy the needs or desires.

The "triggering" need or desire which it is the purpose of the system to fulfill must be identified. In business, this may be a customer's desire for goods or services. In government, it may be the public's requirement that mail be delivered, or that roads be available for travel. In the military, it may be the need to deter or defend against possible enemy aggression.

How is information concerning the triggering need or desire conveyed to the organization which can do something about it? The forms and paths of the communications should be identified. Each message should be traced until it is disposed of or inactivated. It may go through many processes; information may be abstracted, or it may be combined with other information. The flow can be shown graphically by lines connecting "nodes" at which the information is treated in some way.

At each place where information is received a determination should be made as to what is done with it, how long it takes to do this, and what the capacity of the node is for doing what it does. At some points very simple operations such as routing and compiling may be performed. At others information may be collected, tabulated, and analyzed. All the relevant informational inputs and outputs at each node should be identified. At some points along the information paths decisions are made. The location and nature of the decision should be identified. The instructional outputs should be traced in the same way as the informational inputs.

The information in the system and the decisions based on it eventually make contact with the operations of the system; that is, they lead to action. The points of contact should be determined, and each step of the operations should be identified. The rate and capacity of operations at each stage should also be determined. The operations may involve such things as acquisition, transportation, conversion, inspection, and packaging of resources.

The information on decision making and operations is usually best recorded and displayed in one or more flow charts generously sprinkled with explanatory notes.

In light of what has been learned about decisions and operations in the system, determination should be made as to which messages have *no* effect on the activities of interest. These can be eliminated from further consideration.

The activities which are performed between control points (i.e., points at which decisions affect the operations) can be combined into one composite operation.

The resultant information-process-flow chart will show how the system operates, where and how decisions are made, and what they affect and how. Such an analysis may frequently reveal problems of which the decision maker was unaware or even show that the problem which he thinks he has is quite different from the one he actually has. Such cases are discussed in Churchman, Ackoff, and Arnoff (1957, Chapter 4).

The complexity of an analysis such as has been described depends directly on the complexity of the problem context. In the case of an individual confronted with a commonplace problem—for example, which of two routes to take in driving to work—the same components are present: informational inputs, transmission, compilation, decision, and so on. The system, however, is largely contained within the decision maker. His sensory, thinking, and motor processes may or may not be relevant, depending on the nature of the problem. For example, in determining how to design the controls of an automobile the complexities of the human system are relevant. In determining what size shirt a person should wear these complexities are irrelevant.

Since the decision maker is himself a complex system, all problems involve such a system: whether or not the complexity of this or other systems is relevant depends on how many of their characteristics affect the value of the choice that is made. How an individual perceives may not be relevant to the goodness of a shirt's fit, but it is to how he drives a car.

The analysis of the problem's context may be very costly and time consuming. If research funds and time are scarce, the researcher may have to abbreviate the procedure described here and/or the procedures involved in other phases of the research. How best to allocate scarce research resources in problem solving is itself a methodological problem which cannot yet be formulated, let alone be systematically solved. Consequently, an allocation of his resources to the phases of research must be made by the researcher on the basis of judgment and experience. A knowledge of how he ought to conduct each phase if no restrictions existed is necessary for making good estimates of the loss that will be incurred by performing a phase of the research in less than the best way available.

THE DECISION MAKER

It might appear as though the decision maker identifies himself when he brings the problem to the researcher, but this is not necessarily the case: it may be someone else's problem. To mention an obvious example, a research foundation may ask for study of a problem of, say, hospital administration. In such cases identification of the decision maker can be incredibly complex. Witness the difficulty of trying to determine who in a military arm or governmental agency accepts or rejects a new supply policy. In many large systems, particularly public ones, the organization almost appears to be designed to conceal the identity of the decision maker(s) and to confuse him who tries to make the identification.

Where the decision maker acts on behalf of an organization, nothing less than the type of system analysis briefly described in the last section may be required to locate the sources of decisions. Organization charts seldom provide reliable information in this regard; they may show who is "responsible" for control but not who exercises it.

THE DECISION MAKER'S OBJECTIVES

What is the decision maker trying to *attain* by solving the problem at hand? And what is he trying to *retain?* Objectives may involve either getting something one does not have or giving up none or as little as possible of something one does have. The decision maker's desire to retain things he already has is usually formulated as *restrictions* on possible solutions to the problem because they limit the set of courses of action which are acceptable to him.

Despite a popular misconception to the contrary, objectives are seldom given to the researcher. The decision maker seldom formulates his objectives accurately. He is likely to state his objectives in the form of platitudes which have no operational significance. Consequently, objectives usually have to be extracted by the researcher. In so doing the researcher may well be performing his most helpful service to the decision maker.

Direct questioning of the decision maker seldom reveals all the relevant objectives. One effective technique for uncovering these objectives consists of confronting the decision maker with each of the possible solutions to a problem and asking him whether he would follow that course of action if the research results supported it. Where he says, "No," further probing will usually reveal objectives which are not served by the course of action. For example, in one case in which an industrial manager who wanted to diversify his company's production was asked if he would be willing to produce a product closely related to those he already made, he replied, "No." His explanation was, "That would be no fun; we know all there is to know about that product." In this way he revealed an interest in novelty and an opportunity to learn something new. It is worth checking such answers by asking subordinates and other associates what *they* think the decision maker would do in each situation. This may frequently reveal an objective not admitted by the decision maker. For example, in one instance in which a decision maker expressed willingness to accept any of the alternatives proposed, each involving close association with a different person, his associates said that he would not accept one of these (or, if he did, he would sabotage it) because of his deep dislike for the person with whom he would be associated.

This approach to uncovering objectives is based on the observation that a decision maker and his associates are likely to be more certain about what they are willing (or are not willing) to do than about why they are so inclined. Objectives not only determine choices, but also are revealed by choices, though not necessarily without ambiguity. A choice may be explained by many different objectives. Consequently, choices have to be studied collectively in order to find underlying patterns.

Objectives are hard enough to define when they "stand still," but many change frequently. Science has a long way to go before it develops adequate techniques for determining what objectives are relevant in any choice situation, and how and why they change. Nevertheless, it is necessary to formulate them as best we can. By failing to do so we do not avoid a research problem, we merely deal with it unconsciously. Such dealings do not lend themselves to systematic improvement through subsequent examination and analysis. Everything should be done to keep open and encourage this possibility for improvement.

ALTERNATIVE COURSES OF ACTION

Various alternatives may be revealed in discussing the problem with the decision makers and, in more complex situations, by analysis of the system or organization involved. But alternative courses of action may be as illusive as objectives.

Essentially the task of identifying the possible courses of action consists of (a) identifying the variables that significantly affect the outcome of the problem, and (b) determining which of these can be controlled directly or indirectly by the decision maker.

The variables which define the alternative courses of action may be defined either quantitatively or qualitatively. If the variables are defined quantitatively, each possible set of values along the relevant scales specifies a possible course of action. For example, the variables may be the amount of a resource purchased and the price paid. Then each combination of a possible amount and price constitutes a relevant course of action. Each possibility need not be explicitly formulated if the relevant scales and the feasible ranges on each are made explicit. If the variable(s) are defined qualitatively, it is usually necessary to specify each possible course of action explicitly. For example, the single relevant controllable variable may be the mode of transportation. The possible courses of action may then be use of an automobile, train, or plane.

Determination of which variables affect the relevant outcome may require more than a casual analysis. It may involve such procedures as regression analysis or designed experiments. (These subjects will be considered in the discussion in Chapter 10 of ways of establishing the relevance of variables.)

In a development problem none of the available alternative courses of action is considered to be good enough; a better one is sought. Such problems are of two types: *design* and *search*. In a design problem a new material, instrument, or process is sought which is more efficient than any of those available. The alternative designs must be compared with each other and the available courses of action. The designs are differentiated by the values of a set of relevant properties which they incorporate. Aircraft designs, for example, may be differentiated with respect to wing span, type of power plant, length, and so on. These are properties which are relevant to the objectives expressed in such terms as a cruising speed, range, carrying capacity, and rate of climb.

In a search problem the instruments necessary for a better course of action are believed to exist, and they must be identified and/or located. For example, in pharmaceutical research a chemical compound may be sought which has certain properties relative to a specified ailment. Once the compound is found, it may be necessary to design a process for producing it in quantity.

A development problem, then—in a sense—consists of formulating a course of action, whereas a search problem consists of finding one. (This distinction may be difficult to make at times.) Once new possibilities are developed or found, however, they must be evaluated relative to each other and/or previously available courses of action. In either developmental or search problems it may not be possible to specify all the possible courses of action in advance, since the information gained in testing one possibility may be used in formulating the next alternative to be examined. That phase of research which is directed toward the discovery of new alternatives is usually called *exploration*. The system analysis described above is such an exploratory phase of research.

OTHER PARTICIPANTS AND UNCONTROLLED VARIABLES

If participants other than the decision maker(s) are involved in the problem, the courses of action available to them which may affect (cooperatively or in conflict) the outcome of the decision maker's

choice should also be identified. Where these participants are governments, military enemies, or competition, various types of "intelligence" may be required. Available information of this type may be incomplete, and hence "reasonable assumptions" concerning such alternatives may have to be made by the researcher and decision maker working collaboratively. In some instances it is desirable to set up a separate research or decision-making group to *play* the role of the opposition in order to ensure against oversight of important counteractions that might be selected. Military and management games *
are used increasingly for this purpose. (We will discuss the use of such games for other purposes in Chapter 11.)

"Hostile" or "cooperative" action may be taken by other than identifiable participants; for example, nature may "select" bad weather, or the economic system may "decide" to recede. Such acts involve changes in relevant uncontrolled variables. Identification of some of these variables may require sophisticated causal analysis. Such analysis (also relevant to disclosing controllable variables) will be considered in Chapter 10.

Defining Objectives and Associated Measures of Efficiency

The identification of objectives normally consists of *naming* the objectives, but this leaves a great deal to be done. For example, in the military context one might come up with such objectives as minimizing vulnerability and maximizing mobility, reliability, flexibility, or the state of readiness. In industrial problems the objectives may involve maximizing productivity, profit, share of the market, product leadership, growth, or security; or minimizing costs. In government the objective may be to maximize public service, safety, or protection of property. It is a long way between naming these objectives and obtaining suitable measures for the degree to which they are obtained, for all of them are quantitative in character. We shall discuss the problems of definition and measurement in Chapters 5 and 6, but some remarks are necessary here.

The measurement of attainment of some of these objectives may appear to be deceptively simple. Let us consider one concept which most people, particularly business executives, think they understand: profit. On the surface profit seems to be merely the difference between income and costs. However, it is first necessary to determine

---

* See Thomas and Deemer (1957) and Thomas (1961) for discussion of these games and their use in research.

whether one is concerned with gross or net profit: the difference before a portion of the income is withdrawn for such things as taxes (i.e., gross profit), or only that income whose disposition remains in the control of the company (net profit)? Without considering the problems associated with the measurement of either type of profit in detail, let us enumerate some of the difficulties involved in finding a suitable measure for it.

In order to measure the degree to which profits have been maximized it is necessary to select a period with respect to which the measure is to be made. It is clear that in most cases one cannot consider only the short-range effects of a decision but must also consider the longer-range consequences. How far ahead should one look? Once this has been decided, it becomes apparent that a dollar earned today has a different value from one earned some time from now. This is usually taken care of by a discounting procedure, a procedure by which a future dollar's value is reduced by a specific percentage per unit of time. It is necessary, therefore, to select an appropriate discount rate. Furthermore, since many conditions can change which will affect what profits are actually made in the future, there is more uncertainty concerning future profits than there is concerning present ones. Therefore, it is necessary to take the uncertainty into account in evaluating possible future profits.

Each of these questions—the planning period, the discount rate, and the adjustment for uncertainty—is very difficult to answer. The nature of this difficulty is discussed in detail by Churchman (1956).

As indicated, in later chapters we will consider how such objectives (as well as other concepts) ought to be defined and how measures for them ought to be specified. Nowhere in research, however, is it as difficult to approach doing as well as we know how as in obtaining adequate definitions and measures of objectives. The fact is that in much applied research the investigators do not explicitly define the objectives or develop adequate measures of their attainment, but rather they accept the use of convenient *indices*. For example, consider the "state of readiness" of a military force. Here researchers may use a measure of the average number of pieces of equipment which are available for use, and perhaps some measure of the dispersion of the actual number available around this mean. With only minimum reflection the deficiencies of such an index become apparent. Obviously, readiness depends on (among other things) the condition of the equipment involved. Equipment which is likely to be usable for only a short time does not yield nearly as much readiness as equipment which can be expected to operate over an extended period of time. Furthermore, readiness depends on the ability of the force involved to maintain the equipment in operating condition so that some measure of down time for repair should be a part of the measure of readiness. One could continue to point out shortcomings of the index, but it soon becomes apparent that a full-time research effort could be directed at only the question of how to measure this state adequately.

The research at hand would never be completed if we had to solve fully every research problem that arises on the way to solving the problem at hand. Therefore a critical problem in the strategy of research is where to cut off consideration of such problems as arise in defining and finding suitable measures for objectives.

Wherever one stops and however one decides where to stop in the pursuit of these subproblems, it is clear that if future research is to do better than current research it is necessary to report explicitly on the considerations which went into the definitions and measures which are used. The deficiencies which are believed to exist should be made explicit, so that later researchers can begin where this research left off. In this way progress can at least be made gradually, and subsequent researchers can be spared going through the difficulties encountered previously, or at least can know specifically where to take issue with previous work.

As a minimum the measure adopted in the research should be acceptable to the decision maker. It must be one that he is willing to accept. Hence it is important that the decision maker actively participate in the development and/or acceptance of those measures of degrees of attainment of objectives which are to be used in the research. It should be noted that, despite the allusion to the contrary in the discussion of profit, decision makers are usually aware of the shortcomings of suggested measures of attainment of an objective.

We assume in the remaining discussion of this chapter that such measures have been obtained. But we will return to these problems of definition and measurement in Chapters 5 and 6.

MEASURES OF PERFORMANCE

In Chapter 2 the following types of problems and their requirements relative to a measure of performance were considered:

(1) *One qualitative objective.* All that is required is a *measure of efficiency* for this objective.

(2) *Two or more qualitative objectives.* A measure of efficiency for each objective is required and a measure of the *relative value* of each objective.

(3) *One quantitative objective.* A measure of efficiency involving an input and/or output scale is required and a measure of the relative values of points on the scale employed.

(4) *Two or more quantitative objectives.* A measure of efficiency for each objective is required, as well as a way of *transforming units* on the various efficiency scales employed into one "standard" scale, and a measure of relative values of points on the "standard" scale.

(5) *Mixed objectives.* Measures of efficiency and relative value are required and, if two or more quantitative objectives are involved, transformations into a "standard" scale.

There are two different ways of handling the measure of performance. In the first, the *a priori* method, the complete measure P is developed before a model of the problem situation is constructed, so that the model can take the form already referred to:

$$P = f(X_i, Y_j)$$

where, ideally, P is a measure of expected value. In the second, the *a posteriori*, approach, the outcome is expressed either as a measure of expected efficiency for one objective or as an expected effectiveness. In the former case, the model is solved by optimizing relative to one control variable for a variety of assumed values of the other control variables. This yields what is called an *efficient surface* or *curve* from which a point is chosen by the decision maker. In the latter case, the transformation function is itself treated as a variable, so that an "effectiveness surface" or "curve" is obtained from which a point is chosen. In either case the choice of a point at which to operate contains an *implicit* transformation and evaluation of scales, as contrasted with the *explicit* transformation and evaluation in the *a priori* method.

We will first consider the steps involved in the *a priori* method.

A *Priori* Transformation Functions

In order to demonstrate the various methods of transforming one scale into another we shall consider situations which arise very commonly in applied research, ones involving the conflict of two objectives. One of these objectives normally takes the form of minimizing the expenditure of a valuable resource required to perform a desired task. The other involves minimizing the inability to perform that task because of lack of resources. The first objective, then, involves the conservation of resources, and the second the avoidance of an undesirable outcome. For example, in business a manufacturer may want both to minimize the cost of his operations and to fill any customer's order when it arrives and, hence, minimize delay. The conflict between such objectives arises out of the fact that the chances of avoiding the undesirable event can be increased only at the expense of the resource to be conserved. The transformation problem, then, involves evaluating the "occurrence of the event to be avoided" along the same scale on which the "resources to be conserved" are measured.

Objective transformations

The behavior of the process itself involved in the problem can be used in some cases to provide the information required to obtain the desired transformation function.

Consider the following simplification of a real case. A merchandising firm receives mail orders for goods selected by customers from a catalogue. The orders are filled by clerks who draw the required goods from stocks, package, and mail them. In this case the company involved wanted to determine how large a staff of order clerks it should maintain. Two objectives were involved: the company desired to minimize the cost of its operations (conservation objective), and it also sought to minimize the time the customer must wait for receipt of the goods ordered (avoidance objective).

It seemed clear that to express the (negative) value of delay to the customer as a cost would be desirable. Consequently, the research team studied the system to determine how much order-filling delay cost the company. First, records were examined to determine what proportion of orders were returned to the company by the customer because of delay and how this proportion varied for various delays in

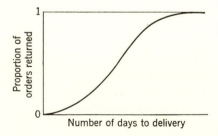

FIGURE 3.1.

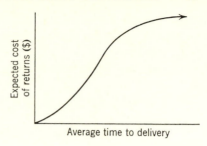

FIGURE 3.2.

receipt of goods by the customer. This analysis revealed a function of the form shown in Figure 3.1. That is, delays of up to a few days had practically no effect on the return rate; then for increasing delays the proportion of returns increased at a relatively constant rate. Beyond a certain delay the return rate remained relatively constant, rising almost imperceptibly.

Next an analysis was performed to determine whether the value of the goods was in any way related to the delay in shipment. No relationship was found. This meant that the length of a delay in shipping did not depend on the size or value of an order.

It was now necessary to determine the cost of a returned order. This cost involves both direct outlays and customer dissatisfaction. Hence, an analysis was made of the salvage value of returned orders. Salvage value was expressed as a percentage of the sale value and was found to be relatively constant.

By studying the distribution of the sizes of orders it was then possible to determine the average dollar loss resulting from a returned order. To this expected cost was added the cost of shipping itself. Finally, by multiplying this combined cost of return by the probability of return a function of the form shown in Figure 3.2 was obtained. This, then, provided a transformation function in which the expected cost associated with various delays could be obtained.

The question remained as to whether or not customers were lost by long delays and, consequently, whether loss of future sales had to be taken into account. It was found, on examination of the records, however, that delays of the frequency and magnitude actually experienced by customers did not affect the amount or frequency of their orders. Therefore the transformation could be used without adjustment for loss of future business. It was very likely, of course, that repetitive delays of long duration would affect future business, but the range of delays within which the company was willing to operate made the probability of a sequence of long delays very unlikely.

The underlying principle in this procedure is very simple: it attempts to determine *what is the loss of the resource to be conserved in the occurrence of the event to be avoided.* Determination of this loss, however, may be very complicated or even impractical. If, for example, in the case just considered, customers were lost due to repetition of delays, it would have been a much more difficult problem, though not necessarily an impossible one.

In another problem in which the event to be avoided was the cancellation of a scheduled flight of a commercial airline it was not possible (and, as it turned out, not necessary) to determine the effect on future business of such a cancellation. A variation of the transformation procedure just described was used.

The problem of the commercial airline involved determining how many stewardesses should be located at each base. The objectives were "to minimize the cost of stewardesses" (the size of the stewardess staff at each base) and "to minimize the number of instances on which stewardesses were not available for a scheduled flight." If a stewardess is not available for a flight, it cannot be flown.

An examination of the past history of the company revealed—to the surprise of the research team—that a flight cancellation due to lack of stewardesses had never taken place. This was surprising because it could be shown that with the existing staff the probability of running out of stewardesses was not negligible. It turned out, however, that the stewardess administrators at each base had advance knowledge as to when such a run-out would occur and therefore could take some preventive action. The administrator would obtain the aid of an ex-stewardess who lived in the city and who could be enlisted on a special emergency basis at an additional cost to the company. In this case, then, the cost of a run-out was the cost of the emergency measure (expediting) which was taken.

This cost is not a linear function of the number of simultaneous run-outs. That is, it becomes increasingly difficult for the administrator to obtain emergency stewardesses as the number required increases. An examination of the records indicated that these costs increased approximately as the square of the number of stewardesses required; that is, quadratically.

It should be observed that the cost of prevention might exceed the cost of the event to be avoided. But if it is the correct policy to prevent rather than incur the undesirable outcome, the "cost" of such an event as "running out" is the cost of preventing that outcome if the event occurs.

A similar problem arose in connection with production control in a pharmaceutical company. Here the objectives were "to minimize production and inventory costs" and (again) "to minimize the lateness of delivery of customer orders." An examination of past records indicated that delays beyond promised delivery dates practically never occurred. The reason was that, when there was a shortage of a product relative to an order in hand, a special production run was initiated and expedited under the direction of a manager so as to be sure the promised delivery date was met.

Here the cost of expediting involved two components: the cost of the labor (managerial and otherwise) required to perform the necessary expediting, and the cost added to scheduled production by the interruptions in the schedule. In this case the second component of cost was difficult but possible to determine.

The general logic of this second procedure for making an objective transformation then is *to determine the cost* (in terms of the resource to be conserved) *of avoiding or preventing the event to be avoided*. This method assumes that avoidance is always possible. Justification of this assumption may be difficult but is nevertheless necessary for the application of this procedure.

Subjective transformations

If an objective procedure cannot be used, then the researcher can ask the decision maker(s) to sketch a transformation function, using his best judgment.

This subjective but explicit procedure at least opens the possibility for future objective evaluation of the transformation function obtained. It is important to remember that a decision involving quantitative objectives measured on different scales requires transformations. Transformations cannot be avoided, but they can be submerged in unconscious processes and hence can be kept from objective examination in the future.

A *Priori* Evaluation of Objectives

Efforts to measure the relative value an individual places on objects, events, or states date back at least a century and a half. In 1789 Jeremy Bentham attempted to construct what he called a *calculus of values*. Since then economists have speculated continuously on the measurement of *utility* (their term for "value"). In the last twenty-five years psychologists have directed their attention to the measurement of *attitudes*, a concept closely related to that of value.* But it has been only in the last decade that a major scientific effort has been made to develop and apply such measures. Recent efforts have received their principal stimulation from either the work of von Neumann and Morgenstern (1953) in the development of the theory of games, or the work of E. A. Singer, Jr., in the development of his philosophy of *experimentalism* (1924, 1936, and 1948).

A completely general measure of relative value (one that is applicable in all situations) has yet to be developed. But progress has been rapid, largely because of a high degree of methodological self-consciousness which has characterized the work.† The measures which are available all make rather strong assumptions concerning the nature of values and human choices. An increasing number of different techniques of measuring value based on different assumptions offer the researcher a growing store from which to make a selection.

Contemporary scientists inherit a strong disinclination to involve themselves in questions concerning values. The majority of scientists and philosophers alike have argued in the past that questions of value are not reducible to or translatable into scientific questions. A minority has argued to the contrary. But this argument is not immediately relevant to the problem at hand. The argument concerns the scientific determination of what people *ought* to value, not what they do value. Even if we grant that science ought not to concern itself with what people ought to desire,‡ we have not established the impropriety of science determining what people *do* value. Nevertheless, some of the scientific disinclination to deal with what people "ought to value" rubs off on the question of what they do value.

This disinclination is manifested in applied research by a tendency to consider only one—generally the most important—objective in seeking solutions to problems. This means that only a measure of efficiency need be used to find a "solution," no measures of value. The important point about such "simplification" is that it does not obviate the evaluation problem. In effect such a simplification consists of an implicit assignment of maximum value to one objective and zero value to all other relevant objectives. Such a procedure is likely to introduce more distortion of the real problem than even uncontrolled guesses by the decision maker as to the relative values of the objectives. This simplification constitutes a *resolution*, not a solution, of the evaluation problem. Evaluation cannot be avoided, but it can be pushed down below the level of research consciousness.

* See Arrow (1958).
† For the most complete methodological analysis to date see Churchman (1961).
‡ I am not willing to grant this assumption. See Ackoff (1949).

Since a large proportion of the currently available measures of value are based on the work of von Neumann and Morgenstern, we will first consider their measure and the theory on which it is based.

von Neumann-Morgenstern measure of utility

In order to avoid introducing a new set of symbols we shall translate the theory of von Neumann and Morgenstern into symbols we have already used, with only a few additions.

(a) O_1, O_2, O_3, $\cdots$ represent outcomes, objects, or anything to be evaluated.

(b) $O_1 > O_2$ means that O_1 is preferred to O_2, and $O_1 < O_2$ means O_2 is preferred to O_1.

(c) α, β, γ, $\cdots$ represent real numbers between 0 and 1. (These will be subsequently interpreted as probabilities.)

(d) $(\alpha, O_1{:}O_2)$ represents a choice of either O_1 with probability α or O_2 with probability $(1 - \alpha)$. This expression represents what is called a *gamble*.

(e) $O_1 = O_2$ means that neither is preferred to the other; the decision maker is *indifferent* as between O_1 and O_2.

The following postulates make explicit the assumed nature of evaluation:

(1) For any O_1 and O_2, either $O_1 > O_2$, $O_2 > O_1$, or $O_1 = O_2$. This asserts that any pair of outcomes can be ordered preferentially, that is, ranked.

(2) If $O_1 > O_2$ and $O_2 > O_3$, then $O_1 > O_3$. This asserts that the relation "is preferred to" is transitive.

(3a) If $O_1 > O_2$, then $O_1 > (\alpha, O_1{:}O_2)$, for any α. This asserts that if O_1 is preferred to O_2, then certain attainment of O_1 is preferable to any gamble in which there is some probability of less than 1 of getting O_1 or getting a less desirable outcome with one minus the probability of obtaining O_1. Suppose, for example, that a person would rather have a new wrist watch than a new fountain pen. Now suppose that he is given a choice of a wrist watch or taking a gamble in which he obtains either a wrist watch or fountain pen. It is asserted that he would prefer the wrist watch to the gamble. (This assumption implies that the decision maker places no value on the act of gambling itself. This implication will be discussed below.)

(3b) If $O_1 < O_2$, then $O_1 < (\alpha, O_1{:}O_2)$.

(4a) If $O_1 > O_2 > O_3$, then there exists an α $(0 < \alpha < 1)$ such that $(\alpha, O_1{:}O_3) > O_2$. Suppose that a wrist watch is preferred to a pen and the pen is preferred to a pencil. Then this postulate asserts that it is possible to find a gamble involving the watch and pencil that is preferred to the pen.

(4b) If $O_1 > O_2 > O_3$, then there exists a β $(0 < \beta < 1)$ such that $O_2 > (\beta, O_1:O_3)$. Using the same example as above, this asserts that it is also possible to find a gamble involving the watch and pencil such that the pen is preferred to it. (In general α will be "high" and β will be "low.")

(5) $(\alpha, O_1:O_2) = (1 - \alpha, O_2:O_1)$, for any α. This asserts that the order in which the choices are offered has no effect on preferences.

(6) $[\alpha(\beta, O_1:O_2):O_2] = (\alpha\beta, O_1:O_2)$. This asserts that probabilities can be multiplied, and hence compound gambles can be formed which obey the preceding postulates. Algebraic expansion of the left-hand expression gives the right-hand expression.

If the decision maker's values conform to these assumptions and if his choices satisfy two other conditions to be discussed below, his values can be measured as follows.

Consider three objectives which are ranked by the decision maker in order of preference as O_1, O_2, and O_3. Arbitrarily assign a value to O_1 of 1 and a value to O_3 of 0. Now find the α for which

$$\alpha O_1 + (1 - \alpha)O_3 = O_2.$$

Then $V_2 = \alpha$. For example, if the objectives are (in order) watch, pen, and pencil; and if it is found that

$$0.7V \text{ (watch)} + 0.3V \text{ (pencil)} = 1.0V \text{ (pen)},$$

then if V (watch) is set at 1.0 and V (pencil) is set at 0,

$$0.7(1.0) + 0.3(0) = 1.0V \text{ (pen)}, \quad \text{and} \quad V \text{ (pen)} = 0.7.$$

In his detailed evaluation of this theory Churchman (1956) has found "reasonable" grounds to question the general validity of each postulate cited above, and he has considered tests which might be used to establish or reject these postulates. Others have also called these postulates into question. Our concern here, however, is with the assumptions concerning the decision maker's choices rather than his scale of values.

The von Neumann-Morgenstern procedure assumes that the subject knows what the true probabilities are; that is, that the "chances" associated with the various outcomes which he believes to exist correspond exactly with the "objective" probabilities. Here again there is considerable experimental evidence to indicate that this is not true in general.* This evidence has driven some to develop value-measurement procedures which do not have this property. One such effort will be considered later.

Certain practical considerations in the use of such a measuring procedure are involved. The choices presented to the decision maker are difficult for him to comprehend. In addition, the procedure is awkward to extend to more than three objectives and becomes increasingly difficult as the number of objectives increases.

Davidson-Siegel-Suppes measure of utility

As one would expect, following the initial pioneering of von Neumann and Morgenstern into the no-man's land of values, a number of efforts were made to find measures which were in some sense better than the one presented above. One of the most sophisticated is the procedure developed by Davidson, Siegel, and Suppes. In a paper by Siegel (1956, pp. 212–213) the procedure is succinctly described as follows:

Davidson, Siegel, and Suppes,† in a study designed to measure the utility of money in the sense of an interval scale, developed an event which, for most people, has a subjective probability of one-half. Such an event is difficult to find because of the prejudices and superstitions which most people hold concerning familiar events, e.g., heads on coins, evens on dice, etc. The event used here is produced by means of specially made dice. On three faces on the die, the nonsense syllable *ZOJ* is engraved, and on the other three faces *ZEJ* is engraved. Similar dice were made with pairs *WUH*, *XEG*, and *QUG*, *QUJ* on their faces. These syllables were selected from Glaze,‡ who reports these pairs to have practically zero association value. The dice were tested with each subject; in every case the expectation of zero association was upheld, i.e., each subject was indifferent about which nonsense syllable he would bet on or which one would be the winner. The use of these dice will be discussed further in the following section.

Careful and considered choices between the probability-combinations presented to a subject were assured by "realistic" conditions. That is, when books were used as entities to be scaled, the subject was assured of getting a book or books. The identity of the book he received was a function of *all* of his choice behavior. Therefore he was highly involved in each choice. When amounts of money were used as the entities, the subject was given a sum of money (usually one dollar) at the start of the session. He gambled with that money, keeping all funds in his possession at the end of the session.

The essential device that defines operationally how the subject's choices

---

* See Edwards (1954).

† D. Davidson, S. Siegel, and P. Suppes, "Some Experiments and Related Theory in the Measurement of Utility and Subjective Probability," *Report* No. 4, Stanford Value Theory Project, 1955.

‡ J. A. Glaze, "The Association Value of Nonsense Syllables," *Journal of Genetic Psychology*, **35** (1928), 255–267.

determine ordered metric scaling is a one-person game * in which the subject chooses between two alternatives, each of which is a probability-combination of two outcomes. The format for each offer is:

	Alternative 1	Alternative 2
If event E occurs:	you get w	you get x
If not-E occurs:	you get z	you get y

The subject chooses the column; the outcome of event E determines the row. Event E might be *ZOJ*, in which case not-E would be *ZEJ*.

Suppose $w > x > y > z$. If the subject chooses Alternative 1, then

$$(w, z; p) > (x, y; p). \tag{1}$$

If $u(w)$ is read as "the utility of w," and is interpreted as the subjective value of w, i.e., its worth to the person, then (1) can be written:

$$p \cdot u(w) + (1 - p) \cdot u(z) > p \cdot u(x) + (1 - p) \cdot u(y). \tag{2}$$

If p is understood to be subjective probability, and is known to be one-half, then (2) may be written:

$$u(w) + u(z) > u(x) + u(y), \tag{3}$$

and

$$u(w) - u(x) > u(y) - u(z), \tag{4}$$

i.e.,

$$\overline{wx} > \overline{yz}, \text{ when } (w, z; p) > (x, y; p). \tag{5}$$

That is, w and x differ in utility more than y and z.

It should be noted that the distances are *directed* distances. That is, $\overline{xw}$ is the negative of $\overline{wx}$. To simplify comparisons, the convention has been adopted of always deriving the distance from the more preferred to the less preferred entity. [For example, from (3) above we could get $u(z) - u(y) > u(x) - u(w)$. But since $w > x > y > z$, we multiply through by -1 to get (4) as shown.]

From a practical point of view this procedure is reported to work well in laboratory situations. Siegel reports that, on the average, the time required to obtain the measurements for five entities is twenty minutes. There has, as yet, been no report of efforts to apply the method in "real" situations.

It should be noted that, though this procedure probably reduces the hazard of assuming the equivalence of subjective and objective probability, it does not remove it. It also assumes, as indicated above, that choice is made so as to maximize expected value.

Both the von Neumann and Davidson procedures assume that no value is placed on the act of gambling itself. Evidence of such value

---

* D. Davidson, S. Siegel, and P. Suppes, "Some Experiments and Related Theory in the Measurement of Utility and Subjective Probability," *Report* No. 4, Stanford Value Theory Project, 1955.

has been found by Royden, Suppes, and Walsh (1959), who then added this consideration to their gambling model of value. They tried the "enriched model" on a group of sailors and college students. It led to better predictions for the former but worse for the latter.

Churchman-Ackoff approximate measure of value

The third procedure to be presented, unlike the preceding two, is not based on the concept of a gamble and hence makes no assumptions about subjective probability or maximization of expected value. Although developed independently, it resembles a procedure used in chemistry for estimating values of a property of each of a set of objects where only comparative evaluations are possible. The procedure first appeared in Ackoff (1953). The underlying assumptions were presented in a subsequent paper by Churchman and Ackoff (1954).

The procedure is perhaps best understood by example. We will consider a case involving four outcomes. The steps are as follows:

(1) Have the subject rank the four outcomes in order of importance and then assign numbers to each which reflect his relative evaluation of them. Let O_1, O_2, O_3, and O_4 represent these outcomes, ordered from the most to the least important.

(2) Determine which is preferred, O_1 or the combination of O_2, O_3, and O_4. If the combination is preferred, then

(2a) Determine which is preferred, O_1 or the combination of O_2 and O_3.

(3) Determine which is preferred, O_2 or the combination of O_3 and O_4.

(4) Determine whether or not the numbers assigned in step (1) are consistent with the preferences expressed in steps (2) and (3). If they are, the procedure is completed; if not, confront the subject with the inconsistency and have him modify either the numbers or the preferences until they are consistent.

Suppose, for example, that the subject has assigned the numbers 6, 4, 3, and 1 to O_1, O_2, O_3, and O_4, respectively; and that he has expressed the following preferences:

$$O_1 > (O_2 \text{ and } O_3 \text{ and } O_4)$$

$$O_2 > (O_3 \text{ and } O_4).$$

The numbers are inconsistent with both expressions of preference. If he changes the numbers to 8, 4, 2, and 1, the results would then be consistent.

This procedure has been adapted to situations involving large numbers of outcomes. Without such adaptation the procedure as described becomes unmanageable when more than about six outcomes are involved. The procedure for evaluating larger numbers of outcomes is as follows:

(*a*) Select one of the outcomes at random.

(*b*) Assign the remaining outcomes at random to groups of approximately five each—the groups need not be equal—and add the outcome selected in step (*a*) to each group.

(*c*) Evaluate each group by the procedure described in steps (1) to (4) with the following modification: after the subject has evaluated the first group, assign the number that he has associated with the outcome that appears in each group to the same outcome in the other groups. Subsequently, in assigning (and adjusting) numbers assigned to outcomes in the other groups he must leave this number alone.

Reliability of this procedure can be checked easily by repeating the process, selecting a different "common" outcome and different groupings. Applications of these procedures and use with groups of decision makers are discussed in detail by Churchman *et al.* (1957, Chapter 6).

The assumptions underlying this procedure are as follows:

(1) For each outcome, in a set of outcomes in a specified situation, there corresponds a real nonnegative number V_j, to be interpreted as a measure of the true *relative* value of O_j in *that* situation. (Each V_j, then, is relative to the set $\{O_j\}$ and the situation.)

(2) If O_j is more important than O_k, then $V_j > V_k$, and if O_j and O_k are equally important, then $V_j = V_k$.

(3) If V_j and V_k correspond to O_j and O_k, respectively, then V_j plus V_k corresponds to the combined outcome O_j and O_k.

This additivity assumption will fail if O_j and O_k are logically incapable of occurring simultaneously. For example, if O_j is "to earn exactly \$10" and O_k is "to earn exactly \$20," these cannot simultaneously occur and the assumed condition fails.

In many cases where the outcomes appear to violate the additivity assumption they can be reformulated so that the assumption is applicable. Consider, for example, a case in which an individual values both salt herring and chocolate cake taken separately, but not in combination. His desire for these foods may be formulated as "to have salt herring at a meal not involving chocolate cake" and "to have chocolate cake at a meal not involving salt herring." The values of these outcomes may satisfy the condition of additivity, since they do not involve a combination of the foods at the same meal, but rather a combination of meals.

The additivity assumption, not present in the von Neumann and Davidson procedures, has the following corollaries:

$(3a)$ If $O_j > O_k$ and $O_k > O_l$, then $(O_j$ and $O_k) > O_l$.

$(3b)$ $(O_j$ and $O_k) = (O_k$ and $O_j)$.

$(3c)$ If $(O_j$ and $O_k) = O_k$, then $V_j = 0$.

If an O_j exists satisfying this last condition, then there is a zero point on the scale which is invariant with any transformation of the value scale. This is not true for the two methods presented earlier.

Another property of this procedure should be noted. It does *not* assume that subjective and objective probabilities correspond; probabilities are not involved. It does, however, make the assumption of additivity and hence is applicable only to qualitatively defined outcomes. The gambling models are not so restricted.

In effect, this method requires the decision maker to express a preference between paired sets of outcomes. By the assumptions stated, these expressions give rise to a system of inequalities among the V's. Thus the value of each outcome may not be uniquely determined. Consider, for example, a system of three outcomes, O_1, O_2, and O_3, where the decision maker has expressed the following preferences:

(1) $O_1 > O_2$,
(2) $O_2 > O_3$, and
(3) $O_1 > O_2 + O_3$.

This gives rise to the corresponding inequalities:

(1) $V_1 > V_2$,
(2) $V_2 > V_3$, and
(3) $V_1 > V_2 + V_3$.

Even if it is assumed that $0 \leqq V_i \leqq 1$, and

(4) $V_1 + V_2 + V_3 = 1$,

there is no unique solution to this system. In fact, each possible triplet of values may be considered to be a point in three-dimensional space. It can be shown that the set of all such points is a convex set. There are methods, however, for expressing analytically this solution set.

Although the solution, using this method, is not necessarily unique, the method does provide two important inroads on the problem of measuring value. First, it provides a systematic method for determining whether or not the decision maker's expressions of preference are internally consistent and consistent with his quantitative judgments of relative value; that is, the numbers assigned. Second, the procedure provides a method for determining the bounds or limits on the estimates of value that are consistent with the preference expressions. In some cases, depending upon the nature of the efficiency matrix, even though the solution set may be fairly large, any point in it will lead to the selection of the same course of action as will any other point.

The techniques of linear programming can be used for finding all the possible sets of values which can be assigned to outcomes consistent with the preferences expressed by the decision maker.

In the von Neumann, Davidson, and Case * methods the judgments of the decision maker are applied to outcomes which are assumed (explicitly or implicitly) to be exclusive and exhaustive; in the Churchman-Ackoff procedure the outcomes are assumed to be neither. In many problems the outcomes as initially formulated may not satisfy the exclusiveness and exhaustiveness requirement. Consider a commonplace situation in which an individual wants black coffee and sugar. If obtaining coffee and obtaining sugar are treated as outcomes, they are not exclusive. To obtain a set of exclusive and exhaustive outcomes we combine the two "primitive" outcomes into "compound" outcomes by means of a Boolean expansion:

(1) Coffee and sugar.
(2) Coffee but not sugar.
(3) Sugar but not coffee.
(4) Neither sugar nor coffee.

In general, if there are n primitive outcomes, they can be combined into 2^n compound outcomes that are exclusive and exhaustive.

Suppose that the primitives are quantitative outcomes, say the amount of coffee and the amount of sugar obtained. Clearly, the value of an amount of coffee depends on the amount of sugar that is available; that is, these values are not independent, and hence they

---

* This procedure is considered in the next section.

cannot be added to obtain the value of a combination. Put another way,

$$V(C \text{ and } S) \neq V(C) + V(S),$$

where $V(C \text{ and } S)$ is the value of an amount of coffee, C, and an amount of sugar, S; and $V(C)$ is the value of an amount of coffee, C, with no sugar; and $V(S)$ is the value of an amount of sugar, S, with no coffee. Hence, various combined amounts of coffee and sugar should be considered as outcomes. This means that the outcome is multidimensional and that the value of combinations when plotted is a surface or volume rather than a line.

Case measure of relative value

This fourth type of measure shares with von Neumann's theory applicability to both quantitative and qualitative outcomes, or to a combination of them. If transitivity is assumed, it also yields an interval scale. If transitivity is not assumed, the measure can be used to determine whether or not the values obtained are transitive. This procedure requires less complex judgments than those required by either the von Neumann or the Davidson procedure.

Consider a set of exclusive and exhaustive outcomes $(O_1, O_2, \cdots, O_n)$. Assume that one can obtain from a subject judgments which yield a set of probabilities $(P_1, P_2, \cdots, P_n)$ such that the choices $P_1O_1, P_2O_2, \cdots, P_nO_n$ are equally preferred.* Then, on the assumption that the subject is trying to maximize expected value, we can conclude that

$$P_1V_1 = P_2V_2 = \cdots = P_nV_n, \tag{6}$$

where V_1 is the relative value of O_1, V_2 is the relative value of O_2, and so on.

Now let $\sum V_j = K$, where K is some arbitrarily selected constant, say 1.0. It follows from $P_1V_1 = P_2V_2$ that

$$V_2 = \frac{P_1}{P_2} V_1. \tag{7}$$

Similarly

$$V_3 = \frac{P_1}{P_3} V_1 \tag{8}$$

* In each case where P_j refers to the probability of attaining O_j, the alternative outcome with probability $(1 - P_j)$ is assumed to be in effect: "no change in the present state of the environment" or "maintaining the status quo."

or, in general,

$$V_j = \frac{P_k}{P_j} V_k. \tag{9}$$

Then

$$V_1 + \frac{P_1}{P_2} V_1 + \frac{P_1}{P_3} V_1 + \cdots + \frac{P_1}{P_n} V_1 = 1.0. \tag{10}$$

From this we obtain

$$V_1 \left(1 + \frac{P_1}{P_2} + \frac{P_1}{P_3} + \cdots + \frac{P_1}{P_n} \right) = 1.0 \tag{11}$$

$$V_1 = 1 \bigg/ \left(1 + \frac{P_1}{P_2} + \frac{P_1}{P_3} + \cdots + \frac{P_1}{P_n} \right). \tag{12}$$

Once the numerical value of V_1 is thus established, the relative values of V_2, V_3, $\cdots$, V_n are easily obtained.

For example, consider four outcomes in which the preference equalities are

$$0.4O_1 = 0.3O_2 = 0.2O_3 = 0.1O_4.$$

Then

$$V_1 = \tfrac{4}{3} V_1 + \tfrac{4}{2} V_1 + \tfrac{4}{1} V_1 = 1.0.$$

Hence,

$$V_1 = 1/(1 + \tfrac{4}{3} + 2 + 4) = \tfrac{3}{25}.$$

Therefore,

$$V_2 = (\tfrac{4}{3})(\tfrac{3}{25}) = \tfrac{4}{25}$$

$$V_3 = 2(\tfrac{3}{25}) = \tfrac{6}{25}$$

$$V_4 = 4(\tfrac{3}{25}) = \tfrac{12}{25}$$

and

$$V_1 + V_2 + V_3 + V_4 = \tfrac{3}{25} + \tfrac{4}{25} + \tfrac{6}{25} + \tfrac{12}{25} = 1.0.$$

If three outcomes are involved, we could proceed by finding the values of P_1, P_2, and P_3 such that

$$P_1 O_1 = P_2 O_2 \quad \text{and} \quad P_1 O_1 = P_3 O_3 \tag{13}$$

or

$$P_1 O_1 = P_2 O_2 \quad \text{and} \quad P_2 O_2 = P_3' O_3. \tag{14}$$

For the first case, as we have shown,

$$V_3 = \frac{P_1}{P_3} V_1. \tag{15}$$

In the second case,

$$V_3 = \frac{P_2}{P_3{}'} V_2 \tag{16}$$

and

$$V_2 = \frac{P_1}{P_2} V_1. \tag{17}$$

Hence,

$$V_3 = \frac{P_2}{P_3{}'} \frac{P_1}{P_2} V_1 = \frac{P_1}{P_3{}'} V_1. \tag{18}$$

Now, if we proceed by using both sets of comparisons and if the rankings of the two sets—P_1, P_2, P_3 and P_1, P_2, $P_3{}'$—are identical with respect to the subscripts 1, 2, and 3, the preferences are transitive; if not, the preferences are not transitive. For example, $P_1 > P_2 > P_3$ and $P_1 > P_2 > P_3{}'$ yield transitivity, but $P_1 > P_2 > P_3$ and $P_1 > P_3{}' > P_2$ do not.

In addition, by comparing the values P_3 and $P_3{}'$ we obtain a good measure of the reliability of the judgments of the subject.

The fundamental question which this and the other methods of measuring value raises concerns the possibility of developing a procedure which makes no assumptions concerning the nature of values or the criterion of selection actually used by the decision maker. Churchman and Ackoff attempted to define such a procedure (1947). Churchman (1961) has re-examined this suggestion in light of the recent developments of such measures as have been discussed here. The procedure requires the ability to measure such properties of the evaluator as his familiarity with and knowledge of the courses of action available to him. At the present time these are at least as difficult to measure as is value. The procedure, then, cannot be applied in practice at present, but it represents a first effort to provide a completely general standard for the measurement of relative value.

Minimal information required on relative values

Although the criterion of maximum expected value is defined as

$$\max_{} \sum_j E_{ij} V_j, \text{ where } \sum_j E_{ij} V_j = E(C_i), \tag{19}$$

it is not always necessary to know the numerical value of the V_j's in order to find the course of action which yields this maximum. If only two outcomes are involved, O_1 and O_2, and they are defined so as to be exclusive and exhaustive in the relevant environment, then we need only know if $V_1 > V_2$, $V_2 > V_1$, or $V_1 = V_2$. This can be shown as follows:

(1) Since O_1 and O_2 are exclusive and exhaustive, $E_{11} + E_{12} = E_{21} + E_{22} = 1.0$. (By convention let $E_{11} > E_{21}$; then, $E_{22} > E_{12}$.)

(2) Therefore, $E_{11} - E_{21} = E_{22} - E_{12}$.

(3) Now, $E(C_1) > E(C_2)$ if $E_{11}V_1 + E_{12}V_2 > E_{21}V_1 + E_{22}V_2$, or $E_{11}V_1 - E_{21}V_1 > E_{22}V_2 - E_{12}V_2 = V_1(E_{11} - E_{21}) > V_2(E_{22} - E_{12})$.

(4) But, since $E_{11} - E_{21} = E_{22} - E_{12}$, this last condition reduces to $V_1 > V_2$.

Hence, if $V_1 > V_2$, $E(C_1) > E(C_2)$.

If $E_{11} = E_{21}$, then $E_{22} = E_{12}$ and $E(C_1) = E(C_2)$ whatever the values of the V_j's.

If as few as three objectives are involved, however, we can show that is may be necessary (and it is always sufficient) to be able to express the ratio of differences in the V_j's as numbers, and hence as values on (what will be shown in Chapter 6 to be) an *interval* scale.

Consider the following case:

	O_1	O_2	O_3	$\sum_j E_{ij}$
C_1	E_{11}	E_{12}	E_{13}	1.0
C_2	E_{21}	E_{22}	E_{23}	1.0

where $E_{11} > E_{21}$, $E_{22} > E_{12}$, and $E_{13} > E_{23}$; and $V_1 > V_2 > V_3$. We wish to determine whether

(1) $E(C_1) - E(C_2) = V_1(E_{11} - E_{21}) - V_2(E_{22} - E_{12}) + V_3(E_{13} - E_{23}) > 0$.

(2) Consequently, $V_1(E_{11} - E_{21}) + V_3(E_{13} - E_{23}) > V_2(E_{22} - E_{12})$.

(3) But $(E_{11} - E_{21}) + (E_{12} - E_{22}) + (E_{13} - E_{23}) = 0$, and therefore $(E_{11} - E_{21}) + (E_{13} - E_{23}) = -(E_{12} - E_{22}) = (E_{22} - E_{12})$.

(4) Then, substituting in (2), we get $V_1(E_{11} - E_{21}) + V_3(E_{13} - E_{23}) > V_2(E_{11} - E_{21}) + V_2(E_{13} - E_{23})$, and hence

$$V_1(E_{11} - E_{21}) - V_2(E_{11} - E_{21}) > V_2(E_{13} - E_{23}) - V_3(E_{13} - E_{23})$$

$$(E_{11} - E_{21})(V_1 - V_2) > (E_{13} - E_{23})(V_2 - V_3).$$

(5) Finally,

$$\frac{(V_1 - V_2)}{(V_2 - V_3)} > \frac{E_{13} - E_{23}}{E_{11} - E_{21}}.$$

Since the E_{ij}'s are numbers, the right-hand term will be a number, and it is necessary to know whether the ratio of the differences of the V_j's is greater than this number. Now it remains to show that, if the ratio of the differences of the V_j can be asserted to be larger or smaller than some specified number, this is sufficient for selecting that course of action which maximizes the expected value, given the efficiencies, E_{ij}.*

Let $\{O_j\}$ be a finite set of n exhaustive and exclusive objectives or consequences. Then, $\sum_j E_{ij} = 1.0$. By convention, let

$$O_1 \geq O_2 \geq \cdots \geq O_n, \text{ and hence } V_1 \geq V_2 \geq \cdots \geq V_n.$$

Now compare two courses of action, C_1 and C_2, to determine whether the expected value of C_1, $E(C_1)$, is greater than or equal to the expected value of C_2, $E(C_2)$. If $E(C_1) - E(C_2) < 0$, then C_2 should be selected. If $E(C_1) - E(C_2) > 0$, C_1 should be selected. If $E(C_1) = E(C_2)$, it makes no difference which is chosen. By convention then, if $E(C_1) \geqq E(C_2)$, select C_1.

Now,

$$
\begin{aligned}
E(C_1) - E(C_2) &= \sum_{j=1}^{n} E_{1j}V_j - \sum_{j=1}^{n} E_{2j}V_j \\
&= \sum_{j=1}^{n-1} (E_{1j} - E_{2j})V_j + (E_{1n} - E_{2n})V_n \\
&= \sum_{j=1}^{n-1} (E_{1j} - E_{2j})V_j - V_n \sum_{j=1}^{n-1} (E_{1j} - E_{2j}) \\
&= \sum_{j=1}^{n-1} (E_{1j} - E_{2j})(V_j - V_n). \quad\quad (20)
\end{aligned}
$$

Then, if $V_1 = V_n$, from equation (20) and the fact that $V_1 \geqq V_2 > \cdots \geqq V_n$,

$$E(C_1) - E(C_2) = 0 \quad\quad (21)$$

and either C_1 or C_2 (say C_2) may be dropped from consideration. If $V_1 > V_n$, from equation (20), we obtain

$$\frac{E(C_1) - E(C_2)}{V_1 - V_n} = \sum_{j=1}^{n-1} (E_{1j} - E_{2j})\frac{V_j - V_n}{V_1 - V_n}. \quad\quad (22)$$

* The following proof is due to my colleague, Peter Fishburn (1961).

If all the V_j's are measured on an interval scale, then all terms

$$\frac{V_j - V_n}{V_1 - V_n} \tag{23}$$

are invariant on this scale, and their values are known. Then

$$\sum_{j=1}^{n-1} (E_{1j} - E_{2j}) \frac{V_j - V_n}{V_1 - V_n} \tag{24}$$

is known, and moreover is invariant.

Since $(V_1 - V_n) > 0$, it follows from

$$\sum_{j=1}^{n-1} (E_{1j} - E_{2j}) \frac{V_j - V_n}{V_1 - V_n} \geq 0 \tag{25}$$

that

$$E(C_1) - E(C_2) \geq 0. \tag{26}$$

It follows from

$$\sum_{j=1}^{n-1} (E_{1j} - E_{2j}) \frac{V_j - V_n}{V_1 - V_n} < 0 \tag{27}$$

that

$$E(C_1) - E(C_2) < 0. \tag{28}$$

This proves the sufficiency of the ability to express the ratio of differences between V_j's as a number for selecting that one of two courses of action which maximizes expected value. If more than two courses of action are involved, comparisons between them can be made pairwise, and the surviving one is "best." Hence this ability is sufficient for any finite number of courses of action.

In some cases involving three or more outcomes it may not be necessary to have more than a ranking of the V_j's in order to select the best course of action; for example, if for three outcomes, $E_{11} > E_{21}$, $E_{12} > E_{22}$, and $E_{23} > E_{13}$. Here,

$$E(C_1) - E(C_2) = V_1(E_{11} - E_{21})$$
$$+ V_2(E_{12} - E_{22}) - V_3(E_{23} - E_{13}) > 0. \tag{29}$$

Since

$$(E_{23} - E_{13}) = (E_{11} - E_{21}) + (E_{12} - E_{22}), \tag{30}$$

it follows that

$$[V_1(E_{11} - E_{21}) + V_2(E_{12} - E_{22}) > V_3(E_{23} - E_{13})] = V_1(E_{11} - E_{21})$$
$$+ V_2(E_{12} - E_{22}) > V_3(E_{11} - E_{21}) + V_3(E_{12} - E_{22}). \tag{31}$$

Then, clearly this last inequation holds if $V_1 > V_2 > V_3$.

In some cases where a ranking of the V's is not sufficient to determine whether $E(C_1) - E(C_2) \gtreqqless 0$, a ranking of adjacent differences of the V_j, such as $V_1 - V_2 > V_2 - V_3$, will be sufficient.* For example, suppose that the previous illustration is modified so that $E_{11} > E_{21}$, $E_{22} > E_{12}$, $E_{13} > E_{23}$ and $E_{11} - E_{21} > E_{13} - E_{23}$. Further, suppose that in addition to $V_1 > V_2 > V_3$ we know $V_1 - V_2 > V_2 - V_3$. Here we write

$$E(C_1) - E(C_2) = (E_{11} - E_{21})(V_1 - V_2) - (E_{13} - E_{23})(V_2 - V_3), \quad (32)$$

obtained from

$$E(C_1) - E(C_2) = (E_{11} - E_{21})V_1 + (E_{12} - E_{22})V_2$$
$$+ (E_{13} - E_{23})V_3 \quad (33)$$

by setting

$$E_{12} - E_{22} = -(E_{11} - E_{21}) - (E_{13} - E_{23}). \quad (34)$$

Here $E(C_1) - E(C_2) > 0$ is the same as

$$(E_{11} - E_{21})(V_1 - V_2) > (E_{13} - E_{23})(V_2 - V_3), \quad (35)$$

which is valid since

$$E_{11} - E_{21} > E_{13} - E_{23} > 0 \quad (36)$$

and

$$V_1 - V_2 > V_2 - V_3 > 0. \quad (37)$$

But without the information that $V_1 - V_2 > V_2 - V_3$, we can clearly not conclude that

$$(E_{11} - E_{21})(V_1 - V_2) > (E_{13} - E_{23})(V_2 - V_3). \quad (38)$$

The point of these observations is that, once we know what the values of the E_{ij} are, we can determine the minimum amount and kind of information required about the V_j's. Then, by waiting until we know what the E_{ij}'s are, we may reduce the work required in evaluating objectives. Correspondingly, if it is easier to measure the V_j's than the E_{ij}'s, we should wait until the V_j's have been determined to learn what information about the E_{ij}'s is required.

A *Posteriori* Approach to Decision Making

In the *a posteriori* approach to decision making the outcomes are expressed only in terms of the efficiency or effectiveness of courses

* This is called an *ordered metric scale* and is also discussed in Chapter 6.

of action, and the decision maker must select that course of action which in his judgment yields the best combination of these measures, where "best" is not explicitly defined.

The first procedure (use of efficiency curves) which we will consider employs only measures of efficiency which are expressed on different scales. The second procedure (retrospective optimization) resembles the first except that past decisions are used to determine what trade-offs (transformations) would have made these decisions maximize expected effectiveness. The third procedure (use of effectiveness curves) deals with the ratios of measures of efficiency, which measures are not made explicit but are assumed to be expressed on the same scale.

Efficiency curves

This approach has been described by Hanssmann (1961, p. 237) as follows:

Suppose there are only two conflicting objectives. Then the levels of achievement, O_1 and O_2, are dependent on each other. This dependence may be exhibited by a curve (see Figure [3.3]). It is argued that—at least subconsciously—every decision-maker makes use of such relationships when he chooses between conflicting objectives. He does not make his value decision in a vacuum. It is further argued that the shape of the curve will greatly influence his decision. Suppose that in the case of the solid curve he chooses the compromise designated by the solid dot which ensures him of the level a for O_1. In the case of the lower curve he might very well settle for a much lower value of O_1, since the value a must be paid for with a much higher loss in terms of O_2 than is the case for the upper curve. This being the case, it seems essential that the decision-maker use the best possible curve. The best possible curve obviously is the one which for each given value of O_1 maximizes O_2. Maximization is, of course, with respect to all degrees of freedom left within the restrictions of the problem. This particular curve we call the 'efficient curve.' In the case of more objectives, an 'efficient surface' can be defined in completely analogous fashion by maximizing one given objective for fixed levels of all others. For objective functions with rather

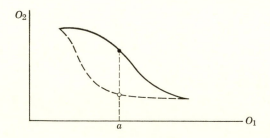

FIGURE 3.3.

general convexity properties, the efficient surface also has the stronger property of maximizing *each* objective for fixed levels of all others.

To understand how this procedure works let us consider an example in detail: the simple lot-size problem. This problem consists of finding the value of the *decision variable*

q = the number of units to be produced in a production run

which will minimize the sum of two costs: (1) the inventory investment per year and (2) the cost of setting up equipment for a production run per year. In effect, then, there are two objectives: (1) to minimize average inventory, and (2) to minimize the number of setups per year. To make these objectives commensurate (i.e., to provide the necessary transformation) the dollar scale is ordinarily used as a standard. Then the *cost parameters* are

C_1 = the cost of holding one unit in inventory per year

and

C_2 = the setup cost per production run.

The *item parameter* is

R = required number of units per year.

The *outcome variables* are

$$y_1 = \frac{q}{2} = \text{average inventory} \tag{39}$$

and

$$y_2 = \frac{R}{q} = \text{the number of runs per year.} \tag{40}$$

The total cost, then, is given by

$$TC = C_1 y_1 + C_2 y_2 = C_1 \frac{q}{2} + C_2 \frac{R}{q}. \tag{41}$$

Note that the two objectives (to minimize average inventory and to minimize the number of setups) have been transformed into a common (dollar) scale by use of C_1 and C_2. To find the value of q which minimizes the total cost, we proceed as follows:

$$\frac{dTC}{dq} = \frac{C_1}{2} - C_2 \frac{R}{q^2} = 0. \tag{42}$$

Solving, we get

$$q_o = \sqrt{2R\frac{C_2}{C_1}}. \tag{43}$$

The minimum total cost is then

$$TC_o = C_1\frac{q_o}{2} + C_2\frac{R}{q_o} = \frac{C_1}{2}\sqrt{2R\frac{C_2}{C_1}} + \frac{C_2R}{\sqrt{2R(C_2/C_1)}}$$

$$= \sqrt{2RC_1C_2}. \tag{44}$$

Now, if R, C_1, and C_2 were known, q_o and TC_o could be determined. But suppose that we do not want to transform the second objective (to minimize setups) into a cost yet. Then, according to the *a posteriori* procedure, we can treat C_2 as a variable and find the values of TC_o for various values of C_2. For example, if $R = 200$ and $C_1 = \$25$, we would get the "efficient" curve shown in Figure 3.4.

The decision maker is then asked to select the point at which he wants to operate, and the corresponding value of q_o is used.

Retrospective optimization

A weaker procedure than that described in the use of efficient curves may be employed when (*a*) the time necessary to calculate the efficient surface is not available, and (*b*) past decisions of the type under study are available for examination. The procedure consists of "using the model in reverse" on past decisions of the kind under study. Past decisions are assumed to have been optimal. Then by use of the decision model (to be discussed in the next chapter) a determination is

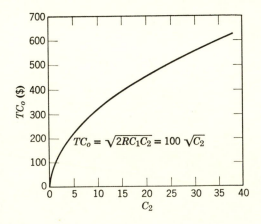

FIGURE 3.4.   An efficient curve.

made as to what transformation of values would have been necessary to have made the past decisions optimal. This procedure is repeated for several past decisions, and the results are compared. If
they have been relatively consistent, then the researchers have a
general notion of the location of the equal trade-off point. If the
results are not consistent, the decision maker may judge which past
decision was best and the trade-off associated with this decision can
be used.

In a study involving a public utility the question was raised concerning the number of service garages from which men were dis-
patched to answer calls from customers whose electricity was "cut
off." The problem involved two familiar objectives: minimization
of cost of operation and minimization of service delays to the customer. The cost of delays to the customer could not be obtained by
either objective or subjective analyses. The procedure for evaluating
a course of action involved a complex and time-consuming simulation
which could not be repeated for a variety of assumed delay policies.
The time allotted for the research prevented making such computations.

In the past, however, the company had made two decisions of the
kind under study. These were assumed to be optimal, and a determination was made as to what range of values in dollars of an average minute's delay to the customer made these past decisions optimal.
The ranges obtained from the two past decisions were almost identical. Consultation with management disclosed no basis for questioning the reasonableness of the results. The average midrange was
then used to find the "best" decision in the current decision situation.

Retrospective optimization is obviously the weakest of the transformation procedures described. It assumes that the decision maker
has performed optimally in the past. The obvious question is, if this
is assumed, why not let him make this decision in the same way he
has decided previously? The principal advantages of this procedure
are that it makes consistent decisions (though perhaps inefficient ones)
more likely in the future and that it raises past implicit transformations to consciousness, where they are likely to receive more careful
consideration in the future.

Effectiveness curves

Suppose that in the example used in connection with efficiency curves
the researcher is not only unwilling or unable to express C_2, the setup
cost per production run, but also unwilling or unable to do so for C_1,
the unit inventory-holding cost per year. He feels, however, that

the ratios C_1/C_2 and C_2/C_1 are nevertheless meaningful to the decision maker. He could then follow a procedure described by Feeney in 1955.

The optimal values of the outcome variables, y_1 and y_2, may be expressed as follows:

$$y_{1o} = \frac{q_o}{2} = \frac{\sqrt{2R(C_2/C_1)}}{2} = \sqrt{\frac{C_2}{C_1}}\sqrt{\frac{R}{2}} \qquad (45)$$

$$y_{2o} = \frac{R}{q_o} = \frac{R}{\sqrt{2R(C_2/C_1)}} = \sqrt{\frac{C_1}{C_2}}\sqrt{\frac{R}{2}}. \qquad (46)$$

Then

$$y_{1o}y_{2o} = \sqrt{\frac{C_2}{C_1}}\sqrt{\frac{R}{2}}\sqrt{\frac{C_1}{C_2}}\sqrt{\frac{R}{2}} = \frac{R}{2}. \qquad (47)$$

Assuming $R = 200$ as before, we can now plot the *effectiveness curve* shown in Figure 3.5.

Feeney (1955, p. 75) offers the following explanation of the effectiveness curve: *

Any point of the curve is attainable through the decision rule . . . derived and is efficient in the sense that the outcomes associated with that point yield a minimum total variable cost for some cost parameter ratio $[C_1/C_2]$. Thus any relationship between inventory investment and [number of setups per year] that lies on this curve may be attained and will be the lowest cost relationship for some set of cost parameters. Conversely, for any given cost parameters used in the decision rules, the resulting outcomes must lie at a point on this [effectiveness curve].

He goes on (p. 77) to evaluate this procedure as follows:

This mechanism is the mind of the decision maker himself. We conclude, therefore, that in situations in which it is not possible by direct methods to obtain meaningful measures of the cost parameters contained in the decision rules the [final] decision might best be made by confronting the [decision maker] with a picture of the [effectiveness curve]. In essence, we present him with the set of all possible alternatives that have the property of being optimal under some set of costs. If, as is generally the case, the [effectiveness curve] is convex, we may make a very strong statement with respect to the properties of these alternatives, namely, that so long as total variable cost is non-decreasing over the range of each of the outcome vari-

* The bracketed expressions are substitutes for Feeney's terminology, with which that used here has not been consistent.

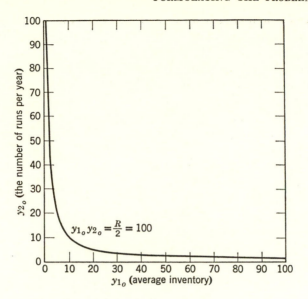

FIGURE 3.5. An effectiveness curve.

ables the [effectiveness curve] derived under a linear cost model *must* contain the optimal outcome regardless of the nature of the cost function that is actually employed by the decision maker. That is, even if the cost function is non-linear and the outcome variables themselves are subject to a multitude of complex restrictions, some point on the [effectiveness curve] must provide minimum total variable cost.

Returning to the simple lot size formulation that was explored earlier, the curve shown in Figure [3.5] (or some modified form of this curve) might be presented to the executive. He could be told that under the rules that have been developed any relationship between inventory [average inventory] and [number of setups] per year that lies on this curve can be attained and that regardless of the factors that are actually taken into account, some point on this curve must be the best available outcome for the company. He would be told also that the final selection of a point on this curve as a target for company inventory operations is a decision that he himself must make. This picture might be elaborated through such things as an indication of the outcome attained through existing controls to provide some perspective, and perhaps by an indication of the point or points along the curve that would be selected through a cost accounting study of the underlying cost parameters. We believe through the use of such an approach the analyst provides the best available basis for executive decision making and avoids the undesirable practice of working beyond the limits of his methodology.

The *a posteriori* methods just described have a great deal of appeal to researchers because they appear to be relieved of the generally difficult tasks of finding transformation and value functions. They are so relieved, but at a price. It is this price that we want to examine now.

If any of the variables in a problem situation and its model are probabilistic, then the outcome is also probabilistic. This is handled in the *a posteriori* method by dealing with *expected* values rather than distributions of values, and hence deterministically. Consequently, even if the point chosen by the decision maker maximizes expected effectiveness (or minimizes expected ineffectiveness), it will maximize (minimize) expected value (loss of value) only if the value function of the scale involved is linear and monotonically increasing in the case of maximization and monotonically decreasing in the case of minimization problems. Therefore, determination of a value function is avoided by assumptions, assumptions which seldom turn out to be valid where value functions are explicitly derived. For example, because of the threat of monopolistic charges by the government the value of increasing share of the market for most companies is not monotonically increasing. The infrequency of linear-value functions has already been referred to.

If the problem is truly deterministic, then the linearity assumption concerning values is not required, but the assumption of monotonicity is.

If three objectives are involved, the efficiency and effectiveness surfaces can still be represented in two dimensions. An example of such a surface, taken from Feeney (1955), is shown in Figure 3.6. If, however, more than three objectives are involved, graphic representation is virtually impossible and the decision maker must be confronted with extensive tabulated data the significance of which is almost impossible for him to understand. The evaluations asked of him under these circumstances are considerably more difficult to make than those involved in obtaining explicit subjective transformation functions or value functions.

Finally, the computational requirements for the *a posteriori* method where three or more objectives are involved become very great. Use of a high-speed computer is almost essential. Although this may not be prohibitive, the alternative use of time to find the transformation and value functions explicitly should be carefully considered.

Despite the shortcomings of the *a posteriori* method the researcher may be forced to use it, as Feeney has observed. If he does so, he should be aware of the assumptions involved and these should be explicitly formulated. The decision maker should be informed completely of them and their significance before he is asked to reach any decision.

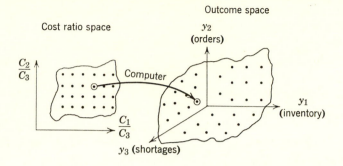

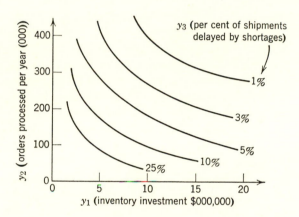

FIGURE 3.6. Effectiveness surface.

A SATISFICING PROCEDURE

In some situations it may not be practically feasible to use either the *a priori* or *a posteriori* method. For example, limitation of resources for the research (e.g., time or money) may preclude the necessary effort to perform the required transformations, evaluations, or computations. In such cases the following procedure is commonly used. The most important objective (judged in some qualitative way) is selected as the basis for the measure of performance of a course of action. Minimal levels of acceptable performance (subjectively determined) are imposed as restrictions on an acceptable solution. Such a level may, for example, be the level of performance attained in the past.

Consider a case in which the decision maker wants to reduce costs and improve service. Suppose that a transformation or evaluation is precluded on practical grounds. The decision maker may be willing to settle for this criterion of performance: to minimize costs subject to the condition that the quality of service does not deteriorate below the current level. If service is improved, fine; this is a bonus. But it will not be permitted to get worse.

Such a procedure combines the principles of optimization and satisficing; optimizing with respect to costs, satisficing with respect to service. If alternative optima relative to costs are found, that action which does best relative to service is selected.

The principle involved here consists of reducing all objectives but one to a constraint, an objective to be retained or a qualitative objective that must be attained. Since optimization is not involved here, satisficing is; that is, doing at least as well as some specified level of performance relative to the objectives involved. Then optimization takes place with respect to only one of the objectives. This procedure eliminates the need for transformations, but not necessarily for evaluation of the scale used in connection with the optimization objective. In order to select among the efficiency functions for alternative courses of action it may be necessary to know at least some characteristics of the value function of the scale (e.g., if it is monotonically increasing).

The satisficing procedure is not to be recommended except where the *a priori* and *a posteriori* procedures cannot be carried out. It embodies very strong assumptions concerning the value functions of the alternatives. It assumes that performance better than the acceptable level relative to the objective to be satisficed has negligible value relative to improved performance on the scale with respect to which optimization is performed.

If, of course, an action can be found which performs best with respect to both scales, it is the best course of action regardless of the transformations and evaluations which might be performed. Such a uniformly best alternative is not likely to be found from among a large set. The existence of such an alternative depends entirely on the consistency of the decision maker's objectives. But most problems are characterized by some incompatibility (conflict) between objectives.

BIBLIOGRAPHY

Ackoff, R. L., "On a Science of Ethics," *Philosophical and Phenomenological Research,* **9** (1949), 663–672.
———, *The Design of Social Research.* Chicago: University of Chicago Press, 1953.

Adams, E. W., "A Survey of Bernoullian Utilities and Applications," Behavioral Models Project, *Technical Report* 9, Columbia University, 1954.

———, and Robert Fagot, "A Model of Riskless Choice," *Behavioral Science,* **4** (1959), 1–10.

Arrow, K. J., "Utilities, Attitudes, Choices: A Review Note," *Econometrica,* **26** (1958), 1–23.

Bentham, Jeremy, *Introduction to the Principles of Morals and Legislation,* 1789.

Bernoulli, Daniel, "Exposition of a New Theory on the Measurement of Risk" (translated by Louise Sommer), *Econometrica,* **22** (1954), 23–26.

Churchman, C. West, *Prediction and Optimal Decision.* Englewood Cliffs, N. J.: Prentice-Hall, 1961.

———, and R. L. Ackoff, "An Experimental Definition of Personality," *Philosophy of Science,* **14** (1947), 304–332.

———, and ———, "An Approximate Measure of Value," *Operations Research,* **2** (1954), 172–180.

———, ———, and E. L. Arnoff, *Introduction to Operations Research.* New York: John Wiley and Sons, 1957.

Davidson, D., S. Siegel, and P. Suppes, "Some Experiments and Related Theory on the Measurement of Utility and Subjective Probability," Applied Mathematics and Statistical Laboratory, *Technical Report* 1, Stanford University, Stanford, 1955.

———, ———, and ———, *Decision Making: An Experimental Approach.* Stanford, Calif.: Stanford University Press, 1957.

Edwards, Ward, "The Theory of Decision Making," *Psychological Bulletin,* **5** (1954), 380–417.

———, "The Reliability of Probability Preferences," *American Journal of Psychology,* **67** (1954), 68–95.

Feeney, G. F., "A Basis for Strategic Decisions on Inventory Control Operations," *Management Science,* **2** (1955), 69–82.

Fishburn, P. C., *A Normative Theory of Decision under Risk,* Ph.D. thesis, Case Institute of Technology, 1961.

Hanssmann, Fred, "Operations Research in National Planning of Underdeveloped Countries," *Operations Research,* **9** (1961), 230–248.

Royden, H. L., P. Suppes, and K. Walsh, "A Model for the Experimental Measurement of the Utility of Gambling," *Behavioral Science,* **4** (1959), 11–18.

Savage, L. J., *The Foundations of Statistics.* New York: John Wiley and Sons, 1954.

Siegel, Sidney, "A Method for Obtaining an Ordered Metric Scale," *Psychometrika,* **21** (1956), 207–216.

Singer, E. A., Jr., *Mind as Behavior.* Columbus, Ohio: R. G. Adams and Co., 1924.

———, *On the Contented Life.* New York: Henry Holt and Co., 1936.

———, *In Search of a Way of Life.* New York: Columbia University Press, 1948.

Suppes, P., and M. Winet, "An Axiomatization of Utility Based on the Notion of Utility Differences," *Management Sciences,* **1** (1955), 259–270.

Thomas, C. J., "Military Gaming," in *Progress in Operations Research,* I, ed. by R. L. Ackoff. New York: John Wiley and Sons, 1961, 421–464.

———, and W. L. Deemer, Jr., "The Role of Operational Gaming in Operations Research," *Operations Research,* **5** (1957), 1–27.

von Neumann, J., and O. Morgenstern, *Theory of Games and Economic Behavior.* Princeton, N. J.: Princeton University Press, 3rd ed., 1953.

INTRODUCTION

The word *model* is used as a noun, adjective, and verb, and in each instance it has a slightly different connotation. As a noun "model" is a *representation* in the sense in which an architect constructs a small-scale model of a building or a physicist a large-scale model of an atom. As an adjective "model" implies a degree of *perfection* or idealization, as in reference to a model home, a model student, or a model husband. As a verb "to model" means *to demonstrate*, to reveal, to show what a thing is like.

Scientific models have all these connotations. They are representations of states, objects, and events. They are idealized in the sense that they are less complicated than reality and hence easier to use for research purposes. These models are easier to manipulate and "carry about" than the real thing. The simplicity of models, compared with reality, lies in the fact that only the *relevant* properties of reality are represented. For example, in a road map, which is a model of a portion of the earth's surface, vegetation is not shown, since it is not relevant with respect to the use of the map. In a model of a portion of the solar system the balls representing planets need not be made of the same material or have the same temperature as the planets themselves.

Scientific models are utilized to accumulate and relate the knowledge we have about different aspects of reality. They are used to reveal reality and—more than this—to serve as instruments for explaining the past and the present, and for predicting and controlling the future.   What control science gives us over reality we normally obtain by application of models.   They are our descriptions and explanations of reality.   A scientific model is, in effect, one or a set of statements about reality.   These statements may be factual, law-like, or theoretical.

In science, as well as in ordinary activity, we employ different types of models: the *iconic* model, the *analogue,* and the *symbolic* model.

Iconic models are large- or small-scale representations of states, objects, or events.   Because they represent the relevant properties of the real thing by those properties themselvs, with only a transformation in scale, iconic models *look like* what they represent.   For example, road maps and aerial photographs represent distances between and relative positions of places and routes between them.   With respect to these relevant properties such maps or photographs look like the real thing; they differ from it with respect to these properties only in scale.   Flow charts which show the processing of material or information may also be iconic models, as may be floor plans or other types of diagram.

In most cases if we want to show relief (i.e., the third dimension, elevation) on a map we do not produce a three-dimensional map; rather we resort to colors or to contour lines which by their distance apart convey information about grades.   Or, if we want to show the kind of road, we use color or shading and provide an appropriate legend which explains the transformation of properties.   In these cases, one property is used to represent another, and hence the necessity of a legend.   In such cases the model is an *analogue.*

An electrical system may be represented by a hydraulic system. In such a case the flow of water may represent the flow of electrical current.   The slide rule is a familiar analogue in which quantities are represented by distances proportionate to their logarithm.   Graphs in which such properties as costs, time, numbers of people, and percentages are plotted are also analogues.

Finally, there are *symbolic* models in which the properties of the thing represented are expressed symbolically.   Thus, a relationship shown in a graph (as an analogue) can also be shown in an equation. The equation is a symbolic model.   Models in which the symbols employed represent quantities are usually called *mathematical models.*

Iconic models are the most specific and concrete of the three types of model but are usually the most difficult to manipulate for purposes of determining the effect of changes on the real thing.   In the analogue easier-to-manipulate properties are usually substituted for the real ones. As a consequence such models are more abstract and general. For example, if we examine a graph in which distance and time are plotted, it is not likely that we can identify the phenomena involved unless the graph is labeled appropriately. Symbolic models are the most abstract and general and are the easiest to manipulate. In general, the amount of analysis required to construct a model is inversely related to the ease of manipulating it once it has been constructed.

Science employs all three types of model. In general, however, it uses iconic models and analogues as preliminary to the development of symbolic models. Iconic models and analogues are also used widely by scientists for pedagogical purposes, since they are easier to understand.

VARIABLES

Mathematical models in science usually take the form of equations $(=)$ or inequations $(>, <, \geqq, \leqq)$. On the left side of the equality or inequality sign we normally place the variables whose past values we are trying to explain or whose future values we want to predict or manipulate. These variables may be thought of as describing an outcome or *output* of a process. The variables on which these values depend are placed on the right side of the equality. These may be thought of as *inputs*.

In the familiar gravitational model

$$s = \tfrac{1}{2}gt^2$$

s (the distance traveled by a freely falling body) is the variable to be estimated, g is the gravitational constant, and t is the number of seconds elapsed from the start of the fall. By an algebraic transformation we can get

$$t = \sqrt{2s/g}.$$

By such transformations we can convert the role of a variable in a model. We do not obtain a complete description by naming the dependent and independent variables; a description of their relationship is also required. We can write

$$s = f(g, t),$$

which says that s is a function of g and t, but f must be specified. This is done by the appropriate insertion of $\frac{1}{2}$ and the square.

The gravitational equation is a model of a class of phenomena but is not a model of a problem situation.

MODELS OF PROBLEM SITUATIONS

Models of *problem situations*, as we have discussed them, should always take the following special form:

$$V = f(X_i, Y_j), \tag{1}$$

where V = the measure of the value of the decision that is made (i.e., the action taken).

X_i = the variables which are subject to control by the decision; the *decision variables* define the alternative courses of action.

Y_j = the factors (variable or constant) which affect performance but which are not subject to control by the decision maker within the scope of the problem as defined; these we shall call "parameters."

f = the functional relationship between the independent variables and constants, X_i and Y_j, and the dependent variable V.

A model of a problem situation has two essential characteristics. First, at least one of the "input" variables is subject to control by the person(s) confronted by the problem (i.e., it must model his possible choices of action). Second, the "output" variable must be a measure or index of the value of the alternative choices to the decision maker. Models which satisfy these two conditions may be called *decision* or *problem* models.

In some problem situations the values of the decision variables are constrained or limited. For example, in problems involving the allocation of resources, the amount of resources that can be allocated cannot exceed the amount available. The total amount of time a person can allocate to various types of activity cannot exceed the amount of time available to him. If t_i is the amount of time allocated to the ith activity, then the constraint can be represented by the inequation

$$\Sigma t_i \leq T,$$

where T is the total amount of time available. More than one constraint may exist, and consequently more than one equation and/or inequation may be required as part of the model. The decision model, then, may consist of a set of equations and inequations, the core of which takes the prototype form

$$V = f(X_i, Y_j).$$

It should also be observed that in some problem situations the choice available to the decision maker cannot be represented by a quantitative variable; rather the choice is between discrete qualitative alternatives. For example, which of several brands of an instrument should be used in a control system? In such a case the available brands cannot be conveniently represented as a quantitative variable. In these cases, then, the model may be expressed as a set of equations of the form

$$V_1 = f(X_1, Y_j)$$

$$V_2 = f(X_2, Y_j)$$

$$\begin{matrix} \cdot & \quad & \cdot \\ \cdot & \quad & \cdot \\ \cdot & \quad & \cdot \end{matrix}$$

(2)

where X_1, X_2, $\cdots$ represent the discrete choices, and V_1, V_2, $\cdots$ represent their performances.

Decision models may be applicable to the decision maker's problem or to decisions which the researcher must make either in trying to find a solution to the decision maker's problem or in answering a question. We shall call the latter *research* models. "Optimizing research decisions," then, requires the construction and solution of appropriate research models. We are not yet capable of constructing all the relevant models, nor are we capable of solving all the models we can formulate. In this book we will try to go as far as possible in the construction and solution of such models.

The general discussion provided here about decision models is equally applicable to the special type of decision model, research models.

In the construction and use of decision models many other models may be required. In some cases we incorporate other models into a decision model, and in other cases we use them as preliminary steps in the construction of a decision model. To illustrate the former, consider a model of the operation of the toll booths at the entrance to a bridge or tunnel. One variable that is very likely to appear is the "average waiting time of a motorist." To determine what this average waiting time is, it may be necessary to construct a model which expresses this average time as a mathematical function of the number of toll booths in operation, the service rate of each booth, and the rate of customer arrivals. This waiting-time submodel can then be substituted for the waiting-time variable in the more general model.

Models as a Source of Control

A model which can be used to predict a future outcome may not be suitable for use in controlling that outcome. It may, however, be useful in developing a model which permits control. For example, consider the following digest of an actual research project. An oil company wants to determine where to locate its service stations and what types of service stations to build so as to maximize its sales volume.* The researchers found that no adequate theory exists to explain the volume of business that a service station obtains. They drew up a long list of factors which may affect sales volume. The most important of these seemed to be the volume of traffic that passes the service station. The researchers decided to concentrate initially on determining the extent of the effect of traffic on sales volume. They selected a number of the company's service stations which are located at intersections of two streets meeting at right angles, at which intersections no other service stations are located. (The number of adjacent stations is another variable that was investigated subsequently.) It was observed that traffic can come into the intersection from four different directions and can leave the intersection in any of four directions, assuming that a turn-around is possible, as it is through a service station. Consequently, there are sixteen different routes through this type of intersection. Data were collected on the number of cars passing through the intersection on each route and on the percentage of cars in each route that stopped at the station. These data were tabulated and analyzed, and it was found that the percentage of cars from each route which stop at the station varies significantly. By regression analysis an equation was constructed that predicted the volume of sales as a function of the average number of cars traveling in each route per unit time. These predictions were not perfect, of course, because many variables were omitted. But it turned out that the predictions obtained from the regression equation were considerably better than those obtained from the predicting procedure then in use by the company, even though the latter took into

---

* The objective is deliberately simplified in this discussion.

account a greater number of variables. The regression equation could easily be adapted for selecting sites for service stations. Traffic volumes could be determined at prospective sites, and those with the highest predicted sales volume could be selected. Hence the model could serve as a basis for deciding which of a set of alternative sites to select. But the model thus developed for site selection could *not* be used for affecting the sales volume at a specific site, since the model of a site's sales volume contained no control or decision variables. Traffic volume could not be manipulated by the company.

The researchers were not satisfied with the description or prediction of sales volume at a site; they wanted to understand the wide variation in the percentages of cars from each route that stopped at a service station. An examination of the relative contributions to sales of the various routes suggested that the differences could be explained by the differences in the amount of time that drivers lose in stopping at the service station. Data were then collected on these times, and it was found that as this lost time decreases the percentage of drivers that stop increases. The model was then reconstructed. In addition to the variables representing the volume of traffic in each route the expected lost time of stops for service was included. This new model turned out to predict better than the first; but, more important, it appeared to *explain* the volume of business, at least in part. But the model still did not explicitly contain any control variables. The researchers could ask, however, how the service time at the station could be affected by controllable station characteristics. If the theory were correct, then, for example, the number and location of entrances and exits to a station, and the number and location of pumps, should affect sales volume. Further study revealed these and other significant controllable variables which could eventually be incorporated into a new model which made control, rather than mere choice, possible; not only could good sites be selected, but also stations could be designed which exploited the potentiality of the sites.

The first model which made it possible to select the best of a set of alternative sites was an *evaluative* model. The second model made it possible to manipulate the sites so as to get best performance out of them. This was a *developmental* model. A developmental model, unlike one that is evaluative, must contain a causal relationship between a controllable variable and the outcome measure. The nature of causal relationships will be considered in Chapter 10.

In the case in which we do not understand the phenomenon involved—that is, do not know how to manipulate the outcome of the decision—we normally begin by listing all the variables that we believe might be causally related to the outcome. In such cases it is better to include doubtful variables than to exclude them because—as we shall see—it is subsequently much easier to identify and delete an irrelevant variable than to identify and insert a relevant one.

What we do next depends on whether or not we can manipulate the variables listed. If we can bring the phenomena into the laboratory or can control them in their natural setting, we can then conduct experiments to determine which variables are causally related to the outcome and how. If such control is not possible or practical, we must restrict ourselves to the data available from the "natural" (i.e., in context) behavior of the phenomena and we must usually resort to the methods of regression and correlation analysis or variations thereof.

In the service-station case referred to above, initially there was no acceptable explanation of sales volume, and one had to be developed in order to determine which properties of a service station should be manipulated so as to affect its sales, and how to manipulate them. Initially, then, all variables (recognized by those involved in the problem) which might affect sales were listed. Each variable had to be *defined* in such a way that the observations required to test its relevance were specified. Such definitions had to specify how *measures* (quantitative observations) of the variable were to be made. The service stations to be observed had to be specified (i.e., the *population* defined) and a decision made as to how many and which stations to observe (the *sampling* design). The procedure for making the observations, recording the results, tabulating, and *analyzing* them also had to be designed. In subsequent chapters we will consider each of these phases of the research in detail. That is, we will consider defining, measurement, sampling, estimation, and procedures for analyzing these data.

In the case in which we can control the values of the "candidate" variables (i.e., those in question) these same procedures are involved; but rather than sample elements, situations, or events under natural conditions, we can specify the conditions under which they are to be observed and either how these conditions are to be constructed or how they are to be found, if they exist. Here the problem is one of *experimental design,* to which subject Chapter 10 will also be devoted.

Sometimes an explanatory model can be constructed without first either developing a descriptive model or conducting experiments. These are cases in which a different type of observation and analysis of the phenomenon involved can lead one directly to an explanatory model. Required for such cases is a certain amount of prior information about the process and—relative to our state of knowledge—a certain simplicity of the phenomenon involved.

Consider the problem of a newsboy who must decide how many newspapers to order each day. He makes a certain amount of profit on each newspaper he sells and incurs a certain loss on each paper he returns. His losses and gains depend on how many newspapers he sells. This quantity varies from day to day, but is predictable in the sense that past data provide estimates of the probability that any specified number of papers will be sold on any given day.

We can begin the construction of a model of this problem situation by listing the relevant factors and assigning a symbol to each:

n = the number of newspapers ordered per day.
a = the profit made on each newspaper sold.
b = the loss incurred on each newspaper that is returned.
r = the number of requests from customers for newspapers.
P = net profit per day.

If P is negative, the newsboy has sustained a loss. On any particular day his profit can be expressed as

$P = ra - (n - r)b$, if he orders more than are requested, and
$P = na$, if he orders less than are requested.

To determine how many newspapers the boy should order we must consider more than one day; that is, the average effect of his decision. In order to do so we must introduce the following concepts:

$P(r)$ = the probability that r requests will be made on a day.
$\bar{P}$ = the average net profit per day.

Now we can construct a general decision model for the situation:

$$\bar{P} = \sum_{r=0}^{n} p(r)[ra - (n - r)b] + \sum_{r=n+1}^{\infty} P(r) \cdot na. \qquad (3)$$

In this model $\bar{P}$ is the measure of performance, n is the decision variable, r is the uncontrolled variable, and a and b are uncontrolled constants. The problem, in this case, is to find the value of n which maximizes $\bar{P}$.

In the illustration the structure of the problem situation is rather apparent, and hence a causal model can be obtained directly from a description of the situation. But this may not be the case even for a situation that can be described simply. For example, an industrial sales manager may want to divide his available funds between advertising and selling effort so as to maximize sales volume. Since the relationship between sales and advertising, for example, is not known, research would first have to be conducted to uncover this relationship.

MODELS AS APPROXIMATIONS

All models of problem situations are approximate representations of these situations. They are generally simpler than the situations they represent, which are usually so complex—although in many cases, fortunately, only in unimportant detail—that an "exact" representation (even if possible) would lead to hopeless mathematical complexity. Therefore, the problem confronting the model builder is to attain a best or good balance between accurate representation and mathematical manageability. Practical considerations (e.g., limited time, money, personnel, or computing facilities) almost always require some compromise of accuracy.

The mathematical manageability of concern here is of two types: one involving the researcher, and the other the decision maker. On the one hand, construction of a model that the researcher cannot solve because of mathematical complexity is of little value. On the other hand, the derivation of a solution which is too complex mathematically for the decision maker to use is also of little value.

The simplifying assumptions on which model approximations are based should be made explicit so that the researcher can determine in what direction they falsify the problem situation and by how much. Such a determination is essential in the justification for the approximation.

Complete justification of an approximation, however, requires a comparison between the "cost" arising from mathematical complexity and the cost of lost performance of the course of action selected by use of the model as compared with a less approximate model. The cost of the mathematical complexity includes not only the cost to the researcher arising out of computational difficulty but possibly also the cost to the decision maker in applying the solution if he must do so himself, as may be the case in repetitive decision making.

These approximation costs are likely to be more difficult to determine in practice than to discuss in principle. The complete cost of approximation would require an "exact" model with which to compare the approximation. The exact model is seldom if ever available. Hence, the calculation of costs in practice, if at all possible, must be based on a comparison of two models, both approximate but to different degrees. Differences in computational and analytic costs generally have to be determined by trying the alternatives. Determination of costs due to loss of performance can also be determined either exactly or approximately by analysis or computation. In the examples which follow such determinations will be considered.

Approximations are used in two ways in model construction:

(1) To "sneak up" on the problem by successively more complex approximations. This procedure is likely to be used when the researcher cannot initially grasp all the complexity of the real situation. For example, in discussing his approach to modeling the operation of complex systems Glen D. Camp (1957–58, p. 10) said:

> I prefer to start with two or a small number of the crudest and simplest models which appear to offer any hope of representing the major features of the operation under study, choosing them so as to "surround" the real operation as well as possible (that is, attempting to falsify the two or more models in opposite directions so as to bound the real operation). These models can usually be "operated" by simple desk calculations, the results being used to judge the desirability of further refinements and the directions which these should take if deemed desirable.

(2) To move down from a model that is too complex to handle to successively simpler approximations until one is obtained that is both manageable and accurate enough. This procedure will be illustrated in the case (which will be discussed in the next section) involving production of a chemical.

The researcher who uses the second of these procedures (complex to simple) has an explicit standard against which to judge the simplicity of successive models. In the first procedure (simple to complex), judgments of simplicity are based on an implicitly formulated complex model. This does not mean that the second procedure is better. Whether one should approximate "up" or "down" is largely a matter of personal preference and the complexity of the problems at hand. Ideally, the net result should be the same.

Approximations can be applied to any of the components of a

model: the variables, relations, and limitations or constraints. We will consider each of these in turn.

Omitting Decision Variables

Variables known to be relevant may be deliberately omitted, generally because their impact on performance is small and their contribution to mathematical complexity is large. This is equally true of decision (controlled) and uncontrolled variables.

Omission of decision variables is illustrated in a model which was developed to control the production of a biochemical. The process yields three products which we shall refer to as "Crude Q," "Finished Q," and "R." Crude Q and Finished Q are products for human consumption; the former is made in bulk and semifinished form. R is made for animal consumption. The production process involves approximately fifty distinct chemical operations. This number made it impractical (from both the accounting and the mathematical point of view) to construct a cost equation for the process in which the cost of each operation was treated separately. It was decided, therefore, to construct a less complex diagram to describe the process, a diagrammatic analysis which grouped operations around the points at which the process is controlled. This diagram (Figure 4.1) was also designed to group the operations so as to permit acquisition of cost data in a convenient way and yet show all possible channels of production.

The discs in Figure 4.1 indicate points at which there is a division of material on the basis of its usability. At such separation points, some material may be suitable only for the R processes, some may be suitable for both the Q and the R processes, and some may have to be disposed of as waste. Waste, as it is shown on each of the charts, includes material sewered (because it is uneconomical to reprocess) and process losses resulting from each operation. At each separation point in the Q process a portion of the material is suitable for R processing, but it requires further processing or recycling to be suitable for Q. The small dark rectangles in Figure 4.1 indicate where control decisions regarding the allocation of usable materials to various channels must be made by those in control of the process. Then, in addition to the decision as to how many fermentors to set, there are six control decisions involved in the production process (shown in Figure 4.1 as A through F):

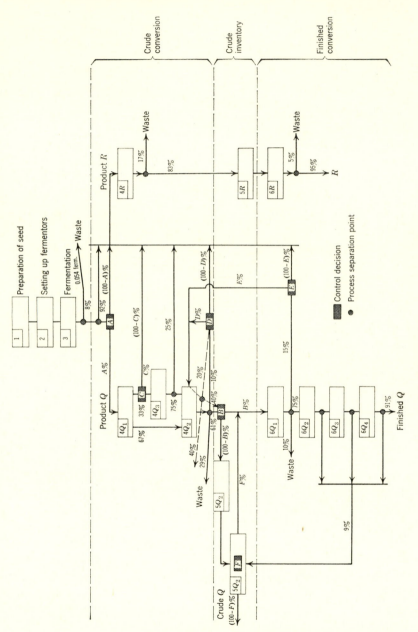

FIGURE 4.1.   Flow diagram of a biochemical process.

Control-Decision Symbol	Control Decision
A	Determination of the portion of materials suitable for both Q and R production that is to be sent through the Q process.
B	Determination of the portion of the materials suitable for the Finished and Crude Q production that is to be sent to the Finished Q production.
C	Determination of the portion of the materials suitable for R production that is to be sent to special process $4Q_3$ which eventually makes more material available for Q processing.
D	Determination of the portion of the materials suitable for R production or recycling that is to be recycled after the Crude Q conversion process.
E	Determination of the portion of the materials suitable for R production or recycling that is to be recycled after the Finished Q conversion process.
F	Determination of the portion of the Crude Q inventory that is to be recycled through the Finished Q conversion process.

A model of the problem was constructed which expressed the cost of the process as a function of the six decision variables. The result was an equation that was much too complex to handle even with the aid of an electronic computer. The principal reason for the complexity arose out of the "recycling" possibilities; that is, decisions C, D, E, and F, at which points the material could be returned for reprocessing. If these controllable variables could be omitted, the model would become manageable. Could such omission be justified?

An analysis was made to determine how the control decisions affected the yield of the process. Six extreme cases were defined. In the first case all suitable material is sent to Finished Q at every control decisions; the material not suitable at B is sent to Crude Q; and what is not suitable at C, D, and E is sent to R processing, and no Crude Q is reprocessed. (That is, $A = 100$, $B = 100$, $C = 0$, $D = 0$, $E = 0$, and $F = 0$.) This case involves no recycling. This and the other five cases are shown in Table 4.1, as well as the yields of each product expressed as percentages of the fermentation yield (X).

Table 4.1 shows that the more material recycled the greater is the waste. Specifically, a comparison of no recycling with complete recycling for daily settings of one or two fermentors, after allowance for nonrecoverable fermentors has been made, shows that there is 6.2 per cent (38.7 per cent − 32.5 per cent) more fermentor yield available for processing from the same amount of raw material. For a

TABLE 4.1. USABLE PRODUCT EXPRESSED AS A PERCENTAGE OF
FERMENTATION YIELDS (X) FOR VARIOUS CONTROL DECISIONS

Control Decisions, percentages					Fermentor Yields						
					Finished Q		Crude Q		R		Waste *
A	B	C	D	E	Per cent of X	Per cent of finished product	Per cent of X	Per cent of finished product	Per cent of X	Per cent of finished product	Per cent of X
100	100	0	0	0	25.7	38	2.5	4	39.3	58	32.5
100	100	100	0	0	35.2	56	3.4	5	24.8	39	36.6
100	100	100	100	0	37.5	60	3.6	6	21.3	34	37.6
100	100	100	100	100	39.7	65	3.8	6	17.8	29	38.7
† 73.8	100	0	0	0	20.2	29	2.0	3	48.1	68	29.7
† 73.8	100	100	100	100	31.2	49	3.1	5	29.0	46	36.7

* This quantity is the total of the expected losses in the system, consisting of the process-phase losses plus unusable quantities which are sewered. In addition to this waste, there is also an expected waste of 0.054 fermentor per day at the fermentation stage.

† Since the number of fermentors that can be sent to Q processing per day is limited by the nature of the process, if the maximum number of daily settings is made, A can be no greater than 73.8 per cent.

maximum daily setting of fermentors, 7.0 per cent (36.7 per cent − 29.7 per cent) more fermentor yield is available.

The fact that recycling decreased yield was known to management. But the amount of this decrease was not known. A study was then made to determine how the reduction of waste through the elimination of recycling would affect total production costs and income. The results are shown in Table 4.2. The income was computed by assuming that all material produced is sold at the average market prices.

The difference between income and process cost is defined as a related net income. (Note that this is not a net profit.)

Table 4.2 shows that, compared with complete recycling, production without recycling yields twice as much related net income for minimum fermentor settings, and one and one-third times as much for maximum fermentor settings.

That production economy results from eliminating recycling was firmly substantiated by these results. It was then necessary to determine whether sales requirements could be met if recycling were eliminated.

A comparison of annual process capacity with shipments for 1950, 1951, and 1952 was made. The results are shown in Table 4.3, where 1950 shipments for Finished Q are equated to 1 and are used as a base. All other figures are expressed as multiples of this figure.

Table 4.3 shows that enough of each product could have been produced to meet annual sales requirements in 1950, 1951, and 1952. This is not conclusive, however, for it does not show whether sales requirements could have been met on a day-to-day basis. To determine whether short-run requirements could be met, and to determine the cost of so doing, it was necessary to develop a detailed procedure for controlling the production process without recycling. This was done, but the model involved was based on the simplified conception of the

TABLE 4.2.   RECYCLING COST ANALYSIS

Control Decisions, proportions					Fin-ished Q Units	Crude Q Units	R Units	Total Units	Process Cost, $	In-come, $	Related Net In-come, $	Per Cent
A	B	C	D	E								
1	1	0	0	0 *	17.0	1.7	22.9	41.6	2247	3,939	1692	100.0
				†	39.1	3.9	92.7	135.7	4638	13,062	8424	100.0
1	1	1	0	0 *	23.3	2.3	13.3	38.9	2294	3,588	1294	76.5
				†	53.6	5.3	70.6	129.5	4732	12,255	7523	89.3
1	1	0	1	0 *	18.2	1.8	20.5	40.5	2273	3,814	1514	89.5
				†	41.7	4.1	87.1	132.9	4658	12,750	8092	96.1
1	1	0	0	1 *	18.0	1.8	20.7	40.5	2305	3,816	1511	89.3
				†	41.4	4.1	87.6	133.1	4694	12,773	8073	95.9
1	1	1	1	1 *	27.2	2.7	5.0	34.9	2305	3,137	832	49.2
				†	62.5	6.2	51.6	120.3	4744	11,219	6475	76.9

Processing:
    * Minimum fermentor setting per day.
    † Maximum fermentor setting per day.

TABLE 4.3. MAXIMUM ANNUAL YIELDS WITHOUT RECYCLING COMPARED
WITH ANNUAL SHIPMENTS

| Product | Annual Yield $A = 0.738$ | | Annual Shipments | | |
	$B = 0.5$	$B = 0.95$	1950	1951	1952
Finished Q	3.6	7.4	1.0	1.8	7.0
Crude Q	5.6	1.2	5.3	1.2	1.0
R	16.6	16.4	6.6	13.4	11.0
Total	25.8	25.0	12.9	16.4	19.0

process (shown in Figure 4.2) which resulted from the elimination of the four decision variables involving recycling.

Omitting Uncontrolled Variables

Omission of uncontrolled variables is illustrated by the usual model employed to determine "economic production quantities" which was developed in equation (41) in Chapter 3:

$$TC = C_1 \frac{q}{2} + C_2 \frac{R}{q} \tag{4}$$

where TC = total incremental cost per year, where "incremental" refers only to costs affected by the production quantity.

C_1 = cost of holding one unit in inventory per year.

q = number of units to be produced in a production run.

C_2 = the setup cost per production run.

R = required number of units per year.

This model omits in-process inventory cost; that is, those costs involved in carrying the investment of money in labor and material in the parts being produced. The larger the production quantity, the longer is the production time and hence the larger is the in-process inventory cost. An accurate model of this cost is generally very complicated and, if added to the simple equation (4), frequently makes it unmanageable. In most cases, however, even tripling the production quantity will result only in an increase of the in-process inventory cost that is a small fraction of 1 per cent of the total cost of the part. Costs can seldom be estimated with an accuracy that justifies (on

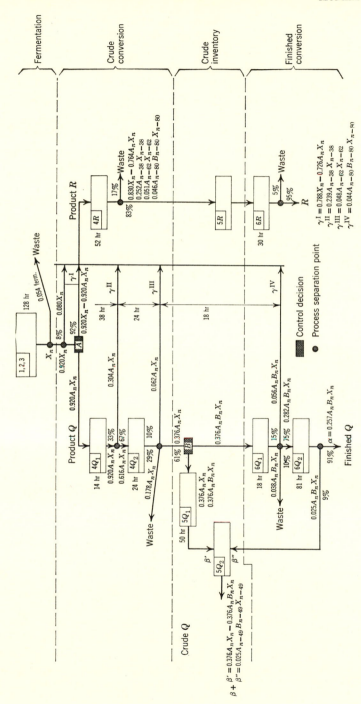

FIGURE 4.2. Flow diagram—final simplification.

practical grounds) inclusion of this small in-process inventory cost. Omission of this cost from the model, however, should be justified by a determination of its magnitude.

The aggregation of several variables does not exactly omit any of the variables, but it does reduce the number that have to be considered. For example, in some inventory-supply systems hundreds of thousands of items are involved. It is not feasible to determine the best stocking quantity for each of these separately, even if all the required models could be constructed. The parts are sometimes grouped into four classes:

> (a) High usage, high cost.
> (b) High usage, low cost.
> (c) Low usage, high cost.
> (d) Low usage, low cost.

In most inventory situations only a small percentage of the items carried falls in class (a), but these items generally account for most of the investment in inventory. Therefore, there is generally good economic reason for treating these items separately and for using average characteristics of items in the other classes. An estimate of the error introduced by the "averaging" approximation can be made.

In some cases where usage and cost do not vary widely over different items the principle of "essentiality" is used to classify them. For example, in determining a policy for stocking replacement parts for discontinued models of heavy industrial equipment the following classification was used:

(a) Parts without which the equipment could not operate at all.

(b) Parts without which the equipment could perform some but not all its functions.

(c) Parts without which the equipment could perform all its functions but only at inconvenience to the operator or at lower efficiency.

(d) Parts without which the operation of the machine was unaffected.

Models are then prepared for only these classes, again using average values for each class.

Where variables are aggregated, the error (in the estimate of the outcome) which is introduced is roughly proportional to the ratio of the within-aggregation variance to the between-aggregation variance. Put another way, it is desirable to make the variables aggregated as homogeneous as possible and the aggregations as heterogeneous as possible.

Glen Camp (1957–58, p. 12) discusses this principle of aggregation and illustrates it as follows:

The labor of solving problems increases roughly *exponentially* with the number of variables, and hence it is important to begin with as few variables as seems likely to yield a useful representation. To this end, we often aggregate variables and it is therefore important to be able to estimate the errors which this will yield. Packaging-storage-distribution problems often involve hundreds of different products, each in several different packages, and hence thousands of variables may be required for an accurate representation. A brief examination of the product-package items often shows, however, that they can be grouped by classes either according to the facilities used to produce and/or package them, their weight or value, frequency of demand, etc. The effect of such aggregation can then be estimated. . . . Items are grouped because of an approximate similarity of properties and hence the dispersion of these properties over the group plays much the same role as fluctuations in arrival rate at a server, etc. Since fluctuations tend to add like approximately perpendicular vectors, rather than numerically, the effects of quite large dispersions are often considerably less than might at first glance have been supposed. For example, if a total of one million quart cans of different lubricating oils must be canned per month, it makes little difference what kinds of oils go into the cans provided batch sizes are reasonably large. Owing to differences in viscosity, canning rates may be different (or provision for heating may be installed); however, good bounds will be obtained by grouping and using the average for an optimistic lower bound and this average plus the standard deviation for an approximate upper bound.

Changing the Nature of Variables

The mathematical characteristics of the variable may be changed to simplify its handling. This may be done in many ways; for example, a continuous variable may be treated as discrete, or conversely; and a variable may be treated as a constant and therefore its fluctuations are ignored.

For example, in bracketing the required server capacities in a queueing process, we may neglect fluctuations in the input and get a clean lower bound by using the unaltered average input rate, and can get a tentative upper bound by using an arrival rate equal to the average plus the standard deviation. If the standard deviation is not too large, and if server capacity is not too expensive, this may be good enough; it will almost always be good enough until other important aspects of the operation have been similarly "roughed in."

It might be argued that this crude procedure ignores the rare peak fluctuation which may exceed a storage or production capacity, etc. However, in most cases a rigid upper limit on storage or production capacity is itself a model approximation. The nominal capacity of a warehouse can be exceeded, for example, by piling goods on platforms or leaving them in freight cars, at an infrequent added cost of extra handling, spoilage, theft and/or demurrage charges, etc.; and production capacity can often be increased at the added cost of overtime, subcontracting, etc. In short, most nominal capacities are not rigid but can be increased at a price, and hence we are seldom dealing with a qualitative yes-no question but, rather, with a simpler quantitative question as to where the balance lies between excess capacity which lies idle most of the time and an occasional but possibly very costly expansion of nominal capacity. The order of magnitude of these effects can usually be estimated to sufficient accuracy to decide whether they need be taken into the initial tentative models or can be left for a later stage of refinement. [Camp (1957–58, p. 11)]

In some problems involving the amount of equipment required to perform a task, it is much simpler to treat the control variable (number of pieces of equipment) as a continuous variable rather than as one whose value must be an integer. When a noninteger is obtained, it is rounded off. In many cases it can be shown that this approximation introduces only very minor distortion in the measure of performance.

The effect of treating the decision variable as continuous in the model and of rounding off the solution to the nearest integer can usually be determined quite simply. For example, suppose that we have the following model:

$$V = X + \frac{Y}{X}, \tag{5}$$

in which X is the decision variable, and Y is independent of X. We find the optimal value of X as follows:

$$\frac{dV}{dX} = 1 - \frac{Y}{X^2} = 0 \tag{6}$$

$$X_o = \sqrt{Y}. \tag{7}$$

Therefore, the minimum value of V is

$$V_o = \sqrt{Y} + \frac{Y}{\sqrt{Y}} = 2\sqrt{Y}. \tag{8}$$

In rounding off we add a positive or negative fraction, a, where $0 \leq a \leq 0.5$. Then the V actually obtained, using the rounded-off value, $X_o + a$, is

$$V' = \sqrt{Y} + a + \frac{Y}{\sqrt{Y} + a}. \tag{9}$$

The round-off error is then

$$V' - V_o = \sqrt{Y} + a + \frac{Y}{\sqrt{Y} + a} - 2\sqrt{Y}$$

$$= a + \frac{Y}{\sqrt{Y} + a} - \sqrt{Y}$$

$$= \frac{a(\sqrt{Y} + a) + Y - \sqrt{Y}(\sqrt{Y} + a)}{\sqrt{Y} + a} = \frac{a^2}{\sqrt{Y} + a}.$$

$$(10)$$

As Y approaches infinity, the error approaches zero. As Y approaches zero, the error approaches a.

The replacement of a discrete variable by a continuous one is sometimes referred to as *fluidization*. Its advantages are cited by Glen Camp (1957–58, p. 7) in the context of problems involving waiting lines (queues):

The "fluid" approximation, in which discrete variables n_1, n_2, . . . representing the number of items in various queues are replaced by continuous variables, is very useful in some cases, since it converts mixed derivation and finite difference equations into partial derivative equations of diffusion processes, and thereby permits extensive knowledge of the properties of these latter to be effectively applied. At first glance it might appear that this approximation would be useful only when the expected queue sizes are large compared to 1. In this case, the "fluid" approximation dose indeed give excellent results; however, it can also be used to establish upper and lower *bounds* even where expected queue sizes are quite small.

Situations arise in which what seems to be a discontinuous variable may be continuous. Consider the ships in a port which require loading or unloading. The ship operators must ask for a discrete number of gangs of longshoremen because union regulations require this type of "order." But the work required is really a continuous variable in gangs, which the system rounds off to an integer. Hence, for example, one may represent the work requirement as a negative exponential, even though the number of gangs worked is discrete.

In some cases a variable can be treated as a constant. The value selected for the constant is usually the expected value of the variable. The outcome may then also be expressed as an expected value. For example, if in the model

$$V = X + \frac{Y}{X}$$

the expected value of the uncontrolled variable, $\overline{Y}$, is used, the model would generally be written as

$$\overline{V} = X + \frac{\overline{Y}}{X}. \tag{11}$$

Such a model ignores the penalties associated with values of $Y \neq \overline{Y}$. For example, in the economic lot-size equation in which average demand is used as a constant, the costs of less demand in a specific period (additional inventory-carrying cost) and of more demand (shortage costs) are ignored. This is equivalent to assuming that the standard deviation of demand is equal to zero. The error introduced by this approximation depends on how large the standard deviation really is and on the magnitude of the shortage and inventory-carrying costs.

Modifying the Function

A model may frequently be simplified by modifying the functional form of either the entire model or of expressions within it. Since linear functions are the simplest to deal with, particularly when a number of functions are involved, as in a set of simultaneous equations, nonlinear functions are frequently approximated by linear functions so that the matrix manipulation is facilitated. In some cases it is necessary to use a linear approximation only in the region of interest. In others where the region is large and the function has a great deal of curvature, a series of linear approximations is applied to sub-regions of the nonlinear function. These approximations are quite common where use is made of linear programming, a technique for solving a set of linear equations subject to a set of linear constraints.

In a model containing several control variables which is to be solved by finding a minimum or maximum outcome by means of the calculus, a quadratic form is frequently used because the partial derivatives constitute a set of linear equations. In quadratic programming, for example, all cost and payoff subfunctions are assumed to be quadratic for this reason.

Many other functional approximations are commonly used. Discontinuous functions are frequently assumed to be continuous; discrete distributions (e.g., the binominal and Poisson) are approximated by continuous ones (e.g., the normal). Limited distributions (e.g., ones with no negative values) are sometimes approximated by unlimited distributions (e.g., the normal, which allows negative values).

It should be realized that fitting a function to a set of data is almost always an estimation procedure and hence an approximation. The researcher, however, exercises freedom as to how "approximate" his fit is.

Changing Constraints

Approximations can be attained by the manipulation of constraints. These may be added, subtracted, or modified so as to simplify the model.

It is quite a common practice to ignore constraints in initially solving a model to see whether the solution satisfies the constraints even when obtained in this way. If it does, no harm has been done. If it does not, the constraints can be added one at a time (in an order dictated by mathematical convenience) and the model re-solved until an acceptable solution is obtained. It is sometimes easier to adjust a solution once obtained back into the constrained area than it is to find a solution subject to constraints. For example, in determining the most economic production quantities for a number of products made on one machine, these quantities can be obtained ignoring the limited time available on the machine. If the solutions obtained require more time than is available, it is possible to determine for each part how its cost increases as the production quantity decreases. With this information, the originally obtained production quantities can be cut back so that the time required is acceptable and the cost added by so doing is approximately minimized. This, then, yields a set of quantities which are approximately optimal and which satisfy the time limitations.

In the biochemical production process considered earlier, the level of production can vary depending on the number of fermentors which are set up. The plant is operated by crews of fixed size. The number of crews required to operate the plant is discrete and depends on the level of production. There is a considerable cost associated with changing the number of crews in the plant because of hiring, firing, and training. These changes are complicated by a seniority system that requires shifting an average of five workers every time one is added or subtracted from the system. Determination of this cost and its inclusion in the model were incredibly complex. In this case, it was much simpler to *add* a constraint, that the number of crews remain constant. Since it was possible to improve the plant's performance significantly with this constraint and because employment stability was desired, the approximation was acceptable to those in control of the process.

In general, the omission of constraints yields an optimistic solution, and the addition of constraints a pessimistic one. Consequently, by the manipulation of constraints, one can obtain upper and lower bounds on the problem solution.

Problem situations are frequently so complicated that one model of the entire situation cannot be feasibly constructed. In such cases the problem may be broken into parts so that each part can be modeled separately. The interactions between the outputs of the models can then be specified and taken into account. We consider first a case in which only two models are required, where the output of the first becomes the input to the second. For example, consider a problem involving determination of the number of maintenance shops which the Army should maintain in order to service inoperable construction equipment.

First a model was constructed for determining for any specified number of shops, n, the optimal number of men that should be assigned to each shop, taking into account the fact that, as the work force increases, the amount of equipment waiting for repairs decreases. The model minimizes the sum of the shop cost (cost of men operating shops) and queue or waiting-line costs. The operation of this model is shown schematically and graphically in Figure 4.3.

This model is used repetitively for a range of assumed numbers of shops. For each assumption the minimal total cost is computed. These results then become the input to a second model used for determining the optimal total number of shops. This second model is shown schematically and graphically in Figure 4.4.

The same procedure of breaking a problem into parts for modeling

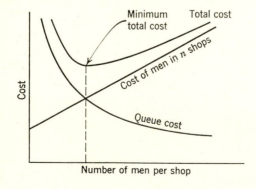

FIGURE 4.3

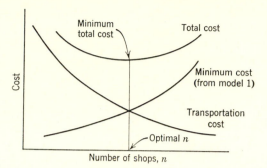

Cost

Minimum total cost

Total cost

Minimum cost (from model 1)

Transportation cost

Optimal n

FIGURE 4.4

Number of shops, n

is illustrated on a larger scale in the following selection from the report of the study from which the previous example was selected.*

The total expected incremental cost of the maintenance system (C) can be expressed as

$$C = P + E + S + T, \tag{12}$$

where P = the total expected cost of *parts* (ordering, purchase cost, stocking, excessing, etc.).

E = the total expected cost of the *end-items* [major equipment] in the system.

S = the total expected *shop* cost (including direct personnel, indirect personnel, tools, facilities, etc.).

T = the total expected cost of *transporting* supported equipment to and from the shops.

Ideally, one would expand equation [12] by expressing each of the above costs as functions of the controllable and uncontrollable variables. Then by mathematical methods, one would seek to minimize the total expected incremental cost by selecting the proper values of the controllable variables. However, this approach is not mathematically feasible. Consequently, an alternative approach was developed. It involves constructing three "submodels": one for *shops*, one for *parts*, and one for *method of repair* [sub-assembly versus part replacement].

In order to break this problem into three parts certain interactions between these parts had to be accounted for. First, the number and size of the parts inventory required depend on the number of shops and hence the number of inventory locations. It was found, however, that for the alternative number of shops which are feasible, the effect of this number on parts inventory requirements is sufficiently small so that the optimal solution is not significantly altered by considering these variables independently.

Secondly, the method of repair affects both the parts and shops costs. Decisions concerning parts inventory and the number and size of shops are

* *Maintenance Logistics for Major Mechanical Equipment,* prepared by the Operations Research Group of Case Institute of Technology for the U.S. Army Corps of Engineers, 1960, pp. 8–9.

made assuming parts replacement. Then the possible improvements to be obtained by sub-assembly replacement are considered.

A separate submodel is not required for the cost of end-items. The additional end-item requirements (above availability requirements) can be broken down into

(1) equipment waiting for repairs,
(2) equipment being repaired,
(3) equipment in transit, and
(4) equipment waiting for parts.

The costs associated with these four types of additional end-items . . . appear in the shops and parts submodels.

SEQUENTIAL-DECISION MODELS

In practical problems involving probabilistic variables a model is constructed involving assumptions concerning the distributions of probabilistic variables relative to either their form (e.g., normal, Poisson, exponential) or the values of the distribution's parameters. At least one additional assumption is made: that the characteristics of the distribution which pertained in the past will also pertain in the future. In general, such an assumption becomes less justified as the time of applying the model becomes more distant from the time at which the model is developed. There are advantages, therefore, to making the decision at the last possible moment.

Put briefly, there is an obvious advantage to making the decision as late as possible because at that point of time the maximum amount of relevant information is available. There is a very important and not so obvious consequence of delaying the decision: it is then possible to treat the particular state of affairs at the time of the decision and not deal with the "average" characteristics of such situations. This frequently allows research economies and better decisions to be made. This fact, for example, is the basis for the power of sequential sampling. In normal sampling procedures, the sample size is determined on the bases of previously available information. In sequential sampling, the sample size is not fixed in advance, but observations are made one at a time or in small blacks and after each observation or block a research decision is made as to whether enough information is available to make the estimate required or whether the collection of data should be continued. Those who developed sequential sampling realized that the data which are obtained during sampling can be used in order to determine more efficiently how large a sample is required. As a consequence sequential sampling, where applicable, saves about one-third the observations required by a fixed sampling plan relative to any specified degree of precision.*

Sequential-decision models, then, do not "average" over future decisions situations on the basis of past experience; they deal with each situation separately. For example, in some inventory situations the average demand and the average time to replenish stock are used to determine reorder quantities and frequencies. These average quantities and frequencies are then used regardless of what happens in any particular period. In sequential-inventory models an advanced decision as to when to order (e.g., every week or every month) is not determined, but the reorder point is specified by a certain stock level. This level is determined using average replenishment times. But the time of ordering becomes a variable in this treatment, a variable which reflects the characteristics of the period at hand. Here, then, the sequential concept is introduced in a limited way. If the stock level at which reordering takes places is also permitted to vary as a function of production or purchasing experience during the current period, another sequential element is introduced.

To see the significance of sequential models in a more dramatic context consider a replacement problem involving a large number of low-cost items that fail. A number of identical items such as light bulbs, vacuum tubes, and air filters are installed at a certain time, $t = 0$. These are subsequently subjected to usage at an identical rate for all. All have the same probability-density function of length of life, $f(t)$. When an item fails it is immediately replaced by an identical item of age zero.

Given a population of items such as that described above, it is often desired to carry out the replacement process in some optimal manner. In military applications it is customary to specify that replacements should be made so as to maximize the mean time to failure of the individual items. In industrial applications, where cost rather than reliability is considered, a policy of replacement which minimizes the total cost of operation should be adopted. In this illustration we deal only with the problem of cost minimization.

Two alternative policies may be considered:

(a) Individual replacement of items as soon as they fail.

(b) Group replacement of all items plus individual replacement of failed items between successive group replacements.

---

* The maximum exploitation of available information and its continuous revision and re-evaluation lie at the root of what is called the *Bayesian approach* to statistics. This approach to estimation theory will be discussed in Chapter 8. For further discussion of this type of statistics see Chernoff and Moses (1959).

The usual procedure of deriving the best replacement policy involves three steps:

Step   I: Determine the total expected cost (TEC) for the individual-replacement policy.
Step   II: Determine the optimal replacement period and hence the optimal TEC for the group-replacement policy.
Step III: Choose the policy with lower TEC.

Such a policy provides a complete specification of the group-replacement times for the future. It assumes that the probability-density function $f(t)$ is known, both its form and parameters. There are two good reasons to question this assumption.

(1) If the data on which these assumptions are based come from the manufacturer, the chances are that he obtained them under conditions different from those in which the user will operate. For example, he may have tested light bulbs by burning them continuously to failure under relatively constant environmental conditions. But it is known that lamp life depends on frequency of turning the lamps off and on, temperature changes, jarring, and so on; in brief, conditions in the laboratory differ from those in the installation involved in the problem.

Furthermore, even if the data were obtained from the installation itself, operating conditions may vary significantly from period to period (e.g., winter and summer) and hence the distribution of times to failure may vary significantly from period to period.

(2) The distribution of life spans, even if accurate, is obtained for a very large sample, and hence the actual distribution of failures for a smaller number of bulbs may vary significantly from it.

Use of a sequential model involves observing the failures as they occur and using this information to decide, at the time of a failure, whether to group-replace or continue replacing individually. We can distinguish among the following cases:

Case	Form of $f(t)$	Parameters of $f(t)$	Stability of $f(t)$ and Parameters
1	Known	Known	Stable in time
2	Known	Unknown	Stable in time
3	Unknown	Unknown	Stable in time
4	Unknown	Unknown	Unstable in time

Some preliminary research by Rutenberg (1961) on the first case has demonstrated the advantages of sequential models. A technique has been developed which takes advantage of random fluctuations of failures about the mean of a given distribution; group replacement is not carried out at a point in time corresponding to the *minimum expected* cost but at a time at which the actual sequence of failures is estimated to yield a *minimum cost for that particular sequence.*

Some other problems which can be approached by sequential models are the following:

(1) A publisher puts out a new book and watches sales week after week. On the basis of the sales information he wants to make the following decisions: should a new edition be printed, and, if so, how large?

(2) A theater puts on a new show and counts the tickets sold each night. Should the show be continued or dropped?

(3) An enemy missile is detected on the radar screen. As more radar observations are obtained, its trajectory can be determined with better accuracy; on the other hand, precious time is lost. When should the countermeasures be activated?

(4) In certain servicing operations (e.g., operation of a fleet of delivery trucks) additions to facilities can be made on short notice (e.g., by renting trucks and hiring drivers by the day). Here, too, observations on accumulation of units waiting for service can be made until a change in requirements is indicated. Hence, there is a possibility of using sequential-decision procedures for a large class of *queuing* problems.

A number of characteristics are common to the above examples:

(*a*) The information available at the outset is general in nature [a general demand function of a probabilistic nature in examples (1) and (2), the laws of motion and error function in example (3), and the distribution of arrival and service times in example (4)], but the parameters are estimated, not known. As more information is collected, a more precise estimate of the parameters may be obtained.

(*b*) A cost is attached to errors of estimation.

(*c*) A cost is attached to deferring the decision in order to collect additional information.

(*d*) It is desired to obtain a sequential-decision rule which will optimize an objective function.

The methodological implications of such a decision rule are as follows:

(1) Control of the solution is inherent in the decision process itself instead of being dependent on an external-control procedure such as is discussed in Chapter 13.

(2) Situations in which very little information is available at the outset can nevertheless be approached in a systematic fashion, and may undergo continuous improvement as time goes on and more basic information (such as the distribution of parameters) becomes available. Thus, in effect, a learning process is introduced in the use of a sequential model.

THEORIES, LAWS, AND DECISION MODELS

Theories and laws in pure science are frequently expressed in the form of mathematical models. Such theories and laws may play an important role in decision models because the phenomena involved in the problem situation may behave in accordance with certain theories and laws. For example, a decision model which is constructed for use in selecting between alternative designs of equipment will generally contain physical laws which relate the performances of the various types of equipment to their characteristics.

The discussion of various types of models and approximations contained in this chapter is also applicable to the construction of quantitative theories and laws. Here too mathematical manageability and accuracy must be brought into balance. For example, the Ptolemaic (epicyclic) geocentric theory was replaced by the Copernican (circular) heliocentric theory largely because of the greater mathematical manageability of the latter

The pressures of time and the limited mathematical abilities of those who use the research output are not likely to be major factors in determining the form of pure laws and theories. But even in pure science research resources (men, money, material, machines, and time) are likely to be limited, and short cuts may be necessary.

It is important to realize, however, that the possibility of future improvements of decision models, and of pure laws and theories, depends critically on the explicit formulation of the approximations which have been made and of the assumptions and evidence which justify or explain their use. It should become increasingly feasible to evaluate approximation procedures and to develop general principles for model construction to guide researchers into "best" approximations in any given situation.

For detailed discussion of laws and theories in science see Campbell (1952 and 1957) and Churchman (1961).

CONCLUSION

It should be apparent that there is considerable flexibility in model construction. It is unlikely that different researchers confronted by the same problem will emerge with identical models, although their models should be similar in most cases. As yet few principles have been developed to assist the researcher in this phase of his work, but a means for developing such principles is becoming increasingly available: simulation of a wide variety of even complex phenomena on electronic computers. It is possible to use a simulated phenomenon as "reality" and to try different modeling techniques on it. Since, in such cases, "reality" is known, it is possible to evaluate alternative models and ultimately to extract principles of model construction from such trials, if they are conducted in a controlled way. The simulator can also serve as an effective pedagogical instrument in teaching students of science and engineering how to construct models.

Two aspects of a decision situation, in which research is being performed for the decision maker by others, are not usually, if ever, incorporated in the model even approximately: (1) the probability associated with each possible course of action; that is, the probability that the decision maker will follow that course if the research so indicates; and (2) the likely amount of distortion the course of action will be subjected to in application if accepted. The reason for the omission of these aspects of the decision maker's behavior is obvious: the inability of the researcher to quantify them. To be sure, the effective researcher takes these factors into account in deciding what approximations to use and in designing the implementation of a solution derived from the model; but he does so qualitatively and often un-self consciously. The science of psychology will have to advance a great deal more before these factors can be handled quantitatively and consciously. In the meantime they can at least be handled consciously, and ways of doing so are discussed in Chapter 14.

Construction of a model involves continuous testing of its adequacy. To see what is involved in the testing procedure we consider the ways in which the model can be in error.

(1) The model may contain variables which are not relevant; that is, have no effect on the outcome. Their inclusion in the model, then, makes the predicted outcome depend on factors on which it has no dependence in reality.

(2) The model may not include variables which are relevant; that is, ones that do affect the outcome.

(3) The function, f, which relates the controllable and uncontrollable variables to the outcome may be incorrect.

(4) The numerical values assigned to the variables may be inaccurate.

If these deficiencies are a result of ignorance rather than of deliberate approximation, they should be uncovered and corrected. In the following six chapters we shall consider each of these types of error in detail and procedures for minimizing them. First we will consider the evaluation of variables. This discussion will involve the subjects of *defining, measurement, sampling,* and *estimation.* Next we will consider the relevance of variables, and this will include a discussion of correlation analysis and causal analysis (*experimentation*), and the *testing of hypotheses.*

BIBLIOGRAPHY

Beach, E. F., *Economic Models.* New York: John Wiley and Sons, 1957.

Camp, G. D., in *Operations Research for Management,* Vol. II, ed. by J. F. McCloskey and J. F. Coppinger. Baltimore: The Johns Hopkins Press, 1956.

———, "Approximation and Bounding in Operations Research," in *Operations Research,* II, Record of the 1957–58 Seminar in Operations Research, University of Michigan.

Campbell, N. R., *What Is Science?* New York: Dover Publications, 1952 (first published in 1921).

———, *Foundations of Science.* New York: Dover Publications, 1957.

Chernoff, H., and L. E. Moses, *Elementary Decision Theory.* New York: John Wiley and Sons, 1959.

Churchman, C. W., *Prediction and Optimal Decision.* Englewood Cliffs, N. J.: Prentice-Hall, 1961.

Rutenberg, Y. H., *Sequential Decision Models,* Ph.D. thesis, Case Institute of Technology, 1961.

5

DEFINING

INTRODUCTION

The symbols in a symbolic model represent variables, constants, and the relationship between them. In its symbolic form the model represents only the structure of the problem and the phenomena involved. The model takes on *meaning* or *content* only when the symbols and the things which they represent are defined.

Definitions of variables or constants are required for working with them effectively, but all too often these definitions are not explicitly formulated. This not only makes it difficult to understand the model and the results derived from it but also suppresses the criteria for relevance of observational data.

Scientific defining has always received attention from the philosophers of science and scientists, but with the appearance of Bridgman's theory of defining, *operationalism*, in 1927 this interest was greatly increased. This theory has been at the center of most discussions of defining ever since.

There are two types of defining in science: *conceptual* and *operational*. Conceptual defining is sometimes called *constitutive* [Caws (1959), p. 5] or *contextual* [Pap (1959), p. 178]. This type of definition relates the concept being defined to one or more other concepts and generally takes a form similar to that of dictionary definitions. Operational definitions, on the other hand, relate a concept to what would be observed if certain operations are performed under specified conditions on specified objects.

The conceptual definition of "father," for example, would be "male parent." In this definition the concept "father" is equated to the concept "male parent" and hence may be written as

$$\text{Father} = \text{male parent.}$$

In an operational definition of "father," however, the concept would be equated to some function of one or more observations made under certain specified conditions.

By showing the relationship between concepts in conceptual definitions the relevance of various types of knowledge to the study of the concept being defined is demonstrated. Such definitions allow us to develop a conceptual system through which the various types of inquiry in science are related. In a later section of this chapter this aspect of defining will be illustrated when we begin with concepts of geometry, kinematics, and mechanics and derive a wide range of other types of concept from them.

In a sense, then, conceptual definitions tell the scientist what to think about in relation to a concept, and operational definitions tell him what to do about answering questions involving the concept.

OPERATIONAL DEFINING

According to Bridgman (1927, p. 5) "in general, we mean by any concept nothing more than a set of operation; *the concept is synonymous with the corresponding set of operations*." S. S. Stevens (1935, p. 323), operationalism's principal spokesman in the behavioral sciences, echoed, "Operationism [he contracted the term] consists simply in referring any concept for its definition to the concrete operations by which knowledge of the thing in question is had." The first task of the operationalist is to define an *operation* and, as Stevens observed (1935, p. 323), "If we are to be consistent, we must define it operationally. An operation is the performance which we execute in order to make known a concept."

Further, according to Bridgman (1927, p. 6), "we must demand that the set of operations equivalent to any concept be a unique set, for otherwise there are possibilities of ambiguity in practical applications which we cannot admit." It is pointed out that different sets of operations give different concepts even though the results may be the same. When such is the case, the concepts are considered to be "practically" the same, though not "actually" so, whatever this distinction means.

Strictly speaking, length when measured by light beams should be called by another name, since the operations are different [from measuring by a measuring rod]. The practical justification for the same name is that within our present experimental limits a numerical difference between the results of the two sets of operations has not been detected. (1927, p. 16)

Bridgman provided no criterion for determining when two sets of operations are the same or different. Consequently, it is difficult to see how two sets of operations can ever be exactly the same in every respect. They must at least differ in either time or the operator— and if they need not be exactly the same, then by how much and in what respect may they differ?

Concern with such questions led Stevens (1935, p. 325) to note:

If the eye could distinguish between lengths of infinitesimal size, it would be impossible to find two objects between whose lengths the eye could distinguish no difference. However, the capacity for discrimination in human observers is limited, and also variable. This limitation has as a direct consequence the fact that all operations are at best only approximations. A penumbra of uncertainty surrounds even the most precise and obvious operations.

Here Stevens admits that discrimination is subject to error, and that no precise specification of an operation can ever be perfectly satisfied. Yet his doctrine asserts that we must restrict ourselves to operations which can be performed: "Science is concerned with the formulation and determination of concepts which are based upon operations which can be carried out" (1935, p. 324 fn). It is therefore implicitly admitted that, since no precisely defined operation can be carried out without error, such operations are *imaginary*. But, according to Stevens, "to admit the possibility of defining certain concepts by 'imaginary' operations . . . detracts from the rigor of operationism as a procedure for determining empirical definitions" (1935, p. 324 fn).

To determine whether or not two operations are the same requires that we make explicit the sense in which we want *sameness* to be taken. This requires an explicit statement of the purpose for establishing difference or similarity between two or more operations.

These comments on the ambiguity and inconsistency of operationalism as it relates to defining have more than academic significance. It can safely be said that there are few problems in contemporary science as critical as that of preparing instructions which will be carried out in the "same" way by different observers. This point has been illustrated over and over again in the so-called "exact" sciences.

For example, in World War II, the "same" type of a specific article was made in a number of different places. The government, which "consumed" these articles, attempted to set up very precise instructions for measuring their "hardness." It set up "round-robin" tests to determine whether different laboratories obtained the same results on the same items by following the "carefully worded" set of instructions. In this particular case, as in many others, the results obtained by different laboratories were so varied as to invalidate the whole process of testing. One "simple" operation, for example, involved counting the grains in a well-marked area on a brass strip. The laboratories differed significantly in their counts. Apparently there is something in the individual laboratory's training of its observers which is "added to" the instructions.

One might argue that, in the case cited, the instructions were not precise or complete enough. But, if we want to avoid the tautology, "Make them precise and complete enough to give reliable results," we must turn to some other theory of defining. Stevens tried to avoid such an alternative by seeking an ultimately simple operation that could be performed identically by all. When operations are not understood by someone, he argued (1935, p. 327):

We should then describe the operations in terms of others which appear simpler to him by reason of his own experience. These operations may again be defined in terms of still simpler operations until we come at last to operations which seem to be at present, though not necessarily always, fundamental and unanalyzable. This process might be called the *operational regress*. It is not infinite. In practice, the operational regress need be pursued only until agreement is reached. . . . Description of a concept may, at a certain level, be made in terms of constructs with little obvious relation to what we see or hear, but, when the description of the constructs themselves must be given, inevitably appeal is made to objects or events to which we can point.

The inadequacy of pointing as an ultimately simple operation, however, is dramatically illustrated in the following anecdote of J. H. Weeks,* related by Ogden and Richards (1947):

I remember on one occasion wanting the word for Table. There were five or six boys standing round, and, tapping the table with my forefinger, I asked, "What is this?" One boy said it was a *dodela*, another that it was an *etanda*,

---

* J. H. Weeks, *Among Congo Cannibals*, p. 51.

a third stated that it was *bokali*, a fourth that it was *elamba*, and the fifth said it was *meza*. These various words we wrote in our notebook, and congratulated ourselves that we were working among a people who possessed a language that had five words for one article.

At a later stage Mr. Weeks discovered:

One lad had thought we wanted the word for tapping; another understood we were seeking the word for the material of which the table was made; another had an idea that we required the word for hardness; another thought that we wished for a name for that which covered the table; and the last, not being able, perhaps, to think of anything else, gave us the word *meza*, table—the very word we were seeking. [Ogden and Richards (1947), pp. 77–78]

A case has also been reported in which the informants, instead of giving disparate names to the "same" object, gave the same name to every object at which the anthropologist pointed. It turned out that they were giving the word for "finger."

In order to avoid such ambiguity in pointing we would at least have to confront the observer with two things different in every respect save the one we were pointing to and then make clear that we wanted him to observe the common property. This is not only *not* simple; it is also impossible. If operational defining must depend on the existence of a set of irreducible and completely unambiguous operations, it is not possible.

Bridgman was aware that, if operational defining is a process of reduction, what we ultimately reduce to is not a set of operations but a set of assumptions. For example, in discussing the measurement of distance between too widely separated points he observes (1927, pp. 14–15):

We assume that a beam of light travels in a straight line. Furthermore, we assume in extending our system of triangulation over the surface of the earth that the geometry of light beams is Euclidean.

Therefore, scientific definitions, like laws and facts, are not isolated islands floating in the sea of science, but are bits of ground firmly anchored to the land mass of scientific theory, laws, and facts, and hence are no less subject to change than any of these.

In "reducing" a concept to a set of assumptions and a set of (not irreducible) operations, the definer has a great deal of choice. What considerations should dictate these choices? Bridgman suggested an answer the implications of which he never fully explored. He observes that the assumptions "to which we made reduction and which we accept as ultimate . . . depend to a certain extent on *the purpose in view*, and also on the range of previous physical experience" (1927, p. 39, italics ours).

Defining, then, is not an impersonal mechanical operation; it is an operation imbued with all the richness of both the researcher's purposes and experience and, as we shall see, his culture's purposes and experience as well.

Bridgman and Stevens failed to provide a workable theory of operational defining, but they made a significant contribution to the development of such a theory through their insistence that concepts used in science should be operationally defined. They were reacting against the exclusive use of conceptual definitions which do not directly relate concepts to experience or experiment. They tended to neglect the important function which conceptual definition can perform, but it is not hard to understand why. In the newer branches of science, in particular, it has become increasingly common to define one concept in terms of others which, if anything, are less well understood than the one being defined and whose operational significance is even more obscure. This is illustrated in the following definition of a personality "trait":

. . . a generalized and focalized neuropsychic system (peculiar to the individual), with the capacity to render many stimuli functionally equivalent, and to initiate and guide consistent (equivalent) forms of adaptive and expressed behavior [Allport (1937, p. 295)].

Bridgman and Stevens object to such a definition because it does not tell the scientist how to determine whether or not he is observing a trait. Although the details of their own proposals for defining procedures have been beset by difficulties of their own, the validity of the objection to traditional defining which their theory tries to overcome has been sustained.

One of our objectives in this chapter, then, is to develop an operational theory of defining which provides a more satisfactory basis for determining what the *content* of conceptual and operational definitions in science should be.

THE CONTENT OF DEFINITIONS

A definition, of course, is made up of words, and these words convey *meaning*. In determining what meaning the definition of a concept should convey two considerations are involved: (1) the purposes of the researcher for which the concept is being defined (i.e., how and for what he intends to use the concept), and (2) the way the concept has commonly been used both in and out of science.

The Purposes of the Definer

The relevance of the purposes of inquiry to scientific defining had been recognized long before Bridgman observed it. For example, F. C. S. Schiller (1912, p. 71) wrote:

The essence . . . which every definition tries to state is simply the point which it is for the time being important to elucidate. It follows that the essences and definitions of things are necessarily plural, variable, and "relative" and never "absolute". . . . A single, unmistakable and absolute definition of a thing, true without reference to any context, would have to be one that would serve for any purpose for which it is convenient or possible to use the term. Such a definition is barely conceivable, but quite incredible, and assuredly not extant.

Schiller's observations are illustrated by an experience of the author, who was once involved in determining the accuracy of results obtained in a survey designed to determine the number of rooms in dwelling units. The survey had been conducted without an explicit definition of "room." He met with the designers of the survey and asked what definition they had used implicitly. They were impatient with the question, observing, "Everyone knows what a room is." The author persisted, and one of those present offered: "A room is a space enclosed by four walls, a floor, and a ceiling." The conversation then proceeded much as follows:

The author asked, "Can't a room be triangular?"
"Sure. It can have three or four walls."
"What about a circular room?"
"Well, it can have one or more walls."
"What about a paper carton?"
"A room has to be large enough for human occupancy."
"What about a closet?"
"It must be used for normal living purposes."
"What are 'normal living purposes'?"
"Look, we don't have to go through this nonsense; our results are good enough for our purposes."
"What were your purposes?"
"To get an index of living conditions by finding the number of persons per room in dwelling units."
"Doesn't the size of the room matter?"
"Yes, we probably should have used 'square feet' of floor space, but that would have been too hard to get."
"Doesn't the height of the room matter?"
"I guess so. Ideally, we should have used volume."

"Would a room with 10 square feet of floor area and 60 feet high be the same as one with 60 square feet of floor area and 10 feet high?"

"Look, the index is good enough for the people who use it."

"What do they use it for?"

"I'm not sure, but we've had no complaints."

This conversation makes clear that without an explicit statement of the purposes of the inquiry there are no criteria of the adequacy of defining.

The accuracy of an estimate of the average number of rooms per dwelling unit, for example, depends at least in part on the precision of the definition. On the other hand the degree of accuracy required can be used to determine how precise the definition has to be. If we want an estimate of the average number of rooms per house in a city that is within 10 per cent of the true value, we require a less precise definition than if we want an estimate within 0.1 per cent. In the first case we might not worry, for example, about enclosed porches, but these might be critical in the second case.

The role of purpose in this sense is as relevant in pure science as in applied science. In the former the scientific purposes dictate the degree of accuracy required.

This is not to say that definitions need *only* serve the researcher's or decision maker's purposes; they must serve the communication objectives of science and society as well. For this reason definitions must also be related to past and present usage of the concept involved.

Past and Present Usage of Concepts

The meaning of a concept should, in addition to serving the research purposes, take cognizance of historic and current usage. Otherwise the objective of communicating results, which is present in every research effort, will not be effectively realized.

The meanings of concepts evolve and are as dynamic as any other aspect of science. Past definitions reveal intended meanings. They may not, however, have successively added precision to the meaning of the concept. One of the purposes of this discussion is to establish a procedure which, if followed, would tend to increase the rate at which precision in defining is attained.

Historical analysis of the use of a concept can often reveal a trend in the evolution of the concept or a consistent theme of meaning which persists through numerous variations. This is very well illustrated by E. A. Singer's (1929) penetrating analysis of the meaning of *consciousness*. Unfortunately the analysis is too lengthy to reproduce here in full, but perhaps the following condensation will give some of its flavor.

Singer observes (p. 568) that the history of the concept can be divided into two parts:

. . . a classic expansion from a most special to a most general use; and a modern . . . contraction from a most general to a most special use. . . . It shall be shown (1) that while the story of *the conscious* carries an idea from a narrowly restricted beginning to a narrowly restricted end, yet never was the idea further from its first state than in its last; and (2) that though *the conscious* thus grows and diminishes in extension, there yet runs through its history a continuous thread of intension. In this unchanging implication of *the conscious* lies its real value to humanity. . . . The task it was born to perform . . . *is the task of distinguishing the state of mind knowing another state of mind.*

Singer notes and documents a succession of three classical uses of the concept:

(1) The primitive meaning, *knowing something with another:* ". . . in its primitive meaning the term requires at least two knowers if one is to be called *conscious* . . ." (p. 569).

(2) A more general meaning, obtained by extension of the meaning to include *knowing something in one's self.*

. . . "knowing with" is made to include not only the case of knowing with another self, but also the case of knowing with one's other self . . . (p. 569). . . . The semantic transition from the conscious sharing of another's mind to the conscious sharing of one's own must have come about without sensible jolt or thrill of invention. . . . If with like continuity the gap memory is supposed to span in rendering a present *conscious* to its past be imagined to diminish by insensible degrees, there is no point at which the *con* can lose meaning till the limiting case can be reached. But it is common enough for the mathematician to require that meanings which hold good for all terms of a convergent series shall also hold good for the limit. (p. 570)

This limiting case provides (3), the most general possible meaning of *conscious*. Here the term includes not only the cases of knowing with another and with oneself one's own past, but also knowing one's own present state.

Turning to the modern period, Singer observes (pp. 571–572):

English use . . . set out to continue *the conscious* in all its ancient functions. . . . Then a curious thing happens. The special denotations gradually required by the ancient *conscious* are lost to the modern *consciousness* in the very order of their acquisition, until, in English philosophy at least, no use for *conscious* is retained save that "limiting case" of immediate self-knowledge to which the Latin *conscious* seems never to have attained.

Singer documents this modern contraction of meaning of the *conscious* and concludes his account with the following quotation from Reid (*Essays on the Intellectual Powers of Man*, I, 1, 1785, pp. 17 f.):

> *Consciousness* is a word used by philosophers, to signify that immediate knowledge which we have of all our present thoughts and purposes, and, in general, of all the present operations of our mind. Whence we may observe, that consciousness is only of things present. To apply consciousness to things past, which sometimes is done in popular discourse, is to confound consciousness with memory; and all such confusion of words ought to be avoided in philosophical discourse.

Having concluded his analysis, Singer observes (p. 574):

> The story of *the conscious* carries its hero from a narrowly restricted beginning to a narrowly restricted end, the first and last state of that word being of all its states the most opposed in character, while through this varied story runs a continuous thread of implication: *being conscious* is the state of mind knowing another state of mind.

He then uses this analysis to construct his own definition of *consciousness*, which retains this historic thread but converts the concept into one that has operational and observational significance.

This discussion of the content of definitions may be summarized by the following instructions:

(1) Examine as many definitions of the concept, past and present, as possible. Keep in mind the chronology of the definitions examined.

(2) Try to identify the core of meaning toward which the definitions seem to be evolving.

(3) Formulate a tentative definition based on this core.

(4) Examine usage of the concept in the context of the problem or question to which the research is directed and determine if the meaning you have formulated will serve the decision maker's or research objectives. If not, make necessary revisions.

(5) Submit the definition to as wide a critical appraisal as possible and make any justifiable revisions suggested by the criticism.

We have a final observation relative to the purposes of defining: if two different (physical) sets of operations yield results which are equivalent from the point of view of the purposes of the determination, then these sets of operations are functionally equivalent; that is, practically it would make no difference which set is used. It is possible, therefore, to have two (or more) different but equivalent operational definitions of a concept. No one has argued against the possibility of there being two or more different but equivalent conceptual definitions of a concept.

FORM OF OPERATIONAL DEFINITIONS

The notion of the operationalists that scientific definitions should specify operations is one that we will try to preserve without incurring the difficulties in their theory. Operational definitions should be *directive;* they should tell the researcher how to investigate that which is conceptualized. It is not enough to provide definitions which "clarify" a concept; not only should conceptual definitions employ more understandable concepts than the one being defined, but also the concepts used should themselves be capable of receiving operational definition.

The traditional approach to clarification of meaning has consisted in "reducing" a concept to be defined to a set of concepts whose meaning is immediately known without ambiguity and uniformly over the population. The search for such primitive concepts, like the search for primitive operations, has been fruitless. [For a detailed discussion see Churchman and Ackoff (1950, Chapter XIII).] Concepts are required to specify operations and operations to specify concepts; it is only through the interaction of concepts and operations that meaning is clarified. Suppose that we follow up our earlier discussion of this point, and contrast the following definitions:

(*a*) An individual is said to possess, or to be characterized by, a certain personality trait when he exhibits a generalized and consistent form, mode, or type of reactivity (behavior), and differs (deviates) sufficiently from other members of his social environment, both in the frequency and intensity of behavior, for his atypicality to be noticed by relatively normal and impartial observers, themselves members of the same environment . . . [Vernon (1933, p. 542)].

(*b*) The International Prototype Metre is a bar of platinum iridium alloy (90% platinum, 10% iridium) of a special winged X-form section devised by G. Tresca to give maximum rigidity in relation to the weight of metal used; the neutral plane of the section is exposed throughout the length of the bar, and the metre is defined as the distance between two transverse graduations on the neutral plane, near the ends of the bar, when the latter is at the temperature of 0° C. . . . [Darwin, Sears, *et al.* (1946, p. 152)]

It is necessary, of course, to maintain a close control and make accurate measurements of the temperature of the bars during comparison. For this reason the comparator is arranged so that the bars can be immersed, during measurement, in the inner compartment of a double water-bath, provided with stirring devices to maintain a uniform temperature. . . . Since different bars will have different coefficients of thermal expansion, it is necessary to determine these and make allowances for them in computing the results of comparisons actually made at other temperatures. (p. 154)

Although it is true that the first definition (*a*) is vague in its reference to operations, and (*b*) is precise, we note that (*b*) does not tell us how to determine in any practical situation whether or not an object is one metre long. This definition tells us how we *ought to* make such a determination in an ideal situation. Such defining specifies the best *conceivable* (not necessarily obtainable) conditions under which, and procedures by which, values of the variable can be obtained. "Best conceivable" is, of course, a relative concept; it means the best that *we can* conceive, *not* the best that will ever be conceived.

At first glance, such a step might appear to be very impractical. Why bother to specify operations which we may not be able to carry out? The answer lies in the fact that specification of *ideal* (or *optimal*) observational conditions and procedures is quite important if we want to know how good are the results we eventually obtain. Further, and more important, the ideal conditions and procedures act as a *standard* by means of which we can compare observations made under different conditions using different operations by making *adjustments* in the results so that they represent what would have been obtained under the standard conditions. The use of *idealized operational definitions* for the adjustment of actual data is not new to science. Consider a familiar physical example: the determination of the acceleration of a freely falling body. The idealized operation for measuring such an acceleration requires (among other things) a perfect vacuum in which the body can fall with complete freedom. Actually, the physicist can never create a perfect vacuum, but he can conduct his experiment in such a way as to estimate how a body *would* fall if it were in a perfect vacuum. He determines how acceleration is affected by variations in the density of the atmosphere. He uses mathematical functions to relate changes in the atmosphere to changes in acceleration. Then, by extrapolation, he determines what would occur in a complete vacuum, and thereby infers the acceleration of an ideally freely falling body.

An operational definition of a concept, then, should state explicitly the conditions under which and the operations by which questions concerning the concept involved ought to be (ideally) answered. This notion of operational defining does not require fundamental or irreducible operations or concepts. It requires the specification of a *standard* procedure under *standard* conditions, deviations from which can be measured. The effect of these deviations on the results obtained should be determinable. Consequently, effective scientific defining requires capabilities for measurement and adjustment of data. Progress in defining, then, is closely related to progress in measurement and in the development of the theories and laws on the basis of which adjustments of data can be made. The latter constitute the definitional assumptions to which Bridgman refers.

There are many cases in science where we can develop the standards necessary for good operational defining but where we may not yet have either the necessary techniques of measurement of deviations from these standards or the theory and laws necessary for adjusting for these deviations even where they can be measured. The definition of "value" developed in Chapter 3 is a case in point. But by constructing such definitions we point up deficiencies in available measurement techniques, laws, and theories, and by so doing we accelerate their development. Until they are developed, we may have to use very rough approximations or even guesses, in order to adjust data, but if these approximations are made explicit they may attract the attention of other researchers and hence increase the chances of research effort being directed to them.

Types of Variables and Constants

The variables and constants which appear in a model, theory, or law are essentially of two types: (1) a *number* of objects or events, a count or enumeration; and (2) the *amount* of a property which an object or event possesses. For example, the arrival rate of customers at a service point is the number of customers arriving per unit time; the duration of a process is the amount of time (the number of units of time) it takes. Hence, in defining the variables and constants which appear in a model we define *objects, events*, and *properties* of these.

As we shall see, objects and events are defined in terms of their essential properties, and hence all scientific definitions should "reduce" to operational definitions (in the sense we have developed) of properties. Before considering the formal properties that such definitions should have, however, some observations about definitions of objects and events are necessary.

Objects

In defining objects for the purpose of counting them it is necessary to define the *class* of objects which are to be counted. This means specifying the properties which are sufficient for determining whether or not any particular object is a member of the class of interest. This may be done in either of two ways: (1) by *identifying* the objects to be counted, a *denotative* definition, or (2) by individuating the class of objects, a *connotative* definition. Identification is normally accomplished either by specifying the space-time coordinates of an object or by naming it, where applicable. Thus we can speak of counting all the objects on a particular shelf at a particular time or of counting all the people named Smith. The ability to identify all the relevant objects in an inquiry, however, presupposes a criterion of relevance, and this in turn is based on a specification of "essential" properties. Ultimately, then, a definition of a class of objects in terms of its essential properties is required. Once we have such a definition we can resort to identifying the members of the class.

The "essential" properties of an object are those properties which are individually necessary and collectively sufficient for inclusion in the class to be counted. For example, "four legged" is not a necessary property of a chair, since some chairs may have three or other numbers of legs. "Having a back," however, is necessary, for if we remove the back of a chair it becomes something else, a stool. This property, however, is not sufficient for being a chair because a sofa also has a back. Therefore, another necessary property of a chair is that it is intended for use by only one person at a time.

The scientist cannot afford the looseness that characterizes dictionary definitions. For example, one dictionary defines a chair as "a seat, usually movable, for one person. It usually has four legs and a back, and may have arms." The scientific definer must decide whether or not the four legs, arms, and back are necessary. This decision must be made in light of the research objectives and common usage. If the researcher's purpose is to determine the number of people who can now be seated *comfortably* in a specified room, his definition might be quite different from that used in a situation where comfort is not an objective and a future date is involved.

The definition of a class of objects, then, should consist of a specification of properties each of which is necessary and all of which are sufficient for differentiating the class of interest from all other classes. The selection of these properties should be dictated by the research objectives, and the name by which the class is identified should be chosen with past and present terminology in mind.

Events

An event is something which happens to one or more objects. That which happens can always be described in terms of a change in properties. For example, the *meeting* of two people can be defined in terms of changes in their location or their awareness of each other. An object can be said to be *burning* when certain of its physical properties change in a specified way. A drill can be said to be *dulling* when its rate of cutting decreases, and so on. In defining an event, then, it is necessary to specify the object(s) involved, their relevant properties, and the changes in these properties to be observed.

Types of properties

There are a very large number of ways in which properties can be classified, most of which have no methodological significance. One, however, does: the classes based on the distinction between *structural* and *functional* properties. In loose common terms a structural property is one which refers either to the matter (or material) of which a thing is composed or to its form, or both. For example, if a certain type of ball is defined as a "round rubber" object, both "round" and "rubber" are structural properties. Functional properties, on the other hand, refer to how a thing or event came into being, or what it does or can be used for. For example, another type of ball is defined as a "globular missile." "Globular" is a structural concept, but "missile" is functional, since it refers to a use to which the ball can be put.

Although one might be inclined to think of structural concepts as the domain of the physical sciences and functional concepts as the domain of the life and behavioral sciences, this pairing breaks down rapidly on reflection. For example, a *catalyst* is usually defined as a substance which accelerates a chemical reaction and which may be recovered practically unchanged at the end of the reaction. The essential characteristic of a catalyst, then, is what it does rather than its form or substance. Most physical instruments (e.g., scales, balances, thermometers, barometers, ohmmeters) are defined in terms of what they do or are used for rather than in terms of their structures.

As a consequence of the growing importance in the physical sciences of such concepts as communication, control, and systems, physicists have become increasingly self-conscious relative to their use of functional concepts. This new awareness was evidenced in a classical article by Rosenblueth, Wiener, and Bigelow (1943) and in the contemporary philosophy of science developed by E. A. Singer, Jr. (1959). In the Rosenblueth *et al.* article it is made clear that functional concepts are applicable to mechanisms, even that special kind of function called "purpose." The early thesis of these authors is likely to be accepted today with little if any argument in light of the wide variety of functional properties (e.g., memory and learning) commonly attributed to electronic computers. [See Frank (1949).]

The significance of this distinction for defining will lie in the fact that definitions of structural properties are essentially deterministic in character, whereas those of functional properties are essentially probabilistic. We shall also find other distinctions within these classes of concepts which are significant to defining.

A complete analysis of the distinction between structure and function would take us well beyond the limits of this work. [See, for example, Singer (1959.] It is necessary, however, at least to sketch the major aspects of such an analysis.

The Nature of Structure. Let us begin by assuming an understanding of spatiotemporal concepts; that is, the concepts of geometry (e.g., point and distance) and kinematics (e.g., duration). Let us also assume an understanding of the concept of *mass* (as a measure of inertia). It is possible now to construct the concept of a point particle which can be identified by its mass and its space-time coordinates. This is the fundamental element of classical mechanics.* A mechanical property of a point particle can be defined as a property of such a point which can be expressed as a mathematical function of its space-time properties and mass. For example, the *average velocity* of a point particle is expressed by dividing the length of its travel by the time of travel. Its *acceleration* at a moment of time is the rate of change of its velocity at that moment.

Now a physical body can be conceptualized as a set of point particles individuated by its space-time coordinates. The *physical* properties of such bodies are ones which can be expressed completely as mathematical functions of the mechanical properties of the point particles of which it is composed. For example, the temperature of a body can be defined as the mean squared velocity of its point particles. The mass of the body can be expressed as a simple function of the mass of its particles, and its density as its mass per unit volume.

When we speak of two bodies having the *same* physical property, we refer to values of that physical property which are identical within some specified degree of variation. For some purposes bodies which have a temperature within a thousand degrees of each other may be considered the same; in other cases a difference of a thousandth of a degree may be significant. When we classify by means of physical properties, then, we use a range of values along the scales measuring

---

* For our purposes here the more familiar concepts of classical mechanics (as contrasted with quantum mechanics) are easier to deal with. A complete translation of this discussion into the concepts of quantum mechanics, however, is possible; and hence the distinction between these types of mechanics is not significant in this discussion.

the properties, a range of the researcher's choosing. A specified range on a physical scale specifies what is called a *morphological* property. These properties are the types we normally deal with in the physical domain. Morphological properties may be qualitatively treated as well as quantitatively; for example, hot, warm, and cold, and heavy, medium, and light.

Now structural properties may be defined as the class of geometric, kinematic, mechanical, physical, and morphological properties of physical objects and, hence, events.

The Nature of Function. In order to make the transition from structural to functional properties it is necessary to use the *producer-product* relationship. We have considered this relationship in Chapter 1 and will reconsider it in more detail in Chapter 10. For our purposes here we need only review its principal characteristics.

Members of one class of objects, events, or properties (X) in an environment (E_1) are said to be producers of members of a class of objects, events, or properties (Y) in an environment (E_2) if members of X are necessary but not sufficient in E_1 for the subsequent appearance of members of Y in E_2. Therefore, if no member of X is present in E_1, a member of Y will not appear in E_2. If a member of X is present in E_1, a member of Y may or may not subsequently appear in E_2, depending on other conditions. The other necessary conditions are *coproducers* of Y. For example, pushing a button produces the ringing of a bell if the bell is not in a vacuum; therefore, the presence of air is a coproducer of the bell's ringing.

The producer and the product may be members of the same class, in which case the productive process is called *reproduction*. Also, E_1 and E_2 may be the same environment.

The relative frequency with which members of X in E_1 produce members of Y in E_2 is the probability that members of X in E_1 produce members of Y in E_2.

The importance of classification in the producer-product relationship should be emphasized. Acorns, for example, are producers of oaks, but they are not producers of trees because they are not necessary for all trees (e.g., maples). But acorns are members of a larger class of objects which are tree producers.

Let M_1, M_2, $\cdots$ represent a set of morphologically distinct objects, events, or properties. Suppose that the producers of these things are all members of the same morphological class or are the same individual. Then the set, M_1, M_2, $\cdots$, has the common property of having been produced by members of the same morphology and hence can be said to have a common *passive function*. In this sense all the products made by a particular company, however different they are in morphology, belong to a passive functional class defined as products of that company. In the same sense the writings of an author, however varied their form or content, and all the graduates of a particular college would constitute passively functional classes.

Now consider the case in which each of the morphologically distinct elements, M_1, M_2, $\cdots$, has a common product; that is, each of them produces objects, events, or properties of a common morphology. For example, consider an automobile, train, plane, horse and wagon, sleigh, and dirigible. These morphologically distinct elements constitute a functional class by virtue of the fact that they are all producers of transport. Similarly, watches, hour glasses, and sundials, which have different structures, constitute an active functional class defined by a common product, time telling.

Now suppose that the elements which constitute a functional class are all acts or behavior patterns of (events produced by) a single individual. Then that individual can be said to have the function that defines the class of its behavior. For example, a person who uses matches and mechanical lighters to start fires has the function of producing fires.

An object which has a function by virtue of its membership in a class of morphologically different elements which have a common property of production is said to have an *extensive* function, because possession of this property depends on other things. On the other hand, an object which is said to have a function by virtue of its own behavior is said to have an *intensive* function. For example, the time-telling function of a watch is an extensive function, but the "fire-starting" function of a person is an intensive function because he can start a fire in different ways. The watch, of course, can tell time in only one way. In order for a thing to have its own function (i.e., an intensive function) it must be capable of displaying morphologically distinct behavior patterns which have a common (morphological) product.

Intensive functions are of two types: *nonpurposive* and *purposive*. An object has a nonpurposive intensive function if (*a*) it can display only one type of behavior in any environment but (*b*) it can display morphologically distinct behavior in different environments, and (*c*) if these different behaviors have a common product. For example, a ship's automatic pilot will behave differently for each different deviation of the ship from a specified course. But its behavior in each of these instances has the same product: bringing the ship back on course. Similarly a production-control device which maintains a process at a constant temperature despite environmental changes also displays a nonpurposive intensive function.

A purposive intensive function, or simply a *purpose,* is displayed by an object if the following conditions are satisfied: the object can display morphologically different behavior patterns in a single environment, and these behaviors have a common product. The purpose is defined by the common property of the outcome. For example, suppose that we observe a person who in the same environment at different times nails, screws, or glues wood together. We can say that his behavior is purposeful and his purpose is to join wood together.

Purposive behavior is not restricted to human beings or even living things. It is now quite commonplace to program computers so that they display purposive behavior (e.g., in a game setting), the purpose being to win the game. In this program the computer has different courses of action available to it in each situation, and although probabilities can be associated with each of its moves even the programmer cannot predict with certainty which move it will make.

In purposive behavior the alternative courses of action are frequently called *means,* and the common property of the outcome is called an *end* or *objective.*

If the distinctions between the types of functions are kept in mind, then the definer can, by classifying the functional concept with which he is dealing, establish some requirements of its definition. For example, suppose that we want to define the property "aggressiveness." Without knowing precisely what this concept means, it seems clear that it refers to a property that we attribute only to objects capable of displaying purposeful behavior. In defining this concept, then, we must specify the class of behavior to be observed and the circumstances under which it will be observed. On the common-sense level we would say that a person is aggressive if he enters into conflict with others without provocation. We can make this notion more precise as follows:

An individual A is aggressive if

(*a*) when he shares an environment with another individual or individuals, *B*; and

(*b*) *B*'s behavior has no effect on the efficiency with which *A* can pursue his desired objectives; and

(*c*) *A* has equally efficient alternative courses of action which fall into one of two classes: (i) those which reduce *B*'s efficiency for his objectives, and (ii) those which do not,

A has a greater probability of selecting courses of action of the first class (i) than of the second (ii). The degree of *A*'s aggressiveness can be defined as the probability that he chooses a means of type (i). (Aggressiveness with provocation is generally called *ascendancy*.)

We turn now to a more detailed consideration of formal requirements on operational definitions of structural and functional properties.

Definitional forms of structural properties

Our interest in structural properties may be of three types: (1) in the property of a body at a moment of time, (2) in the change or rate of change of such a property under constant conditions, and (3) in the change or rate of change of such a property under changing conditions.

An operational definition of a structural property of a body at a moment of time should contain specification of

(*a*) the object or class of objects to be observed,

(*b*) the conditions (environment) under which the observations should be made,

(*c*) the operations, if any, which should be performed in that environment,

(*d*) the instruments, if any, and the metric standards which are required to perform the specified operations, and

(*e*) the observation(s) which should be made.

Suppose, for example, that we want to define what is meant by the assertion that a particular object "is red." We might proceed as follows. (*a*) We identify the object whose color is to be determined. (*b*) We specify the environment in which its color is to be determined; for example, the atmospheric conditions, temperature, and lighting conditions. These conditions are determined by the purposes of the inquiry. (*c* and *d*) We specify where the object should be located in the environment, and what instruments (e.g., spectroscope) should be used and how. (*e*) We designate the spectral range of wave lengths (say 0.00006 to 0.00008 cm) into which the reflected light should fall.

The second type of definition involves a change in a structural property over time in a constant environment. Such a definition requires the same five types of specification as in the preceding case plus a specification of the time interval over which the observations are to be made, the timing of the observations, and the way in which the data obtained are to be treated. "Rate of dissolution," for example, is such a property. It involves the length of time required for an object to change certain of its structural (e.g., chemical) properties under constant conditions (e.g., while immersed in a specified liquid). "Rate of deformation" of a structural member of a building under constant load is a similar property. The so-called *life properties* of goods, tools, and equipment fall into this class of structural properties. The life of a lamp bulb, for example, might be defined as the length of time it emits light in a specified constant environment.

The third type of structural property involves changes of a property under changing conditions. The form of this definition is similar to the preceding one with the additional requirement for specification of what changes in the environment should be made and how they should be timed. Observations always involve reactions to these changes. The coefficient of linear expansion of an object is an example of such a property, as is the coefficient of volume expansion and the coefficient of compressibility. So-called *sensitivity* properties all fall into this class as well. The sensitivity of photographic paper to light, of an explosive to impact or heat, of a structure to shock, and so on, can all be defined within the form described.

Definitional forms of functional properties

Since the meaning of function is rooted in the meaning of the producer-product relationship, it is not surprising that the essence of all functional concepts lies in a measure of probability of production. This probability may be of either of the following types:

(1) The probability that an individual object or group will select a specified course of action.

(2) The probability that a specified course of action will produce a specified outcome.

These probabilities correspond roughly to measures of *preference* and *efficiency*. The measure of every functional property reduces to a measure of one or both of these types of probability. For example, in the concept of aggressiveness discussed above, the degree of aggressiveness was defined as the probability that an individual would select a type of action which reduces the efficiency of a co-occupant of his environment.

Functional properties are of three general types, corresponding to the types of structural properties already considered:

(*a*) the property of something at a moment of time,

(*b*) the change or rate of change in a property under constant conditions, and

(*c*) the change or rate of change in the property under changing conditions.

Definitions of the first type should contain specification of

(1) the object or class of objects to be observed,

(2) the conditions (environment) under which the observations should be made,

(3) the operations, if any, which should be performed in that environment,

(4) the instruments, if any, which are required to perform the specified operations,

(5) the observations which should be made, and

(6) the treatment of the data obtained.

This is quite similar to the form of the definition of the corresponding type of structural property. If no observational error is involved in the determination of a structural property, only one observation need be made. In the case of the functional property, however, even where no observational error is present, an infinite number of observations are required (in principle) in order to determine the appropriate probabilities without error.

An example of such a property is "the degree of familiarity of an individual with a means to an end." To define this concept we should first identify the individual and objective (end) involved. Next we should specify the conditions under which the observations should be made. These are:

(*a*) A set of alternative courses of action (C_1, C_2, $\cdots$) are available in the environment.

(*b*) Each of the available courses of action has perfect efficiency for the specified objective.

(*c*) The individual has interest in only the specified objective.

In this situation we should observe the frequency with which the individual selects each course of action. Then the degree of familiarity of the individual for a specified course of action, C_i, relative to the objective in that environment is the probability (limiting relative frequency) of his selecting that course.

As can be seen from this definition, "familiarity" is a preference-type property. All functional properties relating to preferences should have definitions of the form indicated. The same is true for "dispositional" properties; for example, hungry, tired, and bored.

The second type of functional property is similar to the first except that our concern is with changes in probabilities under constant conditions over time. These properties are analogous to such structural properties as solubility or rate of deformation under constant load. People, for example, become tired of certain things after a while, or else may become increasingly fond of them. This simply means that their preference patterns change over time. The same may be true of, say, an inspection machine whose probability of rejecting an acceptable item may change with use of the machine. Another set of properties of this type involves changes in the rate of performance of a task with its repetition.

The definitional form of such a property is similar to the first except that the way of measuring the change in the relevant property must be specified, as must the time interval to be covered and the frequency or timing of the observations. For example, one could, measure the change of degree of familiarity with a course of action as the change in this degree between two moments of time, t_1 and t_2; or one could measure the average rate of change of this probability measure with respect to time (i.e., the average derivative with respect to time).

The third and last class of functional properties to be considered involves probability of choice or efficiency under changing conditions and, hence, parallels the third type of structural property considered: *sensitivity* properties. The corresponding functional properties are called *sensibility* properties, because they involve sensation, that is, functionally distinct responses to stimulation. In the case of sensitivity we were concerned with the variations in stimulation necessary to produce certain changes in structural properties. Here we are concerned with the variations in stimulation required to produce certain changes in functional properties. The stimuli may themselves be structural or functional in nature. Sensibility to noise, for example, would involve structurally defined stimuli; whereas sensibility to aggressiveness would involve functionally defined stimuli (i.e., the measurement of aggressiveness is made under conditions where other people's behavior is defined functionally).

The definitional form of this type of property, then, is similar to the second except that it is necessary to specify the stimulus and the operations by which it must be "administered."

AN EXAMPLE OF DEFINING

To illustrate the various points which have been made about the content and form of definitions and to demonstrate the magnitude of the task of defining we will consider in some detail a functional concept which has been receiving increasing attention in scientific literature, *information*. As we shall see, the amount of information contained in a message will be defined in terms of changes in probabilities of choice in the recipient of the message (a stimulus).

As in most definitional efforts, some of the concepts which must be used to define information themselves require definition. Here we shall merely identify these presupposed concepts, but the reader can find an extended discussion of their meaning in Ackoff (1958).

These concepts are:

I: an individual or entity to which purposefulness is to be attributed.

C_i: a course of action; $1 \leqq i \leqq m$.

O_j: a possible outcome or consequence of a course of action; $1 \leqq j \leqq n$.

P_i: the probability that I will select C_i in a specified environment, N; that is, $P_i = P(C_i \mid I, N)$.

E_{ij}: the probability that O_j will occur if C_i is selected by I in N; that is, the efficiency of C_i for O_j in N.

$$E_{ij} = P(O_j \mid C_i, I, N)$$

V_j: the value (importance or utility) of O_j to I.

An individual (I) may be said to be in a purposeful state in an environment (N) if the following conditions hold:

(1) There are at least two exclusively defined courses of action available in N; that is, $m \geqq 2$.

(2) For at least two of the available courses of action in N, the individual's probability of choice is greater than zero; these are called *potential* courses of action.

(3) Of the set of outcomes (so defined as to be exclusive and exhaustive) there is one (say O_a) for which two of the potential courses of action (say C_1 and C_2) have some efficiency; that is, $E_{1a} > 0$ and $E_{2a} > 0$. Furthermore, $E_{1a} \neq E_{2a}$.

(4) The outcome relative to which condition (3) holds has some value to I; that is, $V_a \geqq 0$.

This definition may be summarized less technically as follows: an individual may be said to be in a purposeful state if he wants something and has unequally efficient alternative ways of trying to get it.

If we consider an individual over a period of time it will be convenient to refer to the purposeful states at the beginning and the end of that period as *initial* and *terminal* states, respectively.

Now we can turn directly to the meaning of *information*.

Shannon, his predecessor, R. V. L. Hartley (1928), and most others who discuss information in mathematical terms are concerned with the amount of information * that *can* be communicated rather than with the amount that is actually communicated.   Shannon was primarily involved with systems in which each possible message can be coded into combinations of symbols.   For example, if there are four possible messages and two discrete symbols (0 and 1), the messages can be represented as 00, 01, 10, and 11.   Then, to select one message out of the four, two choices from among the two symbols (i.e., binary choices) may be made.   One binary choice allows two messages (0 and 1), and three binary choices allow eight messages (000, 001, 010, 100, 110, 101, 011, and 111).   In general, x binary choices allow 2^x possible messages.

For Shannon, the amount of information contained in a message is the amount of freedom of choice involved in the selection of the message.   A unit of choice is defined as the selection of one out of two equally available symbols.   Thus, in selecting one of two equally available symbols, one choice unit is involved and the resulting one-symbol message contains one unit of information.

In general, if there are M equally available messages in a state, the selection of one contains x units of information, where

$$x = \log_2 M. \tag{1}$$

Equal availability of the symbols means equal likelihood of choice by the sender.   That is, if there are M possible messages and the probability of each being selected is $1/M$, complete freedom of choice exists.   If the probability of selecting a particular message, P_i, devi-

---

* Because of the pervasiveness of the use of "information" in Shannon's restricted sense, it might seem preferable to use another term here.   But since the usage here conforms more closely to common usage, if a change is required, it would seem preferable to change Shannon's term.   As Colin Cherry (1957, p. 50) notes, "The measure for H_n [average information] from Wiener and Shannon is applicable to the signs themselves, and does not concern their meaning.   In a sense, it is a pity that the mathematical concepts stemming from Hartley have been called 'information' at all."

ates from $1/M$, there is not a completely free choice. In the extreme case, if the probability of selecting any one of a set of messages is 1.0, then there is no freedom of choice and no information can be communicated by the one message which is always selected.

In order to cover cases in which choices are not equally likely (as well as where they are), Shannon derived the following general measure of the amount of information (symbolized by H in his system) contained in a state:

$$H = -\Sigma P_i \log P_i,^* \tag{2}$$

where P_i is the probability of choice of the ith message. If $\log_2$ is used, then H is expressed in binary units which are called *bits*. Thus, a state which contains two equally likely messages contains one bit of information.

The measure of information to be developed here will also be related to freedom of choice; that is, it will be a function of the probabilities of choice associated with the alternative courses of action available to the receiver rather than with the alternative messages available to the sender. The measure here will also be a function of the number of alternative potential courses of action, m.

When we talk of the amount of information that a person has in a specified situation (state), we do so in two different but related senses. First, we refer to the number of available courses of action of which he is aware; that is, to the number of potential courses of action. For example, a person who is aware of four exits from a particular building has more information than the person who is aware of only two when there are four. The act of informing, then, can consist of converting available choices into potential choices. For example, a statement such as, "There are exits at either end of this hall," may convey information in this sense. The person who has this information (i.e., who has these potential choices) may or may not exercise it, depending on his appraisal of the relative efficiencies of the alternative exits. In one sense, then, information is the amount of potential choice of courses of action which an individual has.

The second sense in which we talk of information involves the basis of choice from among the alternative potential courses of action. For example, an individual who knows which exit is nearer than the others has a basis for choice and hence has information about the exits. In-

---

* For an edifying discussion of this measure and its derivation see Cherry (1957, pp. 177–80).

formation in this sense pertains to the believed efficiencies of the alternatives relative to desired outcomes (e.g., a rapid exodus). Suppose, for example, that there are two exits and one is nearer than the other. If this is known and the objective (valued outcome) is to leave the building quickly, the choice is determined in the sense that the individual will always select the nearer exit. If he always selects the more distant exit, then he is obviously misinformed (i.e., he has information, but it is incorrect). If he selects each exit with equal frequency, then he apparently has no basis for choice; that is, no information about the exits. In this sense, then, information is the amount of choice which has been made. Now let us define and develop a measure for information in this second sense.

Consider the case of an individual (I) who is confronted by two potential courses of action, C_1 and C_2. If the probabilities of selecting the courses of action are equal, $P_1 = P_2 = \frac{1}{2}$, the situation may be said to be *indeterminate* for I. He has no basis for choice and hence can be said to have no information about the alternatives. This is clearly the case when one of the alternatives is more efficient than the other. But if the two courses of action are equally efficient, the individual may have information to this effect and select each with equal frequency. Strictly speaking, however, he has no objective choice in this situation, since the alternatives are equally efficient. In a situation like this—a nonpurposeful state—information has no operational meaning. Consequently this discussion has relevance only to situations in which all the alternative courses of action are not equally efficient.

If $P_1 = 1.0$ and $P_2 = 0$, then the situation is *determinate* for I; all the choice that can be made has been made. The maximum amount of possible information is contained in the state. It may not be *correct*, but this is another matter which will be considered below.

We may define a unit of information as the amount contained in a two-choice situation that is determinate.

Let us consider the general case involving m alternative potential courses of action. In order to select one from this set, a minimum of $(m - 1)$ choices from pairs of alternatives is required. Table 5.1 illustrates this fact.

We can conceive of the amount of information contained in a purposeful state, then, as a point on a scale bounded at the lower end by indeterminism (i.e., no choice has been made) and at the upper end by determinism (i.e., complete choice has been made). Location on this scale will depend on the values of P_i.

TABLE 5.1

$m =$	2	3	4	5
	C_1 $\}1$ C_2	C_1 $\}1$ C_2 $\}2$ C_3	C_1 $\}1$ C_2 $\}2$ C_3 $\}3$ C_4	C_1 $\}1$ C_2 $\}2$ C_3 $\}3$ C_4 $\}4$ C_5

In an indeterminate state each $P_i = 1/m$. Therefore, one measure of the distance of a state from indeterminism is

$$\sum_{i=1}^{m} \left| P_i - \frac{1}{m} \right|. \tag{3}$$

For an indeterminate state this sum is equal to zero. In a determinate state one P_i is equal to 1.0, and the remaining $(m - 1)P_i$'s are equal to zero. Therefore, in a determinate state,

$$\sum_{i=1}^{m} \left| P_i - \frac{1}{m} \right| = \left(1 - \frac{1}{m} \right) + (m - 1) \left| 0 - \frac{1}{m} \right|$$

$$= 1 - \frac{1}{m} + (m - 1) \frac{1}{m} = 1 - \frac{1}{m} + 1 - \frac{1}{m} = 2 - \frac{2}{m}. \tag{4}$$

The ratio of (a) the deviation of a specified state from an indeterminate state to (b) the deviation of a corresponding determinate state from that indeterminate state, then, provides a measure of the fraction of the maximum information such a state can contain, to that which it does contain. Symbolically this ratio is

$$\frac{\sum_{i=1}^{m} \left| P_i - \frac{1}{m} \right|}{2 - \frac{2}{m}}. \tag{5}$$

The product of this fraction and the maximum amount of information such a state can contain—that is, $(m - 1)$—provides a measure of the amount of information (here symbolized by A) in that state:

$$A = (m - 1) \frac{\sum_{i=1}^{m} \left| P_i - \frac{1}{m} \right|}{2 - \frac{2}{m}} = \frac{(m - 1) \left(\frac{m}{2}\right) \sum_{i=1}^{m} \left| P_i - \frac{1}{m} \right|}{m - 1}$$

$$= \frac{m}{2} \sum_{i=1}^{m} \left| P_i - \frac{1}{m} \right|. \tag{6}$$

Now the amount of information communicated may be said to be the difference between the amounts of information contained in the state of the receiver immediately preceding the communication (i.e., the initial state) and in the state immediately following the communication (i.e., the terminal state). Let $A(S_1)$ be the amount of information in the initial state, and $A(S_2)$ the amount of information in the terminal state; then the amount of information communicated, A_c, is given by the following equation:

$$A_c = A(S_2) - A(S_1), \tag{7}$$

which may also be written in an expanded form:

$$A_c = \frac{m'}{2} \sum_{i=1}^{m'} \left| P_i' - \frac{1}{m'} \right| - \frac{m}{2} \sum_{i=1}^{m} \left| P_i - \frac{1}{m} \right|, \tag{8}$$

where m is the number of potential courses of action in the initial state, m' is the number of such choices in the terminal state, and P_i and P_i' are the probabilities of choice in the initial and terminal states, respectively.

A_c can take on values from $-(m - 1)$ to $(m' + 1)$. Negative values represent a loss of information (e.g., as in going from a determinate to an indeterminate state).

The concept of negative information may seem objectionable or at least strange. But on reflection this strangeness disappears. Clearly, information can be discarded or lost by forgetting it. A message may undermine a person's acceptance of a piece of information and hence induce him to discard it. In brainwashing we have such communication in a concentrated form.

It should be noted that this measure contains no implication concerning the correctness or incorrectness of the information received. Further, it should be noted that this measure is relative to a specific receiver in a specific state. The same message may convey different amounts of information to different individuals in the same state or to the same individual in different states. Consequently, to specify the amount of information contained in a message it is necessary to specify the set of individuals and states relative to which the measure is to be made. If more than one individual or state is involved, it is also necessary to specify what statistic (e.g., an average) is to be used. Generality of information may be defined in terms of the range of individuals and/or states over which it operates.

It should also be noted that messages are not the only source of information. One may obtain information by observation. For example, one may count the number of exits from a house. The measure of information suggested here is applicable to information obtained by either observation or communication.

In the definitional effort just completed we have fused both conceptual and operational defining. The concept of "information" was derived from other concepts whose meaning is, in general, clearer than that of "information," and, at the same time, the ground work was laid for an operational definition of the concept.

CIRCULARITY OF DEFINING

As is apparent in the definition of *information,* each definition must resort to other concepts. These may be as complex as the concept being defined; hence the search for ultimately simple concepts by Stevens and others. But simplicity is relative, not absolute as Stevens supposes. It may be very simple to determine whether an object is red where the consequences of error are trivial. But if the observer's life depends on the color determination, the problem becomes as complicated as possible.

The denial of ultimately simple concepts seems to imply that all scientific defining is circular. In a sense this is true, but defining takes place in three dimensions, not two. When a full circle has been made, we are *above* our starting point and have brought to it richer and more precise meaning than it had when we started. In effect, when we define one concept, this definition illuminates the concepts on which it depends as well as the concepts which depend on it.

In order to demonstrate this point, in *Psychologistics* (1947) and subsequent writings, Churchman and Ackoff began with concepts of mechanics and derived the principal concepts of physics, biology, psychology, and the social sciences. Then, using the results, they turned back on the scientific circle and defined the concepts of logic, mathematics, and mechanics in terms of psychological and social concepts. The meanings of the mechanical concepts at the end of this cycle were considerably enriched by the process. To illustrate this point let us consider the concepts of temporal precedence, "before" and "after." These have generally been considered to be extremely difficult, if at all possible, to define. We find a typical reaction to this difficulty expressed by Albert Einstein (1923, p. 1):

> The experience of an individual appears to be arranged in a series of events; in this series the single events we remember appear to be ordered according to the criterion of "earlier" and "later," which cannot be analyzed further. There exists, therefore, for the individual, an *I*-time, or subjective time. This in itself is not measurable.

The analysis of the "unanalyzable" and the conception of the "inconceivable" have in the past constituted some of the most important spurts in the progress of science. When concepts are widely regarded as indefinable even by great scientists, this may be an indication of the need for some very basic reorientation in the way these concepts are regarded. The reorientation in the way of looking at "before" and "after" here consists of regarding these concepts as functional rather than structural; that is, of considering them in terms of human purposes.

An interesting and important early attempt to define these concepts in terms of purpose was made by Charles Peirce [in Buchler (1940)]. For Peirce "future conduct is the only conduct that is subject to self-control" (p. 261). This suggested a criterion (p. 343) for distinguishing the past from the future:

> One of the most marked features about the law of mind is that it makes time to have a definite direction of flow from past to future. The relation of past to future is, in reference to the law of mind, different from the relation of future to past. This makes one of the great contrasts between the law of mind and the law of physical force; there is no more distinction between the two opposite directions in time than between moving northward and moving southward.
>
> In order, therefore, to analyze the law of mind, we must begin by asking what the flow of time consists in. Now, we find that in reference to any individual state of feeling, all others are of two classes, those which affect this one (or have a tendency to affect it . . .) and those which do not. The present is affectible by the past but not by the future. . . .
>
> If, of two states, each is absolutely unaffectible by the other, they are to be regarded as parts of the same state. They are contemporaneous.

Roughly, then, Peirce would say that one state preceded another for a person if he treats one as potentially affecting the other, but not vice versa. This is an insight which we want to employ in defining the direction of time, though there are several details we shall refine to avoid getting involved in a vicious circle. The insight is that purposively endowed individuals distinguish the past from the future on the basis of what they think they can control. With respect to the future, there are always things that their present behavior may accomplish, but they do not regard their present behavior as having any potential influence on the past. Even a man in a prison cell, or a complete paralytic, thinks of himself as capable of changing the future in some respect, even though it is only a change in his own behavior: from sitting to walking, or a change of a recollected image.

To refine the conceptualization of the future as that which a purposive individual takes to be potentially affectible by his behavior, we must give a more accurate account of the concepts involved. Such terms as *affect* and *influence* are inappropriate for our present purposes, for they are equivalent to the notion of "produce," which already contains the notion of the future. It will be recalled that, in defining the relation "X produces Y," one of the conditions was that X precede Y. Hence, if we distinguish the future from the past in terms of potential production, we involve ourselves in a fruitless, and hence a vicious, circle: objects existing at one moment of time t_1 are potentially producible by those of a past moment t_0, but this is so simply because "potential production" immediately entails the notion that t_1 comes after t_0.

To avoid this difficulty, we introduce the concept of *essentiality*. X is *essential* for Y if X is necessary but not sufficient for Y; no reference to precedence is made in this definition: nothing is said as to whether or not X precedes Y in time. Of course, it may seem paradoxical to say that, if X comes after Y it can be essential for Y, but actually such usage is possible. For example, not only can we say that an explosion yesterday was necessary for the ruins we see today, but we could also say that the absence of ruins today is essential for there not having been an explosion (a nonexplosion) at a certain place yesterday.

Now, purposive individuals regard some objects and behavior as potentially essential for other objects and events, and do not regard them in this light with respect to other objects and events. If an event takes place at some distant place, then we may not regard our present behavior as potentially essential for that event. If there is one property of an event that is (virtually) sufficient to prevent a person from regarding an event X as potentially essential for an event Y, this property is one of precedence (i.e., Y precedes X).

Put another way, when a person considers the past, he considers it deterministically; that is, the past is connected (for him) with the present by deterministic causal laws. As a result, he does not respond to the existence of alternative behavior patterns which can be considered as potentially essential for the past. If he regarded the future in the same deterministic fashion, then there would be no alternatives with respect to it either. Only one mechanically specified act in the present will completely determine a specified mechanical state later. And here is the crux of the matter. A person generally does not consider the future deterministically. He specifies at least some future states morphologically or functionally, and hence he can relate the present to the future only by necessary but not sufficient conditions (producers), and he considers alternatives. It is to be noted that, in regarding something as potentially essential for something else, we take it as a member of a collection of things which are *not* mechanically identical, and we regard it as existing in one of a collection of environments. In other words, our attitude toward the future is to regard the future process as one of a collection of processes, in some of which current objects and behaviors are essential for future events. We try to choose that behavior which is most likely to be essential for some intended goal of the future. But with respect to the past, we do not take present objects and events to be essential; that is, we do not respond to whatever essentiality they may have with respect to the past.

Hence, we can use the notion of potential essentiality as a basis for defining *before* and *after* as follows: consider two states of nature designated by the momentary (temporal) properties t_1 and t_0. If a person virtually always fails to regard any object of t_1 as potentially essential for t_0, but does regard some things in t_0 as essential for somethings in t_1, then for him t_0 precedes t_1.

This, then, defines what Einstein (above) called subjective time. Objective time is something else. It refers not to how the individual responds to the content of two states, but to the effectiveness of his response relative to his objectives; that is, to whether or not what he does in t_0 does in fact give him some control over the properties of the state at t_1.

It should be noted that even in the case of subjective time it is assumed that the subject (as well as any observer of the subject) can distinguish between two states and hence between two moments of time. He may be able to do this, however, without knowing which one precedes the other, as, for example, when he forgets which of two clearly distinguishable past events preceded the other.

The reader will observe how difficult it is for him to think of the past in nondeterministic terms; that is, to conceive of the past in such a way that alternative essential conditions for past states occur to him. This difficulty is to be expected in light of the definition given, since, in effect, the past is defined in terms of our inability to conceive of alternatives with respect to it.

Since science has made few efforts to define structural concepts in functional terms, it is only natural that a definition such as has just been developed seems awkward or even forced. But with experience in these matters such definitions will eventually be no more strange than the use of structural concepts in defining a functional concept is currently.

SUMMARY

Defining is an aspect of the research process which all too few scientists take very seriously. The meanings of concepts are too often taken for granted. Yet definitions are essential as criteria for relevance of data used in evaluating variables and constants in all types of scientific statements: theories, laws, facts, and decision models. Such criteria can best be provided by idealized operational definitions which specify the conditions under which and operations by which questions concerning the concept involved "ought" to be answered. The "ought" represents the best that we currently know. Such operational definitions provide research standards which serve as a basis for adjusting data obtained under less than standard conditions. In adjusting data, however, the definitions must be supplemented by necessary theory and laws.

The content of (or meaning contained in) a definition should take into account the objectives of the researcher and common and scientific usage of the concept. The former is necessary if the definition is to provide a standard of accuracy required by the inquiry. The latter is necessary if the objective of communicability of results is to be obtained.

Objects are defined by specifying a set of properties which are sufficient for inclusion in the class of interest. Events are defined by specifying a set of changes in properties of designated objects. The definitions of both objects and events, then, depend on the meaning of properties.

The formal requirements for (operationally) defining properties are that we specify what is to be observed, under what (changing and unchanging) conditions the observations are to be made, what operations are to be performed, what instruments and measures are to be used, and how the observations are to be made and treated.

A fundamental distinction was drawn between structural and functional properties. The former refer to the material of which objects are made and their form. The latter refer to the origin or use to which objects can be put or put themselves. The principal distinction between these types of concepts from the point of view of defining is that functional properties all involve measures of probability, either probability of choice or probability that a course of action will produce a specified outcome. For structural properties the measures involved are ideally deterministic.

All definitions use other concepts and hence presuppose their meaning. In general we try to use simpler concepts than the one being defined. But simplicity is a relative concept, not absolute. There are no concepts that are absolutely simple and whose meaning is fixed and known. This does not imply that the meaning of some primitive concepts must be taken for granted and remain undefined. Every scientific concept is potentially definable. This circularity of meaning need not be vicious because in the process of rounding the circle the meaning of initial concepts can be considerably enriched.

The meanings of concepts evolve with use and changes in the context in which they are used. They are also modified by the discovery of interconnections between concepts which are made explicit by trying to round the definitional circle. The progress of science, pure and applied, is as dependent on progress in defining as on progress in any other aspect of inquiry.

BIBLIOGRAPHY

Ackoff, R. L., *The Design of Social Research.* Chicago: University of Chicago Press, 1953.

———, "Towards a Behavioral Theory of Communication," *Management Science,* **4** (1958), 218–234.

Allport, G. W., *Personality: A Psychological Interpretation.* New York: Henry Holt and Co., 1937.

Bridgman, P. W., *The Logic of Modern Physics.* New York: The Macmillan Co., 1927.

———, "Operational Analysis," *Philosophy of Science,* **5** (1938), 114–131.

———, "Science, Public or Private," *Philosophy of Science,* **7** (1940), 36–48.

Buchler, Justus (ed.), *The Philosophy of Peirce, Selected Writings.* New York: Harcourt, Brace and Co., 1940.

Caws, Peter, "Definition and Measurement in Physics," in Churchman and Ratoosh (1959), Chapter 1.

Cherry, Colin, *On Human Communication.* New York: John Wiley and Sons, 1957.

Churchman, C. W., and R. L. Ackoff: *Psychologistics.* Philadelphia: University of Pennsylvania Research Fund, 1947. (Mimeographed)

—— and ——, *Methods of Inquiry.* St. Louis: Educational Publishers, 1950.

—— and ——, "Purposive Behavior and Cybernetics," *Social Forces,* **29** (1950), 32–39.

——, and P. Ratoosh (eds.), *Measurement: Definitions and Theories.* New York: John Wiley and Sons, 1959.

Darwin, C., J. E. Sears, *et al.,* "A Discussion on Units and Standards," *Proceedings of the Royal Society of London,* **186A** (1946), 149–217.

Einstein, A., *The Meaning of Relativity.* Princeton, N. J.: Princeton University Press, 1923.

Frank, L. K., *et al.,* "Teleological Mechanisms," *Annals of N. Y. Academy of Science,* **50** (1949).

Hartley, R. V. L., "Transmission of Information," *Bell Systems Technical Journal,* **7** (1928), 535.

Hempel, C. G., "Fundamentals of Concept Formation in Empirical Science," *International Encyclopedia of Unified Science* (part III). Chicago: University of Chicago Press, 1952.

Jung, C. G., *Psychological Types.* New York: Harcourt, Brace and Co., 1924.

——, *Contributions to Analytical Psychology.* New York: Harcourt, Brace and Co., 1928.

Ogden, C. K., and I. A. Richards, *The Meaning of Meaning.* New York: Harcourt, Brace and Co., rev. ed., 1947.

Pap, Arthur, "Are Physical Magnitudes Operationally Definable?" in Churchman and Ratoosh (1959), Chapter 9.

Rosenblueth, A. N., and N. Wiener, "Purposeful and Non-Purposeful Behavior," *Philosophy of Science,* **17** (1950), 318–326.

——, ——, and J. Bigelow, "Behavior, Purpose, and Teleology," *Philosophy of Science,* **10** (1943), 18–24.

Schiller, F. C. S., *Formal Logic.* London: Macmillan and Co., 1912.

Shannon, C. E., and W. Weaver, *The Mathematical Theory of Communication.* Urbana: University of Illinois Press, 1949.

Singer, E. A., Jr., "On the Conscious Mind," *Journal of Philosophy,* **26** (1929), 561–575.

——, *Experience and Reflection.* Philadelphia: University of Pennsylvania Press, 1959.

Stevens, S. S., "The Operational Basis of Psychology," *American Journal of Psychology,* **47** (1935), 323–330.

Vernon, P. E., "The Biosocial Nature of a Personality Trait," *Psychological Review,* **XL** (1933), 533–548.

6

MEASUREMENT

INTRODUCTION

Scientific defining and measurement are very closely related, as Peter Caws (1959, pp. 3–4) has observed:

Definition and measurement certainly have functional similarities which make it almost inevitable that a discussion of one should sooner or later involve the other. They both have the character of leading to relations which set the entities of science in order with respect to one another. The kind of order that they establish can be broadly differentiated, but they run together in many cases, so that there are times when the two procedures seem to amount almost to the same thing. Definition, in general, is concerned with the systematic order of the conceptual scheme of science, and with the nature of the relations between different entities. Measurement has a more limited function, that of establishing metrical order among different manifestations of particular properties, and of making scientific events amenable to mathematical description. Often the relation between two *different* properties is not clear unless measurements have been carried out on both in some case where they appear together; nowadays much definition is expressed in a mathematical form which presupposes measurement.

This discussion by Caws shows the close relationship between measurement and definition, but it does not make clear the precise nature of this relationship. *Measurement* will be used here to designate the procedure by which we obtain symbols which can be used to represent the concept to be defined. The scientific definition of a concept tells us under what conditions what observations should be made. Measurement is involved in that part of the definition which concerns itself with how the observations should be made and treated so that the concept defined may be represented by symbols with certain properties the specification of which is the subject of this chapter. Therefore, measurement is here taken to be an essential *part* of scientific defining, but not all of it.

A symbolic representation of the concept defined is not necessarily measurement. The property of the symbol most usually cited as being necessary, if not sufficient, to make it a measurement is that it be or contain a number. But, despite its intuitive appeal, as we shall see, this is neither a necessary nor a sufficient condition of measurement.

The term *arithmetization* is sometimes applied to any procedure of assigning numbers to objects, events, or properties. In common usage *measurement* is restricted to processes which involve use of a constant unit of measurement. In science, however, it has become increasingly common to apply the term *measurement* to any process which involves "the assignment of numerals to objects or events according to rules" [Stevens (1946, p. 677)], or "the assignment of numerals to represent properties" [Campbell (1957, p. 267)].

Such a definition of measurement is clearly incomplete, if not incorrect. For example, we can establish rules for assigning random numbers to objects, events, or properties of these, as we commonly do in random sampling. The obvious objection to such a procedure is that on successive applications it does not yield the same, or approximately the same, numbers to the same things. It is quite simple, however, to modify the procedure so that the same random number is always assigned to the same thing.

The purpose of measurement is to represent the content of observations by symbols which are related to each other in the same way that the observed objects, events, or properties are or can be. Numbers are the symbols generally used because their interrelationships have been exhaustively studied in mathematics, and because some of the relationships between them are shared by the observations. But since numbers do have properties which the observations do *not* have, it is important to make explicit which of their properties are and are not shared by the observations. We shall have more to say on this subject below.

In grading a set of examination papers we may express the grades either as numbers (e.g., from 0 to 100), as letters (e.g., *A*, *B*, *C*), or as words (e.g., excellent, good, fair). There is usually a way of transforming from one set of these symbols to another. The same choice of symbols is possible in measuring any property. The use of a letter or a word is no less measurement than is the use of a number provided that we make explicit, as we must in the case of numbers as well, what operations may be performed on the symbols. Clearly, if we want to manipulate the symbols, numbers are the easiest to use, but rules can be set down for performing the equivalent operations on other types of symbols. If they are, then there is no difference in the uses to which these symbols and numbers can be put.

We can spend an indefinite amount of time trying to specify a set of operations which define measurement. History has shown that such efforts are fruitless, since the operations of measurement are changing and developing progressively as are all other types of scientific operation. But we can look at measurement another way. We can define it as a process whose output can be used in a particular way. This makes the essential property of measurement the functional properties of its product, rather than the way it is produced.

As we have indicated, the products of measurement are symbols, knowledge of which is equivalent to knowledge of the properties represented. For example, to know that a carton is 3 feet-0 inch wide and that a doorway is 3 feet-6 inches wide is to know that the carton will pass through the doorway. Measurements allow us to compare the same properties of different things, and the same property of the same thing at different times, and to describe how properties of the same or different things are related to each other. Therefore, in general terms, measurement can be defined in terms of its function: *it is a way of obtaining symbols to represent the properties of objects, events, or states, which symbols have the same relevant relationship to each other as do the things which are represented.*

In this chapter we will concentrate primarily on the use of numbers in measurement. But the reader should not lose sight of the fact that other types of symbols may also be used. The types of measurement we will consider are numbering, counting, ranking, and measurement in the "restricted" sense. As already indicated, the latter refers to procedures which makes use of a constant unit of measurement; it is to this type of procedure that most people refer when they use the term *measurement.* However, we are using the term in a much broader sense.

The numbering of classes of objects or events involves what has come to be known as a *nominal* scale. Ranking involves what is known as an *ordinal* scale. Measurement in the restricted sense involves either an *interval* or a *ratio* scale. We shall consider each of these in turn.

NUMBERING

In its simplest form *numbering* is the process of assigning to objects or events numbers which serve as *signs* or *names* of (i.e., designate) these entities. For example, college students, baseball players, and automobile registrations are assigned numbers for identification purposes. Such a process makes it possible to use uniform and short "names" and facilitates filing and cataloguing information about these entities. In order to number a set of entities they must be distinguishable from each other and they must retain their identity (distinguishing properties) over the period during which the numbers are to be used as names for them.

It is also possible to employ numbers to designate properties. For example, we may have a list of properties to which numbers are assigned: 1 may represent red, 2 may represent yellow, and so forth.

We may, of course, combine these two types of numbering. Part of the number assigned to an entity may designate the entity, and part may represent one or more of its properties. For example, in the assignment of Dewey decimal numbers to books in a library, part of the number designates the book and part designates its subject matter. That is, part of the number designates the *class* of books to which a particular book belongs.

Since numbers are generally assigned serially, they can also be used to represent some ordering property of the entities. For example, house numbers indicate the approximate location of the house on the street, and army serial numbers the approximate time of induction or enlistment of the person involved.

It is important to observe that in the types of numbering we have considered no arithmetical operations can be performed on the numbers to draw any inferences about the entities or properties involved. The fact that we can use letters of the alphabet or other symbol sequences in place of numbering makes apparent this inability to draw arithmetic inferences.

Nominal Scales

As indicated above, not only may we number individual entities but we may also number classes of entities. Classifying entities and numbering them involve what is called a *nominal* (i.e., naming) scale.

Many types of classificatory schemes can be devised, but the type which is most useful in science involves a set of exclusive classes which exhaust the possibilities relative to the properties used as the basis of classification. This can be made explicit as follows.

Let P_j $(1 \le j \le m)$, represent the properties with respect to which a classification is desired. Let n_j represent the number of categories into which the jth property is divided. Then the total number of possible classes which can be constructed is the product: $(n_1)(n_2)$ $\cdots (n_m)$. The classes obtained by forming combinations in this way will be exclusive and exhaustive if the categories of each property are exclusive and exhaustive. For example:

Population	Property	Categories
Living people	1. Sex	1a. Male
		1b. Female
	2. Educational status	2a. Did not graduate from high school or college
		2b. Graduated from high school but not college
		2c. Graduated from college

First, it should be noted that the categories for each property are exclusive and exhaustive relative to the specified population. Every person must fit into one of the categories for each property, and no one can fit into two categories of the same property. If we combine these categories in all possible ways ($1a2a$, $1a2b$, $\cdots$), we have six exhaustive and exclusive classes.

As long as there are some elements in the population, at least two classes should be occupied; otherwise we have not really classified the population.

Elements which fall into the same class are considered to be "the same" or "similar" or "equal" for the purposes of the research which prompted the classification.

In order to classify effectively, the properties involved must be operationally defined and so must the categories. All that was said in Chapter 5 on the subject of defining is relevant here.

Numbers may be used to name or represent classes. This may be done in two ways. Once we have a completed classification we can number each class. On the other hand, we may number the properties out of which the classes are constructed. Then the class number will consist of a combination of the numbers of the properties which define it. The same number may be used for different properties or categories provided we consistently use a particular location in the class number for the number representing a particular property. For example, in a two-digit number, 1 in the first position may represent "male" and in the second position may represent "did not graduate from high school or college."

Once entities have been classified we can count the number of them in each class and compare the resulting distribution of numbers over classes at different times or the distribution of different populations subjected to the same classification. Although we cannot perform any arithmetical operations on the class numbers, it is meaningful to consider the statistic called the *mode* of the distribution of the entities. The mode class is the one with the largest number of members in it.

Counting

Counting, in its simplest form, consists of matching consecutive positive integers to elements of a class. (This is equivalent to assigning "1" to each class member and adding the 1's which have been assigned.) The largest number used is then the number of elements in the class. In some cases the elements (units) may be divisible into parts, in which case counting becomes more complicated. Here we assign appropriate fractions to parts of elements and "1" to each whole unit and add the numbers assigned. Such is the procedure in counting money where the dollar is used as a unit. Determining the appropriate fraction to assign to parts of units may involve measurement in the sense to be discussed; for example, in counting the number of rolls of paper on a shelf where one or more rolls have been partially used.

Although counting is a relatively simple concept, it may involve very complicated operations. The complexity may derive from two sources: defining elements and matching numbers and elements. For example, in counting the number of people who live in a house, it may not be clear who is to be considered as a resident. Should we count a son away at college for eight months out of the year or a maid who sleeps in five nights and spends the others with her family at their home? It is essential to have good definitions of the unit to be counted.

Counting the people in a crowded room may be difficult even though we have no difficulty in identifying a person. This may be due to the fact that they will mill about. To count them we may have to make them stand still or put them in line or have them pass through a door. When we deal with units that move during the period required to count them, it is necessary to find a procedure for counting each one once and only once; otherwise we either *underenumerate* or *overenumerate*. Considerable ingenuity may be required to find or even approximate such a procedure where human beings are involved: witness the taking of a national census. Difficulties may arise even where inanimate things are involved, as, for example, in taking an inventory of material in a factory or goods in a department store which cannot be shut down during the process.

The operation of counting is similar to numbering in that numbers and entities are matched, but, in counting, this is not done in order to "name" the entities. The objective of counting is to obtain a number which represents a property of the class of entities which are involved. The property of the class, of course, is the number of units it contains.

All arithmetical operations are applicable to the numbers obtained by counting.

Probability Measures

It will be recalled from the earlier discussion of functional properties that their measurement always involves the determination of probabilities: either the probability of production (in the form of an individual producing a course of action, of probability of choice, or of a course of action producing an outcome) or some function of such a probability (e.g., the rate of change of probability of choice with respect to time). It will further be recalled that the determination of what were called *objective* probabilities involves the estimate of the limiting relative frequency of a subset of events. The determination of relative frequencies involves two counts: (1) counting the number of instances in which events in a specified subset occur, and (2) counting the number of instances of events in a specified set which contains the subset. Consequently, objective probability determinations are reducible to the ratio of two counts.

All arithmetic operations can be performed on probability "measures," but their meaning (i.e., operational significance) is not necessarily obvious. For example, the sum of the probabilities of two independent (i.e., not causally connected) events occurring $(P_1 + P_2)$ is not the probability that both events will occur simultaneously, but the probability that one or the other or both will occur. The product of these probabilities, $P_1 P_2$, is the probability that both events will occur simultaneously. The calculus of probabilities specifies the significance of each arithmetical operation on probability measures.

RANKING (ORDINAL SCALES)

Ranking involves ordering the elements of a set with respect to some (dyadic) relation or relations defined over the elements. Thus ranking is a way of relating some or all of the elements in a set. To understand the various kinds of ranking it is necessary to understand some of the elements of the *logic of relations*. To facilitate our discussion of relations, we will consider a set, S, of objects and let x, y, z, $\cdots$ be variables ranging over S. That is, the values of these variables are the members of S. We let R denote a relationship; thus, xRy means that x bears the relation R to y. R' is the complement of R; that is, $xR'y$ is true if and only if xRy is false. Thus, if R is the relation $>$, then R' is $\leqq$.

Types of Relations

The four critical properties of relations that are significant from the point of view of measurement are *reflexivity, symmetry, transitivity,* and *connectivity*.

Before defining these concepts precisely it may be helpful to do so loosely. A relationship is *reflexive* if it holds between a thing and itself; for example, the relationship "is equal to" as applied to numbers. A relationship is *symmetric* if, when it relates one thing to a second, it similarly relates the second to the first; for example, "is married to" in a monogamous society. A relationship is *transitive* if, when it holds between one thing and a second and between the second and a third, it also holds between the first and the third; for example, ">" among the integers. Finally, a relationship is *connected* over a set of elements if it applies to every pair of these elements taken in one order or another; for example, ">" over the set of positive integers. Now we turn to more precise definitions. (See Table 6.1 for a summary of these definitions.)

(1*a*) R is *reflexive* (in S) if and only if, for all x, xRx. Examples of reflexive relations are "$=$" (in the set of real numbers), "resembles" (in the set of human beings), and "is similar to" (in the set of closed plane figures).

(1*b*) R is *irreflexive* (in S) if and only if, for all x, $xR'x$. Examples of irreflexive relations are "$<$" (in the set of real numbers), "is married to" (in the set of human beings), and "causes" (in the set of physical events).

(1c) R is *nonreflexive* (in S) if and only if there is an x such that xRx, *and* there is an x such that $xR'x$. Examples of nonreflexive relations are "employs" (in the set of human beings) and "equals the square of" (in the set of real numbers).

(2a) R is *symmetric* (in S) if and only if for all x and y (not necessarily distinct), $xRy \supset yRx$.* Examples of symmetric relations are "$=$" (in the set of real numbers), "is married to" (in the set of human beings), and "is parallel to" (in the set of lines in the Euclidean plane).

(2b) R is *asymmetric* (in S) if and only if for all x and y (not necessarily distinct), $xRy \supset yR'x$. Examples of asymmetric relations are "$>$" (in the domain of real numbers), "is a parent of" (in the set of human beings), and "has greater mass than" (in the set of physical objects).

(2c) R is *nonsymmetric* (in S) if and only if there is a couple, x and y (not necessarily distinct), such that xRy and yRx; *and* there is a couple, x and y (not necessarily distinct), such that xRy and $yR'x$. Examples of nonsymmetric relations are "is less than twice as large as" (in the set of real numbers), "is a brother of" (in the set of human beings), and "is a subset of" (in the set of sets).

In the study of any set of objects, an important consideration is the criterion of identity. That is, we must be able to determine the conditions under which x and y are to be regarded as the same object. The identity relationship is used in the assertion that they are the same. We shall use I to denote the identity relation. Thus xIy means that x and y are identical, and $xI'y$ means that x and y are not identical; that is, they are distinct.

(2d) R is *antisymmetric* if and only if, for all x and y (not necessarily distinct), $[xRy$ and $yRx] \supset xIy$. Examples of antisymmetric relations are "$\leq$" and "is the square of" (in the set of real numbers).

(3a) R is *transitive* if and only if, for every x, y, and z (not necessarily distinct), $[xRy$ and $yRz] \supset xRz$. Examples of transitive relations are "$>$" (in the set of real numbers), "is an ancestor of" (in the set of human beings), and "is north of" (in the set of geographical locations).

(3b) R is *intransitive* if and only if, for every x, y, and z (not necessarily distinct), $[xRy$ and $yRz] \supset xR'z$. Examples of intransitive relations are "is the father of" and "is married to" (in the set of monogamous human beings), "immediately succeeds" (in the set of

---

* The symbol "$\supset$" means "implies." That is, if P and Q are statements, "$P \supset Q$" means "Q is true if P is" or "If P is true, then Q is true."

integers), and "is perpendicular to" (in the set of lines in a Euclidean plane).

(3c) R is *nontransitive* if and only if there is a triplet, x, y, and z (not necessarily distinct), such that xRy and yRz and xRz; *and* there is a triplet, x, y, and z (not necessarily distinct), such that xRy and yRz and $xR'z$. Examples of nontransitive relations are "is different from" (in any set), "is a blood relative of" (in the set of human beings), and "has a nonnull intersection with" (in the set of sets).

(3d) R is *quasi-transitive* if and only if for every triplet, x, y, and z (not necessarily distinct), $[xRy$ and yRz and $xI'z] \supset xRz$. Examples of quasi-transitive relations are "is a brother of" (in the set of human beings), "is parallel to" (in the set of lines in the Euclidean plane), and "is different from" (in any set).

Not all possible combinations of these properties are logically consistent; that is, some involve contradictions: For example, a relationship which is asymmetrical and transitive cannot be reflexive. If a relationship is symmetrical and intransitive, it must be irreflexive. If a relationship is transitive and irreflexive, it is asymmetrical. A relationship cannot be asymmetrical and reflexive.*

Reflexivity is a property of a relation which is useful primarily in establishing similarities, whereas irreflexivity establishes differences. This is apparent from comparing "$=$" and "$>$". If a given relation is symmetric, then all members of pairs bearing this relation to one another may be substituted for each other in an appropriate context. For example, things which "look alike" or "are the same size as" may replace each other in appropriate contexts.

Asymmetry allows us to distinguish or individuate elements, as in "does not look like" and "is a different size from."

Transitivity allows us to join things together in a chain, in a hierarchical or ordered series; for example, "$>$" in the set of integers.

(4a) R is *connected* if and only if, for every x and y, $xI'y \supset [xRy$ and/or $yRx]$. Examples of connected relations are "$<$" (in the set of real numbers), "is older than" (in the set consisting of a given person together with his father, paternal grandfather, paternal great-grandfather, etc.), and "has a larger radius than" (in the set consisting of all circles with a common center).

(4b) R is *nonconnected* if and only if there is an x and y ($xI'y$) such that xRy and/or yRx, *and* there is an x and y ($xI'y$) such that $xR'y$ and $yR'x$; for example, "is the father of" (in the set of people).

---

* The reader should try to verify these assertions.

TABLE 6.1. TYPES OF RELATIONS

Property	Definition (Relative to a Set of Elements, S)	Examples (S = The Set of Positive Integers)
1a. Reflexive	$x: xRx$	$=$
1b. Irreflexive	$x: xR'x$	$>$
1c. Nonreflexive	$[\exists x: xRx]$ and $[\exists x: xR'x]$	Equals the square of
2a. Symmetric	$x, y: xRy \supset yRx$	$=$
2b. Asymmetric	$x, y: xRy \supset yR'x$	$>$
2c. Nonsymmetric	$[\exists x, y: xRy$ and $yRx]$ and $[\exists x, y: xRy$ and $yR'x]$	Is less than twice As large as
2d. Antisymmetric	$x, y: [xRy$ and $yRx] \supset xIy$	$\geq$
3a. Transitive	$x, y, z: [xRy$ and $yRz] \supset xRz$	$>$
3b. Intransitive	$x, y, z: [xRy$ and $yRz] \supset xR'z$	Immediately succeeds
3c. Nontransitive	$\exists x, y, z: [xRy, yRz,$ and $xRz]$, and $\exists x, y, z: [xRy, yRz,$ and $xR'z]$	Is less than twice as large as
3d. Quasi-transitive	$x, y, z: [xRy, yRz,$ and $xI'z] \supset xRz$	Is different from
4a. Connected	$x, y: xI'y \supset [xRy$ and/or $yRx]$	$>$
4b. Nonconnected	$\exists x, y(xI'y): [xRy$ and/or $yRx]$, and $\exists x, y(xI'y): [xR'y$ and $yR'x]$	Immediately succeeds

Read "$x:$" as "for every x," "$\exists x:$" as "there exists an x such that," and "$\supset$" as "implies."

If a relation is connected, then, it "binds together" all the elements of a population.

Types of Ordering

The elements of a population may be ordered in various ways, depending on the properties of the ordering relation. These orderings range from (what may be thought of as) the "weak" to the "strong." The ones presented here are not exhaustive.

Essential to any type of ordering is the ability to differentiate between elements by establishing one-directional differences. Hence ordering requires a relationship that is not symmetric; that is, one that is either asymmetric, nonsymmetric, or antisymmetric. A relation such as "$=$," therefore, cannot be used to order elements because it is symmetric. A relation which is either nonsymmetric or asymmetric and which does not hold between all elements of the population (i.e., is nonconnected) provides the weakest type of ordering.

The ordering is strengthened if the relation holds between all pairs of different elements of the population; that is, if the relation is connected. For example, "$\geqq$" provides such an ordering for real numbers, and "costs at least as much as" for items which are for sale.

A relationship which is transitive and symmetric (e.g., "$=$") allows us to form chains of similar things, but not to order them. To obtain an ordered chain we require that the relation be either asymmetric (e.g., "$>$") or antisymmetric (e.g., "$\geqq$").

A *partial* ordering or ranking is formed by a relationship which is reflexive, antisymmetric, transitive, and nonconnected. For example, "$\geqq$" yields such an ordering of automobile license plates. Some plates which have only letters and no numbers are not comparable with those having only numbers. Thus we get a partial ordering of the population. Partial ordering reflects the multidimensionality of the attributes differentiating the elements in the relevant set.

A *weak* ordering or ranking is formed by a reflexive, antisymmetric, transitive, and connected relation. For example, "$\geqq$" yields such a scale of people's weight. Since some people have the same weight, they are not ordered with respect to each other and hence the weakness of the ordering. Another weak ordering is provided by military ranks. Each rank constitutes an equivalence class, and for any two officers (x, y) either $x \geqq y$, or $y \geqq x$, or both.

A *complete* ordering or ranking is formed by an irreflexive, asymmetric, transitive, and connected relation. For example, "$>$" yields such a scale of the positive integers. Such an ordering is also called a *chain*, a *simple order*, or a *linear order*. It yields a complete ranking of every element of the population.

There are many variations of ordering. One of the more sophisticated procedures, developed by Siegel (1956), has been discussed in Chapter 3. This scale yields a weak ordering of both utilities *and* the differences between them.

Numbers are usually assigned to ordered elements to represent their rank. In the case of a partial ordering this has little value, since some of the elements cannot be ranked. In a weak ordering the same number must be assigned to elements which have the same value of the property involved. In a complete ordering each element can be assigned a number of its own. It is conventional to use "1" to designate either the lowest or highest position in the order and to number serially

TABLE 6.2.   PROPERTIES OF TYPES OF ORDERING

Property	Partial	Weak	Complete
Reflexive	X	X	
Irreflexive			X
Asymmetric			X
Antisymmetric	X	X	
Transitive	X	X	X
Connected		X	X
Nonconnected	X		

thereafter. Arithmetical operations cannot be performed on the numbers so assigned. For example, if three objects are ranked by weight, it does not follow that the weight of the heaviest (3) is equal to the sum of the weights of the lighter two $(1 + 2)$. Nor is the weight of "3" necessarily equal to three times the weight of "1." This is made apparent by the fact that letters $(A, B, C, \cdots)$ can also be used to designate rank without any loss of information.

Table 6.2 summarizes the basic properties of partial, weak, and complete ordering. For further discussion of other aspects of ordinal scales see Coombs (1951), Coombs, Raiffa, and Thrall (1954), and Stevens (1951 and 1959).

MEASUREMENT (IN THE RESTRICTED SENSE)

Measurement in the restricted sense involves the use of a constant unit of measurement. Such a unit is employed in both interval and ratio scales.

Interval Scales

Interval scales correspond more closely than do nominal and ordinal scales with what we normally think of as measurement. Whereas neither numbering, counting, nor ranking explicitly involves a constant *unit of measurement*, the interval scale does. But, as we shall see, the unit of measurement involved in an interval scale is arbitrary.

The essential characteristic of the interval scale is best understood by considering one property of the ordinal scale. Consider three persons, *A, B,* and *C,* such that we have determined that *A* is taller than *B* and *B* is taller than *C.* Then we can rank them as 1, 2, and 3. In the usual ranking procedure we do *not* know whether *A* is as much taller than *B* as *B* is than *C;* that is, we do not know the relationship between *A*'s height minus *B*'s and *B*'s height minus *C*'s. In the higher-ordered metric scale developed by Siegel (1956), these differences are ranked, but the ratio of their magnitudes is not determined. The measures obtained from an interval scale enable us to make assertions about, and draw inferences from, the magnitudes of the differences between the properties of different objects or events.

The centigrade and Fahrenheit scales of temperature are interval scales. Equal intervals of temperature are scaled off by noting equal volumes of expansion of the liquid used in the thermometer.

These scales have the important property of being "unique up to a linear transformation." The meaning of this property can be explained as follows. Suppose that we obtain measurements of a set of elements $\{x_i\}$. These can be transformed into other values $\{x_i'\}$ by the linear equation, $x_i' = ax_i + b$, where $a \neq 0$. The relative magnitudes of the new values are the same as they were originally. Graphically, this is illustrated in Figure 6.1.

These scales do not have any "natural" *zero point.* The zero point is usually set arbitrarily or for convenience and is then accepted by convention. Hence, the centigrade and Fahrenheit scales have different zero points. These scales can be transformed into each other by a simple linear transformation:

$$t_f = \tfrac{9}{5}t_c + 32,$$

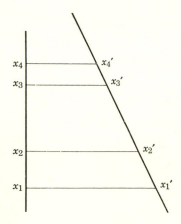

FIGURE 6.1. A linear transformation of scales.

where t_f is the temperature on the Fahrenheit scale, and t_c is the temperature on the centigrade scale.

It can be misleading to say that any value on an interval scale is some multiple of another; for example, that an object at 64° F has twice the temperature of an object at 32° F. That this is misleading is apparent by both example and general considerations. If we transform 32° F and 64° F to the centigrade scale, we obtain 0° C and 17.8° C. The latter are obviously not in a 1:2 ratio. More generally, even if $x_2 = 2x_1$, then, unless $b = 0$,

$$ax_2 + b \neq 2(ax_1 + b)$$

since
$$a(2x_1) + b \neq 2(ax_1 + b)$$

$$2ax_1 + b \neq 2ax_1 + 2b.$$

These will only be equal in the special case where $b = 0$. On the other hand, we can express the *differences* (intervals) between values on the interval scale as multiples of each other (e.g., 64° F is twice as far from 0° F as is 32° F). This can be seen by comparing the intervals between three points, x_1, x_2, and x_3. The ratio of the interval $(x_1 - x_2)$ to the interval $(x_2 - x_3)$ is, of course,

$$\frac{x_1 - x_2}{x_2 - x_3}.$$

If we transform the values of x_1, x_2, and x_3, the value of the ratio is retained:

$$\frac{(ax_1 + b) - (ax_2 + b)}{(ax_2 + b) - (ax_3 + b)} = \frac{ax_1 - ax_2}{ax_2 - ax_3} = \frac{x_1 - x_2}{x_2 - x_3}.$$

The properties measured on an interval scale can be mapped into the real numbers. Although some arithmetical operations cannot be performed on these numbers (e.g., addition and multiplication) without special explanation, most arithmetic operations can be performed on the differences (intervals) between all pairs of these numbers.

The type of interval scale we have considered here is linear, but the interval involved need not be linear. Stevens (1959, pp. 31–34) discusses another type, the logarithmic interval scale, in which the transformation is

$$x' = kx^n.$$

Although use for such a scale has not yet been found, it is of theoretical interest and opens the possibility of development of a wide variety of interval scales.

Ratio Scales

The characteristics of this type of scale have been summarized by Stevens (1951, p. 8) as follows:

. . . Its numerical values can be transformed (as from inches to feet), only by multiplying each value by a constant, that is, $x_1 = ax_1$. An absolute zero is always implied, even though the zero value on scales (e.g., Absolute Temperature) may never be produced. All types of statistical measure are applicable to ratio scales, and only with these scales may we properly indulge in logarithmic transformations. . . .

Measurement on a ratio scale is achieved with a constant but arbitrary unit (standard) of measurement (e.g., feet or meters in measuring length).

Any one value on a ratio scale can be expressed as a multiple of any other. For example, "3 feet" is equal to "3(1 foot)," and this relationship remains invariant with transformations of the type $x' = cx$; that is, "36 inches" is 3(12 inches). Or we may say that one body is twice as dense as another if the ratio of its mass to its volume is twice that of the other body.

All arithmetical operations are applicable to the (real) numbers obtained from measurements on a ratio scale. But some of these operations—for example, addition—may not have the apparent operational significance. For example, the addition of the densities of two bodies, D_1 and D_2, is not equal to the density of the two bodies taken "jointly." That is, $D_1 = M_1/V_1$ and $D_2 = M_2/V_2$ (where M and V represent mass and volume, respectively), but the density of the two bodies taken jointly is not equal to $D_1 + D_2$ or $M_1/V_1 + M_2/V_2$; it is equal to $(M_1 + M_2)/(V_1 + V_2)$. (We shall consider the measurement of density in more detail below.)

SUMMARY OF SCALE CHARACTERISTICS

The characteristics of the four types of scale which we have considered have been succinctly summarized by Stevens and are shown in Table 6.3. Stevens has also summarized the statistical measures which are appropriate to measurements made on each type of scale. These

TABLE 6.3.   A CLASSIFICATION OF SCALES OF MEASUREMENT *

Scale	Basic Empirical Operations	Mathematical Group Structure	Typical Examples
NOMINAL	Determination of equality	Permutation group $$x' = f(x),$$ where $f(x)$ means any one-to-one substitution	"Numbering" of football players Assignment of type or model numbers to classes
ORDINAL	Determination of greater or less	Isotonic group $$x' = f(x),$$ where $f(x)$ means any increasing monotonic function	Hardness of minerals Street numbers Grades of leather, lumber, wool, etc. Intelligence-test raw scores
INTERVAL	Determination of the equality of intervals or of differences	Linear or affine group $$x' = ax + b,$$ $$a > 0$$	Temperature (Fahrenheit or Celsius) Position Time (calendar) Energy (potential) Intelligence-test "standard scores" (?)
RATIO	Determination of the equality of ratios	Similarity group $$x' = cx,$$ $$c > 0$$	Numerosity Length, density, work, time intervals, etc. Temperature (Rankine or Kelvin) Loudness (sones) Brightness (brils)

* (From Stevens (1959, p. 25). . . . The basic operations needed to create a given scale are all those listed in the second column, down to and including the operation listed opposite the scale. The third column gives the mathematical transformations that leave the scale form invariant. Any numeral x on a scale can be replaced by another numeral x', where x' is the function of x listed in column 3.

are shown in Table 6.4. It should be noted that the scientific measures applicable to any type of scale include those listed for the other types of scale located above it in the table; that is, these properties are cumulative.

There is nothing in the nature of the four types of scale which have been discussed to assure their exclusiveness or exhaustiveness. Coombs, Raiffa, and Thrall (1954) have already shown that additional scales can be generated by "forming mixtures." We can expect the construction of new types of scales in the future and, perhaps, a more effective classification of possible types of scales than is currently available.

In examining the scales which have been discussed, one can hardly avoid the impression that they form a hierarchy of some kind. In one sense the nominal scale seems to be the most elementary and simplest type, and the ratio scale the most complex. But despite the complexity of the ratio scale it also *appears* to be more fundamental in some sense; at least it has struck some measurement theorists in this way, particularly N. R. Campbell, whose views we examine later.

TABLE 6.4. EXAMPLES OF STATISTICAL MEASURES APPROPRIATE TO MEASUREMENTS MADE ON THE VARIOUS CLASSES OF SCALES *

Scale	Measures of Location	Dispersion	Association or Correlation	Significance Tests
NOMINAL	Mode	Information, H	Information transmitted, T Contingency correlation	Chi square
ORDINAL	Median	Percentiles	Rank-order correlation	Sign test Run test
INTERVAL	Arithmetic mean	Standard deviation Average deviation	Product-moment correlation Correlation ratio	t test F test
RATIO	Geometric mean Harmonic mean	Per cent variation		

* From Stevens (1959, p. 27).

THE NATURE OF MEASUREMENT

There is anything but common agreement among scientists and philosophers of science as to just what measurement is and how it should be performed. These points of view can be characterized as ranging from the very restricted to the very general. By reference to the work of N. R. Campbell, S. S. Stevens, and C. W. Churchman we shall try to present the more significant points of view and to identify the important methodological problems involved in measurement.

Campbell's Concept of Fundamental Measurement

Campbell, operating in the spirit of others we have considered who have sought simple or irreducible concepts or operations, was preoccupied with what he called *fundamental measurement*. In order to determine whether a property is subject to fundamental measurement, Campbell has set down six conditions on the way that things having the property can be *related*. The relationship must be:

(1) *connected:* for every pair of elements, x and y, either xRy, yRx, or $x = y$;

(2) *asymmetric: $xRy \supset yR'x$*; and

(3) *transitive: $(xRy$ and $yRz) \supset xRz$.*

The relations "is at least as heavy as" and "is at least as dense as" satisfy these requirements for the class of "physical bodies." But "is at least as red as" and "is at least as dark as" are not connected relations. "Some colours are neither redder nor less red than others, two shades of the same blue, for example; and yet they are not 'equal in colour' . . ." [Campbell (1957, p. 272]. Hence, according to Campbell, we must drop color from the class of fundamentally measurable properties, at least with respect to the set of physical bodies.

Next, a fundamental measurement, according to Campbell, has the following properties of additivity:

If α and β represent the numbers assigned to the elements representing the property involved, then

(4) $\alpha + \beta = \beta + \alpha$;

(5) $(\alpha + \beta) + \alpha = \alpha + (\beta + \alpha)$;

(6) $(\alpha + \beta) > \alpha$, where $\beta > 0$.

The measurement of weight by means of a balance, according to Campbell (1957, p. 279), satisfies these conditions:

We state that the weights of two bodies A and B are "equal" when, if A is placed in one pan of the balance and B in the other, the final position of the pointer of the balance is unchanged. We say that the body C is "added to" the body A, when A and C are placed in the same pan of the balance; and that it is "subtracted from" the body composed of A and C in the same pan by removing C from the pan. When we have thus defined "equal" and "added to" in the use of the balance, we can state, corresponding to arithmetical proportions which involve addition and equality, propositions about what will happen to the balance when we place bodies in the pans.

It is clear then that weight satisfies conditions (4), (5), and (6). Density, even though measured on a ratio scale, according to Campbell, does not satisfy condition (6). As already noted, if we "join" two bodies of density α and β, the density of the conjunction is not $\alpha + \beta$, whereas, if α and β represent weights, this would be true. Weight then is a *fundamental magnitude*, but density is *derived*. "It presupposes the measure of mass or volume" [Campbell (1957, p. 277)]. But weight "apparently" involves no other measures and hence is fundamental.

The apparent difference between scales of density and of weight with respect to additivity also appears to exist between scales of "return on investment" and "profit." Return on investment is usually measured as a percentage:

$$(100) \, \frac{\text{net profit in \$}}{\text{total amount invested in \$}}.$$

If a corporation has two companies, each obtaining a 5 per cent return on its investment each year, the total return on investment is 5 per cent, not 10 per cent. On the other hand, if each company makes $1,000,000 profit per year, the total profit is $2,000,000. Profit satisfies all six conditions set down by Campbell but certainly is not a fundamental measure in the sense of depending on no other measures; it depends at least on a measure of expenses and income. On this point we shall have more to say below.

Critiques of Campbell

Stevens, who was so concerned with allowing only definitions containing operations which could be reduced to a fundamental operation (pointing), is not so ardently a fundamentalist when it comes to measurement. He was very disturbed by the Committee of the British

Association for the Advancement of Science, which issued a report on the problem of measurement in 1940. This report, dominated by the participating Campbell's point of view, attacked one of Stevens' sensory scales. One member asserted that "any law purporting to express a quantitative relation between sensation intensity and stimulus intensity is not merely false but is in fact meaningless until a meaning can be given to the concept of addition as applied to sensation" [Ferguson (1940, p. 245)].

Stevens (1946, p. 677) replied as follows:

Paraphrasing N. R. Campbell (*Final Report*, p. 340) we may say that measurement, in the broadest sense, is defined as the assignment of numerals to objects or events according to rules. The fact that numerals can be assigned under different rules leads to different kinds of scales and different kinds of measurement. The problem then becomes that of making explicit (*a*) the various rules for the assignment of numerals, (*b*) the mathematical properties (or group structure) of the resulting scales, and (*c*) the statistical operations applicable to measurements made with each type of scale.

Stevens does not object to the concept of fundamental measurement —in fact, he embraces it—but he does object to restricting the concept of measurement to fundamental measures or ones derived from them. To support his position he defined four types of scales which can be used in measurement (in the broad sense of the word): nominal, ordinal, interval, and ratio. These types have become the focus of most subsequent discussions of measurement, including this one. Stevens would like ultimately to have all measures derived from ones that are fundamental in Campbell's sense, but in the meantime he argues that the "weaker" forms of number assignment are also measurement.

Churchman (1949, pp. 483–485) made a much more "fundamental" attack on the concept of a fundamental scale:

Fundamental magnitudes, he [Campbell] says, are magnitudes "the measurement of which does not depend on any other magnitude." This comes as something of a shock to the reader accustomed to the complexities of physical measurement. Where in nature do we find magnitudes that don't depend on other magnitudes for their measurement?

Whatever these magnitudes are, they must, according to Campbell, involve the simplest kind of operation in their determination. The simplest operation for him seems to be one of adding increments. Hence, fundamental scales have an *additive* property. For scales enjoying the additive property, the magnitude x is "the number of standard things or 'units' that have to be combined together in order to produce the thing equal to x in respect to the property." The additive scales, like all scales, are defined for Campbell by a set of operations; these operations must be such that the objects whose magnitude is to be determined are "ordered." In particular, if we say the operation makes A smaller than B $(A < B)$, then there must not be any prescribed operation leading to $B < A$.

Now it seems to Campbell that lengths, areas, weights, etc., are additive magnitudes, for they are all based on the choice of a certain standard magnitude; the operations consist of taking parts or multiples of the standard.

But none of this substantiates the claim that the measurements of length, weight, etc., are fundamental in the sense that they do not depend on the measurement of any other magnitudes. The natural question we should like to ask someone weighing objects, is whether the arms of the balance are equal and convection currents absent. And, in general, we want to know what variables must be checked to make sure the balance is behaving properly. But to know the answer to these questions it certainly looks as though the experimenter must take measurements of other magnitudes, and hence the determination of weight is not "fundamental" in Campbell's sense. No, says Campbell, all the experimenter need do is follow through the operations and "discover whether interchange of the contents of the pans affects the balance." As a matter of fact, Campbell thinks the question about all the necessary checks on the balance is "actually dangerous." "For the answer must involve in some form the theory of the balance. . . . We are basing our measurements on theory, rather than our theory on measurement, which is a most dangerous procedure." Dangerous for whom? Campbell does not tell us, but we are led to suppose that the danger is for any goodhearted fundamentalist anxious to get his start somewhere. It is interesting to contrast Brown's dictum: "The discovery of the law makes the possibility of exact and accurate measurement rather than the measurement makes possible the discovery of the law." To refute this position, Campbell argues that to check the process of weighing, we "simply try out" the objects on the pans to see if the operations satisfy the formal conditions of additive magnitudes. Well, how many objects must we try? Who shall try them? On what days? On the critical question of judging a result, Campbell asserts that the determination of lengths, for example, "depends on judgments of the contiguity of parts of lines, which is a relation *instinctively perceived*." Do all people instinctively perceive alike? Does one person instinctively perceive alike at different times? Of course, I don't know exactly what Campbell means by "instinctively perceived"; but almost any conceivable meaning of the term would lead to a decided negative to the questions. Different observers *do* perceive "instinctively" in different ways, even when the operations are very carefully specified. Further, different observers get significantly different results on different days, in different laboratories, etc.

I think Campbell's position might be tolerated, even in the light of its lack of rigor, if scientific experience indicated that the results of following operations at different times, by different observers, did not differ very widely.

Measures always presuppose and hence involve other measures. Control of the environmental conditions, which is always necessary to some degree in measurement, itself always requires measurement. Therefore, measurement, like defining, has the appearance of circularity, but it actually cycles in "three-dimensional space," progressing as does defining. In a specific study, however, it is always desirable to specify a measure in such a way that the presupposed measures or other measures required are less difficult than the direct measure in the context of the problem or question. One of the difficulties, for example, in the specification of an idealized measure of value presented in Chapter 3, was that it presupposes a measure of knowledge which is at least as difficult to obtain as is that of value. But, as in this case, the presupposed measures cannot always be more easily attained than the measure directly involved. Even here the presupposed measures should be made explicit so that efforts to improve any one of the interrelated measures take the others into account. Only with a self-conscious treatment of these interrelations can measurement progress more evenly over all the sciences and in all problem areas.

Churchman's critique of Campbell's concept of fundamental measurement is based on the latter's assertion of the existence of measures which presuppose no other measure. Another aspect of Campbell's doctrine is also open to criticism: the concept of additivity. According to Campbell (1957, p. 281),

> In respect to weighing a process of addition and a relation of equality can be found which are similar . . . to the arithmetical process of addition and the arithmetical process of equality, but a process of addition and a relation of equality which are thus similar to the arithmetical processes and relation cannot be found in respect to determination of density.

The fact is that we can find a set of operations which yield additivity of densities, at least under restricted conditions. Consider two containers of equal volume, one containing gas G_1 of density D_1 and the other gas G_2 of density D_2. If G_2 is added to G_1 in the first container, the density of the resulting mixture is equal to $D_1 + D_2$. This suggests the possibility of eventually finding a set of operations which more generally yield additivity of density. This possibility is implicit (but not intended) in an observation made by Campbell (1957): "Thus we may say that A is denser than B if a liquid can be found such that B will float in it and A will sink" (p. 276). To this observation Campbell attached the following significant footnote (p. 276):

> I am inclined to think that this is historically the ultimate meaning of density, that to Archimedes, for example, density was simply the property in virtue of which some bodies floated while others sank, and the discovery that this property was represented by the ratio of the mass (or rather weight) to the volume was a later and independent discovery.

Measures of properties, like their definitions, may go through an evolutionary process. Campbell's observations on density indicate that the measurement of density has progressed from an ordinal to a ratio scale. The possibility of such evolution is explicitly recognized by Stevens (1959, pp. 24–25):

It is an interesting fact that the measurement of some quantities may have progressed from scale to scale. We can imagine, for example, that certain Eskimos might speak of temperature only as freezing or not freezing and, thereby, place it on a nominal scale. Others might try to express degrees of warmer and colder, perhaps in terms of some series of natural events, and thereby achieve an ordinal scale. As we all know, temperature became an interval scale with the development of thermometry, and, after thermodynamics had used the expansion ratio of gases to extrapolate to zero, it became a ratio scale.

We can observe just such an evolution compressed into a short time in the measurement of utility (value). Man undoubtedly first classified things as either desirable or undesirable. Eventually, with the development of preference tests in psychology, ordinal scales were involved. The von Neumann-Morgenstern measure of utility involves an interval scale. Finally, serious efforts are now being made to develop ratio scales of utility. See, for example, Stevens (1959, pp. 52–61).

What conclusions can be drawn from the critiques of Campbell's work? Churchman (1949, pp. 488–492), after his study of Campbell's doctrine, suggested five principles of measurement:

(1) We must stop thinking of scientific method as proceeding from the intuitively simple elements to more complex ones.

(2) Additive scales are not any more "fundamental" than any other type of scale.

(3) All exact measurements take place in an idealized environment; the results of an actual experiment are to be regarded as estimates of what would happen if ideal conditions could be obtained.

(4) The scaling of a property of an object provides information as to the most efficient use of that property in any problem situation.

(5) A scale furnishes the experimenter with a technique whereby he can measure the degree of scientific perfection he has attained.

The significance of these principles will become more apparent as we address ourselves to the following questions, which should be answered in preparation for measurement in research:

(1) *Definition.* What property of what objects or events is being measured? What operations should be performed on these objects or events, and how should numbers be assigned to the property observed?

(2) *Formal properties.* What mathematical and statistical operations can be performed on the measurements obtained?

(3) *Accuracy.* How can we adjust measurements obtained in less than the ideal conditions that are specified in the relevant definition, and what is their accuracy?

(4) *Control.* How can an acceptable level of accuracy be maintained?

Definition of What Is Measured

It may seem unlikely that a procedure can be developed or adopted for measuring something without being able to define operationally that which is being measured. If this can be done, one can reasonably ask, "In what sense can the numbers obtained be called a measurement?" Such a procedure is much more common than one would expect. Suppose, for example, that a series of puzzles are collected and given to a number of persons in a specified order. Each person is scored on the number of puzzles correctly solved within a specified time. Then a number of other characteristics of these persons are determined, such as average annual earnings, rate of advancement, size of family, and IQ. Correlations are then obtained between these characteristics and the score on the puzzle test. If a high correlation is obtained between the test score and any of these characteristics, the score on the test is used to estimate the properties with which it is correlated.

Stevens prefers to call such scores as are yielded by this test *indicants* rather than measures. Indicants are *effects* or *correlates* related to the property in question by unknown laws. According to Stevens (1951, pp. 47–48), the use of indicants

. . . is inevitable in the present stage of our progress, and it is not to be counted as a blemish. . . .

The end of the trail is measurement, which we reach when we solve the relation between our fortuitous indicants and the proper dimensions of the thing in question.

In the meantime we take hold of our problems by whatever handles nature provides. . . . We measure changes in the resistance of the skin and call it an indicant of emotion. . . .

The distinction between measures and indicants disappears, of course, as soon as we learn the quantitative relation between the indicant and the object of our interest, for then the indicant can be calibrated and used to measure the phenomenon at issue. We measure electric current by means of a calibrated indicant composed of a coil of wire suspended by a spring in a magnetic field. . . . The more mature a science, the more it uses *calibrated* indicants.

Recalling that indicants are effects or correlates, it becomes apparent that their appropriateness can be scientifically established only if either the causal connection to the property of interest can be established, or that property can be measured so that a correlation analysis can be performed. Clearly, the former cannot be done if the relevant laws involved are unknown. If these laws are unknown, then the bridge is intuitive and is not objectively founded. Similarly, in most cases where indicants are used, the correlations by which their use is justified are not established objectively but are also based on intuition.

In many a case where indicants are justified on the basis of correlation analysis, observations of the indicants have been correlated with subjective evaluation of the relevant properties. Such an instance will be cited below relative to a "test" of attitudes toward the Church, where test scores are correlated with subjective judgments of the subjects' attitudes.

Despite these shortcomings of most indicants currently employed, they can be useful as a bridge to measurement as long as those who use them do not confuse them with measuring instruments, as is usually done. Even after measurement of a property is attained, however, indicants may be useful because of observational simplicity. For example, we know how to determine the age of a tree by measuring time, but we usually do so by counting the rings in the tree's cross section. The rings are indicants which are causally connectable to age but are easier to count than are the years of life.

One gets the impression from the Stevens quotation that all that is required to bridge the gap between indicants and measures is empirical knowledge. But all the empirical knowledge in the world is not sufficient to connect the resistance of the skin to emotions unless we have an operational definition of emotion. What Stevens attributes to a lack of knowledge is usually due to a lack of definition. If half the effort which is expended in searching for properties that indicants "quantify" were spent in proper defining of concepts, science and its application would progress at a considerably greater rate.

In some cases a loose definition of a concept is used in constructing a measure of it. This always leaves room for doubt as to whether or not the measure actually pertains to the concept involved. For example, consider a fairly common procedure for constructing attitude tests, one described in detail by Thurstone and Chave (1929).

They define an attitude as "the sum-total of a man's inclinations and feelings, prejudice or bias, preconceived notions, ideas, fears, threats, and convictions about any topic" (pp. 6–7). It is clear that the "sum-total" is a figure of speech. Addition in any serious sense is not proposed here. In fact, when a definition provides no explicit criterion for relevance of observations or instructions for making them, it is *not* an operational definition. Furthermore, the definition gives little indication as to how attitudes can be measured.

In the procedure for "measuring" attitudes developed by Thurstone and Chave, statements about the topic involved are selected because they *seem* relevant to the topic. Their relevance cannot be demonstrated objectively. What is normally done is as follows. The statements are submitted to a set of judges who rank them on the basis of their own feelings according to the strength of each statement's favorableness (or unfavorableness) to the topic involved. Those statements which are consistently rated by the judges are combined in a questionnaire. This is given to two groups of people, one "known" to be "favorable" and the other "known" to be "unfavorable" on the topic involved. If the test scores discriminate between members of the two groups, then the test is said to be "validated" and the score to be a measure of the attitude.

Since the test designers and judges have no explicit criterion for determining whether a question or statement is relevant to the particular attitude in question, it is not surprising that the items selected are frequently quite ambiguous. Consider, for example, Thurstone's and Chave's test for "measuring" attitudes toward the Church (1930). Here, not only was "attitude" left ill-defined but the "Church" was not defined at all. In their item 26 ("I regard the Church as a parasite on society") "Church" is apparently used to mean "organized religion." In item 31 ("There is much wrong in my Church, but I feel it is so important that it is my duty to help improve it") "Church" means "either the particular congregation I attend (if any)" or "the denomination with which I associate myself (if any)." Item 34 ("I feel that Church attendance is a good index of the nation's morality") would be agreed to by a religious citizen of a capitalist country, implying that his nation is moral; whereas an ardent Communist in the U.S.S.R. would also agree, but to him high attendance means immorality. Many other ambiguities exist in the items. For this reason different tests of the same attitude may not always yield consistent results, a difficulty which could be avoided by proper definition.

"Measures" of profit in business may also be quite inconsistent, and for the same reason: profit is usually very poorly defined. Different accountants can derive widely divergent profit figures from the same set of industrial transactions.

For the reasons which have been considered, then, it is essential in research that operational definitions be provided for all properties to be measured. Only by so doing can the relevance of observations be assured and a basis for adjustment be provided. In the ideal operations specified in the definition, the relevant measurement standard should be specified. For structural properties measurement standards are usually a matter of convention and hence do not have to be explicitly identified as long as they are known. For example, the metric standard of length is the *meter,* which, by international agreement, is the distance between two scratches on a platinum-iridium bar kept near Paris. The standard of time is the *mean solar second,* which is 1/86,400 of a mean solar day. The metric unit of mass is the inertia of a block of platinum kept near Paris and is called the *kilogram,* and so on. In the United States the Bureau of Standards has responsibility for maintaining appropriate standards by calibrating measuring instruments and specifying the accuracy they must be capable of yielding.

Formal Properties of Measurement

We must be careful not to impute automatically to the numbers obtained by any process of assigning numbers to objects, events, or properties, the properties which these numbers have *as numbers.* We can add the numbers of two houses or of two car registrations, but the question is whether or not the sum has any meaning, and if so what. The numbers of two houses may represent some property of these houses, but the sum of these two numbers may not represent any property of the two houses taken jointly. This is quite apparent in the case of house numbers but may not be so apparent in other cases; for example, the sum of the temperatures of two bodies obtained on a Fahrenheit scale does not represent the temperature of the two bodies taken jointly.

The formal properties of a scale should describe what operations can be meaningfully performed on the properties which are measured on the scale. The scale of weight is said to be additive because we can find an operation (or set of operations) for joining two bodies in such a way that the weight of the union is equal to the sum of the weights of the bodies taken separately. It will be recalled that, in the earlier discussion of density, Campbell argued that such an operation could not be found with respect to density. The formal properties of a scale, then, do not describe properties of that which is being measured, but properties of the operations which can be performed on that which is being measured. Thus, to say that the scale of weight is additive is not to say anything about weight itself, but it does say something about what operations can be performed on objects which have weight. It is this fact that makes the evolution of measurement possible. If temperature itself were not additive, for example, the Kelvin scale would never have been developed. The Fahrenheit and Kelvin scales of temperature yield measures with different formal properties. The formal properties of these scales represent different sets of operations which can be performed on temperature, and not differences in temperature itself.

Put another way, when a procedure for assigning numbers to a property is developed, the properties of the procedure dictate the kind of scale involved, and it is not the scale that dictates what procedures are possible. Translation of the characteristics of measurement operations into formal properties of a scale employed is a safeguard against our treating the numbers obtained in a way which has no operational counterpart.

Accuracy of Measurement

A count, classification, rank, or interval or ratio measurement has little significance (if any) without some knowledge of its accuracy. All types of measurement are subject to error, and an estimate of the magnitude of this error is necessary in order to know whether or not the measures obtained are usable in any specific pure, or applied, research situation.

The value of measurement can perhaps best be appreciated if one realizes that the range of uses to which measurement of a property of an object or event can be put increases with its exactness. A perfectly accurate measurement of a property would make it possible to answer *any* question or solve *any* problem involving only that property; and, furthermore, it allows one to do it *vicariously*. For example, if we want to determine whether we can move a large carton through a doorway, we can, of course, just try. It is generally much simpler, however, to determine the magnitude of the shortest of the carton's three dimensions and the width of the opening and compare them. Similarly, by measuring the dimensions of a table top we can select a tablecloth in a store without having the table present.

If we know that the carton is less than 3 feet wide, this will enable us to determine that it can pass through doorways which are 3 feet wide or more. But it will *not* allow us to determine whether it will pass through doorways which are *less than* 3 feet wide. If, on the other hand, we knew its exact width, we not only could make such a determination for every doorway, but also could use this information to answer any other question in which this property of the carton is exclusively involved.

Accuracy of measurements is not an end in itself. If all we want to know is whether we can move a carton through a 3-feet-wide doorway, all we need know is whether the carton has a dimension of less than 3 feet, not its exact dimensions. In pure science, where the ultimate uses to which a measure might be put by others is not generally known, becoming more accurate than is required by the question at hand can be justified on the grounds that someone else may require this greater accuracy in solving his problem or answering his question. In Chapter 13 we will consider in detail how to determine the degree of accuracy of measurement which is required in a problem context.

There are several possible sources of error in measurement which may contribute to it separately or in combination. These are (1) the observer, (2) the instruments used, (3) the environment, and (4) the thing observed. We will consider each of these in turn.

Error due to the observer

The observer may not follow the required operations either because he is neglectful or because it is not possible practically to do so. In this way he may bias the observations. In particular he may not make the necessary readings as accurately as possible. He may read dials or meters or rules incorrectly. He may not accurately record a response of a subject he has questioned, or he may fail to see what the respondent did. His senses as well as his powers of concentration are not perfect and hence lead to error.

Round-robin tests, in which different observers of the same object using the same instruments obtain significantly different readings, provide strong confirmation of the fact that even in such "simple" operations as counting the observer can be a source of significant error.

Observer error first came to the serious attention of science when Bessel noted what he called the *personal equation*. In the nineteenth century it was observed that in physical measurements the distribution of an observer's errors tends to form a normal curve. The bias and spread (characterized in terms of probable error or standard deviation) differ from observer to observer and for some observers from time to time. This distribution of observer errors, if given any attention at all, is usually assumed to be normal in character without any supporting evidence.

How can the nature of observer error be determined? The answer depends on the nature of the object or event observed. If the property has a constant value over a long enough time to permit a large number of observations, then multiple observations can be made and their distribution analyzed. First, it is necessary to determine the form of this distribution. This involves fitting a curve to the data, a subject to be discussed in Chapter 8. Next the bias and dispersion of the distribution must be determined. (These will be discussed in Chapter 7.) The bias (deviation of the mean of the distribution from the "true" value) can be determined, however, only if the true value is known. Since this is never known in research, observers are usually checked by using a standard object or event under specified conditions. The standard object or event has previously been measured, using the most highly controlled and careful observations possible. The mean of these observations is then *assumed* to be the true value and becomes the basis for computing observer bias. This assumption is important and makes clear the fact that observer bias is never itself measured without error.

If the thing observed is destroyed or significantly changed with respect to the relevant property by the observation process, then the procedure just described cannot be used. It is still widely believed that in such situations the determination of observer error is not possible. This belief is not well founded. This type of problem arises in quality-control work where inspection or testing of an item often involves its destruction, or in social surveys where a respondent may be changed by the first interview. The method for determining observer error in such situations is briefly as follows. The items to be measured (or a random sample * of them) are divided by a random process into groups of (approximately) equal size. Then groups are assigned to observers at random. Each observer classifies or measures the elements in the group assigned to him. The differences in the distributions of the observations are due to both observer error and the differences in the groups assigned. The probabilities associated with differences due to the forming of the groups can usually be determined, and these can be made as small as desired by increasing the size of the groups. These differences can be "subtracted" from the total error, leaving the observer error for examination. The different groups can also be assigned to the same observer at different times if we are interested in his errors rather than in that of a group of observers. For the details of such an analysis see Hanson and Marks (1958).

It may be helpful to describe how observational errors of two dif-

* See Chapter 7 for a discussion of random sampling.

ferent observers were measured in one particular situation. The observation involved in this experiment was of the auditing type. Service-credit-compensation forms of a company were filled out to correspond with their normal usage but some errors were deliberately inserted on approximately 50 per cent of the sheets. Two auditors from the company were selected as subjects. Each auditor was given the same 120 forms containing 61 sheets with errors and was allowed 25 seconds per sheet to classify it as correct or having an error. The auditors were then given 190 forms containing 90 sheets with errors and were allowed 30 seconds per sheet. Similar examinations were made of other batches of forms at 35, 40, 45, 50, 60, and 70 seconds per sheet. The performance times were given to the auditors in random sequence. It took several runs for the observers to settle on an observational procedure. These early sets of observations were consequently eliminated from the analysis. The remaining data are shown in Figure 6.2.

From these data it is clear that the two observers differ signifi-

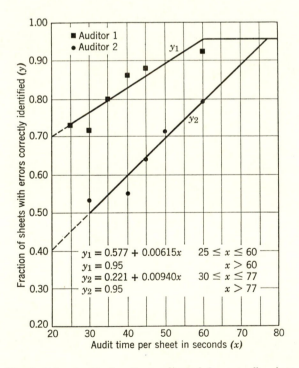

$$y_1 = 0.577 + 0.00615x \qquad 25 \leq x \leq 60$$
$$y_1 = 0.95 \qquad x > 60$$
$$y_2 = 0.221 + 0.00940x \qquad 30 \leq x \leq 77$$
$$y_2 = 0.95 \qquad x > 77$$

FIGURE 6.2. Acuity functions adjusted for cut-off points.

cantly, and statistical tests confirmed this fact. Such data not only permit a selection of observers but also indicate how much time should be allowed for an observation in order to obtain a specified level of accuracy. This experiment should not be interpreted as having general significance for the auditing function; it is used here only to illustrate how determination of observer errors can be made.*

Error due to instruments

The instruments used in making observations, like the observer, may be biased and/or be inconsistent (variable) and hence be characterized by a distribution of errors. The procedure for determining these characteristics is the same as that for an observer.

When an observation involves both an instrument and an observer, they can be considered in combination and a joint observational-instrument error can be determined. It is more difficult to obtain the error functions of each separately, since neither can be held constant with respect to the error, but it can be done by the use of designed experiments such as are discussed in Chapter 10. In such situations, however, we generally want to find the best combination of observer and instrument; this can be determined by an experiment which establishes the error function for each combination.

The improvement of instruments is an important way of reducing observational error arising not only from the instruments themselves but also from the observer, the environment, and the respondent. Mechanization of observation, for example, has contributed to the reduction of error in every branch of science. In astronomy, for example, mechanical means of timing the movement of a star across the field of a telescope has eliminated or at least significantly reduced the error due to variations in reflex time of human observers. Mechanical traffic counters have eliminated or significantly reduced errors due to failure of memory or carelessness of human counters. Hidden cameras and microphones and one-way glass have helped reduce observer influence on human subjects in psychological and social experimentation. Watches are available which are not affected by changes in temperature, moisture, atmospheric pressure, motion, or magnetic fields. One could go on indefinitely enumerating the contribution of instrumentation and mechanization to the reduction of error.

It is important to realize, however, that no matter how highly developed these instruments are they still contribute to error and that a determination of the magnitude of this "contribution" is essential.

* For details on this research see Chambers and Clark (1957).

Error due to environment

The conditions under which the observations are made may vary so as to affect the observer, the instruments, or the thing observed, and, of course, they may fail to correspond to *standard* conditions. In order to determine how these differences and variations affect the accuracy of observations it is necessary to know the laws which connect these changes to the observations. For example, we can correct for variations in observed length of a metal bar due to changing temperature because the linear coefficient of expansion of the metal allows us to compute the resulting changes in length and hence to adjust the observations.

In many areas of inquiry such knowledge is not available, and adjustment of observations to compensate for environmental deviations and changes is not possible. It is essential here to have at least an estimate of the resulting error. This may require experimentation. Only by such experimentation can that knowledge be obtained which will make adjustment for error possible in the future.

Error due to the observed

That which is observed may be either an active or a passive source of error. First, the process of observation may itself affect the behavior of the observed so that we cannot observe its "natural" behavior. Such an effect of the process of observation on the subject of observation has come to be characterized as the *indeterminacy principle*. In quantum mechanics, in which this principle was first formulated, it appears to be possible to reduce the error in the determination of the momentum of a particle at the cost of increasing the error in the determination of its location, and conversely.

The indeterminacy principle has been the center of a major methodological controversy in science since its formulation by Heisenberg. The issue involved concerns the question of whether it is inherent in nature or is a property of our state of knowledge, concepts, and observational methods. There is good reason to believe the latter.

One can maintain that the significance of this principle is that it points up the need for physics to cease thinking of such "elements" as electrons as point particles. In one observational context—the one in which momentum is determined—the electron has no exact position. This does not mean that we have only inexact ways of determining its exact position, but it means that the electron has no exact position. This seems to offend our feeling that all "objects" can be located at some specific place at some specified time. But the new physics requires that we reinterpret the concept "object" in terms dealing with the way it is observed. In effect, an object in the new mechanics is a "state of nature" which is described statistically; it is not a "particle of matter."

One aspect of the new physics is that matter and energy are taken as functions of each other. Matter is no longer conceived of as a substance charged with or discharged of energy. Measurements in this area today involve statistical states and hence are probabilistic in nature. The accuracy of these measures can be reduced without any limit imposed by "principles of nature." As M. Phillips (1949, p. 199) has observed:

It is true that we cannot follow the path of an electron as we can that of a billiard ball; but the reason is that an electron is not a billiard ball. Wave mechanics is concerned precisely with a wave function describing the state of the system, and a wave equation which tells us how this function changes in time.

For detailed discussions of the indeterminacy principle in physics— discussions which argue that continuous reduction of error is not precluded by the principle—see Margenau (1959) and McKnight (1959).

When the object observed is a human being, he may cause much more difficulty (and deliberately so) than does the electron, particularly when he is called on for verbal testimony. This problem has been treated at length in the literature of social-survey methodology. [See, for example, Ackoff (1953, Chapter IX).] Here we can only touch lightly on a few highlights of the subject.

Two types of instruments are used in obtaining verbal behavior from human subjects: tests and questionnaires. In a questionnaire it is assumed that the respondent possesses the information that the observer wants (e.g., his age); in a test such an assumption is not made (e.g., his intelligence).

If a test-design procedure such as is described by Ackoff (1953, Chapter IX) is employed, the consistency of the respondent can be determined by use of duplicate test items. Nothing in a verbal test, however, provides a measure of the accuracy of the responses except in the case where the property under study is the ability to obtain a certain score on the test itself (e.g., in a reading-ability or vocabulary test). In most cases verbal test responses are substitutes for other types of behavior, direct observation of which is difficult or costly to obtain. The definition of the property tested, however, should indicate how such direct observations might be made. The reliance of the pure and applied behavioral sciences on tests is so great that it seems wise to make a serious effort to check the accuracy of test results by use of a standard situation. An experimental check on even a small sample of the population is likely to be very revealing. Without such checks there is no ground for the oft-heard assertion, "Verbal tests are the best practical tool available." Furthermore, unless such evaluations of verbal tests are made, we have no basis for adjusting the test responses; that is, correcting for inaccuracy resulting from the instrument and the respondent.

In using a questionnaire it is assumed that the subject can give us directly the value of the property being investigated.

If a questionnaire is constructed on the basis of an assumed but nonexistent knowledge, then, needless to say, the results are worthless. Therefore, we should be careful, whenever we use a questionnaire, to examine as best we can the legitimacy of such assumptions. This kind of examination may be based on previous studies or on a pretest deliberately conducted to check this assumption.

Once we have decided that we can assume the subject to have knowledge of the points at issue, the problem is primarily one of communication. This means that we want to make sure the subject understands the questions as we want him to, that he tries to give a truthful answer, and that we get his answer recorded accurately.

At present we have no organized science of linguistic communication to help us in these problems, although there are contemporary attempts to construct such a science. [See Cherry (1957).] As yet there are no general criteria to assist in the design of questionnaires. Hence, if we want to evaluate the adequacy of a questionnaire beforehand, in most cases the best we can bring to bear—other than controlled pretesting—is common sense and past experience. Past experience with questionnaires, however, is by no means meager. Numerous articles in the journals provide sound advice for specific types of questions. One of the best of these is authored by Mauldin and Marks (1950). A number of the following remarks and illustrations are borrowed from this article.

Response errors to questionnaire items may, in general, be due to two factors: (1) poor communication and (2) poor recall. "Poor communication" may involve either (a) the failure of the question or the one who asks it to make its meaning clear, or (b) the failure of the respondent to make his meaning clear, or, if he makes it clear, the failure of the recorder of the response to grasp the meaning. The failure of the interviewer to make the question clear may be due to his failure to understand it. This, in turn, may be due to either poor training or lack of ability.

It is obvious and trite to say that questions should use language familiar to the subjects, that they should not be too long, and that there should not be too many of them. The problem, of course, lies in the meaning of "familiar," "too long," and "too many." Several attempts have been made to obtain systematic knowledge on these points by employing linguistic scales [e.g., Terris (1949)]. But, as yet, the designer must rely primarily on unsystematized familiarity with the population to be questioned, common sense, and the pretest.

If there is any doubt as to whether a question or statement contains too much, it is better to break it into two or more questions.

Until recently the Bureau of the Census has asked . . . : "What is the highest grade of school you have completed?" Interpreted literally this question should offer no difficulty for the vast majority of people in answering it correctly. However, many people hear the term "highest grade of school" and immediately think in terms of the highest grade of school they "went to." Some people don't even hear the final word in the question, that is, the word "completed." . . . So we now ask, "What is the highest grade of school you have attended?" Then, the respondent is asked, "Did you finish this grade?" This eliminates part of the response bias for this particular item. [Mauldin and Marks (1950, p. 650)]

Respondents tend to give answers they think the interviewer wants. They may think incorrectly, in which case the respondent's incorrect anticipation should itself be anticipated. The author, for example, once asked a housewife, "Do you raise poultry?" The response was, "No," but it was accompanied by sounds of chickens in the backyard. Further questioning made clear that the housewife thought the question meant, "Do you raise poultry for sale?" She raised poultry only for her own use. The question was subsequently changed to "Do you have any live poultry on this place?" Mauldin and Marks point out that "in evaluating a question it is more important to ask 'How will the respondent interpret this?' than to ask 'What does this question mean?'" (1950, p. 650).

In some cases the question is addressed to the interviewer or observer; that is, he is asked to make a judgment concerning a property of that which is observed (e.g., the condition of a house, the status of a person). In such cases, even if "condition of a house" or "status" is defined, the observer may prefer his own notion as to what this term means. Where this is the case, it is desirable to break the question down into a set of components which can be answered without involving the concept or the observer's prejudices but from which an accurate and reliable judgment can subsequently be derived. For example, it is better to ask questions to determine the extent to which hot and cold water are available than to ask, "Is the supply of water adequate?"

Errors of recall may be due to lack of knowledge or poor memory. In one study, for example, F. F. Smith (1935) asked students to check those books on a list (which he provided) which they had read. The list contained a number of titles of nonexisting books. But over one fourth of the students checked one or more of these. For other similar results see Lucas (1940 and 1942).

We cannot expect a respondent to remember very far back. When he says he has read a nonexisting book, he probably is not lying deliberately; the title sounds familiar, and he concludes that he must have read it, or he has doubts and decides to "play safe."

Response errors can be reduced in many cases by several alternative design procedures. To do so may be costly, and the gain in accuracy may not be worth that cost. Consequently,

In considering the reduction of response error, the fundamental question is how accurate the data should be. Frequently an answer to this question will raise the further problem of how much it is worth (in dollars and in effort) to achieve a given level of accuracy. The level of accuracy required is, of course, dependent upon the uses to be made of the data. For example, much greater accuracy on age is required in preparing life tables for actuarial use than would be required in classifying the population into age groups for an analysis of public opinion trends. [Mauldin and Marks (1950, p. 653)]

We shall return to the question of what level of accuracy is required in Chapters 8 and 13.

Control

Control of observational error consists of periodic checking to determine whether or not the magnitude of this error is changing over the period during which observation is made, during different observational periods, among different groups of observers, and so on. The nature of a control system and the critical methodological questions involved in the design of such a system will be discussed in Chapter 13.

It should be noted that the continuous reduction of error from other sources as well as observation is a major objective of science and is one of the principal measures of its progress.

In Chapter 7, where sampling errors are discussed, we will consider a way of separating observational error from sampling error and of estimating its magnitude.

MULTIDIMENSIONAL PROPERTIES

Some properties cannot be represented by a single measure; two or more are required. Such a requirement can be revealed by careful analysis of the meaning of the concept; that is, the way it is used. The "reliability" of objects or systems is such a property. For example, measurement of the reliability of light bulbs or components of an automobile may involve determination of (a) average life of such components, and (b) the dispersion around this average. The "readiness" of a system is also a multidimensional property. For example, the readiness of a military service may be defined in terms of (a) the average number of pieces of equipment which are available for use at any moment of time, (b) the dispersion of the number available around this average, (c) the expected length of use that can be obtained from equipment usable at any moment of time, and (d) the average time required to make operable any equipment that is not operable at a moment of time.

Ideally we would like to amalgamate these various dimensions into a single measure of the property involved. In principle this is possible if we treat each measure as an objective and try to extract a single measure of performance from all. That is, although it may be necessary to employ several measures to "capture" a property, it may be possible to develop a single measure of value of that property. The procedures discussed in Chapter 2 for obtaining measures of a decision's value are applicable in this context.

CONCLUSION

It is clear from even a cursory examination of current research practices that measurement and measures tend to be taken for granted. In problem and question areas where science has frequently trod no great risk is involved in such casualness because common practice is likely to be based on sound evaluation (of the measures employed) by researchers in the past who established the conventions used in the present. As science moves into new areas, however, the carry-over of this unawareness of problems of measurement can lead to extremely ineffective research. In psychology, for example, only in recent years (largely as the result of Stevens' work) have researchers been giving measurement the attention it deserves. As a result there has been a noticeable tightening of procedures, bringing with it a scientific maturity that reduces the defensiveness which the psychologist must display before the physical scientist. Measurement in applied physical science is likely to be as loose and ill conceived as in any other branch of science. For many of the very important properties used in engineering there are not yet available either adequate definitions or effective measures. This is particularly true in inspection and quality-control procedures, where the relevance of the tests employed and the measures derived from them are frequently ill established.

Measurement, perhaps more than any other research activity, has been the principal stimulus of progress in both pure and applied science.

BIBLIOGRAPHY

Ackoff, R. L., *The Design of Social Research*. Chicago: University of Chicago Press, 1953.

Campbell, N. R., *An Account of the Principles of Measurement and Calculation*. New York: Longmans, 1928.

——, *Foundations of Science*. New York: Dover Publications, 1957 (originally published in 1919 as *Physics the Elements*).

Caws, Peter, "Definition and Measurement in Physics," in Churchman and Ratoosh (1959), pp. 3–17.

Chambers, J. C., and D. F. Clark, "The Determination of Observational Errors Occurring in Information Collection Processes," *Research Memorandum* 4, Operations Research Group, Case Institute of Technology, Cleveland, Ohio, September 30, 1957.

Cherry, C., *On Human Communication*. New York: John Wiley and Sons, 1957.

Churchman, C. W., "A Materialist Theory of Measurement," in *Philosophy for the Future*, ed. by R. W. Sellars, V. J. McGill, and M. Farber. New York: The Macmillan Co., 1949.

——, *Prediction and Optimal Decision*. Englewood Cliffs, N. J.: Prentice-Hall, 1961.

——, and R. L. Ackoff, *Psychologistics*. Philadelphia: University of Pennsylvania Research Fund, 1947. (Mimeographed)

——, and P. Ratoosh (eds.), *Measurement: Definitions and Theories*. New York: John Wiley and Sons, 1959.

Coombs, C. H., "Mathematical Models in Psychological Scaling," *Journal of the American Statistical Association*, **46** (1951), 480–489.

——, "The Theory and Models of Social Measurement" in *Research Methods in the Behavioral Sciences*, ed. by L. Festinger and D. Katz. New York: Dryden Press, 1953.

——, H. Raiffa, and R. M. Thrall, "Some Views on Mathematical Models and Measurement Theory," in *Decision Processes*, ed. by R. M. Thrall, C. H. Coombs, and R. L. Davis. New York: John Wiley and Sons, 1954.

Ferguson, A., *et al.*, "Quantitative Estimates of Sensory Events," *Report of the British Association for the Advancement of Science* No. 108 (1938).

Ferguson, A., "Quantitative Estimates of Sensory Events: Final Report," *Report of the British Association for the Advancement of Science,* **II** (1940), 331–349.

Guttman, L., "A Basis for Scaling Qualitative Data," *American Sociological Review,* **XII** (1944), 139–150.

Hanson, R. H., and E. S. Marks, "Influence of the Interviewer on the Accuracy of Survey Results," *Journal of the American Statistical Association,* **53** (1958), 635–655.

Lazarsfeld, P. F., and A. H. Barton, "Qualitative Measurement in the Social Sciences: Classification, Typologies, and Indices," in *The Policy Sciences,* ed. by Daniel Lerner and H. D. Lasswell. Stanford: Stanford University Press, 1951.

Leonard, H. S., "The Formal Presuppositions of Measurement Theory," a paper read to the University of Michigan Interdepartmental Seminar on Measurement in the Social Sciences, November 30, 1951.

Lucas, D. B., "A Rigid Technique for Measuring the Impression Values of Specific Magazine Advertisements," *Journal of Applied Psychology,* **24** (1940), 778–790.

——, "A Controlled Recognition Technique for Measuring Magazine Advertising Audiences," *Journal of Marketing,* **6** (1942), 133–136.

Margenau, H., "Philosophical Problems Concerning the Meaning of Measurement in Physics," in Churchman and Ratoosh (1959), pp. 163–176.

Mauldin, W. P., and E. S. Marks, "Problems of Response in Enumerative Surveys," *American Sociological Review,* **15** (1950), 469–657.

McKnight, J. L., "The Quantum Theoretical Concept of Measurement," in Churchman and Ratoosh (1959), pp. 192–203.

Nagel, Ernest, *On the Logic of Measurement,* thesis, Columbia University, 1931.

——, "Measurement," *Erkenntniss,* **II** (1931), 313–333.

Phillips, M., "Quantum Mechanics," in *Philosophy for the Future,* ed. by R. W. Sellars, V. J. McGill, and M. Farber. New York: The Macmillan Co., 1949.

Siegel, S., "A Method for Obtaining an Ordered Metric Scale," *Psychometrica,* **21** (1956), 207–216.

Smith, F. F., "Direct Validation of Questionnaire Data," *Educational Administration and Supervision,* **21** (1935), 561–575.

Stevens, S. S., "On the Problem of Scales for the Measurement of Psychological Magnitudes," *Journal of Unified Science,* **IX** (1939), 94–99.

——, "On the Theory of Scales of Measurement," *Science,* **CIII** (1946), 677–680.

——, "Mathematics, Measurement, and Psychophysics," in *Handbook of Experimental Psychology,* ed. by S. S. Stevens. New York: John Wiley and Sons, 1951.

——, "Measurement, Psychophysics, and Utility," in Churchman and Ratoosh, (1959).

Terris, Fay, "Are Poll Questions Too Difficult?" *Public Opinion Quarterly,* **13** (1949), 314–319.

Thurstone, L. L., and E. J. Chave, *The Measurement of Attitudes.* Chicago: University of Chicago Press, 1929.

——, *A Scale for Measuring Attitudes toward the Church.* Chicago: University of Chicago Press, 1930.

7

SAMPLING

REVIEW AND PREVIEW

It may be helpful at this point to review briefly the ground that has been covered and to preview what is to come in the next four chapters.

After an introductory discussion of the nature of science and its methods (Chapter 1) we considered the nature of a problem and the criteria for a best solution to it (Chapter 2). In Chapter 3 we discussed procedures for identifying the controlled and uncontrolled aspects of a problem (X_i and Y_j), and procedures for constructing a measure of the value of the outcome of a decision (V). Chapter 4 was concerned with the symbolic representation of the problem situation in a decision model in which the measure of performance (V) is related to the variables X_i and Y_j by a function f; that is, we considered construction of a decision model of the form:

$$V = f(X_i, Y_j).$$

In Chapter 5 we discussed definition of the components of a model so as to assure relevance of the observations that are made in order to determine their values. Then, in Chapter 6, we considered in more detail how the observations should be made so that they yield symbols (which we called *measures*) that could be used in reaching decisions involving the concept represented.

Now, in order to evaluate an uncontrolled variable or constant (i.e., parameter), we usually must determine what subset of the set of possible relevant observations should actually be made. That is, we must design the *sample* of elements whose properties are to be observed. The design of samples is the subject of this chapter. Next we consider how to combine the data obtained from a sample into an *estimate* of the relevant property (Chapter 8). In some cases an estimate may already be provided by past observations or by a theory. Then the problem is to determine whether or not the value thus provided should be used. This problem, that of *testing a hypothesis,* is discussed in Chapter 9. Tests of hypotheses may also be used in selecting among two or three alternative courses of action or in determining whether or not a parameter is relevant; that is, whether it significantly affects the outcome of a decision. Tests of relevance by *experimentation,* and *regression* and *correlation* analysis, are the subjects of Chapter 10.

This and the next three chapters deal with the various aspects of statistical inference, largely from the point of view of what has come to be called *statistical decision theory.* No attempt is made here, however, to provide comprehensive coverage of the field of statistics. The objective is to analyze the research decisions that are involved, to construct models of them and derive solutions where possible and, where not, to go as far as we can in this direction. The lack of technical details in this treatment is likely to bother the professional statistician; the presence of what technical detail there is, is just as likely to bother the novice. I fear that the median I have struck may not be a happy one, but I hope that it is useful.

INTRODUCTION

Whenever the definition of a concept requires that observations be made of either (*a*) a number of elements in a population, or (*b*) an element in a number of different situations, two questions arise:

(1) How many observations should be taken? This is a question of *sample size.*

(2) Which subset of elements or environments should be selected for observation? This is a question of *sampling design.*

Sampling, then, is concerned with determining what and how many observations are to be made where it is not possible or practical to make all the observations that are ideally desirable.

The techniques of sampling have developed very rapidly in the last quarter century. Knowledge of these techniques is still not widely disseminated among scientists. For this reason it will be necessary to review at least some of this body of knowledge preparatory to discussing the methodological problems which arise in connection with it. This review is not intended as a substitute for a detailed study of the field; its purpose is merely to provide enough background to allow us to discuss meaningfully the methodological problems that arise within sampling. Detailed information on sampling techniques can be found in Cochran (1953), Deming (1945), Hansen, Hurwitz, and Madow (1953), and Yates (1949).

It is difficult, if at all possible, to discuss sampling independently of estimating procedures. For this reason we shall present what is required of estimation theory without comment or question in this chapter. In the next chapter we will discuss estimation theory in detail and bring the methodological problems of sampling and estimation together. In this chapter, however, we shall try to bring together the problems involving observational and sampling error.

To facilitate this exposition it will be helpful to deal with a "toy population." Suppose that the population consists of six children whose ages are 2, 3, 4, 6, 9, and 12 years. The total of these ages is 36 years; the average is 6 years, and the range is 10 years. Our task is to use observations of a sample of these children to estimate the average age of the group.

ACCURACY, BIAS, AND PRECISION

Each possible sample (which is drawn without replacing the elements) and its average are shown in Table 7.1.

For the moment consider only samples of two. Only one of these samples (3, 9) has an average equal to that of the population. Each of the other samples has an average which differs from that of the population, and these sample averages are *inaccurate* estimates of the population average. The inaccuracies consist of *overestimates* and *underestimates* of the population average.

Now assume that we have a way of drawing samples of two from this population so that each possible sample has the same probability of being drawn. Then, if we use this sampling procedure and the sample average as an estimate of the population average, the expected

TABLE 7.1. POSSIBLE SAMPLES OF ONE, TWO, THREE, FOUR, AND FIVE ELEMENTS FROM THE POPULATION: 2, 3, 4, 6, 9, AND 12

1		2		3		4		5	
Sample	Average	Sample	Average	Sample	Average	Sample	Average	Sample	Average
2	2	2, 3	2.5	2, 3, 4	3.0	2, 3, 4, 6	3.8	2, 3, 4, 6, 9	4.8
3	3	2, 4	3.0	2, 3, 6	3.7	2, 3, 4, 9	4.5	2, 3, 4, 6, 12	5.4 *
4	4	2, 6	4.0	2, 3, 9	4.7	2, 3, 4, 12	5.2 *	2, 3, 4, 9, 12	6.0 *
6	6 *	2, 9	5.5 *	2, 3, 12	5.3 *	2, 3, 6, 9	5.0 *	2, 3, 6, 9, 12	6.4 *
9	9	2, 12	7.0 *	2, 4, 6	4.0	2, 3, 6, 12	5.8 *	2, 4, 6, 9, 12	6.6 *
12	12	3, 4	3.5	2, 4, 9	5.0 *	2, 3, 9, 12	6.5 *	3, 4, 6, 9, 12	6.8 *
		3, 6	4.5	2, 4, 12	6.0 *	2, 4, 6, 9	5.2 *		
		3, 9	6.0 *	2, 6, 9	5.7 *	2, 4, 6, 12	6.0 *		
		3, 12	7.5	2, 6, 12	6.7 *	2, 4, 9, 12	6.8 *		
		4, 6	5.0 *	2, 9, 12	7.7	2, 6, 9, 12	7.2		
		4, 9	6.5 *	3, 4, 6	4.3	3, 4, 6, 9	5.5 *		
		4, 12	8.0	3, 4, 9	5.7 *	3, 4, 6, 12	6.2 *		
		6, 9	7.5	3, 4, 12	6.3 *	3, 4, 9, 12	7.0 *		
		6, 12	9.0	3, 6, 9	6.0 *	3, 6, 9, 12	7.5		
		9, 12	10.5	3, 6, 12	7.0 *	4, 6, 9, 12	7.8		
				3, 9, 12	8.0				
				4, 6, 9	6.3 *				
				4, 6, 12	7.3				
				4, 9, 12	8.3				
				6, 9, 12	9.0				
Total	36		90.0		120.0		90.0		36.0
Average	6		6		6		6		6
Per cent between 5.0 and 6.0	17		33		50		67		83

* Deviates by no more than one unit (1) from the population average (6).

value * of such a sampling-estimating procedure would be:

$$\frac{1}{15}\left(\frac{2+3}{2}\right) + \frac{1}{15}\left(\frac{2+4}{2}\right) + \cdots + \frac{1}{15}\left(\frac{9+12}{2}\right) = 6.0$$

In this case the expected value (EV) is equal to the true value (TV). The difference (EV − TV) is the *bias* of such a procedure, which in this case is zero. Hence this procedure is said to be *unbiased*. Note, however, that an unbiased procedure can yield inaccurate estimates. In this case it is more likely to do so than not.

The bias—or lack of it—of a sampling-estimation procedure is independent of the sample size, as can be verified by examining the average of the averages from Table 7.1, assuming that each sample is equally likely.

Now consider the difference between the lowest and the highest estimate yielded by each sample size. These *ranges* of estimates are shown in Table 7.2.

TABLE 7.2.   PRECISION OF VARIOUS SIZE SAMPLES FROM "TOY" POPULATION

Sample size	1	2	3	4	5
Range of estimates of mean	10	8	6	4	2

It is apparent that the estimates become less *variable* (or more *precise* or *reliable*) as the sample size increases.

The most commonly used measure of dispersion of estimates is the *standard error*, which is the square root of the mean of the squared deviations of the estimates from the true value. The standard error of estimates of the mean, $\sigma_{\bar{x}}$, is

$$\left[\frac{\Sigma(\bar{x}-\mu)^2}{k}\right]^{1/2},$$

where $\bar{x}$ = the estimates of the mean based on a sample of specified size.
μ = the true value of the mean.
k = the number of possible distinct samples of the specified size.

Hence the standard error of a set of estimates is its *standard deviation*. Its square, $\sigma_{\bar{x}}^2$, is the *variance*.

In order to simplify this discussion we shall use "per cent of estimates within 1 of the true value" as a measure of dispersion.

* The average of the averages as the number of samples approaches infinity.

SIMPLE RANDOM SAMPLING

The determination of bias and standard error presupposes that each possible sample has a known probability of being drawn. If we drew the elements in such a way that each element had an equal opportunity of being drawn, then this condition would be satisfied. In practice these equal-probability conditions are approximated by uniquely numbering each element of the population and using a table of random numbers * to select the numbers and, hence, the elements. This most common type of sampling is called either *simple* or *unrestricted random sampling*.

SYSTEMATIC RANDOM SAMPLING

Now suppose that the elements of the population or symbols representing them are in some physical order; for example, people standing in line, names listed in a book, items on an assembly line. Each element must be uniquely identifiable by its location in the sequence. Now suppose that there are N elements in the population and that we want a sample of size n. The "sampling ratio" is then N/n. If this ratio is not an integer, it is rounded off to the closest one; call this integer m. Now we can select a number from 1 to m at random; let x represent this number. Then we can select a systematic (random) sample by selecting those elements in the following positions in the sequence:

$$x, x + m, x + 2m, \cdots.$$

If N/n is an integer, then each possible sample will be of equal size. Otherwise some samples will contain one more element than others.

Suppose that there are 1000 members of a population for each of which there is an associated index card numbered from 1 to 1000. If we want a sample of 100, we select a number at random from 1 to $^{1000}/_{100} = 10$. Suppose that it is 7. Then the sample would consist of the members of the population numbered 7, 17, 27, $\cdots$, 997.

For any systematic random sample an unbiased procedure exists for estimating the mean and other characteristics of the population. The variability of these estimates may be greater or less than those yielded by simple random sampling, depending on the way the population is

* See RAND (1955).

ordered. If the ordering is random, then systematic random sampling yields the same variability of estimates as does simple random sampling.

Suppose that the toy population is ordered in the following way: 2, 3, 4, 6, 9, and 12. There are two possible systematic samples of 3 elements: 2, 4, 9 (average = 5) and 3, 6, 12 (average = 7). The range here is equal to 2. If the population order is 2, 6, 3, 9, 4, 12, then the two possible samples of 3 elements are 2, 3, 4 (average = 3) and 6, 9, 12 (average = 9), and the range is 6 (the same as that of simple random sampling). Since the standard error of estimates based on a systematic sample depends on population order and the essential characteristics of this order are often not known beforehand, accurate estimates of standard errors are difficult to obtain without some preliminary data about the population.

For detailed discussion of systematic sampling see Madow (1944 and 1946).

MULTISTAGE SAMPLING

Where the population to be sampled is (or can be) divided into subgroups which are exclusive and exhaustive, it is possible to sample in *stages*. The subgroups would be involved in the first stage of selection, and the elements in the second stage. At either stage we can take either a complete count or a random (simple or systematic) sample. If we take a complete count at both stages, we have, of course, a complete count (100 per cent sample) of the population. Then there are three types of sampling designs for two-stage sampling. These are shown in Table 7.3.

There may be as many stages of sampling as there are levels of classification. In sampling involving three or more stages it is pos-

TABLE 7.3. TYPES OF TWO-STAGE SAMPLES

First Stage (Selecting Groups)	Second Stage (Selecting Items)	Name of Sampling Plan
Sample *	Sample *	Two-stage random sampling
Complete count	Sample *	Stratified sampling
Sample *	Complete count	Cluster sampling

* Simple random sampling or a variation thereof.

TABLE 7.4. POSSIBLE TWO-STAGE RANDOM SAMPLES OF TWO ELEMENTS FROM
TWO OF THREE PRIMARY SAMPLING UNITS: 2, 12; 3, 9; AND 4, 6

Sample	Sample Average	Sample	Sample Average
2, 3	2.5	12, 4	8.0
2, 9	5.5 *	12, 6	9.0
2, 4	3.0	3, 4	3.5
2, 6	4.0	3, 6	4.5
12, 3	7.5	9, 4	6.5 *
12, 9	10.5	9, 6	7.5 *
			17% †

* Deviates by no more than 1 unit from the population average.

† Percentage of sample averages that deviate by no more than 1 unit from the population average.

sible to stratify at any stage before the last and to cluster at the last stage. Such a combination yields a stratified cluster sample. Units sampled in the first stage are called *primary;* those sampled in the second stage, *secondary;* and so on.

Multistage Random Sampling

In this type of sampling a random (simple or systematic) sample is taken at each stage. Unbiased estimates of population characteristics can be obtained from such samples. The standard errors of such estimates can never be less than that obtained from simple random sampling. They can be larger, depending on the *homogeneity* of the groups; that is, the similarity of the groups with respect to the property being investigated. The more homogeneous the groups the less variable are the estimates. See Tables 7.4 and 7.5 for such a comparison.

Where the value of the property under study is correlated with the size of the population (e.g., the total weight or income of a population), variability of estimates can normally be reduced by making the probability of selecting any subgroup of the population proportionate to its size; that is, by making this probability equal to the ratio of the group size to the population size.

The principal advantage of multistage random sampling over simple and systematic random sampling is that every element of the population does not have to be numbered; only those elements in the

TABLE 7.5. POSSIBLE TWO-STAGE RANDOM SAMPLES OF TWO ELEMENTS FROM
TWO OF THREE PRIMARY SAMPLING UNITS: 2, 3; 4, 6; AND 9, 12

Sample	Sample Average	Sample	Sample Average
2, 4	3.0	3, 9	6.0 *
2, 6	4.0	3, 12	7.5
2, 9	5.5 *	4, 9	6.5 *
2, 12	7.0 *	4, 12	8.0
3, 4	3.5	6, 9	7.5
3, 6	4.5	6, 12	9.0
			33% †

* Deviates by no more than 1 unit from the population average.

† Percentage of sample averages that deviate by no more than 1 unit from the population average.

groups which have been selected in the previous stage need to be numbered. Furthermore, if the groups are located in different places, such a sample will generally require less travel than the simpler types of sample. These savings in cost may permit a larger sample to be taken so that either more precision is obtained at the same cost or the same precision is obtained at less cost. Whether or not either of these possibilities is realized depends on the relative costs of observation and of preparing the elements for observation (e.g., numbering).

Stratified Sampling

Stratified samples may yield unbiased estimates of less or more variability than the preceding types for the same sample sizes, depending on the homogeneity of the strata and the division of the sampled elements among the strata. In general, samples of equal size drawn from each stratum yield more variable estimates than do samples which are proportionate to the size of the stratum. This is seen by comparing Tables 7.6 and 7.7. Strata samples of equal size allow us to make more precise comparisons between the strata, but this advantage is obtained at the cost of more variable estimates of population characteristics.

The more homogeneous the strata the less variable are the estimates. This is seen by comparing Tables 7.7 and 7.8. If we have information on the homogeneity of the strata (in the form of the range or variance of the property characteristics among the member ele-

TABLE 7.6.   POSSIBLE STRATIFIED SAMPLES OF THREE ELEMENTS
FROM THE STRATA: (2, 3) AND (4, 6, 9, 12)

Sample	Estimated Average †	Sample	Estimated Average †
2, 3, 4	3.5	2, 6, 12	6.7 *
2, 3, 6	4.8	2, 9, 12	7.7
2, 3, 9	6.8 *	3, 4, 6	4.3
2, 3, 12	8.8	3, 4, 9	5.3 *
2, 4, 6	4.0	3, 4, 12	6.3 *
2, 4, 9	5.0 *	3, 6, 9	6.0 *
2, 4, 12	6.0 *	3, 6, 12	7.0 *
2, 6, 9	5.7 *	3, 9, 12	8.0
			56%

* Deviates by no more than 1 unit from the population average.

† To obtain an unbiased estimate of the population average in disproportionate stratified sampling, the sample average cannot be used. An unbiased estimate can be obtained by taking the average of the sample from each stratum, multiplying it by the size of the stratum, and dividing the sum of these values by the size of the population. For example, in the first sample listed (2, 3, 4) the estimate is computed as follows:

$$\frac{1}{6}\left[2\left(\frac{2+3}{2}\right) + 4\left(\frac{4}{1}\right)\right] = 3.5.$$

TABLE 7.7.   POSSIBLE PROPORTIONATE STRATIFIED SAMPLES OF THREE
ELEMENTS FROM THE STRATA: (2, 3) AND (4, 6, 9, 12)

Sample	Estimated Average	Sample	Estimated Average
2, 4, 6	4.0	3, 4, 6	4.3
2, 4, 9	5.0 *	3, 4, 9	5.3 *
2, 4, 12	6.0 *	3, 4, 12	6.3 *
2, 6, 9	5.7 *	3, 6, 9	6.0 *
2, 6, 12	6.7 *	3, 6, 12	7.0 *
2, 9, 12	7.7	3, 9, 12	8.0
			67%

* Deviates by no more than 1 unit from the population average.

TABLE 7.8. PROPORTIONATE STRATIFIED SAMPLES OF THREE ELEMENTS
FROM THE HETEROGENEOUS STRATA: (2, 12) AND (3, 4, 6, 9)

Sample	Estimated Average	Sample	Estimated Average
2, 3, 4	3.0	12, 3, 4	6.3 *
2, 3, 6	3.7	12, 3, 6	7.0 *
2, 3, 9	4.7	12, 3, 9	8.0
2, 4, 6	4.0	12, 4, 6	7.3
2, 4, 9	5.0 *	12, 4, 9	8.3
2, 6, 9	5.7 *	12, 6, 9	9.0
			33%

* Deviates by no more than 1 unit from the population average.

ments), this information can be used to obtain further reductions in variability of estimates by means of what is called *optimal allocation* of sample size to strata. For example, if we have two strata containing n_1 and n_2 items, with ranges R_1 and R_2, respectively, the proportion of the sample allocated to the first stratum is

$$\frac{n_1 R_1}{n_1 R_1 + n_2 R_2}.$$

Correspondingly, the proportion of the sample allocated to the second stratum is

$$\frac{n_2 R_2}{n_1 R_1 + n_2 R_2}.$$

For example, suppose that the toy population is divided into two strata, (2, 3, 4) and (6, 9, 12); and we want to allocate optimally a sample of four to these strata: for this case both n_1 and n_2 are equal to 3 and $R_1 = (4 - 2) = 2$, and $R_2 = (12 - 6) = 6$. Then the proportion of the sample to be allocated to the first stratum is

$$\frac{(3)(2)}{(3)(2) + (3)(6)} = \frac{1}{4}.$$

The proportion of the sample allocated to the second stratum is

$$\frac{(3)(6)}{(3)(2) + (3)(6)} = \frac{3}{4}.$$

TABLE 7.9. OPTIMUM ALLOCATION (APPROXIMATE) OF A SAMPLE OF FOUR
ELEMENTS FROM THE STRATA: (2, 3, 4) AND (6, 9, 12)

Sample	Estimated Average
2, 6, 9, 12	5.5 *
3, 6, 9, 12	6.0 *
4, 6, 9, 12	6.5 *

* Deviates by no more than 0.5 unit from the population average.

Hence, the number of elements to be selected from the first stratum is $\frac{1}{4}(4)$, or 1, and the number of items to be selected from the second stratum is $\frac{3}{4}(4)$, or 3. Table 7.9 shows the results obtained from using this method.

Cluster Sampling

In general this type of sampling (a complete count of subgroups sampled) yields unbiased estimates of greater variability than any of the other types discussed. Its advantages are as follows. (1) If clusters are geographically defined, cluster sampling generally yields lowest sampling cost per observation. (2) As in multistage random sampling a complete listing is required for only those groups selected for the sample. (3) Characteristics of the clusters which may be relevant can be estimated with no variability due to sampling. (4) A cluster sample may be used over and over again because the subgroups rather than elements are selected, and changes of elements in these subgroups allow us to estimate changes in the population as a whole.

The principal practical difficulty in the use of cluster sampling arises out of the fact that each individual in the population must be capable of being uniquely assigned to one and only one cluster. This requires effective identification of individuals and clusters and the relationship between them. The assignment of individuals to clusters need not be done beforehand; in fact, it is usually done at the time of observation. But this may be a difficult task. For example, in the U.S. Bureau of the Census "Post-Enumeration Survey" conducted in 1950, each individual in the population of the United States had to be potentially assignable to some living quarters as of April 1, 1950. This was extremely difficult to do, for it involved the complex concept of "usual place of residence." For example, it is frequently hard to assign a person who travels in his business to a usual place of residence. Yet this transient portion of the population is important, and each member of it must be assignable to some one cluster. To avoid errors in this assignment, the concept of "usual place of residence" and related notions had to be carefully defined in accordance with the principles given in Chapter 5.

Determination of population characteristics from data obtained by a cluster sample is not a simple statistical procedure. Various types of adjustments of the data are required. To make such adjustments, expert statistical assistance is usually required. A discussion of these technicalities can be found in Deming (1945) and Mahalanobis (1941).

REPETITIVE (OR MULTIPLE) SAMPLING

Up to this point in the discussion of sampling by stages, the decision as to how to draw the sample at any stage is completed before any stage of the sampling is performed. It is also possible, however, to draw one sample from a population, analyze it, and use the resulting information in designing a second sample from the same population. Such a procedure is called *double sampling*. In double sampling the data obtained from the second sample may be used in connection with the data from the first sample to improve the efficiency of estimates of population characteristics. For example, information from the first sample can be used efficiently to stratify the population or to allocate the sample to strata.

In nonrepetitive or single samples a definite decision is always reached only when all the stages are completed. But in double sampling, according to Deming (1950, pp. 548–549):

. . . A small sample would first be taken: if the results are decisive, no further investigation is required. But if the results are not decisive, a further sample would be taken. The results of the first sample would nearly always provide the necessary estimates . . . by which the second sample could be very economically planned and made neither too large nor too small to provide definite and sufficient evidence for a rational decision.

After a small first sample is taken, if the results are not decisive, the next sample taken may also be small. The results of the first and second samples can be combined. If these are not decisive, another sample can be taken, and so on. Each subsample may be so selected, for example, that it constitutes a day's work. Computations can then be made to determine whether another sample is required. Such a procedure is called *group sequential sampling*. It can be used profitably where the treatment of the data is relatively simple and additional samples can be drawn very quickly or are prepared beforehand.

The method of sequential sampling just discussed suggests the following question: would it be possible to make only one observation at a time and decide whether or not the results up to that point are decisive? Such a sequential-sampling procedure is feasible and is in use. In this type of sequential sampling the size of the sample is not determined in advance, but the results of each observation are used to determine whether an additional observation is necessary in order to come to one of a set of specified conclusions. On the average, fewer observations are required by this procedure than by single or double sampling relative to a fixed error. In some cases only half the sample size required in simple random sampling will yield equally good results if sequential sampling is used.

The sequential procedure cannot be used in all cases. The following general conditions are sufficient for its application: (*a*) random sampling can be conducted for any sample size or for subgroups of samples, and (*b*) the number of observations can be increased indefinitely at any stage of the procedure. Condition (*a*) fails to apply in those cases where we doubt that a very small sample can even approximately represent the population. That is, in general, wherever stratification or multistage sampling is desirable, sequential sampling is not an efficient procedure to use. For example, if we were to examine a number of persons for their preferences with respect to some article, we would want to make sure that we had examined several professions, several levels of income, and so on, before we came to any conclusion; hence, we would not apply sequential sampling, at least not until a minimum sample had been obtained. Condition (*b*) fails if it is not possible to draw additional items into a sample after the research has begun. This is true of most social surveys, since it is usually very difficult or expensive to increase the number of subjects during the course of the survey.

Despite these restrictions, there are many cases in which this method is applicable even in the social sciences. For example, in one project it was necessary to determine whether the percentage of inmates in a state mental institution who had a certain characteristic was significantly different from 1.5 per cent. For each patient there was a large envelope on file which contained, among other things, his medical history. This history was generally quite long and required considerable time for a complete reading. In such a case, where the sample was drawn from the file and could be increased with no great difficulty, sequential methods were extremely efficient.

In general, sequential procedures are applicable only where the observations can be made one at a time or in groups without considerable loss of time between observations. This means that in most cases the subjects or data concerning them should be concentrated in a relatively small area and hence be easily accessible. The individual subjects must be uniquely identifiable so that there is no ambiguity about which one is to be selected in each drawing. In effect, this method requires the ability to manipulate efficiently the sample elements, whether these be records, individuals, or groups. It is apparent that satisfactory sequential-sampling conditions are most likely to be encountered in research in which records or very small concentrated populations are involved.

The analysis of data obtained by sequential sampling is different from that applied to nonsequential-sampling procedures. A discussion of analyses applicable to sequential procedures can be found in Statistical Research Group (1946) and in Wald (1947).

JUDGMENT SAMPLING

The probability-sampling procedures which have been discussed up to this point involve either a complete count or a random sample at each stage of the procedure. Because all these procedures have been based on random sampling, it is possible to determine for each procedure the probability that an estimate (which it yields) of a population characteristic deviates by any specified amount from the true value of the characteristic under investigation. This is not true for all methods of sampling at the present time.

In some cases there are well-defined subgroups of a population which seem to be representative of the population as a whole. In other cases practical considerations seem to preclude the use of probability sampling, and the researcher looks for a representative sample by other means; that is, he looks for a subgroup which is typical of the population as a whole. This subgroup is used as a "barometer" of the population. Observations are then restricted to this subgroup, and conclusions from the data obtained are generalized to the total population. This is a type of common-sense procedure. For example, for a number of years many people in the United States believed with respect to presidential elections that "as Maine goes, so goes the nation." This expressed a conviction at the time that Maine's voting behavior was typical of that of the nation as a whole. An election forecaster who restricted his observations to Maine would have taken a *judgment* (or *purposive*) sample.

Judgment sampling is very precarious, because much stronger assumptions must be made about the population and the selection procedure than are required in probability sampling. For example, to select a typical city in a study of consumer purchases for the nation, the researcher may look for a city whose income distribution is similar to that of the nation as a whole, whose industries are typical of those of the nation as a whole, and so on. In effect, he selects a community which is typical with respect to a set of properties, $A, B, \cdots,$ N, from which he assumes that the community is typical with respect to the characteristic X which he is investigating. Now it does not follow that, because a city is typical with respect to $A, B, \cdots, N$, it is typical with respect to X, unless $A, B, \cdots, N$ completely determine X. It is not enough to claim that they are highly correlated. Even if the correlation is high, the city selected may not be typical with respect to the way X is related to $A, B, \cdots, N$. Hence the further assumption is required that in the city selected the relationship between $A, B, \cdots, N$ and X is typical. Assumptions such as these are likely to be very doubtful, and their validation is likely to cost more then the use of a probability sample.

Judgment sampling has another significant shortcoming: sampling errors and biases can be computed only if there is available a record of estimates derived from such samples in the past together with the true values that were being estimated in each case. In such cases the sampling error and bias can be determined empirically, but there is no assurance that future use of such sampling will yield results consistent with these computations. Despite its shortcomings judgment sampling does have its uses. Deming (1960) cites three. First,

> If a sample must be confined to only 1, 6, or 10 units (blocks, tracts, cities, counties, farms, pieces of material), a judgment sample would be preferable to a probability sample. In such very small samples, the errors of judgment are usually less than the random errors of a probability sample. (p. 31)

Second, if "one wishes to discover a minimum or maximum . . . a biased selection may be preferable to a broader coverage by a probability sample" (p. 32). Finally, in some exploratory studies such samples are the only kind one can take the time or trouble to use.

In general, then, judgment sampling should be restricted to situations in which (1) the possible errors are not serious and (2) probability sampling is practically impossible. Data from judgment samples at best only suggest or indicate conclusions; they cannot provide a sound basis either for obtaining statistical estimates of parameter values or for conducting statistical tests such as will be considered in the next two chapters.

OPTIMIZING SAMPLE SIZE

As indicated earlier, the two methodological problems associated with sampling involve determination of the size and type of sample to be used. First we consider the problem of sample size. As we shall see, a decision model of this research problem can be constructed and solved under certain conditions.

In the literature on sampling theory there is a great deal of discussion of optimizing sample size, but the type of optimization involved is usually very limited. Sample size is normally minimized for a specified sampling design and a fixed (specified) sampling error. Conversely, sampling error is minimized in some cases for fixed sample size; for example, in optimal allocation of the sample to strata (see p. 228). Our objective here is to convert sampling error and sample size into commensurable costs the sum of which is to be minimized. In order to accomplish this objective it is necessary to express the cost of error as a function of its magnitude.

First we will consider determination of optimal sample size where the cost of error is assumed to be a quadratic function of its magnitude; that is, under the assumption that the cost of error is given by

$$C(y - Y) = k(y - Y)^2, \tag{1}$$

where $C(y - Y)$ = the cost of the error involved in using an estimate y for the value of a parameter Y.

k = a cost constant.

Note that in this assumption the cost of an error (1) is independent of the true value of Y in that it depends only on the magnitude (not the position) of the error on the error scale, and (2) does not depend on the sign of the error.

The quadratic assumption is generally made because of the resulting mathematical simplicity and not because of conformity with the real situation. After discussing how to optimize sample size under this assumption, we will consider how cost-of-error functions can be derived from a decision model and used in this optimization process.

Simple Random Sampling, Quadratic Cost of Error *

In this and the succeeding cases in which quadratic costs of error are assumed, we will also assume that we are trying to estimate the mean of a normal (or approximately normal) population. In the case of simple random sampling the cost of the sampling is assumed to be given by

$$C(n) = C_1 + nC_2,$$ (2)

where $C(n)$ = the total cost of n observations.
C_1 = the fixed cost of preparing the sample.
C_2 = the cost per observation.

Let S^2 be an unbiased estimate of the variance of the population. Then S^2/n is the variance (mean squared error) of estimates based on samples of size n. From the assumption that the cost of error is proportional to the square of the error the estimated expected cost of error, $E(C)$, is given by

$$E(C) = k \frac{S^2}{n}.$$ (3)

If the true variance, σ^2, is known (in this and succeeding cases), it can be substituted for S^2; then the expected cost of error would be known rather than estimated.

The total expected cost, TEC, of a simple random sample of size n which is designed to estimate the mean of the population is then

$$TEC = C_1 + nC_2 + k \frac{S^2}{n}.$$ (4)

To find the optimum sample size, n_o, we proceed as follows:

$$\frac{dTEC}{dn} = C_2 - k \frac{S^2}{n^2} = 0.$$ (5)

This can be shown to be a minimum point. Then

$$n_o = \sqrt{\frac{kS^2}{C_2}}.$$ (6)

* The material in this section and the others which deal with quadratic costs of error is due to my colleague, Rudolph Reinitz.

Therefore, the minimum total expected cost is given by

$$TEC_o = C_1 + C_2 \sqrt{\frac{kS^2}{C_2}} + \frac{kS^2}{\sqrt{kS^2/C_2}}$$

$$= C_1 + 2S\sqrt{kC_2}. \tag{7}$$

Stratified Random Sampling, Quadratic Costs of Error

The population of N units is divided into L exclusive and exhaustive strata so that

$$N_1 + N_2 + \cdots N_h + \cdots + N_L = N. \tag{8}$$

Here the problem is to select the sample size n_h from stratum h that will minimize the total expected cost of that sample. The total expected cost of the total sample, $n = \sum_1^L n_h$, is minimized if each stratum cost is minimized. Neyman (1934) demonstrated that in stratified sampling the variance of the estimated mean, $S_{\bar{y}}^2$, is smallest for a fixed total sample size if the sample is allocated with n_h proportional to $N_h S_h$, where S_h is the standard deviation of the hth stratum. That is, if

$$n_h = n \frac{N_h S_h}{\Sigma N_h S_h}, \tag{9}$$

we obtain

$$n = n_h \frac{\Sigma N_h S_h}{N_h S_h}. \tag{10}$$

The expression for the minimum variance is

$$\min S_{\bar{y}}^2 = \frac{1}{N^2} \sum \frac{(N_h S_h)^2}{n_h} - \frac{1}{N^2} \Sigma N_h S_h^2. \tag{11}$$

Assume that the cost of sampling is given by

$$C(n_h) = C_1 + \Sigma n_h C_h, \tag{12}$$

where C_h = the cost per observation in the hth stratum. The estimated expected cost of error is obtained from equations (9) and (10).

$$E(C) = k \min (S_{\bar{y}}^2)$$

$$= k \left[\frac{1}{N^2} \sum \frac{(N_h S_h)^2}{n_h} - \frac{1}{N^2} \Sigma N_h S_h^2 \right]$$

$$= \frac{k}{N^2} \sum \left(\frac{N_h^2}{n_h} - N_h \right) S_h^2. \tag{13}$$

Therefore, the total expected cost is

$$TEC = C_1 + \Sigma n_h C_h + \frac{k}{N^2} \Sigma \left(\frac{N_h^2}{n_h} - N_h \right) S_h^2. \qquad (14)$$

To get the optimal sample size for stratum h, we proceed as follows:

$$\frac{\partial TEC}{\partial n_h} = C_h - \frac{k}{N^2} \frac{N_h^2 S_h^2}{n_h^2} = 0 \qquad (15)$$

$$n_{h_o} = \frac{N_h S_h}{N} \sqrt{\frac{k}{C_h}}. \qquad (16)$$

The minimal total expected cost of the sample is obtained by substituting the value of n_{h_o} from equation (16) in equation (14).

Cluster Sampling, Quadratic Costs of Error

In custer sampling the cost of preparing and obtaining the sample may require a very complex expression for its description. [See, for example, Hansen, Hurwitz, and Madow (1953, Chapter 6, Section D).] In the simple case this cost may be expressed as

$$C(m, \bar{n}) = m(C_1 + \bar{n} C_2), \qquad (17)$$

where $C(m, \bar{n})$ = the total cost of preparing and obtaining the sample.
$\qquad C_1$ = the fixed cost of preparing a cluster.
$\qquad C_2$ = the cost per observation.
$\qquad m$ = the number of clusters in the sample.
$\qquad \bar{n}$ = the average number of observations per cluster.

The problem is to find the optimal values of m and $\bar{n}$, m_o and $\bar{n}_o$, respectively.

The unbiased estimate of the variance of the mean of the population is given by

$$V(\bar{y}) = \left(\frac{1}{m} - \frac{1}{M} \right) S_b^2 + \left(\frac{1}{m\bar{n}} - \frac{1}{MN} \right) S_w^2, \qquad (18)$$

where M = total number of clusters in the population.
$\qquad N$ = total number of elements in the population.
$\qquad S_b^2$ = estimated variance relative to y between clusters.
$\qquad S_w^2$ = estimated variance relative to y within clusters.

The total expected cost is then given by

$$TEC = kV(\bar{y}) + C(m, \bar{n})$$

$$= k\left[\left(\frac{1}{m} - \frac{1}{M}\right)S_b{}^2 + \left(\frac{1}{m\bar{n}} - \frac{1}{MN}\right)S_w{}^2\right] + m(C_1 + \bar{n}C_2), \quad (19)$$

where k is the usual cost constant. For simplification purposes, since $\bar{n}$ appears in (19) only in the expression $m\bar{n}$, let $Q = m\bar{n}$. Then, rewriting (19), we get

$$TEC = k\left[\left(\frac{1}{m} - \frac{1}{M}\right)S_b{}^2 + \left(\frac{1}{Q} - \frac{1}{MN}\right)S_w{}^2\right] + mC_1 + QC_2. \quad (20)$$

To find m_o we proceed as follows:

$$\frac{\partial TEC}{\partial m} = -\frac{kS_b{}^2}{m^2} + C_1 = 0 \quad (21)$$

$$m_o = S_b \sqrt{\frac{k}{C_1}}. \quad (22)$$

Now, let us find the optimal value of Q, Q_o:

$$\frac{\partial TEC}{\partial Q} = -\frac{kS_w{}^2}{Q^2} + C_2 = 0 \quad (23)$$

$$Q_o = S_w \sqrt{\frac{k}{C_2}}. \quad (24)$$

Since $\bar{n} = Q/m$,

$$\bar{n}_o = \frac{Q_o}{m_o} = \frac{S_w \sqrt{k/C_2}}{S_b \sqrt{k/C_1}}$$

$$= \frac{S_w}{S_b} \sqrt{\frac{C_1}{C_2}}. \quad (25)$$

By appropriate substitution of the expressions for m_o and Q_o in equation (20) the minimal total expected cost can be found.

Nonquadratic Costs of Error

Now we attempt a general formulation of a model for optimizing sample size, in which the costs of error may take any form.

Let $\overline{Y}$ represent the true average value of a population characteristic, and let $\overline{Y}$ represent an estimate of this mean. Then, if $\bar{y} > \overline{Y}$, there is an error of overestimation, and if $\overline{Y} > \bar{y}$, there is an error of underestimation. Let C_u represent the cost of an error of underestimation, and C_o the cost of an error of overestimation. The values of C_u and C_o will generally depend on the size of the error. That is, C_u is generally a function (g) of $(\overline{Y} - \bar{y})$, where $\overline{Y} > \bar{y}$:

$$C_u = g(\overline{Y} - \bar{y}), \quad \overline{Y} > \bar{y}. \tag{26}$$

Similarly,

$$C_o = h(\bar{y} - \overline{Y}), \quad \bar{y} > \overline{Y}. \tag{27}$$

Then the expected cost of underestimation is

$$\int_{-\infty}^{\overline{Y}} g(\overline{Y} - \bar{y})p(\bar{y}) \, d\bar{y}, \tag{28}$$

where $p(\bar{y})$ is the probability-density function of the estimate, $\bar{y}$. Similarly, the expected cost of overestimation is

$$\int_{\overline{Y}}^{\infty} h(\bar{y} - \overline{Y})p(\bar{y}) \, d\bar{y}. \tag{29}$$

The sum of these two expected costs is the total expected cost of error. The cost of preparing the sample and taking n observations is given by

$$C(n) = C_1 + \theta(n, C_2). \tag{30}$$

We use this form to allow for the possibility that the cost of taking n observations may not be a linear function of n.

The total expected cost, then, is given by

$$TEC = C_1 + \theta(n, C_2) + \int_{-\infty}^{\overline{Y}} g(\overline{Y} - \bar{y})p(\bar{y}) \, d\bar{y}$$
$$+ \int_{\overline{Y}}^{\infty} h(\bar{y} - \overline{Y})p(\bar{y}) \, d\bar{y}. \tag{31}$$

To illustrate the use of this equation consider the following simple case. Assume that the costs of over- and underestimation are a linear function of the magnitude of error. (We shall have more to say on this function below.) Then, letting k_1 equal a unit cost of underestimation and k_2 a unit cost of overestimation:

$$C(\overline{Y} - \bar{y}) = g(\overline{Y} - \bar{y}) = k_1(\overline{Y} - \bar{y}), \quad \overline{Y} > \bar{y} \tag{32}$$

and

$$C(\bar{y} - \overline{Y}) = h(\bar{y} - \overline{Y}) = k_2(\bar{y} - \overline{Y}), \quad \bar{y} > \overline{Y}. \tag{33}$$

We shall again assume that

$$C(n) = C_1 + nC_2. \tag{34}$$

Then, assuming that the estimates are normally distributed about the true value, $\overline{Y}$, equation (31) can be rewritten as

$$TEC = C_1 + nC_2 + \int_{-\infty}^{\overline{Y}} k_1(\overline{Y} - \bar{y}) \frac{\sqrt{n}}{\sigma\sqrt{2\pi}} e^{-n(\bar{y}-\overline{Y})^2/2\sigma^2} \, d\bar{y}$$

$$+ \int_{\overline{Y}}^{\infty} k_2(\bar{y} - \overline{Y}) \frac{\sqrt{n}}{\sigma\sqrt{2\pi}} e^{-n(\bar{y}-\overline{Y})^2/2\sigma^2} \, d\bar{y}. \tag{35}$$

This can be simplified by integration as follows:

$$TEC = C_1 + nC_2 + \frac{k_1\sigma}{\sqrt{2\pi n}} + \frac{k_2\sigma}{\sqrt{2\pi n}} \cong C_1 + nC_2 + \frac{0.4k_1\sigma}{\sqrt{n}} + \frac{0.4k_2\sigma}{\sqrt{n}}$$

$$= C_1 + nC_2 + \frac{0.4\sigma(k_1 + k_2)}{\sqrt{n}}. \tag{36}$$

To find the optimal sample size, n_o, we take the derivative, set it equal to zero, and solve for n:*

$$\frac{dTEC}{dn} = C_2 - \frac{0.2\sigma(k_1 + k_2)}{\sqrt{n^3}} = 0. \tag{37}$$

This value is minimum because

$$\frac{d^2TEC}{dn^2} > 0, \quad \text{for all } n > 0. \tag{38}$$

Then

$$n_o{}^3 = \frac{0.04\sigma^2(k_1 + k_2)^2}{C_2{}^2} \tag{39}$$

and

$$n_o = \left[\frac{0.04\sigma^2(k_1 + k_2)^2}{C_2{}^2}\right]^{1/3}. \tag{40}$$

* n, of course, should be an integer, but here we are treating it as a continuous variable and are rounding off the solution to the nearest integer.

Consider the following numerical example:

$$k_1 = \$0.50$$

$$k_2 = \$0.25$$

$$\sigma = 4100$$

$$C_2 = \$0.50.$$

Then

$$n_o{}^3 = \frac{(0.04)(4100)^2(0.50 + 0.25)^2}{(0.50)^2} = 1,512,900$$

$$n_o = 115.$$

Determining the Cost of Error from a Decision Model

In applied problems, the value of the "cost" of error can be determined from the decision model in terms of loss of performance. For example, consider the following simple decision model:

$$V = XY + \frac{1}{X}, \tag{41}$$

where V is a measure of performance to be minimized (e.g., cost), X is the control variable, and Y is the parameter whose value must be determined. To find the value of X which minimizes V we proceed as follows:

$$\frac{dV}{dX} = Y - \frac{1}{X^2} = 0 \tag{42}$$

$$X_o = \frac{1}{\sqrt{Y}}. \tag{43}$$

Then the minimum value of V is

$$V_o = \frac{Y}{\sqrt{Y}} + \sqrt{Y} = 2\sqrt{Y}. \tag{44}$$

Now, if an estimate y is used for Y, then instead of X_o we get

$$x_o = \frac{1}{\sqrt{y}}, \tag{45}$$

and instead of V_o we get

$$v_o = \frac{Y}{\sqrt{y}} + \sqrt{y}. \tag{46}$$

The cost of the error, $y - Y$, is

$$C(y - Y) = V_o - V_o = \frac{Y}{\sqrt{y}} + y - 2\sqrt{Y}. \qquad (47)$$

It will be observed that in this expression for the cost of error (47) the true value of the parameter, Y, appears. Hence, in this case, the cost of error is not only a function of its magnitude but is also a function of the location of this magnitude on the scale on which Y is measured. Furthermore, this cost-of-error function is not symmetrical; it depends on the sign of the error. This asymmetry will be proven generally in the next chapter. It can be illustrated here by assuming $Y = 4$; then for the indicated values of y the following costs of error are obtained:

y	Cost of Error
$\frac{1}{4}$	$4\frac{1}{2}$
1	1
4	0
9	$\frac{1}{3}$
16	1
25	$1\frac{4}{5}$
36	$2\frac{4}{6}$
49	$3\frac{4}{7}$
64	$4\frac{4}{8}$

As shown, the cost of a particular error of estimation (46) in the illustrative model we have been using depends on the true value of the parameter being estimated, Y, and the estimate of that parameter, y. This is true for the cost of estimating errors associated with parameters in most decision models. Clearly, if we knew Y in advance there would be no need to sample and estimate, and if we knew y we would already have an estimate. The need to know the value of the estimate y can be removed by a knowledge of the distribution of the estimates around the true value, $p(y|Y)$, which is normally provided by the theory on which the estimating procedure is based. Use of this distribution allows us to deal with the expected cost of error provided we know the value of Y. Similarly, if we know the distribution of the true value of $Y, p(Y)$, or can make some reasonable assumptions about it, we can use this distribution as well. That is, the expected cost of error $E(C)$ is given by

$$E(C) = \int_R \int_r C(y - Y) p(y|Y) p(Y) \, dy \, dY, \qquad (48)$$

where R and r represent the range of possible values of Y and y, respectively. The total expected cost (observations plus error) is

$$TEC = C(n) + E(C). \qquad (49)$$

Then, in the example,

$$TEC = C_1 + nC_2 + \int_R \int_r C(y - Y)p(y\,|\,Y)p(Y)\,dy\,dY \qquad (50)$$

In actual practice the distribution of the true value of the parameter can sometimes be estimated. For example, Y may represent the demand for a product in a future month. Actual past monthly demands are known. The average past monthly demand may not be used as a forecast for future demands because a better forecast, y, can be prepared based on information obtained from a sample of potential customers.

But even where $p(Y)$ is known the task of performing the necessary mathematical operations to find n_o may be prohibitively complex, if at all possible. An approximately optimal sample size can be obtained, however, if the following procedure is followed.

(1) First rewrite (50) in a conditional form

$$(TEC\,|\,Y) = C_1 + nC_2 + \int_r C(y - Y)p(y\,|\,Y)\,dy, \qquad (51)$$

where the values of y fall within the range

$$r = [(Y + K\sigma) - (Y - K\sigma)] \text{ standard units.}$$

(2) Since the integral involved in (51) is over a restricted range, it must be normalized. Do this as follows:

$$(TEC\,|\,Y) = C_1 + nC_2 + \frac{\displaystyle\int_{Y-K\sigma}^{Y+K\sigma} C(y - Y)p(y\,|\,Y)\,dy}{\displaystyle\int_{Y-K\sigma}^{Y+K\sigma} p(y\,|\,Y)\,dy}. \qquad (52)$$

(3) Assume a value for Y and solve for n_o by numerical integration.
(4) Continue for a variety of different values of Y.
(5) From the results obtained fit a function:

$$n_o = \theta(Y). \qquad (53)$$

(6) On the basis of the best information available (e.g., from previous study or a preliminary sample) get an estimate y, and as-

sume $Y = y$. Then, using the function obtained in step (5), select the corresponding n_o.

If observations can be taken sequentially and estimates of Y prepared after every one or few observations, then n_o can be determined for each estimate obtained. As soon as an n_o is obtained which is less than or equal to the sample already drawn, the sampling is discontinued. For example, let

$$C_2 = 0.001$$

$$K = 3$$

$$p(y \mid Y) = \frac{\sqrt{n}}{\sigma\sqrt{2\pi}} \exp\left[-\frac{(y - Y)^2 n}{2\sigma^2}\right]$$

$$\sigma = 4.$$

Solving equation (52) and following steps (3) through (5), we obtain the following values of n_o for specific values of Y:

Y	n_o
6	28
8	21
10	18
12	16
14	14

The plot of these data is shown in Figure 7.1.

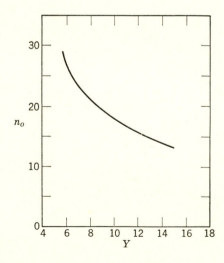

FIGURE 7.1. $n_o = \theta(Y)$, equation (53).

OBSERVATIONAL AND SAMPLING ERROR

Up to this point the discussion of optimizing sample size has not taken observational error into account. Observational error, it will be recalled from Chapter 6, may be due to the behavior of the observer, the observed, the instruments used in observing, and/or the environment in which the observations are made. Now we shall consider such error.

Consider a population of elements whose average value, $\overline{Y}$, of a particular property we wish to estimate. Assume that the true values of the elements, Y_i, are normally distributed with a standard deviation, σ_1. Assume also that observations made on the ith element are normally distributed with mean Y_i and standard deviation σ_2. The standard deviation of observations on each element is assumed to be equal.

It follows from these assumptions and statistical theory that the estimated mean ($\bar{y}$), obtained from observing each item of a sample of n elements exactly once, has a standard error $\sigma_{\bar{y}}$, where

$$\sigma_{\bar{y}} = \left(\frac{\sigma_1{}^2}{n} + \sigma_2{}^2 \right)^{\frac{1}{2}}. \tag{54}$$

Where there is no observational error, $\sigma_{\bar{y}} = \sigma_1 / \sqrt{n}$.

Where both types of error are involved, the unbiased estimate of the true mean $\overline{Y}$ is still the average of the observed values, as long as the distribution of observational error remains unchanged.

The value of $\sigma_{\bar{y}}$ as given in (54) can be substituted for $\sigma_{\overline{Y}}$ in the various cost equations which have been considered. For example, for simple random sampling with a quadratic cost-of-error function, from (4) and (54) we get

$$TEC = C_1 + nC_2 + k \left(\frac{\sigma_1{}^2}{n} + \sigma_2{}^2 \right). \tag{55}$$

As our discussion of observational error in Chapter 6 indicated, this error is usually a function of the time or cost per observation, C_2. That is,

$$\sigma_2 = \theta(C_2). \tag{56}$$

It becomes clear now that C_2 need not be treated as a constant; it may be treated as a variable. Then the more general optimization problem is to find the sample size, n, and the cost per observation, C_2, which minimize the total expected cost.

Continuing with the case of simple random sampling with a quadratic cost-of-error function, equation (55) becomes

$$TEC = C_1 + nC_2 + \frac{k\sigma_1^2}{n} + k[\theta(C_2)]^2. \tag{57}$$

To find the optimum values of n and C_2 we take the partial derivatives of TEC with respect to n and C_2, set each equal to zero, and solve the pair of simultaneous equations. For example, let

$$\sigma_2 = \theta(C_2) = \sqrt{\frac{K}{C_2}}, \tag{58}$$

where K is a constant. Then equation (57) becomes

$$TEC = C_1 + nC_2 + \frac{k\sigma_1^2}{n} + \frac{kK}{C_2}. \tag{59}$$

Proceeding as indicated,

$$\frac{\partial TEC}{\partial n} = C_2 - \frac{k\sigma_1^2}{n^2} = 0 \tag{60}$$

$$\frac{\partial TEC}{\partial C_2} = n - \frac{kK}{C_2^2} = 0. \tag{61}$$

Solving (61), we obtain

$$C_2^2 = \frac{kK}{n}. \tag{62}$$

Substituting (62) in (60), we get

$$\sqrt{\frac{kK}{n}} - \frac{k\sigma_1^2}{n^2} = 0 \tag{63}$$

which reduces to

$$n_o = \left[\frac{k\sigma_1^4}{K}\right]^{\frac{1}{3}}. \tag{64}$$

Substituting (64) in (62), we get

$$C_2 = \left[\frac{K^2k}{\sigma_1^2}\right]^{\frac{1}{3}}. \tag{65}$$

The procedure described can be used where σ_1 and σ_2 are not known but are estimated, by substituting the estimates for the true values.*

THE RELEVANCE OF TIME TO SAMPLING
AND OBSERVATIONAL ERROR

Failure to consider the effect of time on observations can lead to significant sampling and observational errors. First let us consider the relevance of time to sampling a population of elements.

In principle, the parameter of a population to be estimated, Y, is a property of that population at a specific time. For example, the average height of American men and the number of people living in the United States are properties which vary over time. Consequently, the parameter to be estimated should have a time indicator associated with it; for example, Y_t. To estimate Y_t we take a sample of n items and observe each, but these observations are not all made at time t, as they should be ideally. They should, then, be adjusted to what would have been observed at time t.

Necessity for adjusting observations to t is removed by the assumption that Y_t does not depend on t. This may mean either of two things: (1) Y_t may be regarded as independent of t if and only if Y_t is constant for all t; or (2) Y_t is a random variable with a distribution function that does not depend on t. If Y_t is assumed to be constant for all t within the relevant interval of time, then the time of observation is irrelevant. If, however, Y_t is assumed to be a random variable with respect to t, then the time of the observations is important.

In some cases, when the variation of Y with respect to t is small and random, it is supposed that the property being estimated is the mean value of Y over an interval from t_0 to t_1, $\overline{Y}_{01}$. To estimate this parameter properly the time interval should also be sampled. This is seldom done. Rather, one usually acts as though the observations were all made at t. Whether or not it is reasonable to do so depends on how much variance of observations is due to variations in t. This time-related variance may increase with increases in sample size, perhaps more rapidly than sampling error is decreased.

Consider now the case of a single object whose property Y is to be estimated. Here too the time subscript is relevant if Y is not

---

* Marschak (1955) and Radner (1955 and 1959) have also considered the cost of transmitting the observations to a central headquarters or to others in the field for decision-making purposes.

fixed for all t in the period of interest. At best only one observation can be made at time t. If t is relevant, then either (a) controls must be imposed to hold Y constant (as in a laboratory), or (b) adjustments in the observations are required, or (c) time-produced variance should be considered in determining the number of observations to be made.

When the parameter being estimated is a random variable with respect to time, it can be treated as an observational error. This type of observational error does not necessarily decrease as the time per observation is increased.

Although in principle the above remarks are quite obvious, in practice they are frequently ignored with consequences whose significance is left undetermined.

CONCLUSION

In order to construct a decision model of the selection of a sample design it is necessary (a) to be able to express the differences between sample designs in terms of quantifiable variables, and (b) to express errors of estimates yielded by these designs as functions of these same variables. In order to accomplish the latter it is further necessary to know a great deal about the distribution of the property in question among the elements and in the subgroups of the population to be sampled. As yet no such general decision model has been constructed. More specialized models addressed to less general design questions, however, have been constructed. With the development of more and more of these specialized models, we gradually approach a general sampling-design model.

In order to select the best of a set of alternative sample designs, it is necessary at present to determine (or approximate) the optimal sample size for each design, and then select that design which has the least total expected cost. Such an iterative procedure is the only one available to us until a feasible way is developed for representing differences in sampling design by values along one or more scales.

Determination of optimal sample size for any particular sample design requires a knowledge of the cost-of-error function of the variable being estimated. As we showed, this function can be derived from the decision model. Since this cost is generally a function of the true value of the parameter being estimated, it is necessary to use approximation procedures. The consequences of the frequently made assumption that the cost of error is of a particular form (usually quadratic), which is independent of the true value of the parameter being estimated, should be carefully weighed before taking advantage of the mathematical simplicity which such an assumption usually yields.

In "pure" science, where decision models cannot be constructed, some assumptions concerning the cost-of-error function are necessary. These assumptions should be made explicit, and sufficient data should be provided so that users of the results can adjust them appropriately for the context in which they are to be used.

BIBLIOGRAPHY

Cochran, W. G., "The Use of Analysis of Variance in Enumeration by Sampling," *Journal of the American Statistical Association,* **34** (1939), 492–510.

———, "Sampling Theory When the Sampling Units Are of Unequal Sizes," *Journal of the American Statistical Association,* **37** (1942), 199–212.

———, *Recent Developments in Sampling Theory in the United States.* Washington, D. C.: International Statistical Institute, 1947. (Mimeographed)

———, *Sampling Techniques.* New York: John Wiley and Sons, 1953.

Cornell, F. G., "A Stratified Random Sample of a Small Finite Population," *Journal of the American Statistical Association,* **42** (1947), 523–532.

Dalenius, T., "The Problem of Optimum Stratification," *Skandinavisk Aktuarietidskrift,* **33** (1950), 203–213.

———, and M. Gurney, "The Problem of Optimum Stratification, II," *Skandinavisk Aktuarietidskrift,* **34** (1951), 133–148.

Deming, W. E., "On Training in Sampling," *Journal of the American Statistical Association,* **40** (1945), 307–316.

———, *Some Theory of Sampling.* New York: John Wiley and Sons, 1950.

———, *Sample Design in Business Research.* New York: John Wiley and Sons, 1960.

Fisher, R. A., and Frank Yates, *Statistical Tables for Biological, Agricultural, and Medical Research.* London: Oliver and Boyd, 1943.

Hansen, M. H., W. N. Hurwitz, and W. G. Madow, *Sample Survey Methods and Theory.* New York: John Wiley and Sons, 1953.

Horton, H. B., *Random Decimal Digits.* Washington, D. C.: Interstate Commerce Commission, 1949.

Kendall, M. G., and B. B. Smith, "Randomness and Random Sampling of Numbers," *Journal of the Royal Statistical Society,* **101** (1938), 147–166.

——— and ———, "Tables of Random Sampling Numbers," *Tracts for Computers,* No. 24. Cambridge: Cambridge University Press, 1940.

Madow, L. H., "Systematic Sampling and Its Relation to Other Sampling Design," *Journal of the American Statistical Association,* **41** (1946), 204–217.

Madow, W. G., and L. H., "On the Theory of Systematic Sampling," *Annals of Mathematical Statistics,* **15** (1944), 1–24.

Mahalanobis, P. C., "On Large Scale Sampling Surveys," *Philosophical Transactions of the Royal Society,* Ser. B, *Biological Sciences,* **231** (1941), 329–451.

Mahalanobis, P. C., "Recent Experiments in Statistical Sampling in the Indian Statistical Institute," *Journal of the Royal Statistical Society,* **109,** Part IV (1946), 325–378.

Marks, E. S., "Some Sampling Problems in Educational Research," *Journal of Educational Psychology,* **42** (1951), 85–96.

Marschak, J., "Elements for a Theory of Teams," *Management Science,* **1** (1955), 127–137.

Neyman, Jerzy, "On the Two Aspects of the Representative Method," *Journal of the Royal Statistical Society,* **97** (1934), 558–606.

——, "Contributions to the Theory of Sampling Human Populations," *Journal of the American Statistical Association,* **33** (1938), 101–116.

Nordin, J. A., "Determining Sample Size," *Journal of the American Statistical Association,* **39** (1944), 497–506.

Radner, R., "The Linear Team: An Example of Linear Programming under Uncertainty," in *Proceedings of 2nd Symposium in Linear Programming,* Washington, D. C.: National Bureau of Standards, 1955, pp. 381–396.

——, "The Application of Linear Programming to Team Decision Problems," *Management Science,* **5** (1959), 143–150.

RAND Corp., *A Million Random Digits with 100,000 Normal Deviates.* Glencoe, Ill.: The Free Press (1955).

Statistical Research Group, *Sequential Analysis of Statistical Data: Application.* New York: Columbia University Press, 1946.

Stephan, F. F., "History of the Uses of Modern Sampling," *Journal of the American Statistical Association,* **43** (1948), 12–39.

——, "Sampling," *American Journal of Sociology,* **55** (1950), 371–375.

Stock, J. S., and L. R. Frankel, "The Allocation of Sampling among Strata," *Annals of Mathematical Statistics,* **10** (1939), 288–293.

Tippett, L. H. C., "Tables of Random Sampling Numbers," *Tracts for Computers,* No. 15. Cambridge: Cambridge University Press, 1927.

Wald, Abraham, *Sequential Analysis.* New York: John Wiley and Sons, 1947.

Yates, Frank, "A Review of Recent Statistical Developments in Sampling and Sampling Surveys," *Journal of the Royal Statistical Society,* **109** (1946), 12–32.

——, *Sampling Methods for Censuses and Surveys.* London: Chas. Griffin Co., 1949.

8

ESTIMATION*

INTRODUCTION

The parameters in a decision model, Y_j, represent either the property of a single thing (object, event, or state) or the property of a collection (population) of these things. Multiple observations of a single thing may vary for either or both of two reasons: (1) observational error, and/or (2) temporal error. The latter error is introduced by the fact that observations cannot be made simultaneously and the property being observed may change over the period of observation. In the case of a collection of things, the observations may vary not only for the two reasons cited but also because of variation between the properties of the items being observed.

If a scientific observer finds no variation among his observations, he accepts this not as the attainment of perfection, but rather as an indication of a serious imperfection. He may suspect that his measuring instrument is jammed or that he is not making his readings precisely enough. He investigates to find the cause of conformity and "corrects" it so that he gets variation among observations. This process yields ever-increasing accuracy of observation.

* The material in this chapter is based largely on research at Case Institute of Technology, sponsored by the Office of Naval Research, Navy Contract No. NONR–1141(08). Most of the work on this project was performed by Dr. Shiv K. Gupta (1960) and Professor Fred Hanssmann. Portions of their various write-ups of this work have been incorporated into this chapter with their permission.

Given a set of numerical observations of a property Y (y_1, y_2, $\cdots$, y_n), what particular number should be used to represent the property involved? This is the problem of estimation. Put another way, the problem is to find a number y, where

$$y = \phi(y_1, y_2, \cdots, y_n)$$

such that this number is the "best" estimate of Y. To solve this problem we obviously require one or more criteria of "best" in this context. Statistical estimation theory has been concerned with developing estimating procedures and criteria for evaluating them.

SOME IMPORTANT ESTIMATING PROCEDURES IN STATISTICS

Three major (but by no means the only) estimating procedures are:

(1) The analogue method or method of moments.
(2) The maximum-likelihood method.
(3) Bayes strategies.

The Analogue Method or Method of Moments

This method, which was developed by Karl Pearson, may be described loosely as a procedure of estimating a parameter or property of a probability distribution by the same property of the sample. For example, the mean $\overline{Y}$ of a finite population is

$$\frac{1}{N} \sum_1^N Y_i,$$

where N is the number of elements in the population; its analogue estimate is

$$\bar{y} = \frac{1}{n} \sum_1^n y_i,$$

where n is the number of elements in the sample. More precisely, using the method of moments, we estimate a parameter Y_k, which is equivalent to the expected value of the kth moment * of Y, by y_k, where

* In general, a moment is the mean value of a power of a variate. Therefore, the kth moment of a variate Y with a cumulative distribution $F(Y)$ is

$$\int_{-\infty}^{\infty} Y^k \, dF(Y),$$

and its moment about a particular value a is

$$\int_{-\infty}^{\infty} (Y - a)^k \, dF(Y).$$

The first moment about the mean is zero, and the second moment is the variance.

$$y_k = \frac{1}{n} \sum_1^n y_i{}^k,$$

which is the kth moment of the sample. Similarly the analogue estimate of the variance of Y, $\sigma_Y{}^2$, which is equivalent to the expected value of $(Y - \overline{Y})^2$, is

$$s_Y{}^2 = \frac{1}{n} \sum_1^n (y_i - \bar{y})^2.$$

The median of a sample is an analogue estimate of the median of the population, and an observed proportion is an analogue estimate of a probability.

The Maximum-Likelihood Method

Let Y_n represent a particular random sample of size n which has been drawn for the purpose of estimating the value of the population parameter Y. Then the likelihood of a particular value of $Y(Y_1, Y_2, \cdots)$ is defined as the conditional probability of drawing the particular sample Y_n, given Y; that is, $p(Y_n|Y)$. The maximum-likelihood method consists of estimating the value of Y by that one of its possible values which maximizes the likelihood function.

For example, suppose that Y can take on three possible values, Y_1, Y_2, Y_3, and suppose that there are three possible samples ($y_1, y_2,$ and y_3) with probability-density function $p(y_i|y_j)$ as shown in Table 8.1. It is clear that, if the sample y_1 is obtained, the likelihood $p(y_1|Y_i)$ is maximum for Y_1. Similarly, Y_2 and Y_3 yield maxima likelihood for y_2 and y_3, respectively. Hence, the values of $Y_1, Y_2,$ and Y_3 are maximum-likelihood estimates corresponding to the samples $y_1, y_2,$ and y_3.

TABLE 8.1

	y_1	y_2	y_3
Y_1	0.70	0.20	0.10
Y_2	0.30	0.50	0.20
Y_3	0.15	0.25	0.60

Normally, of course, Y can have infinitely possible values, but the same logic applies.

In some cases * the sample mean $\bar{y}$ is a maximum-likelihood estimate of $\bar{Y}$. The observed ratio of m outcomes of a particular type to n trials (i.e., m/n) is a maximum-likelihood estimate of the probability of that particular type of outcome.

Bayes Strategies

Suppose that on some grounds we have an *a priori* distribution of possible values of Y, $p'(Y)$. Then the sample obtained can be used to revise these so as to obtain an *a posteriori* probability distribution $p(Y)$. In so doing, the true value of Y is regarded as a random variable, and hence the cost of using an estimate y when the true value is Y, $C(Y, y)$ may be regarded as a random quantity with a distribution which depends upon $p(Y)$. The value of y which minimizes the expected cost of error, $E[C(Y, y)]$, where the expectation is based on the *a posteriori* distribution, $p(Y)$, may be called a *Bayes estimate*.

For example,† suppose that there are two possible values of Y, Y_1 and Y_2, and three possible sets of observations (y_1, y_2, and y_3) with the conditional *a priori* probabilities shown in Table 8.2.

Then the (unconditional) *a priori* probability of obtaining each estimate, $p'(Y)p(y_i|Y)$, can be computed as is done in Table 8.3.

The *a posteriori* probability for each possible value of Y and for each possible sample is determined as shown in Table 8.4.

Now suppose that the costs of error are as shown in Table 8.5. Then the *expected* costs of error can be computed, and for each possible observed state we can find the Bayes estimate; that is, the one that minimizes the expected cost of error. The computations are shown in Table 8.6.

Up to this point we have considered only the case in which a decision depends on the value of one parameter. Now consider the case in which the decision depends on estimates of two unconnected parameters, Y and Z. To illustrate the logic of the Bayes estimate in this case, assume that Y and Z can each take on only two values, Y_1 and

* For these cases, see J. M. Keynes, "The Principal Averages and the Laws of Error Which Lead to Them," *Journal of the Royal Statistical Society,* **74** (1911), p. 322.

† This example is adapted from Chernoff and Moses (1959, pp. 280–281).

TABLE 8.2.   CONDITIONAL *A Priori* PROBABILITIES

	y_1	y_2	y_3	$p'(Y_i)$
Y_1	0.60	0.25	0.15	0.60
Y_2	0.20	0.30	0.50	0.40

TABLE 8.3.   UNCONDITIONAL *A Priori* PROBABILITIES, $p(y_i)$

	y_1	y_2	y_3
Y_1	$0.6(0.60) = 0.36$	$0.6(0.25) = 0.15$	$0.6(0.15) = 0.09$
Y_2	$0.4(0.20) = 0.08$	$0.4(0.30) = 0.12$	$0.4(0.50) = 0.20$
$\Sigma p'(Y)p(y_i|Y) = p(y_i)$	0.44	0.27	0.29

TABLE 8.4.   *A Posteriori* PROBABILITIES

	y_1	y_2	y_3
$p(Y_1|y_i)$	$\dfrac{0.36}{0.44}$	$\dfrac{0.15}{0.27}$	$\dfrac{0.09}{0.29}$
$p(Y_2|y_i)$	$\dfrac{0.08}{0.44}$	$\dfrac{0.12}{0.27}$	$\dfrac{0.20}{0.29}$

TABLE 8.5.   COSTS OF ERROR

		$y =$	
		Y_1	Y_1
$Y =$	Y_1	0	4
	Y_2	3	0

TABLE 8.6. DETERMINATION OF BAYES ESTIMATES

Sample Drawn	If y Is Taken Equal to	Expected Cost of Error Will Be	Bayes Estimate
y_1	Y_1	$0\left(\dfrac{0.36}{0.44}\right) + 3\left(\dfrac{0.08}{0.44}\right) = \dfrac{0.24}{0.44}$	$y = Y_1$
	Y_2	$4\left(\dfrac{0.36}{0.44}\right) + 0\left(\dfrac{0.08}{0.44}\right) = \dfrac{1.44}{0.44}$	
y_2	Y_1	$0\left(\dfrac{0.15}{0.27}\right) + 3\left(\dfrac{0.12}{0.27}\right) = \dfrac{0.36}{0.27}$	$y = Y_1$
	Y_2	$4\left(\dfrac{0.15}{0.27}\right) + 0\left(\dfrac{0.12}{0.27}\right) = \dfrac{0.60}{0.27}$	
y_3	Y_1	$0\left(\dfrac{0.09}{0.29}\right) + 3\left(\dfrac{0.20}{0.29}\right) = \dfrac{0.60}{0.29}$	$y = Y_2$
	Y_2	$4\left(\dfrac{0.09}{0.29}\right) + 0\left(\dfrac{0.20}{0.29}\right) = \dfrac{0.36}{0.29}$	

Y_2, Z_1 and Z_2. Suppose, further, that there are three possible sets of independent observations on each (y_1, y_2, y_3) and (z_1, z_2, z_3). Now the *a priori* conditional probabilities can be displayed as shown in Table 8.7 (compare with Table 8.1). The probability entered in the upper left-hand cell, for example, would be the product

$$p(y_1 \mid Y_1)p(z_1 \mid Z_1).$$

TABLE 8.7

	y_1, z_1	y_2, z_1	y_3, z_1	y_1, z_2	y_2, z_2	y_3, z_2	y_1, z_3	y_2, z_3	y_3, z_3
Y_1, Z_1									
Y_2, Z_1									
Y_1, Z_2									
Y_2, Z_2									

If these probabilities are not independent, appropriate adjustments can be made.

The subsequent steps in this case now correspond to those shown in Tables 8.3 to 8.6.

STATISTICAL CRITERIA OF "GOOD" ESTIMATING PROCEDURES

The criteria most frequently used to evaluate estimating procedures are:

(1) Lack of bias.
(2) Invariance under transformation of parameters.
(3) Consistency.
(4) Efficiency.
(5) Sufficiency.

We want to define each of these criteria and to evaluate the estimating procedures with respect to them.

Lack of Bias

An estimate y of a parameter whose true value is Y is said to be *unbiased* if its expected value, $E(y)$,† is equal to Y. Hence, the measure of bias is $E(y) - Y$. For an unbiased estimator, $E(y) - Y = 0$.

For example, $\bar{y} = \dfrac{1}{n} \sum_1^n y_i$ is an unbiased estimate of $|\bar{Y}$; $s_Y^2 = \dfrac{1}{n-1} \sum_1^n (y_i - \bar{y})^2$ is an unbiased estimate of σ_Y^2. On the other hand, it can be shown that $\bar{y}^2$ is a biased estimate of $\bar{Y}^2$.

Invariance under Transformation of Parameters

An estimating procedure which yields y as an estimate of Y is *invariant under transformation of parameters* if it estimates some transformation of Y, $Y^* = g(Y)$ by $y^* = g(y)$. For example, let Y be the length of an object in inches and Y^* be its length in centimeters. Then $Y^* = 2.540Y$. The "invariance" condition asserts that

---

† The expected value of y, $E(y)$, is the limiting value of the average of the estimates obtained as the number of samples of the same size approaches infinity.

if we estimate Y by y we should estimate Y^* by $2.540y$. The maximum-likelihood and (if the cost function and prior distributions are invariant) Bayes estimators satisfy this condition, but in some cases the analogue method does not.

The criteria of unbiasedness and invariance may not both be simultaneously satisfied. For example, although $\bar{y}$ is an unbiased estimate of $\bar{Y}$, $\bar{y}^2$ is a biased estimate of $\bar{Y}^2$. The criterion of invariance is generally taken to be the more fundamental.

Consistency

An estimating procedure is said to be *consistent* if the estimates which it yields tend to approach the true value more and more closely as the sample size is indefinitely increased. More precisely, the probability that the estimates converge on the true value must approach 1.0 as the sample size approaches infinity:

$$p(y \to Y) \to 1.0 \quad \text{as } n \to \infty.\dagger$$

A consistent estimator is almost always unbiased in the limit (i.e., when $n = N$, the population size), but for any sample size less than that of the population (i.e., $n < N$) it may yield biased estimates.

All three methods of estimation which we have considered yield consistent estimates of separately estimated parameters.

Efficiency

An estimator is said to be *asymptotically efficient* if the distribution of estimates which it yields tends to normality with the least possible standard error (i.e., standard deviation of the estimate) as the sample size is increased. Therefore, the standard error of estimates yielded by an efficient estimator must be no greater than that yielded by any other consistent estimator which approaches normality in the limit. An efficient estimator must also be consistent, but it may yield biased estimates where $n < N$.

The analogue method does not always yield efficient estimators, but the maximum-likelihood and Bayes methods generally do. In fact, if we start with any probability-density function of Y, which has positive density for all values of Y, the maximum-likelihood estimator and the Bayes estimator (assuming a smooth cost-of-error function) will be extremely close to one another for large samples.

---

† The symbol "$\to$" represents "approaches the value of."

Sufficiency

An estimating procedure yields *sufficient* estimates if no other statistic can be derived from the sample which yields any additional information concerning the parameter being estimated. More precisely, if $y_1, y_2, \cdots, y_n$ is a sample from a population with density $p(y|Y)$ and if $\phi(y_1, y_2, \cdots, y_n)$ is such that the conditional distribution of $y_1, y_2, \cdots, y_n$ given ϕ does not depend on Y, then ϕ is a sufficient estimator. Such estimators are generally considered to be the most desirable but they exist only in rather special cases.

A sufficient estimator is usually efficient and consistent. It can be shown that, if there are sufficient estimators of a parameter Y, the maximum-likelihood method will yield one.

Reviewing the three methods briefly, the analogue method is usually the easiest to apply. It requires the least information; it does not need complete knowledge of the probability-density function. Although it always yields consistent estimates, it does not generally yield efficient ones. Both the maximum-likelihood and Bayes methods require knowledge of $p(y|Y)$. Both generally yield efficient estimates which are invariant under transformations of parameters. If sufficient estimators are possible, the maximum-likelihood method will yield one. The Bayes method additionally requires knowledge of the probability distribution $p(Y)$ and the cost-of-error function $C(Y, y)$. Because of the complexity of the Bayes method (which we will consider in more detail below), it has been used primarily as a theoretical tool, whereas the other two methods have had wide practical application.

PRAGMATIC CRITERION FOR BEST ESTIMATES

An estimating procedure which yields unbiased estimates with minimum variance will yield the minimum expected cost of (estimating) error only if the cost of error is a quadratic function of its magnitude; that is, if

$$C(Y, y) = k(y - Y)^2.$$

Assuming that the cost of error is quadratic, a biased estimate with a small variance may be preferable to an unbiased estimate with a large variance. For this reason Hansen, Hurwitz, and Madow (1953) suggest use of the *mean square error*, which they define as "the variance of the estimate plus the square of the bias" (p. 56). An estimator which minimized mean square error would minimize the expected cost of error whether it yielded biased estimates or not, but *only if* the cost-of-error function is quadratic. The quadratic function is normally assumed for three major reasons.

First, many smooth [cost-of-error] functions which vanish at [$y = Y$] are well approximated by the "squared loss" function, especially for [y close to Y]. Second, the mathematics involved in using this . . . function is relatively simple compared to other . . . functions. Third, for large samples, many reasonable estimators yield estimates whose probability distributions are approximated by normal distributions with mean Y. Such distributions are completely specified by the variance of Y, and the smaller the variance the better the estimator, no matter what the [cost-of-error] function may be (so long as [$C(Y, y)$] increases as y moves away from Y). [Chernoff and Moses (1959, p. 276)]

The second reason, mathematical simplicity, is generally valid; but the other two reasons are not. The first is largely a matter of wishful thinking. Most cost-of-error functions generated from a decision model (as we shall do below) are not well approximated by a quadratic form because, among other reasons, they are very seldom symmetrical. As for the third reason, it is true that "the smaller the variance the better the estimator" no matter what the cost-of-error function may be (under the stated conditions); but the estimator with the smallest variance is *best* for only certain types of cost-of-error functions.

From any particular decision model one can extract the cost-of-error function for a specified parameter and hence can also determine whether it is symmetrical. For example, consider again the very simple decision model used in Chapter 7:

$$V = f(X, Y) = XY + \frac{1}{X}, \tag{1}$$

where V = total cost, X is the control variable, and Y is the parameter. To find the optimizing value of X we differentiate with respect to X, equate the result to zero, solve for X, and obtain

$$X_o = g(Y) = \frac{1}{\sqrt{Y}}. \tag{2}$$

The minimum cost, therefore, is

$$V_o = f[g(Y); Y] = X_o Y + \frac{1}{X_o} = 2\sqrt{Y}. \tag{3}$$

In normal scientific practice an estimate (y) of Y is obtained and substituted for Y in equation (2), which yields an estimated optimizing value of X:

$$x_o = g(y) = \frac{1}{\sqrt{y}} \tag{4}$$

and the following minimum cost is obtained:

$$v_o = f[g(y); Y] = \frac{Y}{\sqrt{y}} + \sqrt{y}. \tag{5}$$

Thus, the difference between the estimated and the actual minimum cost, the cost of error, is

$$C = f[g(y); Y] - f[g(Y); Y]$$
$$= Yy^{-\frac{1}{2}} + y^{\frac{1}{2}} - 2Y^{\frac{1}{2}}. \tag{6}$$

As indicated in Chapter 7, the cost of error for this decision model depends upon the sign of $(y - Y) = \Delta Y$, the error made in estimating Y, and hence is not symmetrically distributed. This is true because otherwise we must have

$$\frac{Y}{\sqrt{Y + \Delta Y}} + \sqrt{Y + \Delta Y} - 2\sqrt{Y}$$
$$= \frac{Y}{\sqrt{Y - \Delta Y}} + \sqrt{Y - \Delta Y} - 2\sqrt{Y},$$

which is true only if $\Delta Y = 0$.

If the cost of error is not symmetrically distributed about the true value being estimated, and if this cost increases with the magnitude of the error, then an unbiased estimate—whatever its other properties—will not minimize the expected cost of error. Furthermore, an estimate which minimizes variance will minimize the expected cost of error only if this cost has a quadratic form. The advantage of the Bayes approach, in principle, derives from the fact that it can yield estimators which minimize this expected cost whatever the cost-of-error function.

After reformulating the problem of estimation in very general terms, we will consider two specific procedures for generating estimates. The first procedure obtains a Bayes estimate by use of the calculus of variations, but it is much simpler than many of the procedures available for obtaining such estimates. The second procedure, the *biasing* method, unlike the variational method, assumes the form of the estimating function but it does not use the *a priori* distribution of the parameter being estimated. However, it does make some assumptions about the parameter.

MATHEMATICAL FORMULATION OF THE ESTIMATION PROBLEM

Determination of the expected cost of (estimating) error requires knowledge of

(1) either the true value of the parameter, Y, or its probability-density function, $p(Y)$;

(2) the probability-density function of the estimates, $p(y|Y)$, and

(3) the cost-of-error function.

If Y is known, of course, it need not be estimated. Its distribution, $p(Y)$, may be known on the basis of past experience. There is another possibility. The expected cost of error may itself be *estimated*, using an estimate of Y. This possibility is used in the biasing method presented below. The distribution, $p(y|Y)$, is provided for most estimators by the theory from which it is derived. Finally, the cost-of-error function can be derived from the decision model in which the parameter appears, as was shown in the preceding section.

When the parameters of a decision model, Y_j, are known with certainty, standard mathematical techniques can be applied to obtain a decision rule which will optimize the performance of the given model. If the decision model has a unique relative minimum (or maximum) for fixed Y_j, then there exist decision functions $X_{i_o} = g_i(Y_j)$ such that the minimum value of $f(X_i, Y_j)$ is equal to

$$f[g_i(Y_j); Y_j].$$

When the exact values of the parameters are not known (as is usually the case), their values are estimated by some statistical procedure. Let the estimated values of Y_j be y_j. Then, the actual performance of the model is given by

$$f[g_i(y_j); Y_j],$$

and the cost of error arising out of the use of the estimated values is

$$C = f[g_i(y_j); Y_j] - f[g_i(Y_j); Y_j].* \tag{7}$$

* Note that this cost is equivalent to the "regret" associated with estimating error.

The problem, then, is to reduce the expected cost of error, $E(C)$. This problem will be considered where the Y_j are constant * but unknown, and the estimates y_j are assumed to have the probability distribution $p(y_j | Y_j)$.

The simplest decision situation involves one control variable and one parameter; that is,

$$V = f(X, Y).$$

In this case, equation (7) becomes

$$C = f[g(y); Y] - f[g(Y); Y].$$

Let $p(y|Y)$ be the probability-density function of y with mean Y and variance σ^2. Then, for any value of Y, the conditional expected cost of error is

$$E(C \,|\, Y) = \int_r \{f[g(y); Y] - f[g(Y); Y]\} p(y \,|\, Y)\, dy, \tag{8}$$

where the integration extends over the range r of the variable y.

More generally, the conditional expected cost of error for a decision function $d(y)$ of the observations is given by

$$E(C \,|\, Y) = \int_r \{f[d(y), Y] - f[g(Y), Y]\} p(y \,|\, Y)\, dy$$

$$= L\{d(y), Y\}, \tag{9}$$

where the functional L is defined by (9). The best estimating procedure, then, can be defined as a decision function $d(y)$ which minimizes the total (unconditional) expected cost of error:

$$E(C) = \int_R \int_r \{f[d(y), Y] - f[g(Y), Y]\} p(y \,|\, Y) p(Y)\, dy\, dY \tag{10}$$

where R is the range of Y.

A PROCEDURE FOR DERIVING A BAYES ESTIMATE

The purpose of using an optimal decision function $d(y)$ can also be stated as that of achieving cost reductions,

$$L\{g(y), Y\} - L\{d(y), Y\}, \tag{11}$$

---

* Over the period to which a particular decision is to be applied.

for all possible values of Y. When the distribution of Y is known, both $L\{g(y), Y\}p(Y)$ and $L\{d(y), Y\}p(Y)$ can be plotted as functions of Y, and the area between these two curves is the area of expected cost reduction. Hence, maximization of this area can be used as a criterion of optimality. This area is obtained by integration of

$$L\{g(y), Y\}p(Y) - L\{d(y), Y\}p(Y) \tag{12}$$

over Y. Therefore this method presupposes a knowledge of the distribution, $p(Y)$.

It is assumed that the researcher can narrow the range of Y down to a plausible finite region, $a \leqq Y \leqq b$. In practice information which makes this possible is almost always available. For example, a cost usually has a lower limit of zero and some plausible upper limit which can be determined in the problem context. The area of reduction taken over the range $a \leqq Y \leqq b$ is given by

$$\int_a^b [L\{g(y), Y\} - L\{d(y), Y\}]p(Y)\, dY. \tag{13}$$

(See Figure 8.1.) Its maximization over the space of all functions $d(y)$ is equivalent to minimization of

$$\int_a^b L\{d(y), Y\}p(Y)\, dY. \tag{14}$$

The functional L is an integral itself where integration is with respect to y. We can assume that the probability distribution $p(y|Y)$ may be set equal to zero outside the range $Y - K \leqq y \leqq Y + K$, where K is a properly chosen constant. Then, the integration in (9) may be

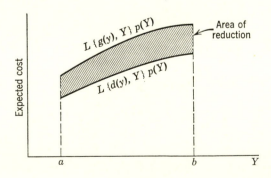

FIGURE 8.1.

restricted to this range of y. For formal reasons, however, we let the integration run over the interval $a - K \leqq y \leqq b + K$. Obviously, this range contains all values of y for which $p(y|Y) \neq 0$.

By (9), the minimization criterion (14) assumes the form

$$M\{d(y)\} = \int_a^b \int_{a-K}^{b+K} C\{d(y), Y\} p(y \mid Y) p(Y) \, dy \, dY. \tag{15}$$

The optimal decision function is found by the minimization

$$\underset{d(y)}{\text{Min}}\ M\{d(y)\} \tag{16}$$

to be taken over the space of all functions $d(y)$ of y above. The problem is one of calculus of variations. However, the classical techniques for minimization of double integrals assume that the unknown function is a function of both integration variables (here y and Y); consequently, the classical approach via the Euler-Lagrange equations must necessarily lead to the useless result $d = g(Y)$ for the unknown function. Therefore, we cannot use the classical techniques. Even without this difficulty, the classical techniques could not be expected to be very helpful, since in most cases the Euler-Lagrange differential equations would be no easier to solve than the original problem in integral form (16).

The minimization of (16) is shown in Appendix I.

The procedure just described is mathematically complex because the estimator is derived before an observed value is obtained. If we delay deriving the estimator until after a value has been observed, we can use the much simpler Bayes *posterior* procedure. This can be seen by reversing the order of integration given by (15) and writing it as

$$\int_{a-k}^{b+k} H[d(y), Y] \, dy,$$

where

$$H[d(y), y] = \int_a^b C\{d(y), Y\} p(y/Y) p(Y) \, dY.$$

Once a value of y has been obtained by observation, we need only minimize H. Since H is nonnegative, this is done by defining $d(y)$ to be that value of d which minimizes $H[d(y)]$. This is no longer a calculus of variations problem but the much simpler one of finding the minimum of a function of one variable. H has an operational meaning: it is the expected cost of error of taking decision d when the observation is y, the expectation being taken over $p(Y)$. In other words, instead of a calculus of variations problem involving integration over all possible values of y, we need consider only the particular value observed.

The posterior procedure, although less complex, requires derivation of an estimator for each different observed value. If the decision model which contains the parameter being estimated is to be used repetitively by a mathematically unsophisticated decision maker, it may be better to provide him with the simple results of the more complex prior procedure, than to have him solve the less complex integral equation each time he observes a different value, y. In an example given in a later section (pp. 275–276), it will be seen that the prior procedure can yield results that are very easy to use.

THE METHOD OF BIASED ESTIMATES *

The biasing method differs from the Bayes estimating procedure in several respects. First, unlike the Bayes procedure, it assumes that the decision function $d(y)$ has the same form as the decision function $g(y)$ derived from the model, assuming exact knowledge of all parameter values. However, it modifies the function by adding to the estimate of Y a biasing factor β; therefore, $d(y)$ takes the form $g(y + \beta)$.

Second, this method does not assume a priori knowledge of the distribution of Y and hence does not seek to minimize the total expected cost of error. However, it does reduce the cost of error for every possible true value of Y. This method, then, does not yield a best estimate, but it does yield a better estimate than is provided by the analogue or maximum-likelihood method.

In the particular example we have been considering, equation (1), there is a decision function of the form

$$d(y) = g(y + \beta), \tag{17}$$

which is superior to the naïve rule, $g(y)$, in the sense of the criterion given in equation (11). For example, suppose that the estimates y have the following probability distribution, $p(y|Y)$, with mean $Y = 3$:

y	1	2	3	4	5
$p(y\mid Y)$	0.15	0.15	0.35	0.25	0.10

* This procedure is due to Shiv K. Gupta.

When the values of y from this distribution are used in the decision rule given in equation (4), the expected cost of error turns out to be 0.1114.

Now suppose that we keep the *same decision rule* but make a transformation $y + \beta$ of the estimate y and use this transformed value to find the expected cost of error. That is, when an estimate y is obtained, an adjusted value $y + \beta$ is used instead. The calculations shown in Table 8.8 for several values of β indicate that the expected cost of error can be reduced by this biasing procedure.

This example shows the possibility of finding a decision function, $d(y) = g(y + \beta)$, which is superior to the decision rule, $g(y)$, for which the cost relation

$$L\{d(y), Y\} \leq L\{g(y), Y\} \tag{18}$$

holds for all values of the parameter Y.

The method of biased estimates generalizes the example just considered. An optimal decision rule is sought in the form

$$x_o = d(y) = g(y + \beta), \tag{19}$$

where $g(y)$ is the naïve rule and β is not dependent on the true value of Y. It may, however, be dependent on an unbiased estimate of Y, y. As a first step, a quantity β is derived by carrying out the minimization

$$\min_{\beta} L\{g(y + \beta), Y\}. \tag{20}$$

However, the minimizing values of β will in general be dependent on Y:

$$\beta = \beta(Y). \tag{21}$$

TABLE 8.8

Value of β	Expected Cost of Error
0	0.1114
0.3	0.0790
0.5	0.0712
0.6	0.0691
0.8	0.0688 (minimum)
0.9	0.0703
1.0	0.0727

Now comes the critical step. Since the true value Y is not known, the functional relationship, $\beta(Y)$, is first established; then the estimate y is substituted for Y to obtain the decision rule

$$d(y) = g\{y + \beta(y)\} \tag{22}$$

By definition, it is certainly true that

$$L\{g[y + \beta(Y)], Y\} \le L\{g(y), Y\}. \tag{23}$$

However, it is not obvious that

$$L\{d(y), Y\} = L\{g[y + \beta(y)], Y\} \le L\{g(y), Y\}. \tag{24}$$

It should be noted that in (23) β remains constant, since the true value Y is constant. But in (24) β varies during the integration process because y is a variable. Equation (24) is proven if the stronger statement given by

$$L\{g[y + \beta(y)], Y\} \le L\{g[y + \beta(Y)], Y\} \tag{25}$$

is proven. In a few specific cases (25) has been verified numerically. However, a general proof of equation (25) has not yet been obtained.

A set of sufficient conditions for equation (25) are:

(a) The cost function $C(Y, y)$ is convex, so that there is exactly one minimum.

(b) The decision function $g(y)$ is monotonic.

(c) The biasing function $\beta(y)$ is monotonic.

(d) The function $y + \beta(y)$ is increasing.

(e) The condition

$$\frac{d}{dx^2} C\{g[y + \beta(y)], Y\} \le \frac{d}{dx^2} C\{g[y + \beta(Y)], Y\} \tag{26}$$

is fulfilled for all Y.

(f) The probability-density function $p(y|Y)$ is symmetrical about its mean Y.

These conditions presuppose that the function $\beta(y)$ has been established in explicit form. Under this assumption, all conditions are easily verifiable with the possible exception of (e); however, condition (e) will normally be easier to verify in any specific case than is equation (25).

The derivation of $\beta(y)$ according to (20) can be carried out analytically for only relatively simple models. In most cases numerical analysis is required (which may be facilitated by use of a computer).

An approximate solution for β may be obtained by means of a Taylor approximation of the function

$$h(y, Y) = C\{g(y), Y\}. \tag{27}$$

Expanding about the point $y = Y$ and neglecting terms beyond the third, we have

$$h(y, Y) = h(Y, Y) + (y - Y)h'(Y, Y)$$

$$+ \frac{(y - Y)^2}{2!} h''(Y, Y) + \frac{(y - Y)^3}{3!} h'''(Y, Y), \tag{28}$$

where we have defined

$$h^{(k)}(y, Y) = \frac{\partial^k}{\partial y^k} h(y, Y), \quad k = 1, 2, 3. \tag{29}$$

Of course, $h'(Y, Y) = 0$.

We now replace y in (28) by $y + \beta$. After multiplying (28) by the probability distribution $p(y|Y)$ and integrating over y, the expected cost associated with the biased decision rule $g(y + \beta)$ becomes

$$L\{g(y + \beta), Y\} = h(Y, Y) + \int \frac{(y + \beta - Y)^2}{2!} h''(Y, Y)p(y|Y) \, dy$$

$$+ \int \frac{(y + \beta - Y)^3}{3!} h'''(Y, Y)p(y|Y) \, dy. \tag{30}$$

Taking the partial derivative of (30) with respect to β and setting it equal to zero, we obtain

$$\beta h''(Y, Y) + \frac{\sigma^2}{2} h''(Y, Y) + \frac{\beta^2}{2} h'''(Y, Y) = 0, \tag{31}$$

where σ is the standard deviation of $p(y|Y)$. This leads to the solution

$$\beta = \frac{-h'' + \sqrt{h''^2 - \sigma^2 h'''^2}}{h'''}. \tag{32}$$

We have adopted the positive sign for the radical, since we know that $\beta = 0$ for $\sigma = 0$. If $h'' \gg \sigma h'''$, a first-order Taylor expansion of the square root in (32) leads to

$$\beta(Y) = -\frac{\sigma^2}{2} \frac{h'''(Y, Y)}{h''(Y, Y)}. \tag{33}$$

It should be noted that β in (33) is not dependent on any properties of the probability distribution $p(y|Y)$ other than the standard deviation; furthermore, β is proportional to the skewness h'''/h'' (at $y = Y$) of the function $h(y, Y)$. By definition, $h(y, Y)$ measures the cost associated with the naïve decision rule. As one would expect, the optimal bias is zero when $h(y, Y)$ is symmetrical about $y = Y$; that is, when the cost of overestimation is equal to the cost of underestimation.

The Taylor expansion (28) also proves to be a valuable tool in evaluating alternative decision rules. The term $h(y, Y) - h(Y, Y)$ represents the *cost of error* introduced by the naïve decision rule. Equation (28) shows that the expected cost of error is approximated to the second degree by

$$S = \frac{\sigma^2}{2} h''(Y, Y). \tag{34}$$

Clearly, the expected cost of error is an upper bound for the reduction in expected cost which can be achieved by the optimal decision rule. Hence, the quantity S in (34) may be used as an optimistic estimate of savings. The actual savings will usually be of the order of $S/2$.

Multiple Control Variables and Parameters

We have considered only the simple decision model in which

$$V = f(X, Y),$$

but the more general form of a decision model is

$$V = f(X_i, Y_j), \quad i = 1, 2, \cdots, m_1$$
$$j = 1, 2, \cdots, m_2.$$

Now we want to consider cases in which m_1 and m_2 are greater than 1.

Several Control Variables and One Parameter

When V is a function of several control variables and one parameter, we have

$$V = f(X_1, X_2, \cdots, X_{m_1}, Y). \tag{35}$$

Then, for optimum V, we must set

$$\frac{\partial V}{\partial X_i} = 0 \; *$$

for each X_i. By solving these equations, we obtain

$$X_i = g_i(Y), \quad i = 1, 2, \cdots, m_1.$$

If y is an estimated value of Y, then the estimated values of X_i are given by

$$x_i = g_i(y).$$

Substituting these values in equation (35), we have

$$V = f[g_1(y), g_2(y), \cdots, g_{m_2}(y); Y].$$

The cost of error C is, therefore, given by

$$C = f[g_1(y), g_2(y), \cdots, g_{m_2}(y); Y]$$
$$- f[g_1(Y), g_2(Y), \cdots, g_{m_2}(Y); Y] = h(y, Y).$$

It follows, therefore, that this particular generalization can be treated in the same manner as the case in which the model contains only one control variable and is a function of one parameter. That is, one biasing function, $\beta(y)$, is all that is required.

Several Parameters and Several Control Variables

Since the case of several control variables can be reduced to one control variable, it is sufficient to consider the case of one control variable and more than one parameter. In other words, the performance model for this generalization may be written in the form

$$V = f(X; Y_j), \quad j = 1, 2, \cdots, m_2. \tag{36}$$

For optimum V, $dV/dX = 0$; solving for X, we obtain

$$X = g(Y_1, Y_2, \cdots, Y_{m_2}).$$

If y_j is an estimated value of Y_j, then the estimated value of X is given by

$$x = g(y_1, y_2, \cdots, y_{m_2}) \tag{37}$$

* Assuming that the condition of sufficiency is met.

and $f(X, Y_j)$ becomes

$$f[g(y_1, y_2, \cdots, y_{m_2}); Y_1, Y_2, \cdots, Y_{m_2}].$$

The cost of error (C) is, therefore, given by

$$C = f[g(y_1, y_2, \cdots, y_{m_2}); Y_1, Y_2, \cdots, Y_{m_2}]$$
$$- f[g(Y_1, Y_2, \cdots, Y_{m_2}); Y_1, Y_2, \cdots, Y_{m_2}]$$
$$= h(y_j, Y_j), \quad j = 1, 2, \cdots, m_2.$$

If $p(y_j | Y_j)$ are the probability-density functions of y_j, then the expected cost of error is given by

$$E(C) = \int_r h(y_j; Y_j) p(y_j | Y_j) \, dy_j.$$

Now let y_j be biased by an amount β_j, such that $E(C)$ given by

$$E(C) = \int_r h(y_j + \beta_j, Y_j) p(y_j | Y) \, dy_j \tag{38}$$

is minimum.

We shall solve equation (38) approximately after making certain assumptions for the case in which $j = 2$. Then the generalization from $j = 2$ to $j = m_2$ will become obvious.

When $j = 2$, equation (38) becomes

$$E(C) = \int_r h(y_1 + \beta_1, y_2 + \beta_2; Y_1, Y_2) p(y_1 | Y_1) p(y_2 | Y_2) \, dy_1 \, dy_2. \tag{39}$$

Now assume that:

(1) All the probability-density functions $p(y_j | Y_j)$ are independent of each other.

(2) The biasing factor β_1 will be found under the assumption that all Y_j's (in our case Y_2) except Y_1 are known; that is, from equation (37)

$$x = g(y_1, Y_2).$$

Equation (39) then becomes

$$E(C) = \int_r h(y_1 + \beta_1; Y_1, Y_2) p(y_1 | Y_1) \, dy_1. \tag{40}$$

Now β_1 will be a function of both Y_1 and Y_2. Since we have assumed Y_2 to be known, we shall substitute the value for Y_2, $[E(y_2) = Y_2]$, and for Y_1 its estimated value, so that β_1 becomes a function of y_1 only. Hence, $\beta_1 \sim \beta_1(y_1)$. Similarly, we find $\beta_2 \sim \beta_2(y_2)$. Equation (39) now becomes

$$E(C) = \int_r h[y_1 + \beta_1(y_1), y_2 + \beta_2(y_2); Y_1 Y_2]$$

$$p(y_1 \,|\, Y_1) p(y_2 \,|\, Y_2) \, dy_1 \, dy_2 \quad (41)$$

This procedure *does* reduce the expected cost of error, although it does not yield the optimum.

An Example of the Biasing Method

Returning to the model given in equation (1), let $p(y,|Y)$ be normally distributed; that is,

$$p(y \,|\, Y) = \frac{I_0}{\sqrt{2\pi}\,\sigma} \exp -\frac{(y - Y)^2}{2\sigma^2} \quad \text{when } |y - Y| \le \alpha$$

$$= 0 \qquad\qquad\qquad \text{otherwise} \quad (42)$$

where

$$I_0 = \frac{1}{\sqrt{2\pi}\,\sigma} \int_{Y-\alpha}^{Y+\alpha} \exp -\frac{(y - Y)^2}{2\sigma^2} \, dy.$$

The cost-of-error function [see (6)] after biasing is given by

$$h(y + \beta, Y) = Y(y + \beta)^{-\frac{1}{2}} + (y + \beta)^{\frac{1}{2}} - 2Y^{\frac{1}{2}}$$

$$= h(Y + \beta, Y) + (y - Y)h'(Y + \beta, Y) + \cdots + R_n, \quad (43)$$

where R_n is the remainder after n terms and

$$h^n(Y + \beta, Y) = \left[\frac{\partial^n}{\partial y^n} h(y + \beta, Y)\right]_{y=Y}.$$

The expected cost of error is given by

$$E(C) = \int_{Y-\alpha}^{Y+\alpha} h(y + \beta, Y) p(y \,|\, Y) \, dy$$

$$= h(Y + \beta, Y) + I_2 h''(Y + \beta, Y)$$

$$+ \cdots + I_{2n} h^{2n}(Y + \beta, Y) + R_{2n}, \quad (44)$$

where

$$I_{2n} = I_0 \int_{Y-\alpha}^{Y+\alpha} (y - Y)^{2n} \frac{1}{\sqrt{2\pi}\,\sigma} \exp -\frac{(y - Y)^2}{2\sigma^2} \, dy. \quad (45)$$

We solve equation (44) for β for various values of Y such that $E(C)$ is minimum. For $\alpha = 2\sigma$ and $R_{2n} < 0.00001$, Table 8.9 gives the values of β for several values of Y.

Reduction of Variance of the Expected Cost of Error

In the preceding discussion β, the biasing factor, was derived so as to minimize the expected cost of error. We shall now find β so that the variance of the expected cost of error $V(C)$, given by

$$V(C) = \int_r [h(y + \beta, Y) - E(C)]^2 p(y \mid Y)\, dy, \tag{46}$$

is minimum. Equation (46) can be solved for β, using various values of Y such that $V(C)$ will be a minimum; and, as was done before, a relation can be found between β and y; that is,

$$\beta = \beta(y).$$

For example, let the cost-of-error function and the probability-density function be given by equations (42) and (43). Then equation (46) becomes

$$V(C) = \frac{I_0}{\sqrt{2\pi}\,\sigma} \int_{Y-\alpha}^{Y+\alpha} [Y(y + \alpha)^{-\frac{1}{2}} + (y + \beta)^{\frac{1}{2}} - 2Y^{\frac{1}{2}}]^2$$

$$\exp -\frac{(y - Y)^2}{2\sigma^2}\, dy - \left[\frac{I_0}{\sqrt{2\pi}\,\sigma} \right.$$

$$\left. \int_{Y-2}^{Y+2} [Y(y + \beta)^{-\frac{1}{2}} + (y + \beta)^{\frac{1}{2}} - 2Y^{\frac{1}{2}}] \exp -\frac{(y - Y)^2}{2\sigma^2}\, dy \right]^2 \tag{47}$$

TABLE 8.9

Y	β
6	0.78
8	0.59
10	0.46
12	0.37
14	0.33

TABLE 8.10

Y	β
6	.80
8	.77
10	.75
12	.73
14	.68

We solve equation (47) for β for various values of Y such that $V(C)$ is minimum. For $\alpha = 2\sigma$, Table 8.10 gives the values of β for several values of Y.

A COMPARISON OF BAYES (PRIOR) AND BIASED ESTIMATORS

The Bayes prior procedure was also applied to the simple cost model given in equation (1)

$$V = XY + \frac{1}{X},$$

which may be interpreted as an inventory model leading to the economic lot size:

$$X_o = \frac{1}{\sqrt{Y}} = g(Y). \tag{48}$$

The estimate y was assumed to have a rectangular distribution with mean Y and range $2K = 6$; that is,

$$p(y\,|\,Y) = \begin{cases} \frac{1}{6} & \text{for } Y - 3 \le y \le Y + 3 \\ 0 & \text{otherwise.} \end{cases} \tag{49}$$

These assumptions permit one to derive an analytical expression for the optimal biasing function:

$$\hat{\beta}(y) = \sqrt{y^2 + K^2} - y, \quad y \ge 3. \tag{50}$$

The details of derivation are given in Appendix II. Turning to the Bayes method, it was assumed that the true value of the parameter

Y is rectangularly distributed inside the interval $3 \leqq Y \leqq 13$. The length of the interval is $F = 10$. This, then, was the integration interval for Y in the Bayes formulation. As is also shown in Appendix II, the optimal-decision function $u = d(y)$ may be obtained in the following explicit form:

$$u = \begin{cases} \sqrt{\dfrac{1}{K + y/2}} & \text{for } 0 \leq y \leq 2K \\[2ex] \sqrt{\dfrac{1}{y}} & \text{for } 2K \leq y \leq F \\[2ex] \sqrt{\dfrac{2}{F + y}} & \text{for } F \leq y \leq L, \end{cases} \qquad (51)$$

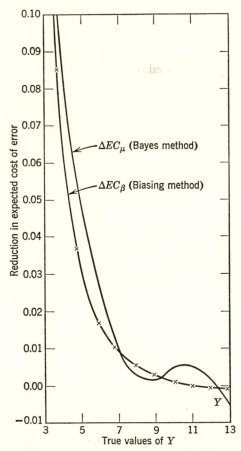

FIGURE 8.2. Reduction of expected cost by biasing and Bayes methods.

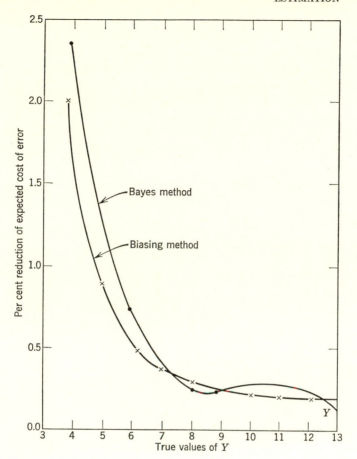

FIGURE 8.3.   Percentage reductions of expected cost of error.

where $L = F + 2K$. The expected cost as a function of Y was then calculated on a computer for the decision functions (50) and (51) as well as for the naïve decision rule (48). Since the computer routine is set up in terms of a biasing function, the decision function (51) was first converted into its equivalent biasing function $\beta(y)$ by the obvious relationship

$$u = \frac{1}{\sqrt{y + \beta(y)}} \tag{52}$$

or

$$\beta(y) = \frac{1}{u^2} - y. \tag{53}$$

The results of the calculations are exhibited in Figures 8.2, 8.3, and 8.4.

The results show that in this particular example the Bayes method gives greater cost reductions (see Figure 8.2), especially in the lower range of Y. It can also utilize additional information about Y, if it is available. For example, if the range of Y were further narrowed down, larger cost reductions could be expected. The biasing method is quite inflexible in this respect. Furthermore, the Bayes method usually requires less computation. Its requirement for knowledge of the distribution of the true value of the parameter, however, may be difficult to satisfy in practice. It should be observed that in this comparison the Bayes method assumed perfect knowledge of the distribution of Y. If this distribution were known with error, as would

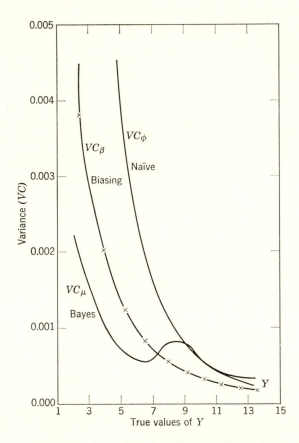

FIGURE 8.4. Variances for three decision rules.

usually be the case, the advantages of the Bayes method would be reduced. Therefore, as the error in our knowledge of $p(Y)$ increases, the relative advantage of the biasing method will also generally increase.

CURVE FITTING

Fitting a curve to a set of data is closely related to the estimation problem. Once the form of a curve (e.g., normal, exponential, or polynomial) has been selected, the remaining task is one of estimating its parameters, to which all we have said about estimation is applicable. The problem of selecting the best form of a curve, however, is another matter. Most of what has been written on curve fitting assumes that the researcher can make a good choice of the type of curve required either on the basis of *a priori* information or by examining a visual plot of the data. This assumption is probably justified for those who have a good vocabulary of functions at their command. The task of picking the *best* form, however, has hardly been discussed, let alone solved. There is no limit to the number of functions which can be fitted to a set of data. There is as yet no way of modeling this choice situation, and hence no way of making an optimal selection. The best we can do is to try different functional forms and compare the resulting distributions of estimating errors. The best form we can select by such a comparative procedure may not be good enough. Therefore, the researcher may have to try a large number of forms before he finds one that is satisfactory.

Fortunately, it has been shown, in many uses of distribution functions, that the resulting distributions of errors are not very sensitive to the form of the distribution function, within a fairly wide range of such types.

CONCLUSION

In this chapter we have considered the various ways of estimating the values of parameters which appear in a decision model and their relative advantages and disadvantages. We showed that the criteria usually applied to evaluating estimating procedures do not necessarily (and in fact seldom) minimize the total expected cost of error. Of the three principal methods of estimation—the analogue, maximum likelihood, and Bayes—only the third directs itself to minimization of the cost of error. Two procedures for obtaining Bayes estimates were provided. Whether the extra computational effort required by Bayes procedures is justified depends on how the cost of such effort compares with the additional expected cost of estimating error resulting from use of other procedures. The Bayes posterior estimator is less complex than the prior estimator, but it requires derivation of an estimator for each different observed value. If the decision model which contains the parameter being estimated is to be used repetitively by a mathematically unsophisticated decision maker, it may be better to provide him with the simpler results of the more complex prior procedure.

We also considered a procedure of producing biased estimates which —although it does not minimize the total expected cost of error—does reduce it, compared with unbiased estimates for every possible value of the parameter, except in the rare case when the cost of error is symmetrical. Unlike the Bayes procedures, it does not require knowledge of the distribution of the true values of the parameter being estimated, but it does use a value of the parameter based on an unbiased estimate of it.

In one case, we saw that the Bayes prior procedure is superior to the biased method, and that both are superior to the unbiased maximum-likelihood estimate. No generalizations are justified by this one case, but the results confirm to what we would expect over a range of problems. Again, it should be noted that the Bayes estimate in this comparison assumed errorless knowledge of the distribution of the parameter being estimated. If this distribution is known with error, the Bayes procedure might have done less well as compared with the biasing and maximum-likelihood methods.

An alternative to the estimating procedures we have described consists of (1) adding the cost of estimating errors to the decision model, (2) using any estimating procedure for which $p(y|Y)$ is known, and (3) solving directly for the optimal value of X, the controlled variable. But even in the case of the toy model, this approach is much more complex mathematically than are the procedures we have considered here.

For any of the estimating procedures we have considered, whether one or more parameters is involved, the conditional probabilities $p(y_i|Y_j)$ play a critical role. It should be kept in mind that these probabilities are a function of the sample design and sample size. Consequently, the estimation problem cannot be effectively considered in isolation. The general problem is to select a sample design, a sample size, and an estimating procedure which minimize the sum of the total expected cost of error and the cost of collecting the data and analyzing them. At present this problem can be approached only iteratively, by "optimizing" the parts of the research process separately, testing their combination, and trying out variations in the design, sample size, and estimating procedure. The time required for such comprehensive optimization is usually prohibitive. The desirability of being able to find such optima in a practical way is so apparent that we can expect significant progress along these lines in the next few years. An effort in this direction involving a simplified type of estimation problem is discussed in the next chapter.

BIBLIOGRAPHY

Chernoff, H., and L. E. Moses, *Elementary Decision Theory*. New York: John Wiley and Sons, 1959.

Deming, W. E., *Some Theory of Sampling*. New York: John Wiley and Sons, 1950.

Fisher, R. A., "On the Mathematical Foundations of Theoretical Statistics," *Philosophical Transactions of the Royal Society*, Ser. A, **222** (1922).

———, "Theory of Statistical Estimation," *Proceedings of the Cambridge Philosophical Society*, **22** (1925).

Gupta, S. K., *A Theory of Adjusting Parameter-Estimates in Decision Models*, Ph.D. thesis in Operations Research, Cleveland, Case Institute of Technology, May 1960.

Hansen, M. H., W. N. Hurwitz, and W. G. Madow, *Sample Survey Methods and Theory*, Vol. 1. New York: John Wiley and Sons, 1953.

Johnson, P. O., *Statistical Methods of Research*. Englewood Cliffs, N. J.: Prentice-Hall, 1949.

Mood, A. L., *Introduction to the Theory of Statistics*. New York: McGraw-Hill Book Co., 1950.

Raiffa, H., and R. Schlaifer, *Applied Statistical Decision Theory*. Boston: Division of Research, Graduate School of Business Administration, Harvard University, 1961.

9

TESTING HYPOTHESES

INTRODUCTION

Testing hypotheses is a special case of estimation in which we are interested in determining which of two (and occasionally three) possible states exist. Where there are only two courses of action (C_1 and C_2) open to the decision maker, he usually groups the possible states into two classes (Y_1 and Y_2) such that, if Y_1 is the true state, C_1 is the best course of action; otherwise C_2 is. Quite frequently the states are described in terms of a single property whose value either is or is not equal to some specified value. The research task is to determine whether Y_1 or Y_2 is the true state. These alternatives are usually formulated as hypotheses; for example, H_0: the true state is Y_1, and H_1: the true state is not Y_1. The fact that only two alternatives are involved simplifies the estimation problem in some respects. This simplification permits us to take the question of sample size (and hence the cost of conducting the test) explicitly into account along with other questions associated with estimation. It is primarily to show how the sample size and the cost of testing can be taken into consideration that this subject, testing hypotheses, is treated separately from estimation.

Tests of hypotheses are useful in selecting the best decision in problem situations that confront either a decision maker for whom the research is done or the researcher himself. On the one hand, some practical problems involve only two possible courses of action.

For example, in inspecting a lot of goods coming off a production line, the choice is either to accept or to reject the lot. In determining whether to acquire a new facility or piece of equipment that is available for purchase, the question is one that requires a "yes" or a "no" answer.

Tests also play an important role in research into problems in which many alternatives are available to the decision maker. In models of such situations the estimates of the relevant variables may not have to be obtained from "scratch;" estimates may be provided by past research or may be deduced from a theory. The problem then is to determine whether or not the "inherited" or theoretically obtained estimate is acceptable. The value given by the theory or past observations is usually called a *hypothetical value.*

Hypothesis testing can be used to determine whether or not the value of a parameter has changed over time, or differs from one set of circumstances to another. This application of hypothesis testing is central in evaluating a model or in controlling its use under changing conditions, which aspects of research are discussed in detail in Chapter 13.

As indicated, such testing also plays a central role in evaluating a theory. A theory is confirmed to the extent that the estimates derived from it are supported by statistical tests, and is disconfirmed to the extent that such confirmation is not obtained.

Hypotheses are not restricted to assertions concerning the value of a parameter. They may also deal with the relevance of a parameter. Experimental design (to be discussed in the next chapter) combined with hypothesis testing provides a test for relevance. The significance of relationships between variables, the fit of a distribution to a set of data, and the randomness or independence of a set of observations may all be tested. Each of these types of test has a significant role to play in the research procedure.

More specifically, among the more commonly used statistical tests are ones which involve hypotheses in which the following types of assertions are made:

(1) The mean or variance of a specified property of a population, or the percentage of population members which have a specified property, is equal to, less than, or greater than some particular number.

(2) The means, variances, or percentages of two different populations are equal, or one is greater than another.

(3) Regression or correlation coefficients, or some other measure of covariation, are equal to zero.

(4) One variable changes or fails to change as another changes.

(5) Two or more qualitative properties (attributes) of elements in a population are independent.

(6) A specified distribution "fits" a set of data.

(7) A set of observations is drawn at random from a single population.

In the discussion that follows, two different conceptual systems are used in discussing tests of hypotheses. The more traditional one is due to Neyman and Pearson (1933) and is generally used today as modified by Wald (1942). This conceptual system is extensively employed in textbooks on statistics. It has considerable computational advantages, but it is a difficult framework within which to make understandable the methodological problems involved in hypothesis testing.

First, we shall take the approach of statistical-decision theory because it exposes more effectively the nature of the underlying methodological problems. However, it does not generally yield practical procedures for selecting a test. Then we will consider the more traditional Neyman-Pearson approach, in which we shall formulate a procedure of testing hypotheses which attempts to approximate optimality.

THE APPROACH OF STATISTICAL-DECISION THEORY TO HYPOTHESIS TESTING

This approach may be formulated as follows.

(1) Let A_1 and A_2 represent the courses of action which are available to the decision maker. Since in this approach we need not classify the possible states into two classes, let Y_1, Y_2, $\cdots$, Y_j, $\cdots$ represent the possible states of nature. There may be an infinity of such states along a continuous scale, but we can consider a finite number of discrete actions and states without loss of generality. However, the procedure to be described can be generalized to the infinite continuous case. Finally, let $V(A_i|Y_j)$ represent the expected value (or loss) to the decision maker of taking course of action A_i, where the true state is Y_j. Now the test situation can be represented by a pay-off matrix such as is shown in Table 9.1.

If the hypothesis-testing situation were to be treated as an uncertainty game against nature, it would be "solved" with only the information provided in a matrix such as is shown in Table 9.1. A minimax, generalized (Hurwicz) minimax, or minimax regret solution

TABLE 9.1. PAY-OFF MATRIX

| Possible Courses of Action | States of Nature | | | |
	Y_1	Y_2	$\cdots$	Y_j	$\cdots$
A_1	$V(A_1|Y_1)$	$V(A_1|Y_2)$	$\cdots$	$V(A_1|Y_j)$	$\cdots$
A_2	$V(A_2|Y_1)$	$V(A_2|Y_2)$	$\cdots$	$V(A_2|Y_j)$	$\cdots$

could be selected at this point. But if observations are to be made and the resulting information is to be used, a modified approach is required. In this case we would proceed to the next step.

(2) Let y_1, y_2, $\cdots$, y_k, $\cdots$ represent possible estimates of Y (or some other computation) obtained from a sample of observations, and $p(y_k|Y_j)$ represent the conditional probability of obtaining an estimate of y_k when Y_j is the true value of Y. These conditional probabilities are usually obtained from the theory of sampling and estimation employed and (in most cases) knowledge or an estimate of one or more parameters of the population from which the sample is drawn. We will subsequently consider in detail how they are obtained. It should be noted here, however, that the conditional probabilities depend on the sample size and estimating procedure, both of which must be selected by the researcher.

The conditional probabilities can be displayed in a tabular form such as is shown in Table 9.2.

TABLE 9.2. CONDITIONAL PROBABILITIES

| Possible Estimates | States of Nature | | | |
	Y_1	Y_2	$\cdots$	Y_j	$\cdots$
y_1	$p(y_1|Y_1)$	$p(y_1|Y_2)$	$\cdots$	$p(y_1|Y_j)$	$\cdots$
y_2	$p(y_2|Y_1)$	$p(y_2|Y_2)$	$\cdots$	$p(y_2|Y_j)$	$\cdots$
$\cdot$	$\cdot$	$\cdot$	$\cdot$	$\cdot$	$\cdot$
$\cdot$	$\cdot$	$\cdot$	$\cdot$	$\cdot$	$\cdot$
y_k	$p(y_k|Y_1)$	$p(y_k|Y_2)$	$\cdots$	$p(y_k|Y_j)$	$\cdots$
$\cdot$	$\cdot$	$\cdot$	$\cdot$	$\cdot$	$\cdot$
$\cdot$	$\cdot$	$\cdot$	$\cdot$	$\cdot$	$\cdot$
Sum	$\sum(y_k|Y_1) = 1$	$\sum p(y_k|Y_2) = 1$		$\sum p(y_k|Y_2) = 1$	

TABLE 9.3.   POSSIBLE STRATEGIES

Possible Estimates	Possible Strategies				
	S_1	S_2	$\cdots$	S_h	$\cdots$
y_1	A_1	A_1	$\cdots$	A_1	$\cdots$
y_2	A_1	A_1	$\cdots$	A_2	$\cdots$
.	.	.		.	
.	.	.	$\cdots$	.	$\cdots$
.	.	.		.	
y_k	A_1	A_2	$\cdots$	A_2	$\cdots$
.	.	.		.	
.	.	.	$\cdots$	.	$\cdots$
.	.	.		.	

Since the set $\{y_k\}$ exhaust all the possibilities, the sum of the probabilities in each column must equal 1.

(3) Let S_1, S_2, $\cdots$, S_h, $\cdots$ represent the possible *strategies* available to the researcher. A strategy is a rule which dictates the course of action to be taken in the event of each possible estimate. These possible strategies are displayed in Table 9.3.

If, for example, only three estimates (y_1, y_2, and y_3) are possible, there would be eight possible strategies. These are shown in Table 9.4.

Clearly, if there are x possible estimates, there are 2^x possible strategies, which we shall designate as m.

(4) Now we want to determine the probability that each course of action will be selected in each strategy for each possible true value of Y_j; that is, $p(A_i|S_h, Y_j)$. These probabilities are computed by obtaining the courses of action associated with S_h from Table 9.3; then the probabilities $p(A_i|Y_j)$ are obtained from Table 9.2 and added for each course of action. These computations yield a table of the type

TABLE 9.4.   POSSIBLE STRATEGIES FOR THREE POSSIBLE ESTIMATES

	S_1	S_2	S_3	S_4	S_5	S_6	S_7	S_8
y_1	A_1	A_1	A_1	A_2	A_1	A_2	A_2	A_2
y_2	A_1	A_1	A_2	A_1	A_2	A_1	A_2	A_2
y_3	A_1	A_2	A_1	A_1	A_2	A_2	A_1	A_2

TABLE 9.5.   ACTION PROBABILITIES

	S_1		S_2		S_3		S_4		S_5		S_6		S_7		S_8	
	A_1	A_2	A_1	A_2	A_1	A_2	A_1	A_2	A_1	A_2	A_1	A_2	A_1	A_2	A_1	A_2
Y_1 Y_2 . . . Y_j . . .																

shown in Table 9.5. For example, using the example in Table 9.4, the action probability associated with S_2, A_1, Y_1 is $p(y_1|Y_1) + p(y_2|Y_2)$ and, with S_2, A_2, Y_1, it is $p(y_3|Y_1)$.

(5) Now for each combination (S_h, Y_j) the expected value, given Y_j, is computed; that is,

$$V(S_h, Y_j) = \Sigma p(A_i|S_h, Y_j)V(A_i|Y_j). \qquad (1)$$

This yields values which can be displayed as in Table 9.6.

TABLE 9.6.   VALUES ASSOCIATED WITH RESEARCHER'S STRATEGIES

	S_1	S_2	$\cdots$	S_h	$\cdots$
Y_1 Y_2 . . . Y_j . . .				$V(S_h, Y_j)$	

Table 9.6 is a revised pay-off matrix in which *expected* gains or losses are shown. In Table 9.1 the pay-offs were simply gains or losses. If the probabilities of each Y_j occurring are known —that is, $p(Y_j)$— then the expected value of each strategy can be determined:

$$EV(S_h) = \sum_j p(Y_j)V(S_h, Y_j). \tag{2}$$

One could then select the strategy which maximizes expected value (or minimizes expected cost). If the $p(Y_j)$ are assumed to be unknown, we again have an uncertainty game against nature, and such criteria as minimax, the generalized minimax, and minimax regret can be applied.

It is also possible to select "mixed" strategies; that is, a selection of each of a set of simple strategies according to some specified probabilities. In any particular case the number of possible mixed strategies is unlimited, since the number of mixes of probabilities is unlimited. In practice, however, it is usually possible, for reasons considered below, to reduce the number of strategies which should be considered.

As indicated, if on the basis of previously available (*a priori*) information the probabilities of occurrence of possible states, $p(Y_j)$, can be estimated, that selection of a strategy can be made which maximizes the expected value. That is, for each S_h and Y_j we can compute $\sum_j p(Y_j)V(S_h, Y_j)$, which is the expected value of S_h, and select that S_h for which this value is maximum. If observations are made, the *a priori* probabilities can be adjusted to obtain *a posteriori* probabilities on the basis of which the expected values are adjusted. These procedures, as one would expect from the discussion of estimation procedures, are referred to as *Bayes strategies*.

Even if the probabilities $p(Y_j)$ are not known, it is clear that we should, if possible, consider only strategies which maximize expected value for some set of possible values of $p(Y_j)$. These may be called *admissible* strategies.* In some (relatively few) cases it is possible to identify all the admissible strategies and hence restrict attention to them.

Both the selection of admissible strategies and the calculation of *a posteriori* probabilities are illustrated in a very simple example of

---

* As Wagner (1957) points out, "In mathematical statistics there is a fine distinction between the classes of admissible strategies and Bayes strategies; further, in special games no admissible strategies may exist" (p. 8 fn). This fine distinction and limitation are not critical in this discussion.

TABLE 9.7. STATISTICIAN'S LOSSES

	States of Nature	
Possible Actions	$Y_1 = 10$ defects per 100 items	$Y_2 = 20$ defects per 100 items
A_1	0	\$20
A_2	\$10	0

this approach given by Wagner (1957, pp. 13–17) which is reproduced here with modification of only the symbols employed.

Small lots of a complex assembly item are to be subjected to an acceptance sampling procedure. It is known from experience that the number of defects per item occurs according to a Poisson probability distribution; and for the sake of simplicity, it is postulated here that Nature "produces" lots after selecting a Poisson distribution with an average of either 10 or 20 defects per 100 items.* In the former case, the lots are acceptable, and in the latter case unacceptable. [Table 9.7] contains the statistician's pay-off matrix. In this example, instead of representing losses as negative numbers employed in a maximizing operation, they are treated as positive numbers, and strategies which minimize loss are to be investigated. It is *assumed* that these monetary outcomes are good approximations to the statistician's ["values"].

The minimax strategy for the statistician, if he does no sampling, is to select A_1 with probability ⅓ and A_2 with probability ⅔. The expected value of the outcome, \$6.66, is then independent of Nature's strategy. If the *a priori* probability $p(Y_1) = $ ¾ and $p(Y_2) = $ ¼, then A_1 is the optimal [minimax expected loss] action, giving an expected value of \$5.00.

Although the size of a sample is a variable which should be subject to economic analysis in a proposed statistical procedure, assume that for various reasons only two items drawn randomly out of the lot are to be inspected. The sample observations will be classified into three categories: $y_1 = 0$ defect, $y_2 = 1$ defect, $y_3 = 2$ or more defects (if two defects are found in either or both items, inspection ceases). The conditional probabilities for y_k are shown in Table 9.8.†

There are 2 possible actions and 3 possible observations; hence $2^3 = 8$ simple strategies exist, Table 9.9. Strategy S_4, for example, specified selecting action A_1 if y_1 occurs, and A_2 otherwise. If Y_1 is the true state of na-

* We utilize the distinction employed in quality control of defect vs. defective. The latter is defined in terms of the particular number of allowable defects per items.

† If the number of defects in 100 items has a Poisson distribution with an average q, then it is postulated that the number of defects in two items is distributed as a Poisson with an average $2q/100$.

TABLE 9.8.   CONDITIONAL PROBABILITIES

Possible Observations	States of Nature Y_1	Y_2
$y_1 = 0$ defect in 2 items	0.82	0.67
$y_2 = 1$ defect in 2 items	0.16	0.27
$y_3 = 2$ or more defects in 2 items	0.02	0.06

TABLE 9.9.   SIMPLE STRATEGIES

Strategies

Observations	S_1	S_2	S_3	S_4	S_5	S_6	S_7	S_8
y_1	A_1	A_1	A_1	A_1	A_2	A_2	A_2	A_2
y_2	A_1	A_1	A_2	A_2	A_1	A_1	A_2	A_2
y_3	A_1	A_2	A_1	A_2	A_1	A_2	A_1	A_2

TABLE 9.10.   ACTION PROBABILITIES FOR SIMPLE STRATEGIES

Strategies

States of Nature	S_1		S_2		S_3		S_4		S_5		S_6		S_7		S_8	
	A_1	A_2	A_1	A_2	A_1	A_2	A_1	A_2	A_1	A_2	A_1	A_2	A_1	A_2	A_1	A_2
Y_1	1.00	0	0.98	0.02	0.84	0.16	0.82	0.18	0.18	0.82	0.16	0.84	0.02	0.98	0	1.00
Y_2	1.00	0	0.94	0.06	0.73	0.27	0.67	0.33	0.33	0.67	0.27	0.73	0.06	0.94	0	1.00

ture, then y_1 occurs with probability .82, and consequently action A_1 is taken with probability .82. Table 9.10 gives the action probabilities for each strategy.*

Finally Table 9.11 combines the previous matrices to give the expected or

* The mathematician states that each strategy defines a "mapping" from the sample space to the action space.

TABLE 9.11. AVERAGE ECONOMIC EVALUATION IN DOLLARS

States of Nature	S_1	S_2	S_3	S_4	S_5	S_6	S_7	S_8
Y_1	0	0.20	1.60	1.80	8.20	8.40	9.80	10.00
Y_2	20.00	18.80	14.60	13.40	6.60	5.40	1.20	0

average losses for each of the strategies. A first glance at Table 9.11 does not reveal which strategies, if any, are inadmissible; a graphical analysis aids in the process, Figure 9.1. The expected losses are plotted as two coordinate points with reference to axes for Y_1 and Y_2. The bottom boundary, which is the lowest convex-to-the-origin boundary defined by strategy points, has the admissible strategies as vertices: S_1, S_2, S_4, S_8.*

* An alternative delineation of admissible strategies may be found in J. D. Williams (1954, pp. 71–72).

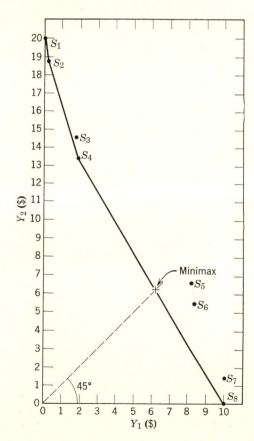

FIGURE 9.1. Display of strategies.

The minimax strategy, found at the intersection of the bottom boundary and a 45° line through the origin, is to select S_4 with probability .46 and S_8 with probability .54. Given *a priori* probabilities, the corresponding Bayes strategy is found either by applying the probabilities to Table 9.11 or by finding at which of the admissible strategies it is possible to construct *tangent* line with slope $-p(Y_2)/p(Y_1)$. If $p(Y_1) = \frac{3}{4}$ and $p(Y_2) = \frac{1}{4}$, S_1 is the optimal strategy.

If a minimax procedure is to be employed, it has been stated that the expected loss without any data is $6.66; with data, the minimax expected loss becomes $6.26. Therefore, it does not pay to take a sample of 2 items unless the sampling cost is less than $.40.* In the case of $p(Y_1) = \frac{3}{4}$ and $p(Y_2) = \frac{1}{4}$, without data the expected loss is $5.00, and with data is $4.70. Hence with this *a priori* information it pays to inspect two items only if the cost of observation is less than $.30. Such considerations are at the heart of selecting a single-stage sample size or a sequential sampling procedure.†

The use of *a posteriori* probabilities to arrive at a procedure identical to the admissible strategy defined in Table 9.11 is illustrated with $p(Y_1) = \frac{3}{4}$ and $p(Y_2) = \frac{1}{4}$, for which S_4 is optimal.

If y_1 is observed [the *a posteriori* probability],
$$p'(Y_1) = \frac{\frac{3}{4} \times 0.82}{\frac{3}{4} \times 0.82 + \frac{1}{4} \times 0.67} = 0.79, \, p'(Y_2) = 0.21; \text{upon applying } p'(Y_1)$$
and $p'(Y_2)$ to Table 9.7, A_1 is found optimal.

If y_2 is observed,
$$p'(Y_1) = \frac{\frac{3}{4} \times 0.16}{\frac{3}{4} \times 0.16 + \frac{1}{4} \times 0.27} = 0.64, \, p'(Y_2) = 0.36, \text{ and } A_2 \text{ is optimal.}$$

If y_3 is observed,
$$p'(Y_1) = \frac{\frac{3}{4} \times 0.02}{\frac{3}{4} \times 0.02 + \frac{1}{4} \times 0.06} = 0.50, \, p'(Y_2) = 0.50. \text{ and } A_2 \text{ is optimal.}$$

On Using a Bayes Strategy

Before turning to the Neyman-Pearson framework it is important to observe that the use of Bayes strategies for testing problems is extremely rare. Even enthusiasts for such strategies assert that they are cumbersome to apply. In addition, they "involve the giving of explicit loss functions, and still more restrictively, require the existence and knowledge of the *a priori* probability" [Chernoff and Moses (1959, p. 274)].

* This statement must be qualified if there is some value in collecting data, say, for making a future estimate of the *a priori* probabilities.

† As the reader may verify, increasing the sample size has the effect of lowering the boundary line in Figure 9.1 toward the origin. But the marginal value of successive observations varies with the form of the probability distribution, the sample size, and the *a priori* probabilities. Hence, depending on the aforementioned considerations and data-processing costs, it may, for example, pay to make two observations where it would not be economical to make one.

Although these strategies are cumbersome to apply, some simplification is possible, as we shall try to show by use of the Neyman-Pearson framework. In a later section we shall also show how the loss functions can be generated from a decision model (following a procedure already discussed in Chapter 8). In connection with the difficulty that is said to be associated with the *a priori* probability, it is useful to recall the discussion of Chapter 2 regarding uncertainty games. It was argued there that a pay-off matrix such as is shown in Table 9.7 cannot be formulated without using or obtaining some knowledge of the probabilities associated with the various possible values of Y; that is, $p(Y)$. This fact is hidden in many statistical-decision theoretic discussions of estimation and hypothesis testing because the data are usually taken as given. Few have inquired, as has Churchman (1961), into what information is needed or assumed in the data-collection process.

For example, consider the following selection from the Wagner quotation given in the last section:

> It is postulated here that Nature "produces" lots after selecting a Poisson distribution with an average of either 10 (Y_1) or 20 (Y_2) defects per 100 items.

How could one ever justify such an assumption without having or assuming knowledge about $p(Y)$? We are back in the black and white ball problem discussed in Chapter 2. That is, how can we determine that a bowl contains only black and white balls without being able to learn something about the percentage of each? To be more specific, the hypothesis being tested makes an assertion about the value of Y; for example, that it is Y_1. The basis for this assertion is either theory or past observations, either of which can be used to estimate the probability-density function of Y.

Some knowledge or assumptions about the *a priori* probabilities are always present in formulating a testing problem. We will consider how this knowledge can be used in the discussion that follows, in which we will use the Neyman-Pearson framework, but the problem of testing will be formulated in a way that is equivalent to that just presented. The discussion will, however, make more explicit the manner in which determination of sample size affects outcome.

THE NEYMAN-PEARSON APPROACH TO TESTING PROBLEMS

The basic logic of the Neyman-Pearson approach to the testing problem is revealed in the way the statistical problem is formulated.

Using common sense, we might ask, for example, "Is the true mean (μ) of a population equal to a?" But in this approach we ask, "If the true mean of the population is equal to a, then how likely are we to obtain a given set of observations?" If it is very likely that we would get the specified set of observations, we may accept the hypothesis, $\mu = a$; otherwise we would reject it. Thus the task of statistical analysis requires determining the probability of obtaining any given set of observations, assuming a specific hypothesis to be true; that is, of determining the $p(y_i|Y_j)$. The ability to make such determinations has been assumed in previous discussions; now we will see how it is done.

Suppose that we are testing the hypothesis that $\mu = 100$ and obtain an unbiased estimate of the mean equal to 101.2. The task, then, is to determine the probability of getting such an estimate if the true mean is equal to 100. To answer this we must know the probability-density function (PDF) of the estimated means. If we know or can make good estimates of the values of μ and σ of the PDF of the element values, we can determine the PDF of the estimated means. If the values of the elements are normally distributed, then the estimated means are also. (Where the PDF of the element values is not normal, the PDF of the estimated means tends toward normality as the size of the sample from which the estimates are made increases.) The mean of the PDF of the estimated means is also μ. The variance of the estimated mean ($\sigma_{\bar{x}}^2$), however, is reduced. That is, if σ is the standard deviation of the population's distribution,

$$\sigma_{\bar{x}}^2 = \frac{\sigma^2}{n}, \tag{3}$$

where $\bar{x}$ is computed from a simple random sample (of size n) with replacement, or, when drawn without replacement,

$$\sigma_{\bar{x}}^2 = \frac{N - n}{N - 1} \frac{\sigma^2}{n}, \tag{4}$$

where N is the number of elements in the population. Thus the estimates become less variable as the sample size increases, a fact we considered in Chapter 7.

If $\bar{x}$ has a normal distribution, the probability that it exceeds any specified number k is given by

$$p(\bar{x} > k) = \int_k^\infty \frac{\sqrt{n}}{\sigma\sqrt{2\pi}} e^{-n(\bar{x}-\mu)^2/2\sigma^2} \, d\bar{x} = \int_k^\infty f_n(\bar{x}, \mu, \sigma_{\bar{x}}) \, d\bar{x}. \tag{5}$$

In testing the ("null") hypothesis, $H_0: \mu = a$, for a population whose variance, σ^2, is known, the usual procedure is as follows. First, a random sample of n items is drawn from the population, and the sample mean, $\bar{x}$, is computed. Let us say that $\bar{x} = b$. The deviation of b from a is converted into standard units, z_b:

$$z_b = \frac{b - a}{\sigma_{\bar{x}}}. \tag{6}$$

If $b > a$, then $z_b > 0$; if $b < a$, then $z_b < 0$; and if $b = a$, then $z_b = 0$. Where $\mu = a$, the probability, $p(\bar{x} > b)$, is given by equation (5). Tables of the normal curve give this probability if entered with the value of z_b.

One can also similarly determine the value of $p(\bar{x} < b)$. If we let $c = |b - a|$, we can obtain the probability that $\bar{x}$ will deviate from a by more than c in either direction; it is

$$p(\bar{x} < a - c) + p(\bar{x} > a + c) = \int_{-\infty}^{a-c} f_n(\bar{x}, \mu, \sigma_{\bar{x}}) \, d\bar{x}$$
$$+ \int_{a+c}^{\infty} f_n(\bar{x}, \mu, \sigma_{\bar{x}}) \, d\bar{x}. \tag{7}$$

Are we in a position yet to accept or reject the hypothesis, $H_0: \mu = a$? Not quite. How small should be the probability that $\bar{x}$ deviates from a by the amount that it does, assuming $\mu = a$, before we reject the hypothesis? This is one of the methodological problems to which we want to address ourselves.

The minimum probability for which a hypothesis is accepted is called the *significance level* of the test and is symbolized by α. The value of α is conventionally taken to be 0.05 or 0.01, but this choice generally has no rational basis. It is such a basis that we seek here.

First let us see precisely what α means. If we test $H_0: \mu = a$ at a significance level α, then we would reject H_0 *when it is true* with a probability equal to α because of deviations of the estimate from a in α proportion of such estimates.

In testing the hypothesis, $H_0: \mu = a$, with a specified α, there are two ways we can proceed: with a *one-sided* or a *two-sided* test. One-sided tests are shown in Figures 9.2 (a) and 9.2 (b), and the two-sided test is shown in Figure 9.2 (c).

For any significance level, α, there is a point on the abscissa, x_α, which is z_α standard units away from a, such that the area on one side of x_α is equal to α and on the other is equal to $1 - \alpha$. Let x_α^+ represent $x_\alpha > a$, and x_α^- represents $x_\alpha < a$. Then

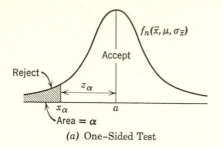

(a) One–Sided Test

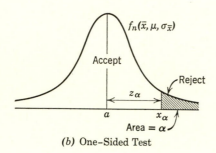

(b) One–Sided Test

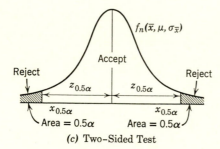

(c) Two–Sided Test

FIGURE 9.2. One- and two-sided tests of H_0: $\mu = a$, assuming $\mu = a$.

$$\int_{x_\alpha^+}^{\infty} f_n(\bar{x}, \mu, \sigma_{\bar{x}}) \, d\bar{x} = \alpha \tag{8}$$

and

$$\int_{-\infty}^{x_\alpha^-} f_n(\bar{x}, \mu, \sigma_{\bar{x}}) \, d\bar{x} = \alpha. \tag{9}$$

In the two-sided test we use $z_{0.5\alpha}$.

That we are inclined to reject a hypothesis when a rare event (i.e., rare if the hypothesis is true) occurs is illustrated by the following coin-tossing example. Even if the probability of getting a head on a toss of a coin is ½, we have some probability of getting 100 consecutive heads. But if we did get this number of consecutive heads we would be more likely to suspect the coin than conclude that we have observed a very rare event. One obvious question is, why not make α as small as possible so that there is practically no probability of rejecting the hypothesis when it is true? The answer lies in the fact that another type of error can be made when testing a hypothesis and that this second type increases as the first decreases.

The error of rejecting a hypothesis when it is true is called a type I error, and its probability is equal to α. A type II error consists of accepting a hypothesis when it is false. As we shall see, there is no simple measure of the probability of this type of error occurring because it depends on what the true value of μ is. If we are testing the hypothesis $H_0 : \mu = 100$, where $\sigma = 10$, we may be quite likely to accept this hypothesis when μ is actually 101, but very unlikely to do so when $\mu = 200$. Furthermore, the probability of making any particular type II error decreases as the sample size increases.

Now suppose that we are conducting a two-sided test of the hypothesis $H_0 : \mu = a$ when μ is actually equal to b $(b \neq a)$. This situation is represented in Figure 9.3. The unshaded area in this figure is equal to β, the probability of accepting $H_0 : \mu = a$ when $\mu = b$, and the shaded area is equal to $1 - \beta$. To determine the value of β under these conditions we must first determine the values of z_β^- and z_β^+.

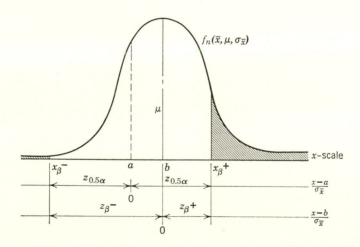

FIGURE 9.3. Testing $H_0 : \mu = a$ when $\mu = b$, $b > a$.

These are given by

$$z_\beta{}^+ = \frac{\dfrac{z_{0.5\alpha}\sigma}{\sqrt{n}} + a - b}{\sigma/\sqrt{n}} \tag{10}$$

$$z_\beta{}^- = \frac{b - a + \dfrac{z_{0.5\alpha}\sigma}{\sqrt{n}}}{\sigma/\sqrt{n}}. \tag{11}$$

By the use of tables of the normal curve we can now find β, the probability of getting an observation $\bar{x}$ which falls between $z_\beta{}^-$ and $z_\beta{}^+$; that is,

$$\beta = p\left(z_\beta{}^- < \frac{\bar{x} - a}{\sigma_{\bar{x}}} < z_\beta{}^+\right). \tag{12}$$

Put another way, since

$$x_\beta{}^- = z_\beta{}^-\sigma_{\bar{x}} + a \tag{13}$$

and

$$x_\beta{}^+ = z_\beta{}^+\sigma_{\bar{x}} + a, \tag{14}$$

then, when $\mu = b$,

$$p(x_\beta{}^- < \bar{x} < x_\beta{}^+) = \int_{x_\beta{}^-}^{x_\beta{}^+} f_n(\bar{x}, \mu, \sigma_{\bar{x}})\, d\bar{x}. \tag{15}$$

Hence

$$p\left(z_\beta{}^- < \frac{\bar{x} - a}{\sigma_{\bar{x}}} < z_\beta{}^+\right) = p(x_\beta{}^- < \bar{x} < x_\beta{}^+). \tag{16}$$

Now let b (in $\bar{x} = b$) be a variable. Then we can express the deviation of a from b in units of the population's standard deviation, σ. Let λ represent this amount. That is,

$$\lambda = \frac{b - a}{\sigma}. \tag{17}$$

Now, if we let λ vary, by use of equation (15) we can obtain a function which describes the type II error. This is called the *power function* of the testing procedure. The plot of this function yields what are called *operating characteristic* (*OC*) *curves* of the testing procedure. A set of such curves for the test we have described is shown in Figure 9.4. Since the curves are symmetrical, only one side is shown.

From an examination of the OC curves as well as the power function it is apparent that the probability of making any particular type II error decreases as the sample size and the significance level increase.

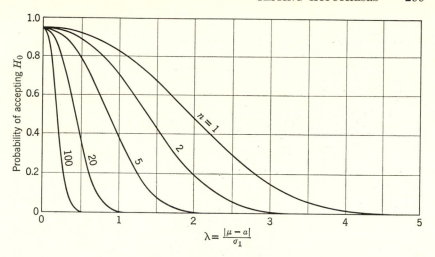

FIGURE 9.4. Operating characteristic curves of the two-sided normal z-test.

The Methodological Problems Involved in Hypothesis Testing

Now we can restate in the Neyman-Pearson framework the nature of the methodological problem involved in testing a hypothesis. The researcher must make three decisions: the sample size (n) and the testing procedure to be used, and the significance level (α) at which the test is to be performed. Ideally these decisions should be made in such a way as to minimize the sum of the following costs:

(1) C_n: the cost of making the observations.
(2) C_a: the cost of the analysis (performing the test).
(3) $E(C_\mathrm{I})$:   the expected cost of type I error.
(4) $E(C_\mathrm{II})$:   the expected cost of type II error.

Expected Cost of Type I Error

In order to determine the cost of a type I error we must know what action is taken if the hypothesis being tested is rejected and what are the consequences of this rejection. For example, suppose that the hypothesis being tested makes an assertion about the average value of a property of items made in lots in a factory. A sample of items from each lot is observed. If the hypothesis, $H_0 : \mu = a$, is accepted, the lot is shipped to a customer; otherwise it is destroyed. The cost of destroying an acceptable lot, C_{I}, can usually be determined without much difficulty. Then the expected cost of a type I error is given by

$$E(C_{\mathrm{I}}) = \alpha C_{\mathrm{I}}. \qquad (18)$$

If, when a lot is rejected, a hundred per cent sample is taken (i.e., a complete count), then—assuming no observational error—the lot would eventually be accepted if $\mu = a$. Here C_{I} is the cost of taking the additional $(N - n)$ observations.

The expected cost of a type I error may be more complex. Suppose, for example, that if a lot is rejected the action taken depends on the value of the estimated mean, $\bar{x}$, and that the cost of error is a function of $\bar{x}$; that is,

$$C_{\mathrm{I}} = \phi(\bar{x}). \qquad (19)$$

Then the expected cost of error for a two-sided test would be

$$E(C_{\mathrm{I}}) = \int_{-\infty}^{x_{0.5\alpha}^{-}} \phi(\bar{x}) f_n(\bar{x}, \mu, \sigma_{\bar{x}}) \, d\bar{x} + \int_{x_{0.5\alpha}^{+}}^{\infty} \phi(\bar{x}) f_n(\bar{x}, \mu, \sigma_{\bar{x}}) \, d\bar{x}. \qquad (20)$$

The corresponding values of $E(C_{\mathrm{I}})$ for one-sided tests are obvious.

Consider the following variation of the simple decision model we have been using illustratively:

$$V = X\bar{Y} + \frac{1}{X}. \qquad (21)$$

Suppose that we are testing the hypothesis, $H_0 : \bar{Y} = a$. We obtain our estimates of $\bar{Y}$, $\bar{y}$, where $\bar{y} = a + \Delta a$. If the hypothesis is rejected, suppose that we substitute for $\bar{Y}$ the value of $\bar{y}$ on the basis of which the rejection occurred. Then from previous analysis (p. 242) we know that

$$C_{\mathrm{I}} = \frac{\bar{Y}}{\sqrt{\bar{y}}} + \sqrt{\bar{y}} - 2\sqrt{\bar{Y}} \qquad (22)$$

and, therefore, the expected cost of error for the two-sided test would be

$$E(C_{\mathrm{I}}) = \int_{-\infty}^{y_{0.5\alpha}^{-}} \left(\frac{\bar{Y}}{\sqrt{\bar{y}}} + \sqrt{\bar{y}} - 2\sqrt{\bar{Y}} \right) f_n(\bar{y}, \bar{Y}, \sigma_{\bar{y}}) \, d\bar{y}$$

$$+ \int_{y_{0.5\alpha}^{+}}^{\infty} \left(\frac{\bar{Y}}{\sqrt{\bar{y}}} + \sqrt{\bar{y}} - 2\sqrt{\bar{Y}} \right) f_n(\bar{y}, \bar{Y}, \sigma_{\bar{y}}) \, d\bar{y}. \qquad (23)$$

Computation of the expected cost of a type I error is, perhaps, most complicated under the following conditions. If each time the decision rule is used, the hypothesis, $H_0 : \mu = a$, is retested, then $E(C_I)$ as given in (21) can be used. If, however, after $\bar{y}$ has been substituted for $\bar{Y}$, we then test the hypothesis, $H_0 : \bar{Y} = \bar{y}$, a much more complex situation arises. We shall consider this situation in Chapter 13 in the discussion of model controls.

Expected Cost of Type II Error

Where we test a hypothesis concerning the value of a parameter, $\bar{Y}$, in a decision model, we can determine for each possible true value of $\bar{Y}$, $a + \Delta a$, the cost of accepting the hypothesis, $H_0 : \bar{Y} = a$. The procedure can be illustrated by use of the decision model

$$V = X\bar{Y} + \frac{1}{X}.$$

If $\bar{Y} = a + \Delta a$ and we use this correct value for $\bar{Y}$, we get

$$X_o = \frac{1}{\sqrt{a + \Delta a}} \tag{24}$$

and

$$V_o = 2\sqrt{a + \Delta a}. \tag{25}$$

If we use $\bar{Y} = a$ when $\bar{Y} = a + \Delta a$, we get

$$x_o = \frac{1}{\sqrt{a}} \tag{26}$$

and

$$v_o = \frac{a + \Delta a}{\sqrt{a}} + \sqrt{a}. \tag{27}$$

Then the cost of a type II error is given by

$$C_{II} = v_o - V_o = \frac{a + \Delta a}{\sqrt{a}} + \sqrt{a} - 2\sqrt{a + \Delta a}. \tag{28}$$

In order to determine the expected cost of type II errors it is necessary to know the probability-density function of Δa, $p(\Delta a)$. Since $\bar{Y} = a + \Delta a$ and a is a constant, this requirement is equivalent to a knowledge of the probability-density function of $\bar{Y}$, $p(\bar{Y})$. If $p(\Delta a)$ were known, the expected cost of type II error would be

$$E(C_{II}) = \int_{-\infty}^{\infty} \left(\frac{a + \Delta a}{\sqrt{a}} + \sqrt{a} - 2\sqrt{a + \Delta a} \right) p(\Delta a) \, d\Delta a. \tag{29}$$

A testing procedure which for any specified n and α yielded a lower probability of making any type II error than any other test would necessarily minimize $E(C_{II})$. This can be asserted even if $p(\Delta a)$ is not known. Such testing procedures are available for most commonly tested types of hypotheses under commonly made assumptions; they are called *uniformly most powerful* (or UMP) tests.

At first glance the existence of such tests might seem to preclude the necessity of test selection. Unfortunately this is not the case because "less powerful" tests may cost less to use and hence may reduce C_a, the cost of analysis, more than they increase $E(C_{II})$. Therefore, without knowing $E(C_{II})$ a complete comparison of alternative testing procedures cannot be made. The difference in C_a between most tests, however, is usually quite small, and hence very little loss if any will be incurred if the UMP test, or the most powerful test available, is used.

For a given testing procedure one must still select the sample size n and the significance level α and these will effect $E(C_{II})$; hence either this cost must be determined or some nonoptimizing alternative procedure found. In some cases past history of the parameter may yield the required *a priori* probability-density function, $p(\Delta a)$; for example, when $\overline{Y}$ is the average daily demand for a product per specified time period (such as a month).

The Optimizing Problem

For any specified testing procedure the total expected cost (TEC) consists of the sum of four cost components previously identified:

$$TEC = C_n + C_a + E(C_I) + E(C_{II}).$$

C_n was discussed and expanded in Chapter 7. $E(C_I)$ and $E(C_{II})$ have been discussed and expanded in this chapter. Then, if the PDF of Y is known, in principle the optimizing values of n and α can be found for any particular test. (Note that this procedure does not provide an explicit formulation of all possible tests, as does the formulation in statistical-decision theory.) If a set of alternative tests is specified, the one that has the least minimum TEC can be selected.

In practice the computations required for such a selection procedure would generally be too difficult and lengthy. Consequently, some simplifications are very desirable. We will consider two simplified procedures which involve (sub)optimizing relative to $C_n + E(C_I)$ and satisficing relative to $E(C_{II})$. C_a is assumed to be too small to be of concern.

Some Suboptimizing Test-Design Procedures

If one can assume that the cost of analysis, C_a, is a small component of the total cost of conducting a test, as it usually is, then if a uniformly most powerful test is available, it must be the best test. We will make this assumption here.

In the first procedure that we will consider we will also assume that a *critical* type II error can be identified and the maximum acceptable probability of making this error can be specified. From this information, the conditional probability of making the critical error can be determined. Once this point of the OC curve is fixed, we need only find the sample size and significance level which minimize the sum of the cost of sampling and the expected cost of type I error. In this procedure the expected cost of type II error is not taken into account explicitly.

The second procedure that we will consider is a slight modification of the first. Here again the critical type II error must be defined, but in this case we require the maximum acceptable probability of making the critical *or a larger* type II error. The conditional probability of making the critical type II error is then derived, and we proceed as in the first case.

Both these procedures require some *a priori* information about the PDF of Y, the parameter whose value is being tested. But the information required is considerably less than complete knowledge of the distribution. In the first procedure it is necessary only to know, estimate, or assume the probability that Y is equal to the value Y' at the critical type II error; that is, $p(Y = Y')$. In the second procedure it is necessary to know, estimate, or assume $p(Y \geqq Y')$.

In order to facilitate the description of the first procedure we assume that we are testing the hypothesis, $H_0 : \overline{Y} = a = 25$, where $\overline{Y}$ appears in the decision model

$$V = X\overline{Y} + \frac{1}{X}.$$

Then we proceed as follows:

(1) *Find the "critical" or "satisficing" value (Y') which is that possible true value of $\overline{Y}$ that is closest to a (on either side of it) for which the decision maker virtually never wants to accept the hypothesis H_0.*

We will refer to the acceptance of H_0 when $\overline{Y} = Y'$ as the "critical type II error."

For example, suppose that for financial reasons the decision maker does not want actual costs to exceed estimated costs by more than 22 per cent. If the researcher assumes $\overline{Y} = 25$ and this is the case, then his correct estimate of the total cost is

$$V_o = 2\sqrt{\overline{Y}} = 2\sqrt{25} = 10.$$

If actual total costs were 22 per cent higher, they would be 1.22 (10) or 12.2. To find the true value of $\overline{Y}$, Y', relative to which the use of $\overline{Y} = 25$ yields a total cost of 12.2, we solve

$$V = 12.2 = \frac{Y'}{\sqrt{25}} + \sqrt{25}$$
$$Y' = 36.$$

(2) *Obtain an estimate of the maximum acceptable probability of making the critical type II error* (Y') *and derive the value of β for Y'.*

The probability of making the critical type II error is

$$p(H_0) = p(Y = Y')\beta. \tag{30}$$

Hence

$$\beta = \frac{p(H_0)}{p(Y = Y')}. \tag{31}$$

Therefore, if the decision maker can supply an estimate of $p(H_0)$ and if $p(Y = Y')$ can be established *a priori*, then the critical value of β at Y' can be established. For example, if $p(H_0)$ is set at 0.005 and $p(Y = Y')$ is known, estimated, or assumed to be 0.500, then $\beta = 0.005/0.500 = 0.01$.

Since it is usually desirable to show the decision maker the consequences of his estimate of $p(H_0)$, it is worth selecting a sample of values of β around its critical value and using them in a way (to be described below) that reveals these consequences. In this case we will use the following values of β: 0.001, 0.005, 0.010, 0.050, 0.100, and 0.200.

(3) *Select the uniformly most powerful test of H_0.*

In the illustration, since $\overline{Y}$ is an average value, if σ is known (as we assume it to be here), we would use the one-sided z-test, since $Y' > a$ (36 > 25). (If σ were not known we would use the t-test.) With the z-test we would reject H_0 if

$$\frac{\bar{y} - a}{\sigma/\sqrt{n}} > z_\alpha,$$

where $\bar{y}$ is the estimate of $\overline{Y}$ based on a sample of n observations, and z_α is the normal deviate corresponding to the significance level α. If we assume in the example that $\sigma = 11$, then we would reject H_0 if

$$\frac{\bar{y} - 25}{11/\sqrt{n}} = \frac{\sqrt{n}(\bar{y} - 25)}{11} > z_\alpha.$$

(4) *Select several possible significance levels and determine for each the number of observations required to obtain each test value of β.*

To do this, the OC curves or the power function must be used. In the example, we would use the power function for the one-sided z-test. We would solve for n, using the following equation derived from the power function:

$$n = \left[\frac{\sigma(|z_\alpha| + |z_\beta|)}{Y' - a} \right]^2, \tag{32}$$

where z_β is the normal deviate corresponding to probability, β.

For test values of α we select 0.001, 0.005, 0.010, 0.025, 0.050, and 0.100. Then, since $a = 25$, $Y' = 36$, and $\sigma = 11$, we can prepare Table 9.12 showing the minimal sample size required for each combination of values of α and β. Since n must be an integer, the numbers shown in Table 9.12 are rounded off to the next higher integer.

TABLE 9.12.   VALUES OF n FOR SELECTED VALUES OF α AND β

α	z_α \ z_β	β 0.001 / 3.090	0.005 / 2.576	0.010 / 2.326	0.050 / 1.645	0.100 / 1.282	0.200 / 0.842
0.001	3.090	39	33	30	23	20	16
0.005	2.576	33	27	25	18	15	12
0.010	2.326	30	25	22	16	14	11
0.025	1.960	26	21	19	13	11	8
0.050	1.645	23	18	16	11	9	7
0.100	1.282	20	15	14	9	7	5

TABLE 9.13. EXPECTED COST OF TYPE I ERROR, $E(C_I)$

α	C_I	$E(C_I) = \alpha C_I$
0.001	2	0.002
0.005	2	0.010
0.010	2	0.020
0.025	2	0.050
0.050	2	0.100
0.100	2	0.200
0.200	2	0.400

(5) *For each significance level determine the expected cost of the type I error.*

To make this determination, it is necessary to know what action will be taken if H_0 is rejected. Suppose, in our example, that in such a case a new estimate of $\overline{Y}$ is prepared using a complete count of the y's. Then, if we assume that no observational errors are made, the error will be detected and the only additional cost is for preparing the second estimate. Assume that this cost is equal to 2.

This cost, as our earlier discussion indicated, may be much more difficult to determine. We will consider a complex case in Chapter 13.

Now we can prepare Table 9.13.

(6) *Determine the cost of observation* (C_n) *for each combination of test values of α and β.*

Let us assume that

$$C_n = C_1 + nC_2,$$ (33)

TABLE 9.14. COST OF OBSERVATIONS, C_n

α \ β	0.001	0.005	0.010	0.050	0.100	0.200
0.001	0.245	0.215	0.200	0.165	0.150	0.130
0.005	0.215	0.185	0.175	0.140	0.125	0.110
0.010	0.200	0.175	0.160	0.130	0.120	0.105
0.025	0.180	0.155	0.145	0.115	0.105	0.090
0.050	0.165	0.140	0.130	0.105	0.095	0.085
0.100	0.130	0.125	0.105	0.085	0.075	0.065

TABLE 9.15. $E(C_{\mathrm{I}}) + C_n$

α \ β	0.001	0.005	0.010	0.050	0.100	0.200
0.001	0.247	0.217	0.202	0.167	0.152	0.132
0.005	0.225	*0.195*	0.185	*0.150*	*0.135*	*0.120*
0.010	*0.220*	*0.195*	*0.180*	*0.150*	0.140	0.125
0.025	0.230	0.205	0.195	0.165	0.155	0.140
0.050	0.265	0.240	0.230	0.205	0.195	0.185
0.100	0.330	0.325	0.305	0.285	0.275	0.265

where C_1 is the fixed cost of preparing the sample, and C_2 is the cost per observation.   Assume specifically that $C_1 = 0.050$ and $C_2 = 0.005$. Then we can prepare Table 9.14, using the values of n from Table 9.12.

(7) *For each test value of β select that test value of α which yields the minimum sum of* $\mathrm{E}(C_{\mathrm{I}})$ *and* C_n, *and plot these against the test values of β.*

Combining Tables 9.13 and 9.14, we prepare Table 9.15.

For the critical value of β, 0.010 in the illustrative problem, we find from Table 9.15 that α should be 0.010 and from Table 9.12 that n should be 22 to minimize $C_n + E(C_{\mathrm{I}})$.   Similarly, a best combination of α and n can be determined for each value of β.   These points are plotted, and a curve drawn through them in Figure 9.5.   We can also show for each value of β that value of $p(H_0)$ for which the indicated β would have been selected.

A graph such as is shown in Figure 9.5 may assist the decision maker in checking his original estimate because he may better understand the consequences of his estimate when confronted with such a figure.   (It should be noted that Figure 9.5 is much like the efficiency function discussed in Chapter 2.)

The second procedure is a slight variation of the one just described, but the kind of probability estimate required of the decision maker and the researcher may be easier to obtain.   The computations required, however, are more complex.

The decision maker now provides an estimate of the maximum acceptable probability of making a type II error equal to or greater than the critical one, $p'(H_0)$.   The researcher must then obtain an estimate of $p(Y \geqq Y')$.   By adapting equation (12) we know that in a one-sided test

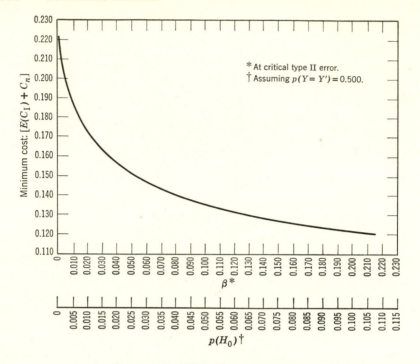

FIGURE 9.5. Minimal costs versus β.

$$\beta = \int_{-\infty}^{\overline{Y}_\beta^+} f_n(\bar{y}, \overline{Y} = Y', \sigma_{\bar{y}}) \, d\bar{y}. \tag{34}$$

Therefore

$$\frac{p'(H_0)}{p(Y \geq Y')} = \int_{\overline{Y} = Y'}^{\infty} \int_{-\infty}^{\overline{Y}_\beta^+} f_n(\bar{y}, \overline{Y} = Y', \sigma_{\bar{y}}) \, d\bar{y} \, d\overline{Y}. \tag{35}$$

Then the value of β is found for which this equation holds. How difficult this is depends on the PDF of $\bar{y}$. If necessary, approximations can be used.

CONCLUSION

The discussion of sampling, estimation, and hypothesis testing emphasizes the central role of mathematical statistics in modern research. To many researchers, however, mathematical statistics is a mystery, analysis of which they avoid by following "conventional" procedures. As long as this is the case, inference itself is a mystery to them, no matter how knowing they may appear to be.

After one has struggled to an understanding of the methodological problems involved in statistical tests of hypotheses and after one realizes how difficult even approximately optimal solutions are to obtain, he may sympathize with the practice of using conventional testing procedures without evaluating them. Yet long- (if not short-) run progress in science depends on our ability to improve these inferential procedures. We cannot evaluate conventional procedures unless we compare them in specific problems with optimal or approximately optimal procedures.

It is important to realize that the detailed analysis we have gone through here did not raise a single question that is not implicitly involved in conventional testing. It has been shown how a decision model can be used to obtain estimates of the costs of errors involved in testing, and how a decision model of the testing procedure itself may be constructed. In pure science one can seldom do other than assume relevant cost functions, but these assumptions should be made explicit so that they are open for future investigation.

Computational complexity is perhaps the major obstacle to optimization of testing procedures. Consequently future progress depends on developing better computational techniques and faster computers particularly well suited for complex integration. An alternative that should be pursued simultaneously is the development of quick but efficient approximation techniques.

Tests of hypotheses play a particularly important role in experimentation, which we consider in the next chapter, and in testing and controlling the model, which we consider in Chapter 13.

BIBLIOGRAPHY

Blackwell, D., and M. A. Girshick, *Theory of Games and Statistical Decisions*. New York: John Wiley and Sons, 1954.

Chernoff, H., and L. E. Moses, *Elementary Decision Theory*. New York: John Wiley and Sons, 1959.

Churchman, C. W., *Theory of Experimental Inference*. New York: The Macmillan Co., 1948.

——, *Prediction and Optimal Decision*. Englewood Cliffs, N. J.: Prentice-Hall, 1961.

Cramér, Harold, *Mathematical Methods of Statistics*. Princeton, N. J.: Princeton University Press, 1945.

Dixon, W. S., and F. J. Massey, Jr., *Introduction to Statistical Analysis*. New York: McGraw-Hill Book Co., 1951.

Duncan, A. J., "The Economic Design of $\bar{x}$ Charts Used to Maintain Current Control of a Process," *Journal of the American Statistical Association,* **51** (1956), 228–242.

Ferris, C. D., F. E. Grubbs, and C. L. Weaver, "Operating Characteristics for the Common Tests of Significance," *Annals of Mathematical Statistics,* **17** (1946), 178–197.

Hoel, P. G., *Introduction to Mathematical Statistics.* New York: John Wiley and Sons, 2nd ed., 1954.

Luce, R. D., and H. Raiffa, *Games and Decisions.* New York: John Wiley and Sons, 1957.

Mood, A. M., *Introduction to the Theory of Statistics.* New York: McGraw-Hill Book Co., 1950.

Mosteller, Frederick, "On Some Useful 'Inefficient' Statistics," *Annals of Mathematical Statistics,* **17** (1946), 377–408.

Neyman, Jerzy, and E. S. Pearson, "On the Problem of the Most Efficient Tests of Statistical Hypotheses," *Philosophical Transactions of the Royal Society,* Ser. A, **231** (1933), 289–337.

Raiffa, H., and R. Schlaifer, *Applied Statistical Decision Theory.* Boston: Division of Research, Graduate School of Business Administration, Harvard University, 1961.

Savage, L. J., *The Foundations of Statistics.* New York: John Wiley and Sons, 1954.

Snedecor, G. W., *Statistical Methods.* Ames: Iowa State College Press, 4th ed., 1946.

Wagner, H. M., "Statistical Decision Theory as a Guide to Information Processing," The RAND Corp., p-1160, Aug. 26, 1957.

Wald, Abraham, "Contributions to the Theory of Statistical Estimation and Testing Hypotheses," *Annals of Mathematical Statistics,* **10** (1939), 299–326.

———, "On the Principles of Statistical Inference." *Notre Dame Mathematical Lectures,* No. 1, Notre Dame, Ind.: University of Notre Dame, 1942.

———, "Statistical Decision Functions Which Minimize the Maximum Risk," *Annals of Mathematics,* **46** (1945), 265–280.

———, "Foundations of a General Theory of Sequential Decision Functions," *Econometrica,* **15** (1947), 279–313.

———, "Statistical Decision Functions," *Annals of Mathematical Statistics,* **20** (1949), 165–205.

Wilcoxon, Frank, *Some Rapid Approximate Statistical Procedures.* Stamford, Conn.: Stamford Research Laboratories, American Cyanamid Co., rev. ed., 1949.

Williams, J. D., *The Compleat Strategyst.* New York: McGraw-Hill Book Co., 1954.

10

EXPERIMENTATION
AND CORRELATION

INTRODUCTION

In the last five chapters we have considered those aspects of research which are concerned with evaluating the parameters appearing in a model. It was implicitly assumed throughout this discussion that the parameters considered were relevant. In this chapter we consider establishing or checking their relevance.

Models can fail to represent phenomena adequately because they either contain irrelevant parameters or do not contain relevant ones. A relevant parameter is a variable or constant which has a significant effect (probabilistically or deterministically) on the outcome variable.

When the researcher deals with a relatively simple phenomenon, his own analysis of it may reveal what variables and constants affect the outcome. For example, in analyzing the amount of savings a man has in the bank one can identify as relevant (a) the amounts deposited, (b) the time of the deposits, (c) the amounts withdrawn, (d) the time of the withdrawals, and (e) the interest rate and the way it is applied. If the relevance of the variables is not as obvious as it is in this example, experimentation can be used to check it.

On the other hand, if the research involves a complex phenomenon which has been extensively studied in the past, the researcher may "inherit" knowledge of its structure. Nevertheless, he may want to check it by experimentation. If, however, the structure is unknown and too complex for analysis by inspection, the researcher may have to use experimentation to determine which of a set of variables are relevant. Therefore, experimentation has two purposes: (*a*) to test the relationships asserted in a model once it is set up, and (*b*) to explore some possibilities before setting up a model.

The discussion of models in Chapter 4 showed that we should seek decision models which contain controlled variables by the manipulation of which the decision maker can affect the outcome of his problem. The model should also contain the uncontrolled variables which affect the outcome. It should assert the causal connections between these variables and the outcome. If analysis of the situation reveals these variables, as in the savings example, a model can be constructed without experimentation. If not, regression and correlation analysis can be used to provide a sort of "candidate" variables, and experimentation can be used to determine whether they affect the outcome, and how.

It will be recalled from Chapter 1 that, in order to establish one variable as the cause or producer of another, we must determine whether one is necessary and/or sufficient for the other. The conditions for establishing necessity and sufficiency were discussed in a general way in Chapter 1. Now we consider them in more detail.

MILL'S CANONS OF INDUCTION

The first systematic effort to specify the conditions under which, and operations by which, one thing, A, can be said to be the cause of another, P, was made by J. S. Mill (1862). He set down five "canons of induction," the first three of which were concerned with establishing one thing as the cause of another. We shall reformulate these rules in our own language.

The Method of Agreement

Let A, B, and C represent a set of conditions or properties which describe a state, and A', B', and C' represent the absence of these conditions. Let P represent some specified phenomena. Then, according to Mill, if

(*a*) P occurs under conditions A, B, and C, and
(*b*) P occurs under conditions A, B', and C',

then A is the cause of P. On the basis of these tests, however, one could not say that A is sufficient for P.

First, it is necessary to know that A, B, and C completely describe the state. Otherwise there may be another condition, D, which is present in both tests and which causes P, rather than A. Thus we require an exhaustive listing of every possible cause of P. In practice it is hard to conceive of a situation in which such a list can be provided.

Second, assume that A, B, and C exhaust all possible state conditions. The two tests (a) and (b) are not sufficient to establish sufficiency even under these conditions. Consider the following example. Let A, B, and C represent milk, bread, and butter, and P be an allergic reaction, say hives. Then, if hives follow a meal of the three and also follow a meal of only milk, in the environment involved, milk would appear to be sufficient for hives, if hives always followed milk. Yet we would not want to call milk a cause of hives unless we knew that hives would not occur unless milk were taken. If hives occurred even if no food were eaten, then clearly milk would not be the cause of hives; or if hives followed any food but did not occur if nothing were eaten, we would call food, not milk, the cause of the hives.

To assert that A is sufficient for P can be interpreted to mean "A, by itself is enough to assure P." But generally we mean something stronger: "A will be followed by P under any set of conditions." Mill's test does not establish sufficiency in this sense even if A, B, and C exhaust the conditions. To establish sufficiency in this sense we would first have to run the following tests with the indicated results:

A, B, C, followed by P
A, B', C followed by P
A, B, C' followed by P
A, B', C' followed by P.

That is, we would have to observe A in every combination of B and C and their absence. We would also have to observe at least one instance in which A' is not followed by P. We must do this in order to establish that P does not occur under any conditions. If it did, the concept of sufficiency would have no significance relative to it.

Finally, the tests assume that conditions A, B, and C are two-valued in the sense that they are either present or absent. This is not always the case. Suppose, for example, that we want to determine whether temperature affects the length of a metal bar. We cannot remove temperature; we can only change it. That is, even the tests we have specified are not adequate where quantitative variables are involved.

The Method of Difference

If A, B, and C are followed by P, and A', B, and C are *not* followed by P, then, according to Mill, A can be said to cause P.

Here the test is designed to determine whether A is *necessary* for the occurrence of P. The test does not accomplish its purpose, for essentially the same reasons that the first method fails. Again we would have to know that A, B, and C exhaust all possible conditions, since the occurrence and nonoccurrence of P may be due to the presence of D in the first instance and its absence in the second. The test also assumes that A can be removed completely. Finally, in order to determine whether A is completely necessary even if B and C completely specify the state, we would have to show that under *any* conditions in which A does not occur, P does not occur. That is

$$A, B, C \text{ followed by } P$$
$$A', B, C \text{ not followed by } P$$
$$A', B', C \text{ not followed by } P$$
$$A', B, C' \text{ not followed by } P$$
$$A', B', C' \text{ not followed by } P.$$

The Joint Method

This combines the first two methods into the following tests:

$$A, B, C \text{ followed by } P$$
$$A, B', C' \text{ followed by } P$$
$$A', B, C \text{ not followed by } P.$$

This is supposed to establish A as a necessary *and* sufficient condition for P. It fails to do so for the reasons already cited. If we now combine the two sets that we (not Mill) said were required, we would get

$$A, B, C \text{ followed by } P$$
$$A, B', C \text{ followed by } P$$
$$A, B, C' \text{ followed by } P$$
$$A, B', C' \text{ followed by } P$$
$$A', B, C \text{ not followed by } P$$
$$A', B', C \text{ not followed by } P$$
$$A', B, C' \text{ not followed by } P$$
$$A', B', C' \text{ not followed by } P.$$

In general, it can be shown that, if n conditions are involved, then 2^n tests would be necessary to establish this strong relationship.

When these tests are displayed as we have done, an important observation can be made. If we want to determine whether B or C is a necessary and/or sufficient condition for P, no additional tests are required, since we have B and B' in all possible combinations of A and C, and C and C' in all possible combinations of A and B. That is, if such testing did establish that A is or is not a cause of P, it would do the same for B and C. This observation, that we can answer many causal questions simultaneously, played a key role in the development of modern experimental design, which we will discuss below.

Collecting our other comments, we can also observe that an adequate testing procedure should

(1) acknowledge the incompleteness of any listing of conditions and account for the undesignated (and hence uncontrolled) conditions, and

(2) allow for quantitative variables as well as qualitative ones.

Satisfaction of the first of these conditions, as we shall see, makes for statistically designed experiments rather than the deterministic ones of Mill. The importance of Mill's contribution, however, should not be minimized because we "know better" today. He made a very important step toward the development of a methodology of experimental design. The contemporary concept of experimentation, to which we now turn, is largely due to R. A. Fisher (1948 and 1949).

MODERN EXPERIMENTATION—THE ANALYSIS OF VARIANCE

In Mill's canons each condition or variable was considered to be two valued: present or absent. But now let us consider two controlled variables A and B, and an outcome variable V, which may have more than two values. They may be temperature and atmospheric pressure or height and age. Suppose that the scales on which these variables are measured are divided into three intervals: a_1, a_2, a_3, and b_1, b_2, b_3. Then we can show all possible combinations of these variable intervals in tabular form. Table 10.1 shows nine possible situations. In general, if A's scale were divided into m intervals and B's into n intervals, there would be mn possible situations.

Let A_1 be the average of the V-values in row a_1, and similarly for A_2, and A_3. Correspondingly, let B_1, B_2, and B_3 be the average of the V-values in each column. Each column average represents a set

TABLE 10.1

	b_1	b_2	b_3
a_1			
a_2			
a_3			

of observations taken under the same conditions; then (under some assumptions which are discussed below) the differences between column averages must be due to the difference in column values. Let $\sigma_c{}^2$ represent the variance of the column averages and $\sigma_r{}^2$ the variance of the row averages. Let $\sigma_T{}^2$ represent the total variance between the nine observations. If the column variable and the row variable were the only two variables which affect V, then the total variance would simply be equal to the sum of the variances due to these two variables; that is,

$$\sigma_T{}^2 = \sigma_r{}^2 + \sigma_c{}^2. \tag{1}$$

But if there are other variables contributing to the variance, then

$$\sigma_T{}^2 > \sigma_r{}^2 + \sigma_c{}^2. \tag{2}$$

Then $\sigma_T{}^2 - (\sigma_r{}^2 + \sigma_c{}^2)$ is the variance due to uncontrolled variables. Let $\sigma_R{}^2$ represent this "residual" or "chance" variance. If the variance due to the row or column variables is no larger than that due to the uncontrolled variables (under assumptions to be listed below), then the variations in V accompanying changes in A and B are no larger than one would expect by "chance." Hence, the effect of the controlled variables is not significant. If these variances are larger than the residual variance, then the effect of these variables is significant.

The variances to which we have been referring are never known but are estimated on the basis of a sample of possible observations in each cell. On the basis of these estimates we can test the two hypotheses:

$$\sigma_c{}^2 > \sigma_R{}^2$$

$$\sigma_r{}^2 > \sigma_R{}^2.$$

This *analysis of variance* is based on the distribution of estimated variances about true variances of normal populations: the F-distribution.

The three assumptions of this procedure can be stated as follows:

(1) Any observation can be considered to be the sum of four components: (*a*) a constant component which is not affected by the column or row variables; (*b*) a component due to the possible influence of the column variable; (*c*) a component due to the possible influence of the row variable; and (*d*) a component due to the residual variables.

(2) The observations are all drawn from normal populations with the same variances.

(3) The residual effects are independent and normally distributed with zero mean (i.e., in the long run the negative and positive effects cancel out) and with the same variance for all observations.

The effects of deviations from these assumptions have been studied extensively by statisticians with the general result of showing that they are not as restrictive as they might appear. For discussion of this problem see Cochran (1947) and Eisenhart (1947).

Acceptance of the hypotheses, $\sigma_c^2 > \sigma_R^2$, does not by itself establish the column variable as a producer of changes in the phenomenon, V. At best, it does so only if the changes in values of the column variable precede those in V; similarly, for the row variable.

Replication and Interaction

Now suppose that in each of the nine cells in the illustrative experimental design two or more observations are taken; that is, *replications* are made. Then another variance is involved; the *within-cell variance*. This variance is due to variations in the uncontrolled (residual) variables. Let this within-cell variance be σ_w^2. We may find now that

$$\sigma_T^2 > \sigma_c^2 + \sigma_r^2 + \sigma_w^2. \tag{3}$$

The remaining variance ($\sigma_T^2 - \sigma_c^2 - \sigma_r^2 - \sigma_w^2$) must be due to something we have not yet considered. It is due to the *interaction* of the row and column variables. Two variables interact if the effect which one has on the dependent phenomena depends on the value of the other. For example, temperature and atmospheric pressure interact relative to the boiling point of water.

It is clear, then, that the residual variance, estimated where only one observation is made per cell, may contain variance due to interactions. But these can be separated only if the variance due to uncontrolled variables can be computed directly from within-cell variance rather than determined as a "remainder."

It should be noted that the classical experimental designs of Mill took no account of interactions. Further, while modern experimental procedures take the uncontrolled variables into account, they do not assume an exhaustive listing of all possible producers of a product. They also take quantitative variables and the statistical character of observations into account.

In order to explore the concept of interaction more completely consider a simple experiment involving two variables—or *factors*, as they are normally called—each at two values or *levels*. The factors are A and B with levels a_1 and a_2, and b_1 and b_2, respectively. Each of the four possible combinations of A-values and B-values is called a treatment. These are a_1b_1, a_2b_1, a_1b_2, and a_2b_2. See Table 10.2. Assume that an equal number of observations, n $(n \geqq 1)$, is made in

TABLE 10.2. SCHEMATIC DISPLAY OF SIMPLE AND MAIN EFFECTS

FACTOR A

Levels	a_1	a_2	Mean	Difference = Simple Effects of A	Mean Difference = Main Effect of A
b_1	1 *	a *	$\dfrac{a+1}{2}$	$a-1$	
					$\dfrac{a-1+ab-b}{2}$
b_2	b *	ab *	$\dfrac{b+ab}{2}$	$ab-b$	
Mean	$\dfrac{b+1}{2}$	$\dfrac{a+ab}{2}$	$\dfrac{a+b+ab+1}{2}$		
Difference = Simple Effects of B	$b-1$	$ab-a$			
Mean Difference = Main Effect of B	$\dfrac{b-1+ab-a}{2}$				

FACTOR B (row label at left)

* Average of observations in this cell.

each cell; that is, for each treatment. Let the means of the observations be represented by 1, *a*, *b*, and *ab*; that is, *a* and *b* represent the second levels, the absence of them represents the first level, and 1 represents the absence of both.

The *simple effects* of a factor are its effects at each level of the other factors. Hence, they are the *differences* of the averages of the observations in the cells differentiated only by levels of the factor whose simple effect is being determined. These are as follows:

$$\text{Simple effect of } A \ (B \text{ at first level}) \quad = a - 1. \tag{4}$$

$$\text{Simple effect of } A \ (B \text{ at second level}) = ab - b. \tag{5}$$

$$\text{Simple effect of } B \ (A \text{ at first level}) \quad = b - 1. \tag{6}$$

$$\text{Simple effect of } B \ (A \text{ at second level}) = ab - a. \tag{7}$$

The *main effect* of a factor is the average of its simple effects:

$$\text{Main effect of } A = \tfrac{1}{2}(a - 1 + ab - b). \tag{8}$$

$$\text{Main effect of } B = \tfrac{1}{2}(b - 1 + ab - a). \tag{9}$$

If the effects of the factors are independent, then the main effect of the factors is the best estimate of their effects because their standard errors are $1/\sqrt{2}$ times the standard error of the simple effects. If the factors are independent, it also follows that the observed differences between their simple effects are due to random (uncontrolled) fluctuations. Consequently to test for independence (and hence interaction) of the factors we test the hypothesis that the difference between simple effects is equal to zero (using the *t*-test). That is, if

$$(ab - b) - (a - 1) = 0, \tag{10}$$

then *A* is independent of *B*. Since the difference between the simple effects of *B* is equal to that of *A*,

$$(ab - a) - (b - 1) = (ab - b) - (a - 1), \tag{11}$$

this also implies that *B* is independent of *A*. If these factors are not independent, then the difference $(ab - a - b + 1)$, usually divided by a numerical factor, is a measure of this *first-order* interaction, *AB*.

Now consider an experiment in which three factors (*A*, *B*, and *C*) are involved, each at two levels. This is represented in Table 10.3(*a*). Tables 10.3(*b*) and 10.3(*c*) show the results for *A-B* combinations at

TABLE 10.3. A THREE-FACTOR TWO-LEVEL EXPERIMENT

Levels	a_1		a_2	
	c_1	c_2	c_1	c_2
b_1	1	c	a	ac
b_2	b	bc	ab	abc

(a) Composite

	a_1	a_2	Difference
b_1	1	a	$a - 1$
b_2	b	ab	$ab - b$
Difference	$b - 1$	$ab - a$	

(b) C at first level

	a_1	a_2	Difference
b_1	c	ac	$ac - c$
b_2	bc	abc	$abc - bc$
Difference	$bc - c$	$abc - ac$	

(c) C at second level

the C_1 and C_2 levels, respectively. It can be seen that the interaction AB (C at first level) is a function of

$$(ab - b) - (a - 1) = ab - b - a + 1 \tag{12}$$

and, the interaction AB (C at second level) is a function of

$$(abc - bc) - (ac - c) = abc - bc - ac + c. \tag{13}$$

The interaction AB is a function of the average of these:

$$\tfrac{1}{2}(abc - bc - ac + c + ab - b - a + 1). \tag{14}$$

By similar algebra it can be shown that the interaction AC is a function of

$$\tfrac{1}{2}(abc - bc + ac - c - ab + b - a + 1) \qquad (15)$$

and the interaction BC is a function of

$$\tfrac{1}{2}(abc + bc - ac - c - ab - b + a + 1). \qquad (16)$$

The interaction of AB with C is a function of

AB (C at second level) $- AB$ (C at first level)

$$= \tfrac{1}{2}(abc - bc - ac + c - ab + b + a - 1). \quad (17)$$

The interactions of AC with B and BC with A are functions of the same expression. This, then, is called the *second-order* interaction, ABC. By extension, higher-order interactions may be obtained when more than three factors are involved.

EXPERIMENTAL DESIGN

Modern experimental techniques allow us to design experiments that effectively serve our objectives. Each of the large variety of experimental designs which are available was created to suit a particular type of experimental situation. We will consider some of the more important of these designs and their relative advantages and disadvantages.

Factorial Designs

All the designs which have been used illustratively up to this point (Tables 10.1, 10.2, and 10.3) are *factorial designs*. In a factorial design observations are made for each possible combination of factor levels. A factorial design involving two factors each at two levels (Table 10.2) is called a 2^2 factorial design since it has 4 cells. Three factors at two levels each (Table 10.3) yield a 2^3 factorial design with 8 cells. The factors need not have equal numbers of levels. If A has 2 levels, B has 3 levels, and C has 4 levels, there will be $2 \times 3 \times 4 = 24$ cells.

Cochran and Cox (1957, pp. 150–151) summarize the advantages of factorial designs as follows:

The advantages of factorial experimentation naturally depend on the purpose of the experiment. We suppose for the present that the purpose is to investigate the effects of each factor over some preassigned range that is covered by the levels of that factor which are used in the experiment. In other words the object is to obtain a broad picture of the effects of the factors rather than to find, say, the combination of the levels of the factors that give a maximum response. One procedure is to conduct separate experiments each of which deals only with a single factor. Another is to include all factors simultaneously by means of a factorial experiment.

If all factors are independent in their effects, the factorial approach will result in a considerable saving of the time and material devoted to the experiments. The saving follows from two facts. First . . . when factors are independent all the simple effects of a factor are equal to its main effect, so that the main effects are the only quantities needed to describe fully the consequences of variations in the factor. Secondly, in a factorial experiment, each main effect is estimated with the same precision as if the whole experiment had been devoted to that factor alone. . . . If there were n factors, all at two levels and all independent, the single factor approach would necessitate n times as much experimental material as a factorial arrangement of equal precision.

Practical considerations may diminish this gain. The experimenter frequently lacks the resources to conduct a large experiment with many treatments, and must proceed with only one or two factors at a time. Further . . . as the number of treatment combinations in an experiment is enlarged, the standard error per unit increases. This standard error is therefore likely to be higher for a large factorial experiment than for a comparable single-factor experiment. This increase in standard error can usually be kept small by the device known as confounding [discussed below]. . . .

The value of factorial experiments when the factors are *not* independent is summarized by Cochran and Cox (1957, p. 151), as follows:

When factors are not independent, the simple effects of a factor vary according to the particular combination of the other factors with which these are produced. In this case the single-factor approach is likely to provide only a number of disconnected pieces of information that cannot easily be put together. In order to conduct an experiment on a single factor A, some decision must be made about the levels of other factors B, C, D, say, that are to be used in the experiment. . . . The experiment reveals the effects of A for this particular combination of B, C, and D, but no information is provided for predicting the effects of A with any other combination of B, C, and D. With a factorial approach, on the other hand, the effects of A are examined for every combination of B, C, and D that is included in the experiment. Thus a great deal of information is accumulated both about the effects of the factors and about their interrelationships.

Latin-Square Designs

If three or more factors are considered to be independent and hence interactions are of no concern, then the factorial design may be modi-

TABLE 10.4. A LATIN-SQUARE DESIGN

	a_1	a_2	a_3
b_1	c_1	c_2	c_3
b_2	c_2	c_3	c_1
b_3	c_3	c_1	c_2

fied so as to require fewer observations in order to obtain estimates of main effects, but at a loss of precision in obtaining these estimates.

Suppose, for example, that we have three factors, A, B, and C, each at three levels. In place of a 3^3 (27-cell) design we can use a 9-cell design such as is shown in Table 10.4. This is called a *Latin square*. In Table 10.4 each cell is defined by 3 values. Each value of C appears exactly once in each column and row. Hence, each value of A is observed under each value of B and C, and the same holds for B and C. That it holds for C is more easily seen by recasting Table 10.4 into its equivalent, which is shown in Table 10.5. Note that although (a_1, b_1, c_3), for example, is not included, (a_1, b_1), (a_1, c_3), and (b_1, c_3) are.

Now averages of the observations obtained for each value of all three variables can be determined, the corresponding variances estimated, and so on. In this type of design (unlike factorial designs) each factor must have the same number of levels.

Greco-Latin squares

We can even go one step further by introducing a fourth variable D with 3 values, d_1, d_2, and d_3. With 9 cells we can still satisfy the requirements of observing each level of each variable for all values of the others. Such a design, the *Greco-Latin square*, is shown in Table 10.6. In this design each value of D also appears exactly once in

TABLE 10.5. A LATIN-SQUARE DESIGN

	b_1	b_2	b_3
c_1	a_1	a_3	a_2
c_2	a_2	a_1	a_3
c_3	a_3	a_2	a_1

TABLE 10.6.   A GRECO-LATIN SQUARE

	b_1	b_2	b_3
a_1	c_1d_1	c_2d_2	c_3d_3
a_2	c_2d_3	c_3d_1	c_1d_2
a_3	c_3d_2	c_1d_3	c_2d_1

each column and row and never appears twice with the same value of C.

The further savings of observations yielded by the Greco-Latin square over the Latin square are paid for by a further loss of precision in the estimates of the main effects of the factors.

The three designs just considered are all directed toward analysis of factor-produced effects. In many cases we are interested in the effects of treatments which consist of combinations of factor levels and not in the effects of the factors taken separately, or the effects of the factors on each other. The next two designs are particularly well suited for study of the effects of combinations of factors.

Completely Randomized Designs

In this type of design the treatments are assigned to the units to be observed at random. For example, suppose that there are four treatments (t_1, t_2, t_3, and t_4), and four replications are desired. Then sixteen units are required. These units are numbered in a random order by use of a table of random numbers; for example,

$$\underbrace{14,\ 11,\ 16,\ 10}_{t_1} \quad \underbrace{7,\ 5,\ 15,\ 2}_{t_2} \quad \underbrace{13,\ 3,\ 8,\ 4}_{t_3} \quad \underbrace{12,\ 9,\ 1,\ 6}_{t_4}.$$

The treatments are applied to the units as indicated and in the order shown.

The advantages of this type of design are:

(1) Any number of treatments can be used, and any number of replications, not necessarily equal for each treatment, can also be used. This makes it possible to utilize all the experiments which can be conducted, even where the number possible is not a multiple of the number of treatments. This is a particularly valuable property in small exploratory experiments.

(2) The statistical analysis of results is easy even if some observations are lost (rejected or missing). The relative loss of information due to lost observations is minimized.

The principal disadvantages of this type of design are:

(1) Since the units receiving the same treatment may be different, a large experimental error may be incurred, but this can be estimated accurately. For this reason, the effectiveness of this design increases with increased homogeneity of the objects or events observed.

(2) Although this type of design is well suited for the laboratory, it may be cumbersome and inefficient to use in the field, where randomized block designs are generally preferable.

Randomized Block Designs

In this design the units to be observed are grouped (as homogeneously as possible) into "blocks." Treatments are then assigned to units in each block at random. For example, suppose that a sample of 5 items is taken from the output of 3 identical machines. Let the units in each of these groups of 5 items be numbered from 1 to 5. These 5 treatments may be assigned by use of random numbers as shown in Table 10.7. If there is a difference between the three groups, and hence the machines, this can also be determined from this design; that is, the replications can be considered as values of a second experimental variable, the machine, and hence, if so considered, this design is equivalent to a factorial design with no replications.

The principal advantage of this type of design is that it generally yields less experimental error than does the completely randomized design. There is no limit to the number of treatments and replications which can be included.

TABLE 10.7. A RANDOMIZED BLOCK DESIGN

Treatment	Replicate 1	2	3
1	5	5	2
2	4	1	3
3	1	3	4
4	3	4	1
5	2	2	5

Cochran and Cox (1957, pp. 106–107) summarize the advantages of this type of design as follows:

1. By means of the grouping, more accurate results are usually obtained than with completely randomized designs.
2. Any number of treatments and any number of replicates may be included. . . .
3. The statistical analysis is straightforward. Mishaps which necessitate the omission of a complete group or of the entire data from one or more treatments do not introduce any complication in the analysis. When data from some individual units are lacking, the "missing-plot" technique developed by Yates enables the available results to be fully utilized. Some extra computational labor is, however, involved, and if the gaps are numerous the design is less convenient in this respect than complete randomization.
4. If the experimental error variance is larger for some treatments than for others, an unbiased error for testing any specific combination of the treatment means can still be obtained.

Confounding

Consider a 2^3 experiment involving three factors, A, B, and C, each at two levels. If this were to be conducted in a randomized block design with three replicates for each treatment, it would appear as shown in Table 10.8. If we are willing to sacrifice accuracy in estimating higher-order interactions, the size of the blocks can be reduced.

The highest-order interaction, ABC, was shown in equation (17) to be a function of

$$abc + a + b + c - ab - ac - bc - 1.$$

Each replicate can now be divided into two blocks with four treatments each, as is shown in Table 10.9. The difference between the

TABLE 10.8.   A 2^3 RANDOMIZED BLOCK DESIGN

Treatments	1	2	3
a			
b			
c			
ab			
ac			
bc			
abc			
1			

TABLE 10.9.   A 2^3 EXPERIMENT WITH *ABC* COMPLETELY CONFOUNDED

Replicate	I		II		III	
Block	1	2	3	4	5	6
	abc	ab	abc	ab	abc	ab
	a	ac	a	ac	a	ac
	b	bc	b	bc	b	bc
	c	1	c	1	c	1

total of blocks 1, 3, and 5 and the total of 2, 4, and 6 provides the basis for estimating the *ABC* interaction, and hence this interaction is said to be *completely confounded* with the blocks. On the other hand, it can be shown that the effects of *A*, *B*, *C*, *AB*, *AC*, and *BC* are independent of block differences and hence are *unconfounded* with blocks and depend only on *within-block* comparisons. The error in estimating the *ABC* effect will generally be larger than in estimating any of the other effects.

It will be recalled that the first-order interactions were functions of the following expressions:

$$AB: abc + c + ab + 1 - bc - ac - b - a$$

$$AC: abc + ac + b + 1 - bc - c - ab - a$$

$$BC: abc + bc + a + 1 - ac - c - ab - b.$$

An experiment can be designed with each of these interactions confounded in one replication. Such a design, with *partial confounding*, is shown in Table 10.10. The interaction *AB* is a function of the difference between blocks 1 and 2, *AC* of the difference between blocks 3 and 4, and *BC* of the difference between blocks 5 and 6. The effects of *A*, *B*, *C*, and *ABC* depend on within-block differences.

TABLE 10.10.   A 2^3 EXPERIMENT WITH *AB*, *AC*, AND *BC* PARTIALLY CONFOUNDED

Replicate	I		II		III	
Block	1	2	3	4	5	6
	abc	bc	abc	bc	abc	ac
	c	ac	ac	c	bc	c
	ab	b	b	ab	a	ab
	1	a	1	a	1	b

[The advantage of confounding] comes from the reduction in the experimental error by the use of a block which is more homogeneous, or which can be subjected to a more uniform technique, than the complete replicate. . . . The disadvantages of confounding consist of (1) the reduction in replication on the confounded treatment comparisons and (2) in some cases, a greater complexity in calculations. . . . No interaction should be *completely* confounded unless there is good reason to believe, either from previous experience or from the nature of the factors to be tested, that the interaction will be negligible. [Cochran and Cox (1957, p. 212)]

There is a wide variety of other confounded designs, of which only one of the more common is presented here.

Split-plot designs

If the units which are assigned randomly to the various levels of one factor (say, a_1, a_2, $\cdots$) can be divided into n parts (called *plots*), then the parts in each unit can be assigned to n levels of a second factor (b_1, b_2, $\cdots$, b_n) at random. For example, where $m = 4$ and $n = 2$, such a design with three replications is shown in Table 10.11. The difference between this and a randomized-block design lies in the fact that in the latter each of the ten combinations of treatments is assigned to each of the ten subplots in a replication completely at random. Here the assignment is more deliberate; the randomness of the assignment is constrained.

If the sub-units are regarded as the experimental units, it is seen that the treatments [a_1, a_2, $\cdots$, a_4] are applied to groups or blocks of two units. Differences among these blocks are confounded with differences among the levels of A; i.e., the main effects of A are confounded. [Cochran and Cox (1957, p. 294)]

As a consequence, in the split-level design the B and AB (interaction) effects can be estimated more precisely than the A effects. The overall-treatment comparison is the same for this design and for randomized block design; therefore it sacrifices precision in estimates of A effects.

. . . the chief practical advantage of the split-plot arrangement is that it enables factors that require relatively large amounts of material and fac-

TABLE 10.11.   EXAMPLE OF A SPLIT-PLOT DESIGN

Replication 1				Replication 2				Replication 3			
a_3	a_1	a_2	a_4	a_1	a_4	a_2	a_3	a_1	a_3	a_2	a_4
b_1	b_2	b_2	b_2	b_1	b_1	b_2	b_2	b_1	b_2	b_2	b_2
b_2	b_1	b_1	b_1	b_2	b_2	b_1	b_1	b_2	b_1	b_1	b_1

tors that require only small amounts to be combined in the same experiment. If the experiment is planned to investigate the first type of factor, so that large amounts of material are going to be used anyway, factors of the second type can often be included at very little extra cost, and some additional information obtained very cheaply. [Cochran and Cox (1957, p. 297)]

Qualitative Variables

Since each variable in an experimental design is broken into classes, even variables which are quantitatively defined are, in a sense, treated qualitatively. Qualitative variables in the usual sense can also be used in experimental designs. For example, A may represent color, and a_1, a_2, $\cdots$, may be red, yellow, and so on. It is necessary to be sure that *different* values of a *well-defined* variable (whether quantitative or qualitative) are used. Suppose that we want to determine whether teachers affect student performance. It would be necessary to test *different* teachers. To assure that the teachers selected are different, the scale(s) along which the difference can be established must be made explicit. In such cases it is common practice to draw a sample of teachers and *assume* that they are different. Sampling cannot assure this difference; hence, the teachers may be alike with respect to the critical variable. If the analysis of variance then showed that there was no "teacher effect," it would not be valid to apply this conclusion to the population of teachers from which the sample is drawn.

It should also be noted that conclusions based on the analysis of variance are applicable only to the range of values of the controlled variables which are used. If, for example, temperature is employed as a controlled variable, and only values between 40° F and 100° F are used, conclusions drawn from an analysis of the results can be applied only to the range of values tested.

For detailed discussions of experimental designs and the analysis of variance see Cochran and Cox (1957), Edwards (1950), Fisher (1948 and 1949), Kempthorne (1952), and Mann (1949).

REGRESSION ANALYSIS

Mill's fifth canon of induction is called the *method of concomitant variations*. It reads as follows:

Whatever phenomenon varies in any manner whenever another phenomenon varies in some particular manner, is either a cause or an effect of that phenomenon, or is connected with it through some fact of causation (1862: III, VIII, Paragraph 6).

Mill's rule is completely qualitative. It was Karl Pearson who provided a measure of the correlation between variables. Correlation analysis is much used and much abused in science. Of those who use it too few understand what a correlation coefficient represents and how it can properly be interpreted.

In order to understand correlation analysis some attention must first be given to regression analysis. Suppose that we are concerned with two variables, X and Y. Situations which are characterized by any specific value of X, x, may also be characterized by a large number of values of Y which are distributed with mean μ_{yx}. Now suppose that the mean values of Y were determined for each value of X. A plot of the means would yield a continuous curve, a *regression curve* of Y on X. If this curve is a straight line, we have a *regression line*.

Let the X-values be represented as deviations from their mean, μ_x; that is, as $(x - \mu_x)$, and let μ_y represent the mean of the distribution means, μ_{yx}. Then a regression line can be described by an equation of the following form:

$$\mu_{yx} = \mu_y + B_{yx}(x - \mu_x),$$

where B_{yx}, the regression coefficient, represents the slope of the line. This is shown schematically in Figure 10.1. Note that the regression line passes through the point (μ_y, μ_x). This follows from the linear-regression equation, since, when $(x - \mu_x) = 0$, $\mu_{yx} = \mu_y$.

If $B > 0$, the line slopes up to the right; if $B < 0$, it slopes down to the right; and if $B = 0$, it is horizontal. In the last case μ_{yx} is independent of X and, hence, X has no effect on Y. From knowledge that $B \neq 0$ we cannot infer that changes in X produce changes in Y; additional information is required which we shall consider below.

In practice we cannot observe all values of X and Y. As a consequence we must select a sample of X-values at which we can observe a sample of Y-values. Then we can estimate μ_y by $\bar{y}$ and μ_x by $\bar{x}$ and B_{yx} by b_{yx}, where

$$b_{yx} = \frac{\Sigma x_i y_i - \dfrac{\Sigma x_i y_i}{n}}{\Sigma x_i{}^2 - \dfrac{(\Sigma x_i)^2}{n}}. \tag{18}$$

The estimated regression line is

$$\bar{y}_x = \bar{y} + b_{yx}(x_i - \bar{x}). \tag{19}$$

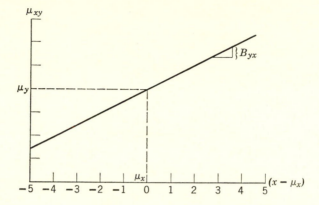

FIGURE 10.1.   Linear regression of Y on X.

The line which is described by this equation has the following important property: the sum of the squared vertical deviations of the observed Y-values from the line $[\Sigma(y_x - \bar{y}_x)]$ is less than the corresponding sum for any other straight line. Hence, it is called a *least-squares fit*.

In practice we do *not know* that the regression is linear, but if it is, equation (19) estimates the line for us. Even if the true regression coefficient is equal to zero $(B_{yx} = 0)$, the estimated coefficient b_{yx} is not likely to be zero because of random fluctuations in the observations. Hence, it is necessary to test the hypothesis H_0: $B_{yx} = 0$, using the estimate and (usually) a t-test.

Two important generalizations of regression analysis should be noted. First, Y-values may be observed in situations described by values of two variables. In such a case a regression *plane* can be derived. Any number of independent variables may be involved; if one or more are, the procedure is called *multiple-regression* analysis.

Second, straight lines need not be assumed. Procedures are available for curvilinear regression as well. [See, for example, Dixon and Massey (1951, pp. 160–162).]

It must be re-emphasized that X cannot be said to produce Y solely on the basis of a statistically significant regression coefficient or a favorable analysis of variance. Even if we know that the condition of precedence is satisfied, a regression equation at best tells us how one variable affects another *if* it affects it, not that if affects it. To establish a causal connection we need to know either that the various X-values occur in situations which are otherwise the same with regard to all other relevant variables (*à la* Mill's method of agreement), or that the other variables are changing in the way assumed in an analysis of variance.

No amount of observation alone can assure us that these conditions are satisfied. Assumptions are always involved in regression analysis and the analysis of variance, and these are part of the experimenter's conception (i.e., model) of the phenomena under study. Strictly speaking, then, cause-effect and producer-product are relationships asserted by a model, not found in data. The observations may lead to acceptance, revision, or complete rejection of the model. But without some kind of model of the situation under study we cannot formulate a relevant experiment or data-collection procedure. Therefore, in order to establish the relevance of variables (i.e., their causal connection with an outcome) we must combine a model of the possible relationship between the variable and outcome with observations. The more carefully designed and controlled the experiment or data collection, the better is the quality of the check.

CORRELATION ANALYSIS

In some instances we are interested in two (or more) variables neither (or none) of which is subject to our control. In a sample of situations in which we have no control over the values of the variables, we can observe the values of both. Since neither of the variables can be controlled, however, the effect of changes in either on the other cannot be determined in that observational context. Let X and Y represent these variables.

The regression of Y on X yields a coefficient B_{yx}. This regression line, it will be recalled, minimizes the sum of the squared vertical deviations (if X is plotted on the abscissa). Similarly the regression of X on Y, and B_{xy}, are theoretically obtainable. This line minimizes the sum of the squared horizontal deviations.

Suppose that X and Y are independent and that their values are normally distributed. Then vertical distances can be expressed as deviations from the mean, μ_y. We know that, if X and Y are independent, a horizontal line through μ_y minimizes the sum of the squared (vertical) deviations of the y's. Correspondingly, the regression of X on Y in this case will be a vertical line drawn through μ_x. The angle between these regression lines is 90°. This is shown in Figure 10.2.

Now consider the other extreme in which X and Y are two ways of characterizing the same property. For example, X may be length in

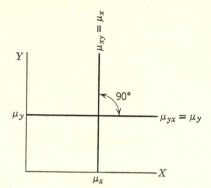

FIGURE 10.2. Linear regression of independent variables.

feet, and Y length in inches. (See Figure 10.3.) All observations will lie on a straight line described by the equation

$$Y = 12X \quad \text{or} \quad X = \tfrac{1}{12}Y.$$

This line minimizes the sum of both the squared vertical and horizontal observations. The angle between the two identical lines is 0°.

The angle between the two regressions can be used to measure the degree of association between values of the two variables. The larger this angle, the less the association; hence it is convenient to use the cosine of the angle, which is 0 for 90° and 1 for 0°. This cosine is called the *correlation coefficient* (ρ), where

$$\rho = \sqrt{B_{yx}B_{xy}}. \tag{20}$$

Then, clearly, if both regression coefficients are zero, as they were in the first case, $\rho = 0$; the variables are uncorrelated. In the second

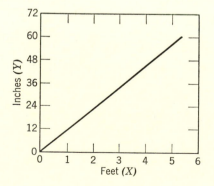

FIGURE 10.3. Regression between equivalent variables.

case, $\beta_{yx} = 12$ and $\beta_{xy} = \frac{1}{12}$. The square root of their product is, of course, 1.

Regression coefficients are negative when the dependent variable decreases as the independent variable increases. If two variables each have negative coefficients relative to the other, then the angle between them is greater than 90° and hence the correlation coefficient is negative. At the extreme the lines overlap on an angle of 180° whose cosine is -1. Thus correlation coefficients vary between -1 and $+1$.

There are several common misuses of correlation against which the researcher should be on guard. First, an estimated correlation coefficient will seldom be zero. This does not necessarily mean that the true coefficient is unlikely to be zero. Consequently, the hypothesis H_0: $\rho = 0$ should always be tested to determine whether or not the correlation estimated from a sample can be considered significant.

Second, correlation analysis presupposes a random sample. When applied to data collected in another way, it may not provide a basis for inferences to the population.

Finally, a significant correlation between variables does not establish either as the producer of the other. If two variables are not correlated, however, we can conclude that they are not causally related. Thus correlation can play an important role in science: the elimination of irrelevant variables.

Correlation has another important use in prediction. The values of one of the two correlated variables may be quite easy to determine, whereas the other may be difficult to determine or else cannot be determined until it is "too late." For example, suppose we know that income and education are positively correlated, and we want to sample a high-income group. If it is difficult to determine income but easy to determine education, we could select a high-education group.

Most economic predictors are based on correlation. In preparing such predictions one must be sure that the variables to be used as a basis of prediction are known *before* the variable to be predicted.

It should also be noted that one is not restricted to two variables in correlation analysis. Any finite number can be treated. Also, the correlations need not be linear; curvilinear procedures are available. For detailed discussion of correlation analysis see Ezekiel and Fox (1959), Johnson (1949), and Kendall (1948).

COMBINING THE ANALYSIS OF VARIANCE
AND REGRESSION ANALYSIS

The analysis of variance and regression analysis can be combined in two different ways. In the first the analysis of variance is applied to data obtained by means of an experimental design in order to determine whether the "experimental variable" has a significant effect on the outcome under study. If it does, the same data can then be subjected to a regression analysis. The following example, taken from Cochran and Cox (1950, pp. 96–97), illustrates this combination of procedures.

A randomized block design involving three replications was used to test the effect of potash (K_2O) on the yield and properties of cotton. Five levels of application were used: 36, 54, 72, 108, and 144 pounds per acre. A single sample of cotton was taken from each plot and four determinations of the breaking strength of fibre were made on each sample. The means of the four observations are shown in Table [10.12].

The analysis of variance indicated that strength of cotton is significantly affected (at the 5 per cent level) by the amount of K_2O per acre. The data also indicate that the strength increases as the amount of K_2O decreases. Consequently a regression analysis of strength on amount of K_2O was performed. It yielded an estimated regression coefficient equal to 0.0050, which is significant at the 1 per cent level. Hence one can conclude that *within the range tested* increased application of K_2O produces a weaker fiber, the strength index declining by (18)(0.0050) or 0.090 for each 18-lb increment in K_2O.

TABLE 10.12. STRENGTH INDEX OF COTTON IN A
RANDOMIZED BLOCK EXPERIMENT

Treatment (pounds K_2O per acre)	Replications			
	1	2	3	Totals
36	7.62	8.00	7.93	23.55
54	8.14	8.15	7.87	24.16
72	7.76	7.73	7.74	23.23
108	7.17	7.57	7.80	22.54
144	7.46	7.68	7.21	22.35
Totals	38.15	39.13	38.55	115.83

The second way of combining regression analysis and the analysis of variance yields an *analysis of covariance*.

THE ANALYSIS OF COVARIANCE

R. A. Fisher is also largely responsible for an important extension of the analysis of variance, the *analysis of covariance*. This procedure is applicable to situations in which a variable affects the observed phenomena but the value of this variable cannot be controlled during the experiment; that is, it cannot be incorporated into the design. For example, suppose that "miles traveled" conditions the performance of automobiles, but that in drawing a sample of automobiles the value of this variable cannot be determined in advance. Then, by the use of the analysis of covariance, the observed performances (V) of the automobiles can be adjusted for the effect of "miles traveled" so that the effect of the controlled variables can be determined.

In some cases the researcher may discover a relevant variable only after the experiment has begun. During the course of the research, for example, it may become apparent that the performances of the cars are affected by how frequently they have been lubricated. If we can determine this frequency, even after the experiment has been conducted, then by use of the analysis of covariance the observed performances can be adjusted for this experimentally uncontrolled source of variation.

The logic of the procedure can be understood by reference to a simple example. Suppose that we want to determine whether values of a property of a phenomenon (V) change when values of a controllable variable A are changed. Suppose that there is another variable, B, which is suspected of having an effect on V, but values of B cannot be controlled by the experimenter. The values of A, however, can be established by the experimenter for each observation. The problem, then, is to cancel out the effect of B on V so that the significance of the independent effect of A on V can be determined.

Assume that A is divided into three intervals: a_1, a_2, and a_3. Assume also that four observations of V are made for each value of a and that the B-value of each observation can be determined at the time of observation. The data obtained may be presented as shown in Table 10.13. These data can be graphed (see Figure 10.4) in such a way as to let the abscissa represent B-values, the ordinate V-values, and the point of origin the average observed B-value, $\bar{B}$, and the average observed V-value, $\bar{V}$.

TABLE 10.13. DATA FOR ANALYSIS OF COVARIANCE

	a_1		a_2		a_3			
	B	V	B	V	B	V		
	2	8	4	10	0	6		
	1	7	3	11	2	5		
	0	7	1	6	4	8	Total	Total
	1	10	4	13	2	5	B	V
Totals	4	32	12	40	8	24	24	96
Means	1	8	3	10	2	6	2	8
							$\bar{B}$	$\bar{V}$

Similar separate plots can be made for the data in columns a_1, a_2, and a_3, as is done in Figure 10.5.

The three plots shown in Figure 10.5 can be superimposed on one another to obtain Figure 10.6. By so doing, the means of each B-column has been superimposed, and similarly for the V-columns. Now the regression line of V on B can be determined for Figures 10.4 and 10.6. The estimated regression coefficient of the former (b_T) is applicable to the observations taken as a whole. The estimated regression coefficient of the latter (b_w) is the within-group regression, since the plot in Figure 10.6 has canceled out between-group variance.

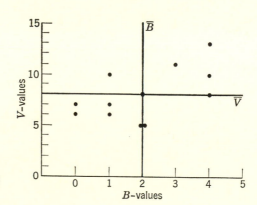

FIGURE 10.4. Plot of all V-values against B-values.

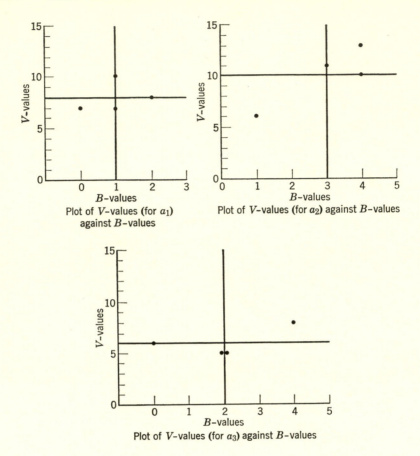

FIGURE 10.5.   Column plots of V-values against B-values.

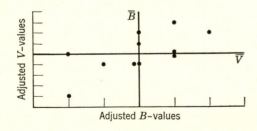

FIGURE 10.6.   Plot of adjusted V-values against adjusted B-values.

If the dispersion about the regression line in Figure 10.6 is significantly less than in Figure 10.4, equating the means of the subgroups had a significant effect on the data. From this it can be inferred that the means of columns a_1, a_2, and a_3 are significantly different in the original data and hence A has an effect on Y. The analysis of variance can be applied to the data, which have been adjusted in the way the data in Figure 10.6 have been. If the change from a_1 to a_2 to a_3 had no effect on V, then equating their means should not effect the dispersion around the regression line.

METHOD OF RESIDUES

The one canon formulated by Mill which has not yet been considered is called the *method of residues*. It reads as follows:

Subduct from any phenomenon such part as is known by previous inductions to be the effect of certain antecedents, and the residue of the phenomenon is the effect of the remaining antecedents (1862, III, VIII, Paragraph 5).

An example of this method occurs in the experiment of Madam Curie in which she discovered radium. She obtained some pitchblende from the mines of Joachimsthal in Czechoslovakia. This ore contained 70 to 75 per cent of black uranium oxide. On examining the ore, she found it to be much more radioactive than other ores of the same uranium content. She came to suspect that the ore contained a radioactive substance other than those with which she was familiar. She eventually removed all the known substances and isolated radium and its effect.

Another example of the method is to be found in the discovery of the planet Pluto. Percival Lowell, after accounting for all the known influences on the planet Uranus, still had an unexplained residual effect on its motion. The existence of another planet was assumed. Its size and location were estimated on the basis of the residual effect to be explained. On January 23, 1930, C. W. Tomaugh discovered the planet Pluto, which satisfied these conditions.

It should be noted that this method presupposes that certain causes and effects are already known, presumably established by other methods. Strictly speaking, this method is a variation of the method of agreement. What we have is a set of "antecedents," say A, B, and C; and a phenomenon consisting of a set of effects, say X, Y, and Z. If C is removed, say Z is also, and similarly for B and Y. Then A

is said to be the cause of X. The presence of the effects Y and Z is really incidental. What we have is

$$ABC \quad \text{followed by } X$$

$$AB'C' \text{ followed by } X,$$

which is the method of agreement. The difference lies in the fact that in the method of agreement the cause is identified in advance, whereas it is "discovered" in the method of residues. Nevertheless, the earlier discussion of the inadequacy of the method of agreement as formulated by Mill is relevant with respect to this method.

CONCLUSION

The relative advantages and disadvantages of different experimental designs generally must be expressed in qualitative terms. Quantitative comparisons between some characteristics of two or more designs can be made in some instances, but the criterion employed is statistical rather than pragmatic (e.g., minimum variance of estimates). Because we cannot yet (1) characterize all the possible experimental designs along quantitative scales and (2) generate cost-of-error functions, comparisons must be made in specific contexts rather than by use of analytic optimizing procedures.

To generate a cost-of-error function for experimentation it is necessary to have a decision model, but it is precisely in order to formulate such a model that experimentation may be required. As yet we have no way of escaping this vicious circularity, as we do in estimation theory. This is not to say that the difficulty may not be overcome eventually.

For the reasons considered, experience remains the best available guide for the selection of experimental designs. This makes the design expert an invaluable asset in conducting any research requiring experimentation.

BIBLIOGRAPHY

Brownlee, K. A., *Industrial Experimentation*. Brooklyn: Chemical Publishing Co., 2nd ed., 1948; London: His Majesty's Stationery Office, 4th ed., 1949.

Churchman, C. W., *Statistical Manual: Methods of Making Experimental Inferences*. Philadelphia: Pittman-Dunn Laboratory, Frankford Arsenal, 1951.

Cochran, W. G., "Some Consequences When the Assumptions for the Analysis of Variance Are Not Satisfied," *Biometrics*, **3** (1947), 22–38.

Cochran, W. G., and G. M. Cox, *Experimental Designs*. New York: John Wiley and Sons, 1st ed., 1950; 2nd ed., 1957.

Dixon, W. J., and F. J. Massey, Jr., *Introduction to Statistical Analysis*. New York: McGraw-Hill Book Co., 1951.

Edwards, A. L., *Experimental Designs in Psychological Research*. New York: Rinehart and Co., 1950.

Eisenhart, Churchill, "The Assumptions Underlying the Analysis of Variance," *Biometrics*, **3** (1947), 1–21.

Ezekiel, M. J. B., and K. A. Fox, *Methods of Correlation and Regression Analysis*. New York: John Wiley and Sons, 3rd ed., 1959.

Fisher, R. A., *Statistical Methods for Research Workers*. London: Oliver and Boyd, 1948.

———, *The Design of Experiments*. London: Oliver and Boyd, 1949.

Johnson, P. O., *Statistical Methods in Research*. Englewood Cliffs, N. J.: Prentice-Hall, 1949.

Kempthorne, Oscar, *The Design and Analysis of Experiments*. New York: John Wiley and Sons, 1952.

Kendall, M. G., *Advanced Theory of Statistics*. London: Chas. Griffin and Co., 1947.

———, *Rank Correlation Methods*. London: Chas. Griffin and Co., 1948.

Mann, H. B., *Analysis and Design of Experiments*. New York: Dover Publications, 1949.

Mill, J. S., *A System of Logic*. Parker, Son, and Bowen, 5th ed., 1862.

Mood, A. M., *Introduction to the Theory of Statistics*. New York: McGraw-Hill Book Co., 1950.

Yates, F., "The Comparative Advantages of Systematic and Randomized Arrangements in the Design of Agricultural and Biological Experiments," *Biometrika*, **30** (1938), 440–466.

11

DERIVING SOLUTIONS
FROM MODELS

INTRODUCTION

The purpose of constructing a model of a problem situation is to enable us to determine what values of the controllable variables (X_i) provide the best measure of performance (V) under conditions described by the parameters (Y_j). Therefore, once we have a model of the form

$$V = f(X_i, Y_j), \tag{1}$$

we want to determine what values of X_i either maximize V (if it is a measure of desirable performance) or minimize it (if it is a measure of undesirable performance). The solution of a problem, then, consists of a set of equations, one for each controllable variable, of the form

$$X_i = g_i(Y_j), \tag{2}$$

where the values of X_i thus specified maximize or minimize V. In this chapter we consider procedures by which optimizing equations of the form shown in (2) can be obtained.

The procedures we will consider are not restricted to problem solving. They can be used also in answering questions involving the maximization or minimization (or, more generally, the evaluation) of any dependent variable which is expressed as a function of a set of one or more independent variables and constants.

Among the procedures we will consider are several which have uses in research other than in deriving solutions from models. At the risk of disrupting the main line of this discussion these other uses will be discussed because they are important.

It should be kept in mind that we are concerned with deriving solutions from models. The value of the solution depends on how adequately the model represents the problem situation; the adequacy of the solution depends on the adequacy of the model. Testing for such adequacy is the subject of Chapter 13.

TYPES OF DERIVATIONS OF SOLUTIONS

Consider the elementary model that was used in Chapters 7 and 8:

$$V = XY + \frac{1}{X}, \tag{3}$$

where $X \geqq 0$. In general, there are two ways of going about solving the model. In the first we proceed deductively, by *analysis*. In the second we proceed inductively; that is, *numerically*. To solve the model analytically we proceed as follows:

$$\frac{dV}{dX} = Y - \frac{1}{X^2} = 0 \tag{4}$$

$$X_0 = \sqrt{\frac{1}{Y}}. \tag{5}$$

Here we have used elementary calculus to find the value of X which minimizes V.* The solution obtained is completely general; it holds for any value of Y. It is also completely abstract, since it did not require knowledge of the value of Y to obtain it.

If we know the value of Y, say 4, then we can obtain the optimal value of X from equation (5), ½. But, if we know that Y is equal to 4, we can obtain the solution by substituting values of X in equation (3) and by trial and error find that one which minimizes V. Graphical techniques may be used to assist in this process. The first procedure, which uses equation (5), consists of a numerical evaluation of a solution that has been obtained analytically. In the second pro-

---

* The conditions which assure this being a minimum (and not a maximum) are satisfied in this case.

cedure, which uses equation (3), the solution itself has been directly obtained in numerical (rather than abstract) form.

In analytic procedures we do not consider any particular set of values of the controllable variables; we proceed directly to the solution. In numerical procedures we try out various values of the controllable variables and select those that yield the best result. For rather obvious reasons analytic procedures are generally preferred where they can be used, but there are many cases where they are either impossible or impractical. In many of these, numerical procedures will yield an exact or approximate solution.

No effort will be made here to survey the large number of mathematical techniques which can be used for deriving solutions from models. Familiarity with their use or availability should be expected of every researcher. Consequently, after a few general remarks about the more common of these techniques we will devote this discussion to more recent developments about which knowledge is not yet generally spread among researchers.

We will not discuss the methodological problem associated with selection of the best analytic or numerical procedure for deriving a solution from a model. In most cases the best choice is relatively apparent to one who is familiar with the alternatives. He must balance the cost of using the technique against the cost of error which it may yield. This is particularly important where approximation techniques are concerned. Furthermore, even if we wanted to, we cannot yet represent the choices in a research decision model.

ANALYTIC PROCEDURES

In equations which contain only one controllable variable, its optimizing value, if there is one and it is obtainable by analysis, can be determined by the use of the calculus, as was done in equation (4). The derivative of the outcome variable is taken with respect to the controllable variable, set equal to zero, and solved. We must take the necessary steps to determine whether the function is at a minimum or maximum point where the derivative is equal to zero, and whether there is more than one maximum or minimum.

If there is more than one controllable variable, the partial derivative of the outcome is taken with respect to each controllable variable and set equal to zero. Then, under certain conditions, solution of the resulting set of simultaneous equations yields the optimizing values of the controllable variables.

If the values of the controllable variables are constrained (restricted) by one or more equations or inequations, and if there are only a few such constraints, we can use Lagrangian multipliers or some variation thereof. When the number of constraints becomes large, numerical procedures are generally required. Here the recently developed techniques of mathematical programming are particularly useful.

Finally, in some cases an optimizing value of a function rather than a variable must be found. In principle the calculus of variations is applicable to such cases, but in practice we can actually solve only very few problems using this technique. Normally we must resort to numerical techniques, particularly the technique of dynamic programming.

NUMERICAL PROCEDURES

The familiar trial-and-error technique has already been referred to as a numerical procedure. Frequently, with the help of graphic plots one can more rapidly determine the neighborhood of the optimum and concentrate one's trials in that region. Since trial and error can be very time consuming, efforts have been made to modify these procedures so that they converge on the solution. A numerical procedure which tends toward a solution on successive trials is called *iterative*. The mathematical programming techniques to which reference has been made are all iterative.

The large amount of computation required even by efficient iterative procedures prohibited their extensive application until the advent of the electronic computer. With the development of computers and techniques for programming them, the use of numerical procedures has become much more widespread.

Recently there has been another development which may make numerical procedures even more accessible. It involves the use of logical techniques to reduce the number of possible solutions which must be considered. For example, consider a problem in which n tasks must be performed, each requiring use of a number of different machines, where only one of each type is available. Which task should be performed first on each machine so that the total time required to complete the n tasks is minimized? If there are m machines involved there are $(n!)^m$ possible solutions. For m and n of any size it would be much too time consuming to try all of these. Akers and Friedman

(1955) have shown how the class calculus (the Boolean algebra) can be used to reduce the cases in which there are 2^m possible solutions to a relatively small number of feasible solutions which satisfy the conditions of optimality. Then only these need be evaluated numerically.

Such instances of the use of logic to reduce computation are still rare, but they hold promise for the future.

Among the important developments in numerical analysis stimulated by the advent of computers one of the most dramatic is *simulation*. It is to this procedure that most of our attention will be given in this chapter.

SIMULATION

With the advent of the computer, simulation has come to attract increasing attention in research circles. It is wrong, however, to associate simulation exclusively with computers because their use is not essential to the procedure. Nevertheless, computers have made simulation possible or practical in many research situations in which previously it was neither.

Simulation has come to mean different things to different people, depending on the use to which they put it. It has been utilized for personnel selection and training, and even for therapeutic purposes. Our concern here, however, is only with its application to problem solving. It has another important research use which will be discussed in Chapter 14: to display research results to those who must be "sold" on these results.

It is much easier to characterize simulation in figurative terms than in literal terms. For example, an essential characteristic of simulation is captured by the observation that a model *represents* a phenomenon, but that simulation *imitates* it. This dynamic aspect of simulation is also caught in the figurative observation that models are photographs and simulations are motion pictures. These figures of speech are not meant to imply that models and simulation are to be contrasted, because simulation is a *way of using* a model. It is, in effect, experimentation on a model rather than on the phenomenon itself; that is, it is *vicarious experimentation*.

In principle, everything that can be accomplished by simulation can be accomplished by experimenting directly on the phenomena involved in the problem. In practice, however, it may be impossible or impractical to experiment on the phenomena themselves.

The conditions under which simulation is useful are summarized by Morgenthaler (1961, pp. 366–367) as follows:

It may not be possible to observe the phenomenon in its desired environment. This is true of studies of the thrust of rocket motors for use in interplanetary space. The phenomenon or system may be too complex to summarize in a compressed mathematical formulation. It has not been possible thus far, for example, to reduce the operation of a large business activity to a few simple equations. Analytical techniques may not exist for solving the mathematical formulation once it has been achieved. This is often the case in solving the diffusion equation or other partial-differential equations when the boundary conditions are time-dependent or complicated by other demands of realism. Even when analysts have the confidence and ability to arrive at a theoretical prediction of the behavior of a large system, it may not be possible to perform validating experiments. You cannot, for example, test conclusions about global strategic war by trying them even once. *When any of these difficulties occur, as they do daily in the attempts . . . to tackle previously untouched, unmanageable problems, some form of simulation is the obvious tool to be tried.*

The principal use of simulation in deriving or testing solutions from decision models occurs when the measure of performance is a statistical parameter of a distribution of outcomes. In many such cases the optimizing values of the controlled variables cannot be derived from the model by either abstract or (the usual type of) numerical analysis. Simulation involves the use of numbers and hence is a type of numerical analysis or, more properly speaking, is an extension of it. In numerical analysis the numerical values of the controlled and uncontrolled variables are inserted in the model and the outcome is calculated by normal arithmetical operations. By trying a number of possible solutions the best (or approximately best) one can be identified and selected. In simulation we also generally try a number of solutions, but the difference from normal numerical procedures lies in the way each solution is evaluated.

The evaluation or testing of a proposed solution to a decision model by simulation consists of running the system on paper or in a computer (i.e., symbolically) for a set of values of the controlled variables in order to generate enough instances of outcomes so that their distribution can be determined. From these "observations" the necessary parameter is estimated. For example, in a "waiting-line" problem it may not be possible to determine analytically how many serving facilities one ought to have so as to minimize the total cost of operation. But for any specified number of facilities we may be able to run the operation on paper by "imitating" arrival of customers, their waiting, their selection for service, their servicing, and their departure. By observing these operations we can estimate the distribution of outcomes (e.g., the daily cost of operation) and calculate the value of a measure of performance based on it. The same holds true for other types of phenomena: the behavior of small physical particles, cells reproducing, the spreading of a disease, people interacting, and societies fighting a peace or a war.

The various uses of simulation in problem solving are best understood with respect to the familiar form of the decision model: $V = f(X_i, Y_j)$. The four principal uses are as follows:

(1) *To determine the optimizing values of controlled variables.* For example, in queuing theory (the stochastic theory of waiting-line processes) models expressing such outcome variables as "mean waiting time" or "mean length of queue" can be expressed as functions of the distributions of arrivals and servicing times, the number of servicing points, the order in which items are served, and so on. But the effect of the number of servicing points on the outcome can be determined analytically only for certain distributions of arrival and servicing times (e.g., Poisson and exponential). For some distributions, the necessary integration cannot be performed. But by simulation in these cases, outcomes can be estimated, and hence solutions to problems involving queuing processes of this type can be approximated.

(2) *To study transitional processes.* In many cases where a model can be solved analytically, the solution specifies only the terminal or steady state that results from changing the values of the variables, and not the intermediate states, the states of transition. Simulation exposes the transition to as careful a study as the researcher may care to make. For example, the solution of a complex inventory problem involving the purchasing, storage, and use of a large number of items (e.g., spare parts for aircraft) may show that the current stock levels of some items are too high and of others are too low. The solution obtained analytically may tell us what the average inventory investment will be after the changes have been made and after the system has settled down to a steady state. In getting to the inventory's steady state from its current state, items which are understocked according to the solution can usually be brought up to the level indicated by the solution rather quickly by buying more of them. But items which are overstocked will be reduced to the appropriate level only with use, and this may take some time. Consequently, although the inventory investment may *eventually* decrease if the solution is followed, it will usually increase during the transition. It may be important to know by how much it will increase and how long the period will be before the steady state is reached. Simulation makes

it possible for us to "map" this transition and determine its characteristics.

(3) *To estimate values of model parameters or the model's functional form.* In some cases we may be able to construct a model but not to evaluate all its parameters (Y_j) because of the lack of data. We may, however, have good and plentiful data on past outcomes and values of the controlled variables. In such cases we can by simulation try out a large number of possible values of the parameters, together with known past values of the controllable variables, until we obtain one or more sets of values which yield outcomes that correspond well with the known past outcomes. The same kind of procedure can be used to explore alternative functional forms of the model.

(4) *To treat courses of action which cannot be formulated into the model.* In some problems the performance of an entity under a set of specified conditions may be one of the important variables, but we may not be capable of enumerating or characterizing all its possible courses of action in advance. Even if we can enumerate them, we may not be able to characterize them by a set of quantitative variables. Such a problem is quite common when such an entity is a decision maker and when the conditions involve other (cooperating or competing) decision makers. When such an entity's performance cannot be modeled, the entity itself may be put into a modeled situation to determine the effects of its behavior as well as of other variables on outcomes. When this entity is human, such simulation is called *gaming.* The best-known examples of such simulation are military games, where real and modeled elements are combined to provide a basis either for predicting the effects of such variables as number and types of forces and equipment of friend and/or enemy, terrain, and weather; or for determining what strategies and tactics (controllable variables when considered relative to "our" side) are available for choice.

Types of Simulation

Simulation procedures can be classified into three main types, depending on the kind of model which is used: iconic, analogue, or symbolic. Since models may have a mixture of these characteristics, so may simulations. The three types may be described as follows.

Iconic simulation

Iconic simulation is the manipulation of an iconic model under real or iconically represented conditions. (An iconic model, it will be recalled, has the same essential properties as that which it represents, but with a transformation of scale.) Such simulation is widely used in problems involving the construction or production of an object, in so-called *hardware* or *design* problems. For example, the testing of a small physical model of an aircraft in a wind tunnel is an iconic simulation. Similarly, the testing of ship models in tow tanks is also an iconic simulation. The construction and operation of pilot plants, a common procedure in the chemical industry, constitute another example.

Analogue simulation

This type of simulation involves the manipulation of an *analogue* model. For example, the Moniac, a hydraulic model of the British economy constructed at the London School of Economics, can be operated to estimate the effects of certain monetary policies of the government. The wide use of analogue computers, particularly in the design and control of continuous production processes, involves such simulation. In the study of queuing processes arrivals of "customers" at service points have been simulated by devices which emit radioactive particles at random.

Symbolic simulation

Symbolic simulation is a process by which equations are evaluated numerically. The essential characteristic of the process is best described with reference to an equation of the following form:

$$W = f(U_i, U_j), \tag{6}$$

where W is a property of a statistical distribution or a distribution itself.

U_i represents one or more (controllable or uncontrollable) variables which are a property of a distribution or a distribution itself.

U_j represents other independent variables and constants.

Symbolic simulation consists of selecting a probability sample of values of each of the stochastic variables U_i and (relative to fixed values of the U_j) calculating a particular value of the outcome w for each set of sampled values of the U_i. Then W is estimated from the resulting set of w's. Thus, the effect of varying the U_j can be determined by repeating this process for different values of them. This requires that the equation in the form of (6) be transformed into a particularized form:

$$w = f^*(u_i, U_j), \tag{7}$$

where u_i represents a set of particular values of the stochastic variables U_i obtained by sampling from the distributions of which U_i are parameters or which U_i represent. The function f^* is a suitably modified form of the general function f.

Random sampling from the probability-density function lies at the heart of symbolic simulation. This application of sampling is called the *Monte Carlo* procedure. As we shall see, this procedure can also be used to evaluate nonstatistical expressions and variables.

Some Simple Examples of the Monte Carlo Technique

In order to provide the reader who is unfamiliar with the Monte Carlo technique with some background for the subsequent discussion we will consider several examples of its use. These examples will show how one can apply the principles of random sampling to the evaluation of deterministic and probabilistic variables. They will also make clear that the Monte Carlo procedure yields statistical estimates which are subject to error, and hence that characterization of this error is a critical aspect of use of this technique.

Consider a roulette wheel on which there are no markings except for one band indicated along the circumference. Suppose that we want to determine the angle whose arc is the marked band, and that no angular measuring devices are available. Assuming that the wheel is unbiased, we could proceed in this way. We spin the wheel and observe whether or not the pointer stops in the marked band. We repeat this process a number of times. The proportion of trials in which the indicator stopped in the band is determined. This fraction can then be applied to 360° to estimate the angle in question. In this way we would have estimated a deterministic quantity by a sampling procedure. The larger the number of spins, the smaller will be the error of the resulting estimate, assuming that the wheel is unbiased.

Now consider the following case, which can be solved either by analysis or by simulation. Suppose that we have a variable $\overline{W}$, which is the mean of a joint distribution of variables U_1 and U_2. Assume that U_1 and U_2 are normally distributed with means $\overline{U}_1 = 10$ and $\overline{U}_2 = 25$, and $\sigma_1 = 1$ and $\sigma_2 = 5$. In this case we know that

$$\overline{W} = \overline{U}_1 + \overline{U}_2 = 10 + 25 = 35$$

but let us see how we can estimate the value of $\overline{W}$ by Monte Carlo procedures.

In column (1) of Table 11.1 is listed the number of each of 15 trials.

TABLE 11.1. An Example of a Monte Carlo Estimate

(1)	(2)	(3)	(4)	(5)	(6)	(7)
Number of Trial n	Random Normal Number r_1	$u_1 = \overline{U}_1 + r_1\sigma_1$	Random Normal Number r_2	$u_2 = \overline{U}_2 + r_2\sigma_2$	$w = u_1 + u_2$	Estimate Mean (Cumulative) $\frac{1}{n}\sum_1^n w$
1	0.464	10.464	0.137	25.687	36.151	
2	0.060	10.060	−2.526	12.370	22.430	
3	1.486	11.486	−0.354	23.230	34.716	
4	1.022	11.022	−0.472	22.640	33.662	
5	1.394	11.394	−0.555	22.225	33.619	
						32.116
6	0.906	10.906	−0.513	22.435	33.341	
7	1.179	11.179	−1.055	19.725	30.904	
8	−1.501	8.499	−0.488	22.560	31.059	
9	−0.690	9.310	0.756	28.780	38.090	
10	1.372	11.372	0.225	26.125	37.479	
						33.145
11	2.455	12.455	−0.323	23.385	35.840	
12	−0.531	9.469	−1.940	15.300	24.769	
13	−0.634	9.366	0.697	28.485	37.851	
14	1.279	11.279	1.698	33.490	44.769	
15	0.046	10.046	0.321	26.605	36.651	
						34.089

In columns (2) and (4) random normal numbers are listed which have been taken from a table of such numbers. Since these numbers are in σ-units, they must be converted into "observed values" as is done in columns (3) and (5). We add to the appropriate mean ($\overline{U}_1$ or $\overline{U}_2$) the product of the random normal number and the appropriate standard deviation (σ_1 or σ_2). We then add the "observed values" u_1 and u_2 to obtain a value of w, shown in column (6). The averages of the first 5, 10, and 15 w's are shown in column (7). The estimated standard error of these estimates may be obtained by usual statistical procedures.

Design Phases of Monte Carlo Technique

Use of the Monte Carlo technique involves three research decisions:

(1) how to obtain a set of random numbers;
(2) how to convert these numbers into random variates from some specified probability distribution; and

(3) how to increase the efficiency of estimates obtained from the sampling process; that is, how to reduce the variance of the estimates.

Random numbers

The basic tool employed in symbolic simulation is a set of random numbers. The numbers which are employed are either supplied by available tables or decks of punched cards prepared from such tables, or they are generated by some arithmetical procedure. Numbers generated in this way are referred to as *pseudo-random* numbers. They are used primarily in simulation involving a computer. Their principal advantage lies in the fact that a large portion of the computer's memory is not then filled with random numbers; only a generating routine is required. In addition, with such a routine it is easy to reproduce the simulation using the same random numbers, thereby allowing more direct comparisons between the effects of different values of the manipulated variables. The disadvantages arise from the possible deviations of pseudo-random numbers from "pure" randomness.*

The most commonly used method of generating pseudo-random numbers is called the *mid-square method*. It consists of taking, for example, a four-digit number, say 3182, and squaring it to obtain 10,125,124. Then one takes the middle four digits, 1251, and squares this number, and so on. The four-digit numbers thus obtained constitute a set of pseudo-random numbers. These numbers eventually come back on themselves; that is, go into a cycle which is generally of the order of 10^4 but may go as high as 10^6. By the use of other procedures, such as the *congruential methods,* cycles as large as 10^{12} have been obtained. The congruential method consists of letting

$$X_{n+1} = KX_n(\bmod M)$$

That is, X_{n+1} is equal to the number that remains after KX_n is divided by M. This method was first reported by Lehmer (1951), using $K = 23$, $M = 10^8 + 1$. This yielded a sequence of eight-digit numbers with a cycle length of 5,882,352. Taussky and Todd [in Meyer (1956, p. 17)] report that in using $K = 5^{17}$, $X_0 = 1$, and $M = 2^{42}$ they get a sequence of approximately 10^{12} numbers before cycling.

Concerning these procedures of generating pseudo-random numbers Marshall [in Meyer (1956, p. 9)] observes that:

---

* For more complete discussion than is provided here of testing and generation of random numbers see Taussky and Todd in Meyer (1956, pp. 15 ff.), and article by K. D. Tocher in "Symposium on Monte Carlo Methods" (1954, pp. 39–61).

The bogus character of the randomness of the generated sequence does not seem to affect the Monte Carlo calculations, just as it is not detected by the various statistical tests to which these sequences have been subjected, and through which they have passed with flying colors.

Random variates from a specified probability distribution

Given a table of random numbers or a set which is generated by a pseudo process, it is necessary to convert these numbers into sampled values from the distribution involved. The general logic of such sampling is quite simple, although the actual operations may be more complex. In principle what is involved is the following. Consider the distribution in question as being plotted in cumulative form. (See Figure 11.1.) The ordinate can then be divided into a large number of small equal intervals, say a thousand parts. Then random numbers are selected from 1 to 1000, and for each number a horizontal line is drawn from the corresponding point of the ordinate to the curve representing the distribution. The value of the point on the abscissa of the curve is then determined. This is the sampled value. The set of values obtained in this way is a random sample from the distribution.

Tables of random variates from the normal distribution are available. See RAND (1955). Marshall reports [in Meyer, (1956, p. 10)] that at RAND the researchers "currently generate random variables having the exponential distribution by taking the logarithm of random numbers." He observes:

It is only gradually that there has developed a practical capacity to generate random variables from a wide class of probability distributions. The choice of any particular scheme of course depends upon the economics of the computation situation.

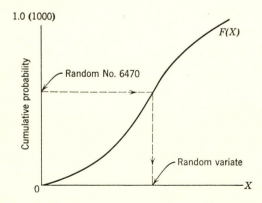

FIGURE 11.1. Conversion of a random number to a random deviate from a specified distribution.

Detailed discussion of this problem can be found in papers by Lytle and Butler [in Meyer (1956)].

Variance-reducing techniques

Kahn [in Meyer (1956)] has provided an excellent survey of the principal techniques of reducing variance of estimates derived from the use of Monte Carlo procedures. His presentation leaves little room for improvement, and hence this discussion is an iconic model of his. The six most useful techniques of variance reduction are:

(1) Importance sampling.
(2) Russian roulette and splitting.
(3) Use of expected values.
(4) Systematic sampling.
(5) Stratified sampling.
(6) Correlation and regression.

The names of the last four consist of terms which have appeared in earlier discussions. Their meaning in this context is closely related to the meanings imputed earlier. Each of the six techniques is equally applicable to normal sampling problems, and several are quite widely used in the normal sampling context.

Kahn illustrates the first five techniques by an example which is very useful pedagogically but which, as he points out, is so simple as to be trivial. The problem is to estimate the probability of obtaining a "3" on a toss of two standard dies. By normal analytic procedures we can determine this probability by observing that there are two ways of "making a '3'": $(2,1)$ and $(1,2)$. Since there are 36 possible outcomes, the probability is $\frac{2}{36}$ or $\frac{1}{18}$.

If the dies are tossed at random, or if we employ pairs of random digits to represent outcomes on each die, we would use a relative-frequency estimate of this probability, p, where

$$p = \frac{n}{N},$$

N is the number of trials, and n the number of occurrences of "3." The variance of this estimate is given by

$$\sigma^2 = \frac{p(1 - p)}{N}.$$

The per cent error is given by

$$\frac{100\sigma}{p} = 100 \sqrt{\frac{1 - p}{Np}}.$$

It is clear that, for fixed N, as p increases the per cent error decreases and that, for fixed p, as N increases the per cent error decreases.

(1) *Importance Sampling.* This is a way of artificially increasing p and adjusting for this increase in making the required estimate. Suppose, for example, that we use two columns of random digits. In addition to letting the pairs $(1, 2)$ and $(2, 1)$ represent a toss of "3," we also let $(7, 8)$, $(8, 7)$, $(8, 9)$, $(9, 8)$, $(9, 0)$, $(0, 9)$, $(7, 0)$, $(0, 7)$, $(8, 0)$, and $(0, 8)$ represent a "3." We now have 12 (or 6 times as many) ways of getting a "3." The estimate of p will now be

$$\frac{1}{6} \frac{n}{N}.$$

The original per cent error would be

$$100 \sqrt{\frac{1 - \frac{1}{18}}{N/18}} = 100 \sqrt{\frac{17}{N}}.$$

The new per cent of error would be

$$100 \sqrt{\frac{1 - \frac{1}{3}}{N/3}} = 100 \sqrt{\frac{2}{N}}.$$

and hence is reduced by $\sqrt{17}/\sqrt{2}$ or by a factor of approximately 3.

In general terms, sampling by importance can be stated as follows. The problem is to estimate the value of

$$Y = \int_{-\infty}^{\infty} g(z)f(z)\, dz,$$

where $f(z)$ is a probability-density function (PDF), and z may be a vector. The problem is to find another PDF, $h(z)$, such that

$$Y = \int_{-\infty}^{\infty} \frac{g(z)f(z)}{h(z)} h(z)\, dz = \int_{-\infty}^{\infty} g^0(z)h(z)\, dz,$$

where the estimate of Y is

$$y = \frac{1}{n} \sum^{n} g^0(z_i)$$

and $z_1, \cdots, z_n$ is a random sample from the population with PDF, $h(z)$.

For the use of multistage sampling in the development of an importance sample see Marshall [in Meyer (1956, pp. 123 ff)]. For a discussion of the use of the variance for measuring accuracy of the results see Walsh [in Meyer (1956, pp. 141 ff)].

(2) *Russian Roulette and Splitting.* Now suppose that we toss only one die at a time or draw only one number at a time. We know that only if we obtain a "1" or a "2" on the first draw do we have any chance of getting a "3." Therefore, we can separate those first draws on which we do not get a "1" or a "2" (*split* the sample) and make a second draw only for the first set. This makes it unnecessary to make the second draw in two thirds of the cases. Hence, the same variance can be obtained with one third less total observations, or with the same number of draws we can decrease the variance.

In some cases it may be neither necessary nor possible to *kill* all the "uninteresting" first draws, in which case a random sample of m of the uninteresting cases can be selected and the estimate based on these observations can be appropriately weighted by m. In addition, each interesting case can be treated as though it were n $(n > 1)$ such cases, and the resulting estimate can also be appropriately weighted by n. This procedure is called *Russian roulette.* The idea is due to von Neumann and Ulam (1945).

The idea of Russian Roulette and Splitting is similar to the sequential sampling schemes of quality control, though quite different in detail. It was first thought of in connection with particle diffusion problems. Particles which get into interesting regions are split into n independent sub-particles, each with one nth of the weight of the original particle. Particles which get into uninteresting regions are, in effect, amalgamated into a fewer number of heavier particles. In this way the calculator achieves his goal of allocating his effort sensibly. [Kahn (1956, p. 147)]

(3) *Use of Expected Values.* In cases where the sampling is done in two stages, even though we cannot compute the relevant probabilities associated with each stage we may be able to do so for the second stage. For example, we may not know the probability of getting a "1" or a "2" on the first toss of a die but we may know this probability for the second toss. Then we need not use the second toss. If we have had a "1" or a "2" on the first toss and know that the probability of getting the other on the second toss is $\frac{1}{6}$, then we can estimate the probability of getting "3" on two tosses as

$$\frac{1}{6}\frac{n}{N},$$

where n is the number of occurrences of "1" or "2" on the first toss, and N is the total number of first tosses. This procedure is referred to as the *use of expected values*.

(4) *Systematic Sampling.* Now suppose that we reverse the situation of the last example; that is, suppose that we know the relevant probabilities on the first toss but not on the second. We would know then that, if we made 600 "first" tosses, the expected number of "1"'s, "2"'s, "3"'s "4"'s, "5"'s, and "6"'s would be 100 each. Therefore we can omit the first toss and assume for the first 100 of the "second" tosses that a "1" came up on the "first" toss. We would assume that a "2" came up on the second 100 "first" tosses, and so on. This eliminates the need for the first toss and reduces the fluctuations in the proportions of "1"'s, "2"'s, and so on, which would occur because of random tosses.

The reduction of the estimating error by this procedure of systematic sampling is generally small: between 5 and 30 per cent. But since it is easy to obtain this gain, it is foolish not to do so where possible. It does require, of course, prior knowledge of the sample size to be drawn.

(5) *Stratified Sampling.* The reflective reader will have asked a question about the preceding example: why make the last 400 tosses, since we know that if there is a "3" or higher on the first toss we cannot obtain a sum of "3" on two tosses? Therefore we ought to divide the total sample into two strata of 300 each. For the first we assume a "1" on the first toss, and for the second a "2."

In theory, this method could be as powerful as Importance Sampling. In actual practice, the fact that you have to sample systematically turns out to decrease sharply the number of places in which it can be used. However, where it can be used, it is usually better than Importance Sampling and in any case never worse. Therefore whenever the costs of the two techniques are comparable, Stratified Sampling is preferable to Importance Sampling. [Kahn (1956, p. 155)]

(6) *Correlation and Regression.* To illustrate this procedure the same coin-tossing example cannot be used. Suppose that we want to determine the difference in average waiting time for customers arriving at a service point with two identical service facilities. It would be possible to conduct two separate simulations, one for each service point, but it is preferable to use the sampled data on arrivals and service for the first facility again in the second case. In the second case we would merely add a sample of service times of the second facility. Then we can compute the difference in waiting time for each customer

and obtain from these results an estimate of the mean difference in waiting times for the two facilities.

This procedure can be extended to cover any number of service facilities. The estimated mean differences would be plotted against the number of facilities at the service point, and a regression line fitted.

Not only does the procedure just described reduce the number of samples which must be drawn, but also it reduces the kinds of chance fluctuations which can affect the results; that is, which can increase estimating error.

Concerning the six techniques just described Kahn (1956, p. 156) has the following methodological observation:

Techniques described under the headings of Importance Sampling, Russian Roulette and Splitting, and Stratified Sampling have the property that in many calculations they will give a tremendous increase in efficiency if properly used; if, however, the intuition of the calculator is faulty and he does not use a reasonable design, then they can be very unreliable and actually increase the variance. The other techniques are more stable in that it is almost impossible for the experimenter to worsen the sampling variance by misusing them, even if he has a bad intuition.

Variance-reducing techniques can in some instances yield startling reductions in the number of computations required to obtain a specified level of precision. In a problem reported by Arnold, Bucher, Trotter, and Tukey [in Meyer (1956, pp. 80 ff)], by the use of a procedure that combines splitting and what these authors call *conditional calculations* they are able to obtain a gain of a factor of about 5000 over standard simple random-sampling techniques.

The following extended quotation from Marshall [in Meyer (1956, p. 8)] provides a succinct summary of the methodological aspects of variance reduction in Monte Carlo procedures:

The increase in the speed of [computing] machines has tended to make variance reducing techniques relatively less interesting, but has by no means eliminated their usefulness. The effect of increased computing speed in the newer machines is to make the cost of designing and coding a problem increase relative to the cost of machine running time. The use of variance reducing techniques shortens running time but at the expense of (1) increasing the time spent in designing the computations so as to adapt the classical techniques to the particular problem or in the invention of a new, more suitable technique, and (2) complicating the coding because of the more elaborate bookkeeping and calculations these techniques usually require. On the whole, however, if there is one thing that would generally increase the usefulness of Monte Carlo it is the discovery of new variance reducing techniques, or the application of known variance reducing techniques as a matter of course to the ordinary run of problems. Not only should these techniques be used whenever it is economical to do so but, in addition, since the variance reducing techniques are not yet well known there should be a bias toward using them even when they are not economical for the problem at hand. This is a way to learn about them for use in later and more suitable problems. The use of new techniques in marginal cases is almost always justified as a method of building intellectual capital. In the long run one would suppose that real thought on the design of Monte Carlo problems will be confined to problems of a basically new type whenever they first appear; standard variance reducing techniques will be available, and used, for other problems on the basis that sub-routines for computing common functions now are.

Here in Marshall's statement concerning "building intellectual capital" we have explicit recognition of the obligation of scientists working on either pure or applied problems to take responsibility for the methodological and technical development of research procedures.

By now it is probably clear to the reader that the problem of reducing variance in Monte Carlo simulations is very similar to that faced in any application of sampling procedures:

> For this reason, it is very valuable to have professional statistical help in designing these calculations. However, if one has to choose between a person who is mainly interested in statistics and one who is mainly interested in the problem itself, experience has shown that, in this field at least, the latter is preferable. This last remark is not intended as a slur on statisticians, but simply to amplify a comment made earlier, that, "the greatest gains in variance reduction are often made by exploiting specific details of the problem, rather than by routine application of general principles." [Kahn (1956, p. 190)]

Variance and Computers in Monte Carlo Simulation

In some instances in which a statistic of two or more distributions is taken jointly, the variance of this statistic can be determined analytically. In most instances in which simulation is required it cannot be. As a consequence the researcher cannot usually determine in advance how many simulation "runs" he will need. For this reason the application of multiple sampling (at least double sampling) is particularly well suited for simulation. When the simulation is done by hand, the variance of the estimate sought can be recomputed after each trial. When a computer is used, however, it is costly and time consuming to divide the simulation into stages. What is frequently overlooked, on the other hand, is that it may be more costly and time consuming to select arbitrarily a sample size and make too many or too few observations. Even where a computer is used, several hand runs of the simulation are usually required in order to check out the computer program. These runs can also be employed to arrive at at least a crude estimate of the variance, which can then be used to estimate the required sample size. Given an estimate of the variance, the procedure described in Chapter 7 for determining optimal sample size can be applied, perhaps with modification to suit the characteristics of the situation. To determine what estimation method to choose, the procedure described in Chapter 8 can be employed.

The question as to whether or not a computer should be used in a simulation involves considerations of economy as well as of accuracy. In complex simulations the opportunities for nonsampling errors are considerable. These errors have the same characteristics, in general, as observer errors and can be analyzed in the same way. (See p. 206.) The cost of using a computer involves not only running time but also programming and the inevitable "debugging." The simulation must be more complex and lengthy than we normally suppose before the use of a computer involves less *human* labor than does hand computation.

The Las Vegas Technique: Marginal-Cost Analysis of Simulation

Simulation, as noted earlier, can be used to evaluate terms in a model so that it may be solved or it may be utilized to find an approximate solution. Where there are a finite number of possible solutions, a solution can always be found in principle by exhaustive trial and error. But for most problems of interest, even with the help of large computers such brute-force tactics are seldom practical. It is obviously preferable to try to find a procedure which will tend to yield closer and closer approximations to a solution. In situations in which the model must be solved at different times for different values of the uncontrolled variables, a converging simulation process (sometimes called the *Las Vegas technique*) may be designed as follows:

(1) A procedure for simulating the model is developed, one which yields a measure of output for a specified set of values of the control variables.

(2) A procedure is developed for examining the performance of the simulated system to locate trouble spots for correction.

(3) Rules are developed for changing the values of the control variables in a way which (on intuitive or other grounds) appears to yield improvements.

(4) If the system is stochastic, repeated trials for a selection of sets of values of the control variables are run to provide an estimate

of within-run variance. Using the estimate thus provided, a determination is made of the number of runs (k) required per set of values to be able to detect differences of a specified magnitude with a specified probability.

(5) Starting with an initial set of values selected on the best basis available, k runs are made. The results are examined (step 2 above), and the decision rules are applied (step 3). A new series of k runs is made for the new set of values; and so on.

(6) The average outcome of each series is plotted against the number of the series. (See Figure 11.2.)

(7) After a large number of series, starting with the first, each point which represents a better performance than any yielded up to that point is circled.

(8) A line is fitted to the circled points. This may be done by free hand.

(9) The cost of k runs for a set of values of the control variables is determined.

(10) The first point on the curve at which the expected increase in performance for the next series is less valuable than the cost of the run is determined.

This, then, establishes the number of series which should be run. The better the search procedure and decision rules (steps 2 and 3), the fewer series of runs will be required to attain some specified amount of improvement over the first series. The length of the simulation also depends on how close to optimal is the first set of values of the control variables which is chosen. Here it may be possible to use even a crude analytic approximation to considerable advantage.

Since there is likely to be considerable variance in the number of series required before the break-even point is reached, it is better to

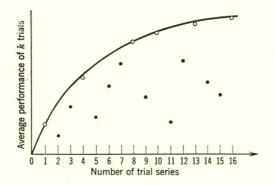

FIGURE 11.2. A Las Vegas plot.

use the Las Vegas technique sequentially than to use one set of series to determine how many series to run on another.

GAMING

A simulation in which decision making is performed by one or more real decision makers is called *gaming*. This term is sometimes restricted to simulations in which two or more *competing* decision makers are involved. The term, however, will not be so restricted in its application here.

Gaming has come into increasing use in the last decade, particularly in the study of complex military and industrial operations. It is now beginning to be used in the study of governmental problems at the municipal, national, and international levels.* Gaming, particularly in the military context, has a very long history, which is described in detail by Young (1957) and Thomas (1961), but its use as a research tool is quite recent. As Hoggatt (1959) observed, its principal application has been as "a teaching device and in making the play of the game interesting for the participants" (p. 192). It is also being used increasingly to select as well as train personnel, to familiarize personnel with the operations of a complex system, and to demonstrate a new idea about a complex system. For discussion of gaming as other than a research tool see Thomas and Deemer (1957) and Cohen and Rhenman (1960). Bibliographies on gaming may be found in Malcolm (1960) and Shubik (1960).

The uses of gaming in problem-solving research fall into three general classes: (1) to help develop a decision model, (2) to help find the solution to such a model, and (3) to help evaluate proposed solutions to problems modeled by the game. Gaming can aid in constructing a model by providing a basis for testing the relevance of variables or the functional form of the model (i.e., the relationship between the variables). It can also be used both to help uncover possible courses of action and decision strategies, and to compare the alternatives. In cases where a completely specified course of action or decision procedure cannot be derived analytically from a model, but a partially specified action or procedure can, the effect of the action or procedure may be determined by gaming.

* Use of gaming in municipal problems is being made by Prof. Nathan Grunstein at the University of Pittsburgh and Prof. Richard Meier at the University of Michigan. An example of its application in the study of international problems can be found in Guetzkow (1959).

The application of gaming in pure research parallels that in applied research. It can be used to help develop theory, to suggest hypotheses to be tested, and to test hypotheses suggested by the game, other experience, or theory. It should be noted that the use of gaming in pure research involves decision making, but not in the context of a particular problem or set of problems of current practical interest.

Gaming is essentially experimentation in which the behavior of decision makers is observed under controlled conditions. It differs from most psychological and social experimentation only in that the conditions under which the "play" is observed represent some situation outside the laboratory about which knowledge is sought. The experimental situation, then, is deliberately constructed as an iconic or analogue model of a type of situation of interest.

The principal methodological problem in the use of gaming lies in the process of inferring from the experimental to the "real" situation. We will consider this problem after we have illustrated and discussed the various research applications of gaming. To facilitate this discussion a particular game (developed by the author and several of his colleagues) will be used for illustrative purposes.

The game to be described was developed as a pure-research tool. It is intended for testing the effect of certain types of variables describing organizations on their performance. The results of the initial use of this game are described in detail in Clark and Ackoff (1959). The game is currently being employed to help develop a mathematical theory which explains the performance of an organization in terms of the variables which are being investigated simultaneously. This use of gaming is by no means unique; for example, see Hoggatt (1959).

An Example of Gaming

There are three basic operations to be performed in this game:

(1) Purchasing: buying letters of the alphabet printed on small wooden "tiles" (which are similar to those used in the game of Scrabble).

(2) Manufacturing: forming words out of these letters.

(3) Selling: playing the words on a board.

Each of these operations is the responsibility of one player, and hence the minimal team consists of three persons.

Each operation involves a cost, and selling yields an income. The

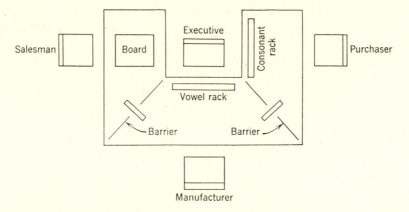

FIGURE 11.3. Layout of gaming situation.

objective of the group is to maximize its profit over a series of plays.

In addition to the Purchaser, Manufacturer, and Salesman, there may be an Executive. The positions of the players around a U-shaped table are shown in Figure 11.3. The Purchaser, Manufacturer, and Salesman are separated by a visual barrier (made of Masonite or plywood) through the bottom of which is a slot. The lettered tiles can be passed through this slot by sliding them along a rack that is provided. The Executive, if present, is the only player who can see all that is going on. At the beginning of a trial, or run, the team is supplied with "$50" in chips. As the Purchaser obtains letters and as the Manufacturer forms words, they must pay the experimenter for these operations out of the team's supply of chips. As the Salesman plays these words, the team receives income in chips, less the Salesman's expenses.

If the team has to "borrow money" at some point in its operations it can do so, but it is charged $1 for every $2 that it borrows.

The Purchaser has before him a rack on which consonants are grouped, valued according to their frequencies of use in the English language, as follows:

$2	$4	$6	$8
JKQXZ	BGPVW	CDFLM	HNRST

In one version of the game, consonants are obtained by buying adjacent pairs within a group.* This is the only way in which they

---

* In other versions of the game "quantity discounts" are provided for large purchases.

can be obtained. The cost per letter is shown above each group, so that the pair HN, for example, cost $16, whereas the pair QX costs only $4.

As the Purchaser buys pairs of consonants, he pays the experimenter for them, records the transaction on his expense form, and then forwards them to the Manufacturer, placing them on the rack which slides through the slot in the barrier.

The Manufacturer has before him the vowels, and the letter Y. As he receives consonants, he may combine them with the vowels in any fashion to make words. When he forms a word, he pays the experimenter $8 per vowel used, and records this operation on his expense form. At this point, the experimenter can declare the word unacceptable if it is an abbreviation, a proper noun, or a misspelling, and remove it from play.

The Manufacturer cannot accumulate more than six consonants. If more than six are available (have already been purchased), he cannot use those most recently bought until the six first acquired have been employed in words. He may "scrap" any of the six available consonants and obtain another from the Purchaser. A scrapped letter cannot be used subsequently.

As words are formed, they are forwarded to the Salesman. He has before him a board (see Figure 11.4). As he receives words from the Manufacturer, he plays them (though not necessarily in the order in which he receives them) on the board, according to the following rules:

(1) Play must begin in the upper left-hand corner of the second row of the board. The first row is filled with a random sequence of letters.

(2) The sequence of play is across the second row from left to right, then across the third row, and so on.

(3) At least one space must be skipped between words.

(4) Every word played must have at least one letter in it that matches a letter directly above it (in either the row above or any previous row if the spaces between the matching letters are not occupied.

For each word that the Salesman plays, the team receives an income of $10 per letter, less $6 per space skipped.

The Executive is responsible for coordinating team effort and directing strategy. There are no restrictions placed on his activity. He may function as a trouble shooter, helping out where bottlenecks occur in the course of play, or as a communications center. His

														Spaces skipped	Letters played		
U	R	R	N	P	F	P	S	G	N	W	S	W	A	N			
J	E	R	K		F	L	A	S	H		B	R	A	G	2	13	
	Q	U	I	P		S	A	G		W	O	R	K	S	3	12	
	B	U	I	L	D		A	L	E		A	R	T		3	11	

FIGURE 11.4. The salesman's board and the tally sheet.

orders must be carried out by the other players. If a player refuses to follow an order, the Executive may "fire" him (for the remainder of that run) and fill in at the position himself.

Play continues in this manner for a period of 10 minutes. At the end of this time, expenses and income are totaled from the records kept by the players, letters are returned to the supply racks, and a new set of letters is placed randomly at the top of the board.

An 8-minute period between rounds allows the players a discussion period of about 5 minutes, in addition to preparation for the next run.

Each player, except the Executive, is scored on his individual performance. His reward (in money) depends on the group's performance and his individual performance. The Executive receives a specified portion of the group's earnings. The Purchaser's objective is to minimize the average cost per letter bought. His score is based on the extent to which he meets this objective. The Manufacturer's objective is to minimize the cost per word, and hence to minimize use of vowels. The Salesman's objective is to minimize the cost of sales, and hence the number of skipped spaces. These objectives create a conflict of interest.

If the Purchaser seeks to minimize his costs by buying inexpensive consonants, the Manufacturer will usually have a harder time making words and will have to use more vowels in the process. Also, the interest of the Salesman in matching letters without skipping more than a minimum number of spaces will often be in conflict with both the Purchaser's and the Manufacturer's attempts to keep their costs low, since he may call for words using more vowels or expensive consonants. Thus some compromise among the player's individual objectives is necessary for effective group performance, and one of the most general strategic problems for an Executive is to determine what sorts of compromise will be both acceptable to the players and efficient for group performance.

Numerous aspects of this organizational situation are subject to experimental control. Some of the more important are the following:

(1) The presence or absence of an Executive.

(2) The fact that the players may have fixed roles or may be rotated.

(3) The fact that the players may be trained as a team or in functional groups.

(4) The amount and type of communication permitted.

(5) The method of compensation.

A brief description of one of the experiments and its results is given in Clark and Ackoff (1959, pp. 291–293):

. . . six 4-man teams were formed. . . .

Two teams were designated "cooperative" teams. The members of these teams were told that they would be competing against other teams; that the team with the highest score would receive a $30 prize, to be divided evenly among the members of that team. Two other teams were called "semicooperative" teams. (These designations were used only among the experimenters.) Members of these teams were told that they would be awarded prize money on the basis of how well they scored in their position as compared to the scores made by players in corresponding positions on other teams. That is, the purchaser was really competing against other purchasers; the manufacturer against other manufacturers, and so on.

The third pair of teams were called "conflict" teams. Members of each of these teams were told that they were competing against each other for prize money. That is, if the salesman did better at his position than the other players at theirs, he would win all the prize money for that team. The other players would win nothing.

Each team went through three sessions. The first consisted of training and practice runs. During the last two, each team engaged in 10 runs.

A t-test showed that the two "cooperative" teams had mean team scores that did not differ significantly. The means of the two "conflict" teams were almost significantly different at the 0.01 level, indicating that it would be preferable not to combine these two groups in subsequent analysis. For the lack of other teams in this classification, however, the scores for these two teams were combined.

Two main analysis-of-variance computations were carried out. One involved two "levels" of competitive effect (cooperative and conflict teams); the second, all three. The "column" contribution to the total variance, then, represented the effect of varying the competitive make-up of the team. The "row" effect represented the effect of trial number, i.e., a "learning" (or, more precisely, a "team improvement") effect. In both analyses, a column or "type-of-team" effect was between the 0.05 and 0.01 significance levels. With all six teams, the learning effect was significant at the 0.05 level. With just cooperative and conflict teams, the learning effect was not significant. This reflects the general lack of improvement in team scores apparent for the two conflict teams. Where the results for all six teams are included in the analysis, the team improvement effect for the cooperative and semicooperative team overbalances its lack in the conflict teams.

A distribution free test, the "Wilcoxon Matched Pairs Signed Rank Test," resulted in finding a difference between "cooperative" and "conflict" team scores significant at approximately the 0.05 level.

The same analysis was carried out for "number of letters played". . . . The "type of team" effect was found significant at the 0.01 level. This occurrence, in view of the set of rules for the game . . . suggests that cooperative team strategy has been to emphasize word output at some expense to the minimization of costs. Where more conflict among group members occurs, and hence more attention may be given to individual costs, total word output may fall considerably, but net team income may not fall proportionately. In fact, a calculation of the average profit per letter played finds one of the "conflict" teams with the highest score.

Since the game under discussion was developed as an experimental tool, it was designed to be flexible enough to permit study of a wide range of variables. This is best seen by noting that the team which has been described is an organizational module which can be combined with similar modules in many ways to create situations for testing a wide range of hypotheses. To illustrate these possibilities consider the following two situations:

(1) To observe two organizations (say, of a business type) under conditions of intense competition the teams are arranged as shown in Figure 11.5. Here the Purchasers must bid (in open auction or closed bidding) for raw materials (letters), and the Salesmen must bid for the right to make the next sale. In this situation teams can be "put out of business." Behavior in this situation is noticeably different from that shown when a team plays without competition.

(2) Two common principles of management are (a) management by function (horizontal structure) and (b) management by end product (vertical structure). To test the relative advantages of these al-

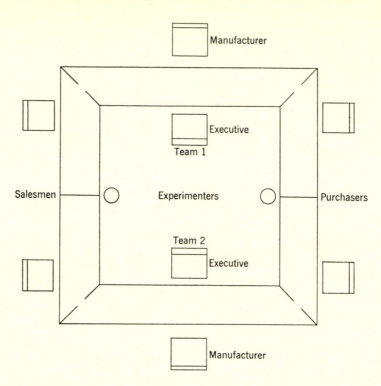

FIGURE 11.5. Layout for directly competing teams.

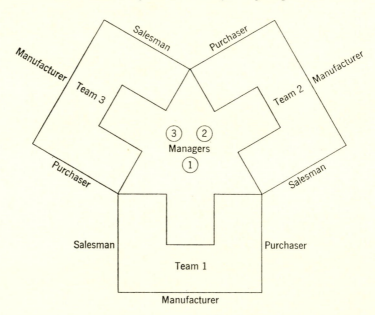

FIGURE 11.6. Setup of game for testing horizontal and vertical structure of an organization.

ternatives the following situation can be created. Let the organizational modules be physically arranged as shown in Figure 11.6. Vertical structure is obtained by having Manager 1 control Team 1; Manager 2, Team 2; and Manager 3, Team 3. Horizontal structure is obtained by having Manager 1 control the three Purchasers; Manager 2, the three Manufacturers; and Manager 3, the three Salesmen. In addition, a super or corporate executive can be established to control these three managers.

There is no limit to the complexity of organization one can develop by manipulating these modules.

The Limitations of Gaming

In many instances games have been developed without any clear notion as to how they can or should be used. Rationalizations for the effort are occasionally offered, but in general these games have been developed either for the scientific exercise involved or for the purpose of exploring the uses to which they can be put. Claims have been made for games as useful training and personnel-selection devices and for demonstrating the operation of complex systems. As yet, however, there has been little or no controlled evaluation of their use for any of these purposes.*

Thomas and Deemer (1957) have provided an extensive discussion of the methodological problems associated with the use of gaming as an applied-research technique. The following quotation is from their article (pp. 19–21):

Beyond [the] difficulty of knowing when one has solved the "right" problem, there is the difficulty . . . of knowing when one has solved any problem. . . . In gaming, generally, there is no way of knowing with certainty when a sample of plays is both strategically and statistically adequate for a required decision. . . .

Despite the absence of logical proof, operational gaming inspires its practitioners with a remarkable confidence in its results. Sometimes an implausible result is accepted with special relish because of its implausibility. The plausible results are often accepted as being now beyond dispute. . . .

In the formulation of a game one is beset by conflicting objectives that induce an ambivalent attitude toward elaboration. On the one hand, it is desirable to formulate a game the solution of which is highly relevant to the competitive situation being investigated. This consideration encourages one to add more and more details in an effort to acquire realism. On the other hand it is desirable to formulate a game the solution of which is possible,

* See Thomas and Deemer (1957) for a detailed discussion of this point. Also see Cohen and Rhenman (1960).

at least to the required accuracy. This constraint tends to inhibit the addition of details. . . .

The common tendency toward excessive elaboration in operational gaming may be regarded as another instance of that misplaced emphasis on the "appearance of reality" . . . it is an easy mistake to make. The search for the "essence of reality" is arduous and difficult, the goal difficult to recognize. One often feels that by incorporating a few more details in a model of reality he is that much more certain of capturing the essence. When, as in operational gaming, the increased difficulty of solution easily escapes notice, the temptation to enlarge the model becomes all the greater.

But this temptation to elaborate should be the more strongly resisted in gaming. For to yield is to court delusion. Not only is there the doubly diminished effectiveness of solution mentioned before as a consequence of excessive elaboration, but there is also another difficulty that arises in interpreting the results of gaming. One tends to forget that the game is not reality itself. The "appearance of reality," so useful in teaching, becomes dangerous in application.

Gaming: Analogy or Analogue?

The fundamental weakness in current gaming lies in the inability to draw strong inferences from the play of the game to decisions in the situation which the game models. Thomas and Deemer argue that the inferences which are drawn are weakened by the complexity of the game. A model, whether an equation or a game, is always a simplification of reality, and for this reason only is it useful in science. It is important, however, to understand the nature and significance of the simplification because only then can we justify inferring from the model to reality.

In current applications of operational games there is, I believe, a tendency to confuse the use of analogies and analogues. These are not the same thing; we can usually draw only very weak inferences (if any) by analogy. The inferences being drawn by analogy, however, are sometimes given a degree of credibility they would deserve only if they had been derived from manipulation of an adequate analogue or other type of model.

It is important to understand the difference between an analogue and an analogy as these terms are used here. In both an analogy and an analogue we use one situation as a model of another. The difference lies in what we know of the correspondence of the models to the "real" situation. In an analogy we know only that two situations have certain properties in common; we know nothing about the correspondence of the *structure* of the two situations. That is, in an analogy we do not know the function f, which relates the outcome to the variables, and hence do not know how well or badly it corresponds to the structure of the real situation. In an analogue we self-consciously design into the model a structure that, based on analysis or experimentation, we believe to correspond to some acceptable degree with the real one.

The structure of a game corresponds to the structure of the modeled situation to the extent that the same types of decisions yield the same performance in both situations. Such correspondence of output for related input must be established before inferences can be drawn from the game to the real situation.

We simply cannot argue from a correspondence of properties to a correspondence of structure. We can construct a game and manipulate its structure until the relationship between its inputs and outputs corresponds to that of the real situation. In this way the game is used to explore structural relationships which yield a particular kind of input-output relationship. But since a particular input-output relationship over a certain set of values of inputs may be produced by a large number of different structures, it is dangerous to infer from the game input-output relationships involving inputs of values different from those that have been tested. Therefore, it is also important to establish the range of inputs over which the structure is asserted to yield outputs corresponding to the real situation. This last observation is similar to one that a linear approximation to an S-shaped curve over a certain region of values of the independent variable may be good, but that it generally fits badly outside that range.

The more aspects of reality which are represented in a game, the more difficult it becomes to analyze its structure (i.e., to represent it by a mathematical model). On the other hand, unless enough of the relevant aspects of reality are included it cannot be an adequate model of reality. Gradation between excessive simplicity and complexity can be attained only by experimenting with the game itself. Considerably more time is generally required to develop a game that will be useful in problem solving, than is required to use the game once it is developed.

If a game fails to correspond adequately with reality or if the degree of the correspondence is difficult to establish, the researcher is likely to become interested in the game for its own sake and not as an analogue. At this point the gaming either becomes "ordinary" experimentation, or it is used for other-than-research purposes, such as training of personnel or demonstration of ideas.

A Game Used Inferentially

Some games have been constructed which can be used to infer approximate solutions to real problems. These are generally simple games which involve a mathematical model of a major portion of the "real" situation. Such games are less dramatic and more modest than those which receive most attention in the literature, but they do point the way to the productive use of gaming for more than scientific exploration. The following is a simple example of such a game developed to help solve a noncompetitive problem.

In an industrial problem reported by Hare and Hugli (1955) it was necessary to find the order in which items requiring production should be processed over an assembly line. The setup costs * associated with each product depended on which item preceded it over the assembly line. The problem, which was to minimize the sum of the setup costs subject to certain inventory requirements, could be represented by a matrix in which the cost of making each product after each other product was shown. The matrix was not symmetrical, since the cost of setting up for product A after product B was not necessarily the same as for setting up for product B after product A. It was recognized that this was an "asymmetrical traveling-salesman problem." A general solution to this type of problem is not yet available. Study of the problem revealed several decision rules which appeared to yield lower costs than one would expect by using intuition and experience to sequence the production runs. The rules, however, did not completely specify the decision to be made in any situation. Some judgment by the decision maker was still required.

The researchers replanned the production of the last three years, using the proposed decision rules and their judgment where required, and compared the resulting costs with those actually incurred. A substantial reduction was obtained. The question remained, however, as to whether such improvements could be obtained by the people who actually planned production in the plant. A game was set up involving the rescheduling of production over a three-year period. The people who actually had scheduled production over that period were taught the new decision rules and asked to reschedule production over the period. They did so, and the results showed the same improvement obtained by the researchers. On the strength of these results the rules were adopted and subsequently showed a continuing improvement over previous methods.

* Costs incurred in adjusting the machinery for a production run.

Few would argue with the inference that the improvement in performance obtained by use of the decision rules in this game was a legitimate basis for forecasting an improvement if the rules were applied in reality. The confidence one has in such an inference derives from the adequacy of the model of the problem situation: the correspondence of the game's structure to the situation it modeled.

Conclusions on Gaming

Gaming is simulation which involves "live" decision makers. It has been used primarily where large complex systems are involved, systems whose structures are not thoroughly understood. In such situations the principal justifiable use of gaming is the exploration of structural relationships. Results obtained from the game should be treated as suggestions or hypotheses which should be more rigorously tested.

In some situations it may be possible to construct an analytic (analogue or symbolic) model which fits a major part of the "reality." Combining such a model with a game can yield approximations to solutions of problems which can be accepted with confidence. Such use of gaming, in effect, is controlled experimentation.

Gaming should not be considered as a substitute for analytic model construction. To the contrary, it should be viewed as a way of obtaining information which can be used to generate models where analysis of or experimentation on the "real" situation is impractical or impossible.

SUMMARY

In this chapter we have been primarily concerned with various ways of deriving solutions from models. First we considered analytic techniques with which an abstract symbolic expression for optimizing values of controlled variables can be derived deductively from an abstract symbolic decision model. By appropriate substitution of numbers for symbols in these expressions the numerical optimizing values of the controlled variables can be obtained.

In some cases the mathematical form of the decision model precludes such an abstract deduction of a solution to the problem. A solution may be obtained, however, by substituting the appropriate numbers for the parameters in the decision model and then "solving" numerically. In some such cases it may not be possible to find directly the best values of the controlled variables, and a number of trials may be required to identify them. Such trials and errors may, in some instances, be conducted so as to converge monotonically or trendwise on the solution; if so, they are called *iterations*.

In still other situations the outcomes that result from using specific numerical values of the controlled variables cannot be calculated, usually because the measure of performance is a parameter of a statistical distribution of outcomes which are in turn a function of two or more probabilistic processes. In these cases we may be able to "run the system on paper" or simulate it in some other way so as to generate a set of outcomes under specified conditions and obtain the required estimates from these observations. Such simulation is experimentation on a representation of the phenomenon under study; that is, vicarious experimentation.

One important advantage of simulation is that it allows us to study the transition of the phenomenon from one state to another. Such transitions can sometimes be studied analytically, but it is usually very difficult to do so.

Finally we considered problem situations which contain decision makers whose behavior cannot be effectively represented in decision models. In these cases simulation can be conducted in which decision makers participate directly. This type of simulation, gaming, was summarized in the preceding section.

BIBLIOGRAPHY

Ackoff, R. L., "Games, Decisions, and Organizations," *General Systems,* **IV** (1959), 145–150.

Akers, S. B., Jr., and J. Friedman, "A Non-Numerical Approach to Production Scheduling Problems," *Journal of the Operations Research Society of America,* **3** (November 1955), 429–442.

Bellman, Richard, C. E. Clark, D. G. Malcolm, C. J. Craft, and F. M. Ricciardi, "On the Construction of a Multi-Stage, Multi-Person Business Game," *Operations Research,* **5** (August 1957), 465–503.

Clark, C. E., *et al.,* "War Gaming, Cosmagon, and Zigspiel," *Staff Paper* ORO-SP-12, Operations Research Office, The Johns Hopkins University, Chevy Chase, Md., May 1957.

Clark, D. F., and R. L. Ackoff, "A Report on Some Organizational Experiments," *Operations Research,* **7** (May-June 1959), 279–293.

Cohen, K. S., and Eric Rhenman, "The Role of Management Games in Education and Research," *Working Paper* No. 22, Graduate School of Industrial Administration, Carnegie Institute of Technology, Pittsburgh, September **1960**.

Cushen, W. E., "War Games and Operations Research," *Philosophy of Science,* **22** (October 1955), 309–320.

―――, "Operational Gaming in Industry," in *Operations Research for Management,* II, ed. by J. F. McCloskey and J. M. Coppinger. Baltimore: The Johns Hopkins Press, 1956.

Glover, W. S., and R. L. Ackoff, "Five Year Planning for an Integrated Operation," in *Case Studies in Operations Research.* Cleveland: Case Institute of Technology, 1956.

Greenlaw, P. S., "The Human Factor in Business Games," *Business Horizons,* Fall (1960), pp. 51–61.

Guetzkow, Harold, "A Use of Simulation in the Study of Inter-Nation Relations," *Behavioral Science,* **4** (July 1959), 183–191.

Hammersley, J. M., "A New Monte Carlo Technique: Antithetic Variates," *Proceedings of the Cambridge Philosophical Society,* **52** (1956), 449.

Hare, V. C., Jr., and W. C. Hugli, "Applications of Operations Research to Production Scheduling and Inventory Control, II," in *What is Operations Research Accomplishing in Industry?* Cleveland: Case Institute of Technology, 1955.

Harling, John, "Simulation Techniques in Operations Research—A Review," *Operations Research,* **6** (May-June 1958), 307–319.

Hoggatt, A. C., "An Experimental Business Game," *Behavioral Science,* **4** (July 1959), 192–203.

Kahn, H., "Use of Different Monte Carlo Sampling Techniques," in Meyer (1956), pp. 146–190.

Lambert, F., "Les methodes de Monte Carlo," *Cahiers du centre d'etudes de recherche operationnelle,* **1** (1958), 7–26.

Lehmer, D. H., "Mathematical Methods on Large Scale Computing Units," *Annals of the Harvard University Computing Laboratory,* **26** (1951), 141–146.

Malcolm, D. G., "Bibliography on the Use of Simulation in Management Analysis," *Operations Research,* **8** (1960), 169–177.

McDonald, John, "Military Operations and Games," in *Readings in Game Theory and Political Behavior,* ed. by Martin Shubik. Garden City, N. Y.: Doubleday and Co., 1954.

Meyer, H. A. (ed.), *Symposium on Monte Carlo Methods.* New York: John Wiley and Sons, 1956.

Mood, A. M., *War Gaming as a Technique of Analysis.* The RAND Corp., p-899, Sept. 3, 1954.

―――, and R. D. Specht, *Gaming as a Technique of Analysis,* The RAND Corp., p-579, Oct. 19, 1954.

Morgenthaler, G. W., "The Theory on Application of Simulation in Operations Research," in *Progress in Operations Research,* I, ed. by R. L. Ackoff. New York: John Wiley and Sons, 1961.

Morton, K. W., "General Principles of Antithetic Values," *Proceedings of the Cambridge Philosophical Society,* **52** (1956), 476.

The RAND Corporation, *A Million Random Digits.* Glencoe, Ill.: The Free Press, 1955.

Riley, Vera, and J. P. Young, *Bibliography on War Gaming,* BRS-7, Operations Research Office, The Johns Hopkins University, 1 April 1957.

Rosenstiehl, P., and A. Ghouila-Houri, *Les choix economiques.* Paris: Dunod, 1960.

Shubik, Martin, "Bibliography on Simulation, Gaming, Artificial Intelligence and Allied Topics," *Journal of the American Statistical Association,* **55** (1960), 736–751.

"Symposium on Monte Carlo Methods," *Journal of the Royal Statistical Society,* Series B, **16** (1954), 23–75.

Thomas, C. J., "Military Gaming," in *Progress in Operations Research,* I, ed. by R. L. Ackoff. New York: John Wiley and Sons, 1961.

———, and W. L. Deemer, Jr., "The Role of Operational Gaming in Operations Research," *Operations Research,* **5** (August 1957), 465–503.

Young, J. P., "History and Bibliography of War Gaming," *Staff Paper* ORO-SP-13, Operations Research Office, The Johns Hopkins University, Chevy Chase, Md., April 1957.

12

EXPERIMENTAL
OPTIMIZATION

INTRODUCTION

There are two situations in which experimentation may be used effectively to locate the optimum of a decision function. First, there is the situation in which simulation (vicarious experimentation) is necessary to find a solution to a model. Second, there are problem situations for which an adequate decision model cannot be constructed. This may be due either to our inability to identify the uncontrollable variables (Y_j) or to a lack of knowledge of the underlying function (f) which relates the outcome to the controllable and uncontrollable variables. It may still be possible to find an optimal solution by means of experimentation. One could, of course, resort to trial and error, but such a haphazard procedure is usually too costly and time consuming. Fortunately, by controlled trials—that is, by experimentation—the researcher may obtain good estimates of the optimal values of control variables in a time- and effort-conserving way.

Designs for seeking optima experimentally fall into two classes: simultaneous and sequential. In simultaneous designs all the combinations of variable values at which observations are to be made are selected in advance, whereas in sequential designs only a few points are so selected. Selection of the remaining points is made after some observations and is based on the information obtained from these earlier observations. Combinations of these types of design are also possible.

Although we will consider the relative advantages and disadvantages of these types of design in later discussion, some general observations are in order here.

In simultaneous experimental designs the observations may be made either simultaneously or sequentially. In sequential designs most, if not all, of the observations are made in sequence. Where observations are made sequentially, the same "subject" may be used over and over again or different "equivalent subjects" may be employed. For example, in experiments to determine what combination of altitude and speed of a bomber yields minimum dispersion of bombs dropped on a point target, different bombs and even different targets may be used.

Where the observations are made simultaneously, different "equivalent subjects" may be used. Either of these requirements or both may be impossible in some problem situations. In marketing research, for example, it may not be possible to duplicate a specific market. Furthermore, a particular market place may be changed by an experiment so that it cannot be used twice. If a sequence of observations is to be made on a single subject, then we have the general requirement that the subject return to the same initial state after each experiment. This means that such changes in outcome as follow the changes in the controlled variables must not be affected by previous values of the controlled variables; that is, the effects must not be cumulative. For example, current sales of a consumer product may be the effect of past as well as current advertising. It may be necessary to have long periods of no change in the controlled variables so as to allow the effects of previous states to diminish or disappear. This is contrary to the practical experimental requirement that changes in the controlled variables can be made relatively frequently.

In general, subjects which can be brought into a laboratory lend themselves better to either simultaneous or sequential experimentation than do subjects which must be observed in their natural habitat.

In either type of design (simultaneous or sequential) the uncontrolled variables must either remain constant or vary in a statistically stable way. That is, the variations in observed outcome must be attributable either to the variables subject to experimental control or to the fluctuations (experimental errors) due to the uncontrolled variables. These errors must be random and measurable. Even if this constancy or stability is attained during the experimentation, it may not continue in the "real" situation. The optimum obtained in experimental optimization is applicable only as long as the environment of the phenomena under study remains constant or stable. Therefore, experimental optimization at best is not a complete substitute for optimization based on a model. The latter can always be appropriately adjusted when the uncontrolled variables change, but this cannot be done with optima derived from experiments alone.

Simultaneous experiments can usually be conducted over a shorter time span than sequential experiments and hence are less subject to distortion due to instability (e.g., time trends) of the uncontrolled variables. But the results of both types are equally subject to such instability when applied to the real situation.

Finally, it should be observed that, in sequential experiments on a single subject, we must be able to change the values of the controlled variables at will and, in general, more frequently than they would normally be changed.

We shall consider two types of simultaneous design: *random* and *factorial;* and two types of sequential design: the *single-factor* and the *steepest ascent.* Only for the method of steepest ascent has a relatively extensive literature been developed. The other designs appear in the literature more as suggestions than as well-developed techniques of optimization. This is due in part to the fact that the method of steepest ascent is considered to be the best available, and hence, since its presentation in 1951, investigation of the other approaches has been curtailed.

In the discussion of these four techniques we will be concerned primarily with their underlying logic rather than with procedural details. Before turning to the techniques, let us set the stage a bit.

Consider again the idealized general form of a decision model:

$$V = f(X_i, Y_j), \quad 1 \leq i \leq m, \quad 1 \leq j \leq n.$$

We observe that the function can be plotted in a space of $m + n + 1$ dimensions. If the Y_j (uncontrolled variables) are not known, then we would have an incomplete model of the form:

$$V = f'(X_i).$$

This can be plotted in a space of $m + 1$ dimensions. In experimental optimization we deal with such incomplete models and assume that the Y_j are constant or statistically stable. Specifically, the "residual" or "chance" effects due to the uncontrolled variables are assumed to be normally distributed, to be independent, and to have the same variance for all observations. Further, it is assumed that the mean of the residual effects is zero; that is, in the long run the negative and positive effects tend to cancel each other.

For illustrative purposes we shall consider only cases involving two control variables, X_1 and X_2, but the conclusions drawn are equally applicable to problems involving any finite number of control variables. In the two-control-variable case the function can be plotted in two dimensions with the use of contour lines. For example, in Figure 12.1 the following simple function is plotted:

$$V = (X_1 - h)^2 + (X_2 - k)^2.$$

The contours are drawn through equal values of the outcome variable, V. The minimum of the function falls at (h, k). If a function has more than one maximum (or minimum), there is no assurance that any of the procedures to be considered finds the greatest of these. In effect, then, these procedures are designed to find *local* maxima (or minima).

RANDOM DESIGN

There are essentially two ways of selecting a random design for experimental optimization. In the first the range of values of X_1 and X_2 from which the selection is to be made is specified. Then random selections of values of X_1 and X_2 are made in pairs. In the second

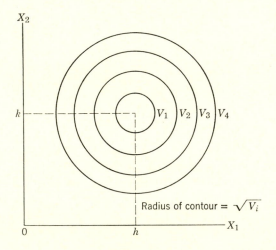

FIGURE 12.1.

procedure, increments along each scale are selected: X_{11}, X_{12}, $\cdots$ and X_{21}, X_{22}, $\cdots$. These values are then combined in all possible pairs: (X_{11}, X_{21}), (X_{11}, X_{22}), $\cdots$, (X_{12}, X_{21}), $\cdots$. A random selection of these pairs is made.

If the variables have one or more natural limits (e.g., zero weight), the task of selecting the sampling range for each variable is simplified. Otherwise such ranges must be selected. It is desirable to make the range large enough to give assurance of including the optimizing values and small enough to minimize the size of sample required. Consequently, the more that is known about the possible region of the maximum the smaller the sampling region can be made.

Once observations of outcomes (which are subject to a random error) have been made at each sampled set of values of the controlled variables, that set is selected which yields the optimal outcome. It may be possible, however, to refine the estimate of the optimizing values in one of several ways. In the two-variable case the observed values of the outcome can be plotted and contours can be sketched through them. By interpolation an improved estimate may be obtained. For any number of control variables it is possible to design a second experiment to explore in detail the region of the observed optimum. If two or more optima are observed which are approximately the same, such further exploration may be necessary in each region in order to determine which is the greatest. Such procedures, of course, become sequential.

If random observations are made sequentially, the Las Vegas procedure of marginal analysis discussed in Chapter 11 can be applied to determine how many observations should be made.

It is apparent that, once the region of the optimum is established, it may be more efficient to probe the area by one of the types of design yet to be discussed. Anderson (1953) has consequently recommended that random designs be used primarily for exploratory work.

Cochran and Cox (1957, p. 367) evaluate random design as follows:

Although this method has no planned strategy, it may have practical possibilities when the number of factors [controlled variables] is large and experimental errors are small. Two goals which the experimenter might hope to accomplish at the end of a moderate series of preliminary trials are (i) to reach a region of relatively high response and (ii) to learn something about the [control] variables that have the greatest influence on [the outcome variable], in order that future experiments can be confined to a smaller number of factors. Suppose that the sub-region in the X-space in which the response is satisfactorily high has a volume which is a fraction a of the volume of the whole X-region which is being explored. If experimental error is ignored, the probability that at least one of the random combinations out of n trials lies in the desirable sub-region is

$$P = 1 - (1 - a)^n.$$

This equation holds irrespective of the number of factors. . . .

Since the levels of the different factors are independently assigned, methods of regression analysis can be applied to provide clues to the factors exerting most influence. This approach must be developed further and compared with other methods before its utility can be assayed.

FACTORIAL DESIGN

Suppose that each of the scales along which X_1 and X_2 are measured is divided into equal intervals. Then the pairs of points can be represented as is done in Table 12.1. Observations made at the pair of x-values represented by each cell constitute a factorial design. Such a design yields a set of observations which are uniformly spaced on a flat surface, but when this pattern is projected on a curved surface those points are furthest apart which fall on the part of the surface with the steepest slope. The observations obtained from this design, like the random one, may be used to contour a three-dimensional surface, or to locate a region of relatively high outcome. This region can then be explored by selecting more closely spaced points, using this or some other experimental design.

By now it will be apparent to the reader that many other types of experimental design can be used in probing for the optimum of a function. Cochran and Cox (1957, p. 366) suggest rotatable second-order designs (which they discuss on pp. 344–347) and use of higher-

TABLE 12.1. A FACTORIAL DESIGN

Values of X_1	Values of X_2			
	x_{21}	x_{22}	$\cdots$	x_{2m}
x_{11}			$\cdots$	
x_{12}			$\cdots$	
.	.	.	.	.
.	.	.	$\cdots$	.
.	.	.	.	.
x_{1n}			$\cdots$	

order polynomials. Which design is best will depend on the nature of the function being explored. Consequently, by means of double (i.e., two-stage sequential) sampling an estimate of the form of the function can be obtained from the first sample and an appropriate design established for the next probe. The logical extension of this principle is a sequential procedure in which we continuously move closer to the region of the optimum and explore each region in a way that is indicated by all the data available before each stage of observation. These principles we will find incorporated in the method of steepest ascent.

If the time between setting the values of the controlled variables and observing an outcome is large, sequential or multiple sampling may be impractical. The experimenter may not have access to the phenomena in question for a long period of time. If, for example, travel is required to make the observations, the cost or time of going back and forth may be prohibitive.

THE SINGLE-FACTOR PROCEDURE

This method, suggested by Friedman and Savage (1947), consists essentially of probing each controlled variable separately in the order of their estimated importance. It may be necessary to perform more than one cycle through the set of controlled variables. The steps involved in the procedure are as follows:

(1) List the controlled variables in the estimated order of their effects on the outcome. Let X_1 represent the most important, X_2 the next most important, and so on to the least important, X_k.

(2) Estimate on the best grounds available (which may be a guess) the optimal combination of values of the controlled variables. Let these values be represented by $x_{11}, x_{21}, \cdots, x_{k1}$.

(3) Fix the value of X_2 at x_{21}, X_3 at x_{31}, and so on. Find the value of X_1 which maximizes the outcome, V.

Observations at from three to five values of X_1 are required, depending on how widely X_1 ranges and how well the region of its optimal value is known. For a discussion of how to space these trials see Hotelling (1941).

If the experimental points straddle the maximum value of V, fit a parabola to the data; for example, if

$$V = b_0 + b_1 X_1 + b_2 X_1{}^2,$$

then, by use of the calculus, the maximizing value of X_1 is found to be

$$x_{12} = - \frac{b_1}{2b_2}.$$

If the experimental points do not straddle the maximum, further observations should be made until the maximum is contained. Then proceed as above.

(4) Fix X_1 at x_{12}, leave $X_3, \cdots, X_k$ at the values $x_{31}, \cdots, x_{k1}$, and repeat step 3 for X_2.

(5) Repeat for the remaining variables.

If at the end of the first round the differences $(x_{12} - x_{11})$, $(x_{22} - x_{21})$, $\cdots$, $(x_{k2} - x_{k1})$ are small, the experiment can terminate. Otherwise conduct a second round, varying X_1 at the fixed values $x_{22}, x_{32}, \cdots, x_{k2}$.

This procedure is illustrated graphically in Figure 12.2. Here only two control variables are involved. The variable X_1 is judged to be the more important, and X_2 is estimated to be optimal at x_{21}. Hence, starting at the point (x_{11}, x_{21}) we probe along the vertical at x_{11} until we find the maximum at x_{22}. Now we probe horizontally at x_{22} until we find the maximum at x_{12}. Then we probe vertically at x_{12} until we find the maximum at x_{23}. Finally, probing horizontally at x_{23} yields no improvement, so we stop at the point (x_{12}, x_{23}), which is estimated to be the optimal combination of values of X_1 and X_2.

The more important the controlled variables are (relative to the un-

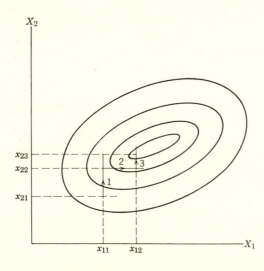

FIGURE 12.2. Single-factor optimization.

controlled variables), the more rapidly this procedure converges on the optimal set of values. The uncontrolled set of variables, it should be re-emphasized, are assumed either to be constant or to be varying randomly about their mean. If these assumptions are not satisfied and if the uncontrolled variables have a significant effect on the outcome variable, this method can lead to a poor approximation of the optimal values of the controlled variables.

It should also be remembered that, if the function has more than one maximum, there is no assurance that more than one will be found or that the optimum occurs at the one that is found.

It can be shown that the advantage of the single-factor procedure over simultaneous designs increases as the number of controlled variables increases. The larger the number of controlled variables the more rapid is the relative rate of convergence on the maximum by the single-factor method. Friedman and Savage (1947, pp. 368–369) suggest a procedure for further accelerating convergence on the maximum during the third experimental cycle if it is required.

. . . After the second complete round it might be desirable to move along the vector defined by the end points of the first two rounds, instead of varying the variables according to the original pattern.

In this suggestion lies the underlying idea of the method of steepest accent, which Box and Wilson were to develop a few years later.

THE METHOD OF STEEPEST ASCENT

In 1951 Box and Wilson first presented a procedure for experimental optimization which permits simultaneous probing of all the controlled variables. In effect, the procedure estimates sensitivity of the outcome to each of the controlled variables and moves in the direction of estimated maximum improvement along all scales simultaneously; it does so by moving along each scale in increments proportional to the estimated sensitivity of the outcome to each variable. The sensitivity is estimated initially by the slope of straight lines fitted to the data obtained in a small factorial experiment. When acceptable linear fits can no longer be obtained, quadratic fits may be used and subsequently, if necessary, fits involving increasingly higher-order polynomials.

In effect this procedure moves along a diagonal which, on the basis of previous observations, is aimed at the optimal set of values. It makes adjustments of its aim as it approaches the target on the basis

TABLE 12.2

Factor	Factor Level	
	-1	$+1$
X_1	$x_{11} - 0.5\Delta X_1$	$x_{11} + 0.5\Delta X_1$
X_2	$x_{21} - 0.5\Delta X_2$	$x_{21} + 0.5\Delta X_2$

of observed errors in the original setting. Since the single-factor method proceeds only along lines normal to the axes, one would expect that this "diagonal" procedure would approach the optimum more rapidly. In most cases it appears to do so.

The initial steps of the procedure can be illustrated by a case involving two control variables, X_1 and X_2. The steps are as follows:

(1) As in the single-factor method optimal values of X_1 and X_2 are estimated or guessed. Let x_{11} and x_{21} represent these values.

(2) An amount by which each factor is to be changed is determined: ΔX_1 and ΔX_2. These amounts should be large enough to show effects on the outcome but not so large as to permit the possibility of much curvature of the function in the interval between values separated by these amounts. A poor choice of ΔX_1 and ΔX_2 can be corrected later, but a good first choice reduces the number of observations required to reach the maximum.

(3) Levels of experimental factors are chosen as indicated in Table 12.2.

(4) These values are arranged into a 2×2 factorial design, and observations are taken at each factor combination. The results are tabulated as shown in Table 12.3, in which v represents the observed values of the outcome.

TABLE 12.3

i	x_{i1}	x_{i2}	v_i	$x_{i1}v_i$	$x_{i2}v_i$
1	$+1$	$+1$	v_{++}	$+v_{++}$	$+v_{++}$
2	-1	$+1$	v_{-+}	$-v_{-+}$	$+v_{-+}$
3	-1	-1	v_{--}	$-v_{--}$	$-v_{--}$
$4 = n$	$+1$	-1	v_{+-}	$+v_{+-}$	$-v_{+-}$
Sum			$\sum v_i$	$\sum x_{i1}v_i$	$\sum x_{i2}v_i$

(5) A linear fit to the data is obtained in the form

$$\hat{V} = b_0 + b_1 X_1 + b_2 X_2,$$

where

$$b_0 = \frac{\Sigma v_i}{n}$$

$$b_1 = \frac{\Sigma x_{i1} v_i}{n}$$

$$b_2 = \frac{\Sigma x_{i2} v_i}{n}.$$

(6) Now probing of X_1 and X_2 begins by changing their values by increments proportionate to b_1 and b_2. For example, if X_2 is changed by increments I_2 equal to $K \Delta X_2$, then X_1 is changed by an increment I_1, where

$$I_1 = K \frac{b_1}{b_2} \Delta X_1.$$

The selection of K is a matter of judgment. If it is too large, the optimum may be passed. Consequently, K is usually made conservatively small. An observation is made at the values $x_{11} + I_1$ and $x_{21} + I_2$. The result is compared with the value predicted by the linear equation [step (5)]. As long as the observed and computed values are relatively close together, further observations are made for additional increments. When they diverge significantly, a new 2^k factorial experiment (k = number of factors) is conducted at the last point. If the new linear fit is good, the procedure is continued until either

(a) the linear fit is good but the coefficients b_i are all small, which indicates that a plateau and hence a maximum has been reached; or

(b) the linear fit is not good, in which case the experimenter proceeds to quadratic fitting. If the initial estimate of the location of the maximum was good, the first linear fit may not be good and the experimenter may have to proceed directly to a quadratic fit.

We will not go into the details of the quadratic phase of the procedure. These may be found in a number of the references given at the end of the chapter, for example, Davies (1956). In some instances the experimenter may have to resort to higher-order fits than the quadratic.

In the method of steepest ascent, as in the single-factor procedure, there is no assurance that in functions involving more than one maximum the optimum has been obtained.

COMPARISON OF THE PROCEDURES

There is no way of making a completely general comparison of these procedures. Their relative values depend on the amount of prior information available and the nature of the surface to be explored. Brooks (1955) did make a comparison of the four procedures for four very simple two-dimensional (i.e., two-controlled-variable) surfaces. He equated the procedures by allowing only the same number of observations in each. In this case the true maximum outcome was equal to 1.0. By making repeated trials with each procedure, he computed the average estimated maximum outcome yielded by each method. The results are shown in the following table:

| | | Surface | | |
Method	1	2	3	4
Single-factor	0.990	0.984	0.926	0.984
Steepest ascent	0.993	0.989	0.979	0.985
Factorial	0.955	0.977	0.927	0.976
Random	0.902	0.911	0.913	0.936

The method of steepest ascent was uniformly the best, although in all but the third case it was only slightly better than the single-factor procedure. As one might expect, the random procedures was uniformly poorest. In the third surface, where the single-factor procedure performed least well relative to the method of steepest ascent, the factorial procedure performed about as well as the single-factor procedure.

General conclusions cannot be drawn from this test, even though it may seem to conform with what one would generally expect. It should be remembered, moreover, that all the surfaces explored in this comparison had only one maximum.

CONCLUSION

Although the development of procedures for experimental optimization is still in its infancy, some of these procedures are quite useful.

To be sure, the range of situations in which application of these procedures is justified is limited, but it is nevertheless extensive. The principal applications to date have been made in the study of such processes as occur in chemical production, metal production, and some areas of agriculture. In general the procedures have been found most applicable to geographically confined phenomena. The opportunities for experimental optimization are best when the observations can be made under such highly controlled conditions as can be created in a laboratory, a pilot plant, or a confined work area.

BIBLIOGRAPHY

Anderson, R. L., "Recent Advances in Finding Best Operating Conditions," *Journal of the American Statistical Association,* **48** (1953), 789–798.

Box, G. E. P., "Multifactor Designs of First Order," *Biometrika,* **39** (1952), 49–57.

——, "The Exploration and Exploitation of Response Surfaces; Some General Considerations and Examples," *Biometrics,* **10** (1954), 16–61.

——, and J. S. Hunter, "Multifactor Designs," Report prepared under Office of Ordnance Contract No. DA-36-034-ORD-1177 (RD) (1954).

——, and ——, "Experimental Designs for Exploring Response Surfaces," in *Experimental Designs in Industry,* ed. by Victor Chew. New York: John Wiley and Sons, 1958, pp. 138–190.

——, and ——, "Multifactor Experimental Designs for Exploring Response Surfaces," *Annals of Mathematical Statistics,* **28** (1957), 195–241.

——, and K. B. Wilson, "On the Experimental Attainment of Optimum Conditions," *Journal of the Royal Statistical Society,* **B13** (1951), 1–45.

——, and P. U. Youle, "The Exploration and Exploitation of Response Surfaces and Examples of the Link between the Fitted Surface and the Basic Mechanism of the System," *Biometrics,* **11** (1955), 287–323.

Brooks, S., *Comparison of Methods for Estimating the Optimal Factor Combination,* Sc.D. thesis, Johns Hopkins University, 1955.

Cochran, W. G., and G. M. Cox, *Experimental Designs.* New York: John Wiley and Sons, 2nd ed., 1957.

Davies, O. L. (ed.), *Design and Analysis of Industrial Experiments.* New York: Hafner Publishing Co., 1956.

DeBaun, R. M., "Block Effects in the Determination of Optimum Conditions," *Biometrics,* **12** (1956), 20–22.

Friedman, M., and L. J. Savage, "Planning Experiments Seeking Maxima," in *Techniques of Statistical Analysis* by the Statistical Research Group, Columbia University. New York: McGraw-Hill Book Co., 1947.

Hotelling, H., "Experimental Determination of the Maximum of a Function," *Annals of Mathematical Statistics,* **12** (1941), 20–45.

Plackett, R. L., and J. P. Burman, "The Design of Optimum Multi-Factor Experiments," *Biometrika,* **33** (1946), 305–325.

13

TESTING AND CONTROLLING THE MODEL AND SOLUTION

INTRODUCTION

Is the model an adequate representation of the phenomena under study? The procedure by which an answer to this question is sought constitutes the testing of the model. This aspect of research is not separated in time from other phases of research but continuously interacts with them, particularly with the construction of the model. While the model is under construction, it should be subjected to continuous testing. Determination of whether the model contains the relevant variables and constants, whether these are evaluated appropriately, and whether the functional form is correct are all aspects of testing as well as of model construction.

The testing of the model that is conducted simultaneously with its construction, however, is usually directed toward parts of the model rather than toward the model as a whole. Once a model is completed, there usually remains the need to test it as a whole. It is this phase of testing with which we are primarily concerned here: the final overall test of the adequacy of the model and the solution derived from it.

In a very fundamental way every model is a predictive instrument. It predicts a value of some outcome as a function of the values of a specified set of variables and constants. Hence, testing the model as a whole consists of testing its ability to predict. Since prediction is itself a procedure for estimating future values of a variable, testing consists of determining the principal characteristics of the estimates which are yielded: bias and reliability. The procedures for testing the model as a whole, therefore, are essentially the same as those involved in the evaluation of any estimating procedure.

TEST FOR BIAS

The model should be compared with the real phenomenon by comparing values of the outcome predicted by the model with actual outcomes, where these can be determined with little or no error. This procedure may be conducted either retrospectively or prospectively. That is, for each set of instances of the phenomenon in question, an outcome is predicted by use of the model, and these predictions should be compared with the actual outcomes. If past instances are used, the test is retrospective; if future instances are used, the test is prospective.

In the use of past data for evaluating a model an effective evaluation cannot be obtained if the model is tested against the same data which were analyzed to obtain estimates of the parameters or the functional form. For this reason it is generally advisable to divide available past data into two parts, one to obtain the necessary information for evaluating the variables and functional form of the model, and the other for testing. If the model stands the test well, then all the data can be recombined to obtain more precise estimates of the variables and the functional form.

It is particularly important to divide the data in the way indicated if the model is empirically derived, using regression or correlation analysis. In most cases an equation which is derived from a set of data can be expected to predict those data reasonably well. The critical question is whether it will accurately predict events not covered by the data from which it is derived. Models have an unpleasant inclination *not* to hold up beyond the period from which they were derived.

In testing the model the difference between the predicted outcome and the actual outcome should be determined for a series of unique events. Let d_i represent these observed differences. By use of these observations two questions can be answered: is the model a biased predictor of the phenomenon in question, and how reliable a predictor is it?

The model would be unbiased if the true average difference between the observed and actual outcomes, $\bar{D}$, were equal to zero. Therefore, the test for bias consists of testing the hypothesis:

$$H_0 : \bar{D} = 0.$$

This test consists of determining, if H_0 were true, the probability that we would obtain the observed average deviation of observed outcomes from predicted outcomes:

$$\frac{1}{n} \sum_{}^{n} d_i,$$

where n is the number of observations made. Standard statistical procedures may be used for this purpose (e.g., the t-test).

If the hypothesis H_0 is rejected on the basis of the test, it is necessary to adjust the model so as to remove the bias. This may be accomplished simply by adding or subtracting a constant equal to the estimated bias. Such an adjustment, however, does not add to our understanding of the phenomena unless we can determine what this constant represents; that is, what relevant aspect of reality is missing from the model or what irrelevant aspect is included. An error in the functional form of the model may also produce a bias. The addition of a bias-correcting constant which is derived from the part of the data that is used for testing purposes makes this portion of the data unfit for further testing of the model. Hence, it is important to determine what causes the bias of the model and not merely to add an empirically derived correction factor.

TESTING FOR RELIABILITY

The reliability of the model can be measured by estimating the variance (or some other appropriate statistic) of the deviations of the observed outcomes from those that were predicted. There are no simple criteria for determining whether the variance is too large; that is, whether or not the model is sufficiently reliable. Practically, the important question is whether the model yields more reliable predictors than alternative models of the same phenomenon. If it does not do so, it does not necessarily follow that it is not good enough. A more reliable model may be more costly to use than the less reliable one; and consequently, when the "cost" of prediction is taken into account, the less reliable model may be preferable. The situation here is the same as that involved wherever an approximation procedure is used. That is, the determination of the adequacy of a model requires consideration of the way it is to be used and the costs involved.

As before, let V represent the true value of the outcome variable and v the value estimated by the model. Then let σ_v^2 represent the true variance of these estimates and s_v^2 the estimate of σ_v^2. Let c_1 represent the "cost" of preparing a prediction using the model. Now it is necessary to determine the expected cost of the inaccuracy of the predictions. We shall examine the procedure for doing so in a moment, but for the time being let c_2 represent this cost. Then alternative modeling techniques can be compared relative to the sum of these costs; that is, the best model is that one which minimizes the sum, $c_1 + c_2$.

Before engaging in the steps involved in testing the reliability of the model, it is frequently desirable to have the model thoroughly scrutinized by other researchers who are knowledgeable in the area involved. Such organized critical sessions are sometimes referred to as "murder boards," since their objective is to "destroy" the model. Evaluation of the criticisms and suggestions generated by such a review is, of course, the ultimate responsibility of the researchers involved. Despite the obvious desirability of such reviews they are not used as much as one would expect. This has led one academic to observe that many researchers would rather publish (and hence publicly display) their errors than reveal them privately to their colleagues.

Determination of c_2, the expected cost of error resulting from use of the model, is usually extremely difficult in so-called pure research, where the uses to which the model is to be put may not be known or cannot readily be evaluated. If this is the case, the scientist must rely on his judgment and experience. In applied research, however, this evaluation can be performed explicitly, since a solution to a problem is involved. In such an evaluation the model and the solution derived from it are treated as a unit and not as separate entities.

Let d_i now represent the deviations of the actual outcome of the phenomenon from that predicted by application of the solution. That is, if V_o represents the true optimal outcome and v_o the outcome actually obtained by use of the solution, then in any specific instance $(v_o - V_o)$ is equal to d. This deviation would be expressed in value units. The expected value of d_i would then be the expected "cost" of error in the model and its solution. Since the true optimal outcome, v_o, is not known, such an idealized evaluation cannot be performed; that is, V_o is a standard of performance which we cannot specify. In situations in which we do not have a standard against which alternatives can be evaluated we must generally compare them with each other. Hence, testing a model and the solution derived from it, in a problem context, involves comparing the performances of two or more solutions. In most problem contexts the comparison can include the decision procedure used by the decision maker before the newly derived solution was obtained and adopted.

Ideally this comparison should be made by solving the problem using the alternative solutions under a set of identical circumstances and by comparing the differences in performance. Such a comparison can sometimes be made by use of test areas, pilot operations, and so on. When it can, the average difference in performance is the relative expected cost of error of the least effective solution. Then, by taking into account the cost of obtaining the solution of each procedure in a specific situation, the sum of the costs for each procedure can be obtained and a comparison made.

In many instances such a controlled comparison between two methods of solution cannot be made. Such comparisons are usually not possible, for example, in problems involving decisions of managers of industrial, governmental, or military enterprises. In such instances we have to approximate a comparison.

Comparison of a proposed method of solving a problem with a procedure that has been in use may be made retrospectively. It consists essentially of determining what the performance of the proposed procedure would have been in instances in which the other procedure was actually used. The difficulty inherent in such a method is that a prediction of what would have happened if the solution had been used must be made by means of the model which is under test. The results, then, yield a comparison which would be perfectly accurate only if the model itself were a perfect representation of the problem situation. This procedure is biased in favor of the solution derived from the model. Yet it is by no means useless.

What such a comparison actually yields, as noted, is a comparison of performance of alternative procedures of solution if the model on which one is based is in perfect correspondence with reality. If the difference observed between the average performances is small, one would have good reason to doubt the superiority of the proposed solution. If it is large, one can then raise some relevant questions which help to support or destroy the apparent superiority of the proposed procedure. For example, if it is assumed that the only errors in the model are ones involving evaluation of variables, it is possible, using the data from the comparison, to determine by how much the estimates of uncontrolled variables would have had to be in error before the proposed solution would perform less well than the procedure with which it is being compared. Such a procedure can be illustrated by using the familiar simplified model:

$$V = XY + \frac{1}{X}. \tag{1}$$

Suppose that we must find the optimizing value of X in this model. As we have shown previously,

$$X_o = \frac{1}{\sqrt{Y}} \tag{2}$$

and hence

$$V_o = 2\sqrt{Y}. \tag{3}$$

Suppose that an estimate of Y, $y = 25$, is obtained. Then the estimated optimal value of X would be

$$x_o = 1/\sqrt{25} = \tfrac{1}{5}.$$

If Y is actually equal to 25, then

$$V_o = 2\sqrt{25} = 10.$$

Now suppose that under these conditions another decision rule yields an actual performance equal to 14.5. Now we can ask, when $Y = 25$, for what value of y is $v_o = 14.5$, where

$$v_o = \frac{Y}{\sqrt{y}} + \sqrt{y}. \tag{4}$$

To answer this question we substitute in (4) and solve:

$$14.5 = 25/\sqrt{y} + \sqrt{y}$$

$$14.5\sqrt{y} = 25 + y$$

$$y - 14.5\sqrt{y} + 25 = 0$$

$$(\sqrt{y} - 2)(\sqrt{y} - 12.5) = 0.$$

Hence,

$$\sqrt{y} = 2$$

$$y = 4$$

$$\sqrt{y} = 12.5$$

$$y = 156.25.$$

Then, if Y actually were equal to 25, we would have to underestimate by $(25 - 4 = 21)$ or overestimate by $(156.25 - 25 = 131.25)$ to do as poorly as did the alternative-decision rule.

Such computations can be repeated, and by so doing we can estimate a distribution of "equalizing estimation errors." Now we can inquire as to whether such a distribution of errors is likely to occur, using a specified estimating procedure for Y. If not, we are relatively sure that the proposed solution yields an improvement even though we do not know precisely how large the average improvement will be.

CONTROL OF THE SOLUTIONS

Control of a model consists of setting up a procedure for detecting significant changes in either (a) the values of the parameters, or (b) the mathematical form (structure) of the model. The model, the solutions derived from it, and the control procedure together constitute a self-maintaining decision-making system. Systems which, on the basis of information feedback on their performance, adjust their parameters so as to improve their performance, are called *adaptive* systems. Those which are also capable of modifying their structure so as to improve performance are said to be *self-organizing*. A dynamic self-maintaining, decision-making procedure, then, is an adaptive and self-organizing system.

If the model and/or the solution derived from it are to be used repeatedly, it may be possible that the values of the uncontrolled variables will change during the interval between applications. Consequently, if it is known that such repetitive use of a decision rule will be made, it is desirable to check the values of the relevant parameters periodically in order to make sure that the proper values are being used; and, if not, to adjust them. Such a procedure we refer to as *control*. Periodic checking of the functional form of the model is also a control procedure.

If the parameter is not statistical in character (e.g., the charge for an hour's labor), no particular problems are created by the control process. Complications arise only when the parameter involved is statistical in character (e.g., an average value, a percentage, or a probability) and where the values are estimated on the basis of a sample. The control procedure in such a case can be characterized as follows:

(1) A significant change in the value of a variable must be defined.
(2) The design decisions involved in a control procedure are

(*a*) the frequency of control checks;

(*b*) the type of sample selected;

(*c*) the size of the sample;

(*d*) the test for significance of change; and

(*e*) the significance level at which the test is to be conducted.

(3) Ideally, these decisions should be made in such a way as to minimize the sum of the following costs:

(*a*) the cost of making the observations;

(*b*) the cost of the test;

(*c*) the expected cost of type I error; and

(*d*) the expected cost of type II error.

The problem is similar to designing a test for a hypothesis with an additional complication arising out of the fact that the test is to be performed repetitively. If we knew the distribution of changes of the true value of the parameter involved with respect to time, it would be possible in principle to optimize the frequency of control checks. Since this information may not be available, it may be necessary to select a frequency of control checks on other grounds.

There is usually little or nothing to be gained by checking the values of parameters any more frequently than the solution is applied (i.e., a decision is made). The only point of checking the value of a parameter less frequently (e.g., at every second or third application of the solution) is that the parameter is extremely stable or that the cost of the control check is very high compared to the cost of possible error. The latter condition is rather rare. Consequently it is generally reasonable to run a control check on each parameter before each application of the decision rule.

The remainder of the control problem is identical with that of testing a hypothesis, but it is necessary to specify the hypothesis to be tested. We would want to change our estimate of the parameter only when the cost of so doing is less than the expected gain in performance. It is necessary, therefore, to determine the magnitude of the least change in the parameter which results in a loss equal to the cost of the adjustment. The cost of the adjustment will vary from problem to problem, depending on the complexity of the solution and on such other factors as whether the process involves a computer program or simple hand computations. In many cases which involve hand computation, the cost of changing the value of a parameter is negligible. Where a computer program would have to be materially changed, however, the cost could be quite large. Once this cost of adjustment, c_a, has been determined, the task that remains is to find for each uncontrolled parameter how large a change in its true value would be required before the loss relative to the outcome variable is equal to c_a. This procedure can be illustrated by use of the model given in equation (1).

Again assume that $Y = 25$ during the last period. Then the optimizing value of X is $1/\sqrt{25}$ or $\frac{1}{5}$, and the minimal V is $2\sqrt{25}$ or 10. To find the critical upper and lower values of Y, Y_U' and Y_L', we proceed as follows.

The cost of error of using $Y = 25$ when Y is actually some other value, Y', is given by the cost of error (C), which is

$$C = \frac{Y'}{\sqrt{Y}} + \sqrt{Y} - 2\sqrt{Y'}. \tag{5}$$

In this case

$$C = \frac{Y'}{5} + 5 - 2\sqrt{Y'}. \tag{6}$$

Suppose that the cost of changing the value of Y is 0.2. Then we set

$$C = \frac{Y'}{5} + 5 - 2\sqrt{Y'} = 0.2$$

or

$$Y' - 10\sqrt{Y'} + 24 = 0.$$

Therefore

$$(\sqrt{Y'} - 6)(\sqrt{Y'} - 4) = 0$$

and

$$Y' = 36 \quad \text{or} \quad 16.$$

Hence, if Y changes in a positive direction by more than $(36 - 25)$ or 11, its value should be changed. If it reduces by more than $(25 - 16)$ or 9, its value should be changed. (The lack of symmetry reflects the asymmetry of the function which gives V.) Hence, in the control process we must check the hypothesis: $16 \leqq Y \leqq 36$.

To illustrate how significant changes can be determined in the two-parameter case, consider the following decision model:

$$V = XY_1 + \frac{Y_2}{X}. \tag{7}$$

The optimizing value of X is found by the calculus to be

$$X_o = \sqrt{Y_2/Y_1} \tag{8}$$

and the optimal performance is

$$V_o = Y_1\sqrt{Y_2/Y_1} + \frac{Y_2}{\sqrt{Y_2/Y_1}} = 2\sqrt{Y_1 Y_2}. \qquad (9)$$

Now suppose that the cost of a change in the solution is 2, and that the last values used for Y_1 and Y_2 were $y_1 = 8$ and $y_2 = 2$. The cost of not changing the solution when these values actually do change is given by

$$C = Y_1\sqrt{\frac{y_2}{y_1}} + \frac{Y_2}{\sqrt{y_2/y_1}} - 2\sqrt{Y_1 Y_2}. \qquad (10)$$

Now, if C is set equal to 2, we can determine for various values of Y_1 what the corresponding values of Y_2 are. For example, let $Y_1 = 1$, then

$$2 = 1\sqrt{\frac{2}{8}} + \frac{Y_2}{\sqrt{2/8}} - 2\sqrt{1 Y_2}$$

$$= \tfrac{1}{2} + 2Y_2 - 2\sqrt{Y_2}$$

$$\therefore Y_2 + \sqrt{Y_2} - \tfrac{3}{4} = 0$$

$$(\sqrt{Y_2} + 1.5)(\sqrt{Y_2} - 0.5) = 0$$

$$Y_2 = \tfrac{1}{4} \quad \text{and} \quad -2.25.$$

Similarly we can compute other values of Y_2 and obtain results as follows:

Y_1	Y_2	
1	−2.25,	0.25
4	0,	4.00
9	0.25,	6.25
16	1.00,	9.00
25	2.25,	12.25
36	4.00,	16.00
etc.		

From this a plot can be obtained such as is shown in Figure 13.1.

Once the significant changes have been determined, the hypothesis to be tested in the control check is that the change in value of Y_j since its last use does not exceed the significant amount.

As the number of parameters in a model increases beyond two, the

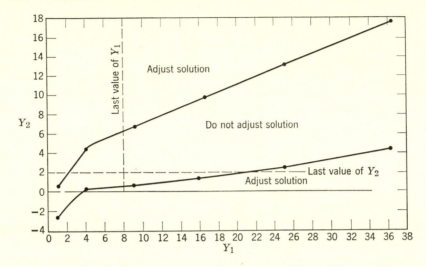

FIGURE 13.1. Bounds on simultaneous changes of two parameters.

number of possible combinations of their value which can constitute a significant change becomes too large to be manageable. In such cases it is generally preferable to determine the effect of any apparent combination of changes when they arise rather than to try to set up criteria in advance.

Once significant changes in the value of a specific parameter in a positive and negative direction have been determined, a control chart —resembling those used in statistical quality control—can be prepared and maintained. Such a chart facilitates the apprehension of trends or other types of nonrandom fluctuations in the value of the parameter. If more than one parameter is involved, the bounds are variable, as has been shown. Even so, it is helpful to prepare a control chart for each parameter separately, assuming reasonable values of the other parameters. The resulting charts should always be studied collectively.

As in quality control, when a significant change occurs, an effort should be made to find the reason for it, the *assignable cause*. If such a cause is found, it may reveal whether or not the change can be expected to persist. In either case it would be desirable to introduce the identified cause of the fluctuation into the model to assure future awareness of significant changes due to its behavior. For example, in a problem containing "change in sales per month" of a pharmaceutical as a parameter, a control chart revealed that this parameter had periodically gone out of control in the past, and had quickly come back into control. Further study revealed that in each such instance a price increase had been announced for the next month. By inserting "change in price for the next month" into the model as a parameter, greater control over the outcome was obtained.

If an assignable cause cannot be found when a parameter goes out of control, close observation should be maintained to determine whether the variation was a random phenomenon, or whether further and more intensive search for the cause should be carried out.

CONTROLLING THE MODEL AS A WHOLE

As an alternative to continuous testing for change of each aspect of the model, such a test can be performed on the model as a whole. At the beginning of this chapter a procedure was described for testing the adequacy of the model. Once the expected error (zero when the model is unbiased) and the standard deviation (or some other suitable measure) of the error has been determined, statistical control procedures can be applied to these errors. If the errors display nonrandomness (e.g., trend) or an unlikely magnitude (under the assumption of no change), the individual aspects of the model can then be examined to determine what specific error caused the observed deviation. Then appropriate adjustments can be made if warranted. The errors can be measured in terms of the output variable; and hence, when the value of the error in question exceeds the cost of adjustment, an adjustment is justified.

CONCLUSION

Even where the most complex models are involved, a considerable amount of control can be obtained by relatively intuitive application of even elementary statistical techniques.* These and more sophisticated procedures are least often used where the mathematical sophistication of the model is greatest, precisely where the greatest gains are to be made by means of *control* procedures.

Finally, it should be observed that the model of a problem situation is a theory which attempts to explain the phenomena involved.

* See references at the end of the chapter for more detailed discussion of these techniques.

The predictions and solutions derived from the model are deduced consequences of the theory. We have, in effect, been discussing theory testing in applied problems. Theory testing in pure science is, therefore, the same in principle as the procedure we have considered here.

BIBLIOGRAPHY

Ackoff, R. L., "The Concept and Exercise of Control in Operations Research," *Proceedings of the First International Conference on Operations Research,* Baltimore, Operations Research Society of America, 2nd ed., 1957, 26–43.

Duncan, A. J., *Quality Control and Industrial Statistics.* Chicago: Richard D. Irwin, 1952.

——, "The Economic Design of $\bar{X}$ Charts Used to Maintain Current Control of a Process," *Journal of the American Statistical Society,* **51** (1956), 228–242.

Grant, E. L., *Statistical Quality Control.* New York: McGraw-Hill Book Co., 1952.

Juran, J. M. (ed.), *Quality Control Handbook.* New York: McGraw-Hill Book Co., 1946.

Littauer, S. B., "Technological Stability in Industrial Operations," *Transactions of the New York Academy of Science,* Ser. II, **13,** No. 2 (1950), 66–72.

——, "The Development of Statistical Quality Control in the United States," *American Statistician,* **4** (1950), 14–20.

Shewhart, W. A., *Statistical Methods from the Viewpoint of Quality Control.* Washington: United States Department of Agriculture, 1939.

Tippett, L. H. C., *Technological Applications of Statistics.* New York: John Wiley and Sons, 1950.

14

IMPLEMENTATION AND ORGANIZATION OF RESEARCH

INTRODUCTION

In each of the aspects of research discussed up to this point it has been possible either to construct a model of the research decisions involved or to make some progress in this direction. When we discuss implementation of research results and organization of the research effort, this is no longer possible. Although an increasing amount of effort is being put into the study of these aspects of research, and even more effort into writing about them, they are still very poorly understood. Since these problems are largely psychological and socio-logical in character, it may be that progress in these currently "artis-tic" aspects of research will have to await further development in the behavioral sciences. In the meantime discussions of implementation and organization of research are more likely to be based on opinion, experience, and wishful thinking than on analysis, experimentation, and systematic observation. Consequently, such discussions, includ-ing this one, ought to be approached with cautious reservation.

How little we know about these problems is particularly well illus-trated by the results of some experimental work of Churchman and Ratoosh (1960) on the problem of implementation. They have devel-oped a game for a four-man team which involves running a small simulated business firm. The underlying model of the market is a simple one which can be explicitly formulated and the optimal solu-tion of which can be derived in a straightforward way. In the main

405

the players have been graduate students in management who have had courses which equip them to construct the model and to derive the solution.

One member of the team is a "plant." He knows the solution to the game. After a number of plays of the game by a team—during which few teams have yet made an effort to construct a model and derive a solution—the "plant" pretends to discover the solution and suggests its adoption by the team. As yet, only a very small proportion of the teams has accepted the suggestion.

The experiments are directed toward finding the conditions under which a suggested solution to a problem will be accepted and implemented. Using what is "known" about these phenomena—most of which is obviously folklore—the experimenters have not yet been able to find a way to present the solution to teams so that it has some significant chance of being accepted.

The moral of this extremely informative and provocative experiment is that at present we do not know enough to assure acceptance of research results and their implementation under what appear to be very simple and favorable conditions.

The fact that the experimenters have had less success in obtaining implementation than most researchers *claim* to have in practice suggests either that the game situation is not as simple or favorable as it appears, or that implementation of research results in practice is less frequent than one would suppose. Nevertheless, until the researcher can solve the implementation problem in situations that are completely under his control, he cannot pretend to have substantial knowledge of implementation in situations which are largely out of his control.

THE RESEARCHER'S RESPONSIBILITY

From the Renaissance up to the recent past society has discouraged entry by the scientist into the realm of practical affairs. Even today the burning of Bruno and the punishment of Galileo are vivid in the scientist's mind. Past persecution and pressure have bred a belief that the scientist is responsible only for producing knowledge and not for the way in which it is used. Since the development of the atomic bomb, however, a gradual transformation has taken place in both the public and the scientific attitude toward the involvement of science in public affairs. The use of science in solving practical problems has been increasing at a considerable rate, and, in fact, many observers have pinned the possibility of continued social and economic progress on just such involvement of science. For example, in his book, *The Scientific Attitude* (1948), C. H. Waddington has written (p. vii):

The aim of this book is to point out some of the contributions which the scientific attitude of mind can make to the creative tasks of social reorganisation with which the world is faced. By this I do not mean merely an enumeration of new devices, new sources of power or techniques of production. The fundamental problems of to-day lie far more in the sphere of ideals and values—in the spiritual sphere, if you are not afraid to use that term— than in the technological. We already have all, or at least most, of the techniques we need to provide a decent civilized life for everybody. They are not yet producing that result, partly of course because the organisational machinery has been smashed in large parts of Europe, and partly because the old political and economic machine was unsuitable, directed to the wrong ends, and in obvious need of thorough overhaul, which unfortunately many people were not yet ready to give it. We now have to decide for what purposes the new organisation shall be designed. And to the discussion of these social ends, science has a good deal more to contribute than has been recognized hitherto.

Recommendations

There are still some persons in and out of science who feel that the researcher should simply determine the consequences of actions of various sorts and not recommend action or take any responsibility for these consequences. The fact is, however, that with the development of an adequate methodology of problem solving, a solution carries with it the prestige of science and is interpreted as a recommendation whether or not the scientist wishes it to be so considered.

To be sure, all solutions to problems are conditional: they depend on the adequacy of the representation of the problem situation by the model employed. That is, at best the solution derived from the model is a solution to the relevant problem only if the model adequately represents the problem situation. The adequacy of the model is clearly the responsibility of the researcher. If the model is less adequate than the researcher would wish, but as adequate as he is capable of producing, he should see to it that the decision maker is aware of the limitations of the model. The ultimate responsibility for decision making, of course, lies with the decision maker, who must evaluate the research and its results. He may also have to supply judgment to cover those aspects of the problem which could not be covered by the research. The decision maker's ultimate responsibility, however, does not relieve the researcher of any responsibility for consequences of action which follows logically from the research findings.

The fact is that decision makers who sponsor research into their problems *expect* recommendations from the research that they support. They will not continue to support applied research which does not yield recommended solutions to their problems.

Implementation

Even some of those who would accept the necessity of the researcher's providing recommendations will deny his responsibility for carrying them out. Such a position ignores important practical and scientific considerations. The principal practical consideration is that a decision maker who sponsors research usually expects and requires the scientist's participation in implementation and frequently selects scientists for applied research on the basis of their ability to follow through. To the scientist who wants to study real problems but not to manipulate the real world, this expectation of decision makers may not seem to be a potent reason for allowing himself to be so used.

There is, however, an important scientific consideration involved in the implementation issue. It is only through implementation that many research conclusions can be tested because an increasing proportion of research is concerned with phenomena that cannot be brought into the laboratory. For such research, application of its results in the "real" world can provide the strongest test of their validity. If implementation is in the hands of nonscientists, modifications in the research results are inevitable, and they are likely to be made in such a way that the usefulness of the application as a test of the research is destroyed. Modifications of problem solutions are generally required in practice because of changing conditions, but such amendments should be made under the direction of those who are thoroughly familiar with the way the research was conducted.

The researcher's role in implementation should be much the same as the architect's in the construction of a building he has designed: that of active supervision. Just as the architect is the only one who knows enough about a building to supervise its construction adequately, so the researcher is the only one in a position to supervise implementation of most research results.

THE PLAN FOR IMPLEMENTATION

Planning for the implementation of research results should begin when the research itself begins; it should not wait until the results are obtained. Specifically, the technical abilities of those who will use the results and the facilities at their disposal should be taken into account in determining the form and nature of the research results which should be sought. It would be foolish to expect a clerk to solve an equation requiring the calculus of variations; a nomograph or a table may be necessary. But a nomograph or a table may be able to provide only very approximate solutions to equations. An approximation which is used, however, will produce better results than an exact solution which is ignored.

The extent to which research results are distorted in use, or the likelihood that they will be used at all, depends critically on the extent to which those who will use these results understand them and can carry them out. Hence, it is important to formulate and solve a problem in such a way as to yield a type of solution which is operationally—not merely logically—feasible.

In order to assure that the research results are carried out as intended, it is necessary to develop a detailed plan for their implementation. This need is generally acknowledged where the action ultimately to be taken is to be performed by a computer. In such a situation the researcher recognizes his responsibility for developing a program for the computer. What is not as well recognized is that almost as detailed a program is required for human operators. It is necessary to specify exactly who is to do what, when they are to do it, and how. The *who* and *when* can normally be shown on a flow chart which indicates the way that the relevant operations are to be conducted. The *what* requires detailed instructions in terms of operations that can be performed by the kinds of people involved.

An example of implementation instructions

To illustrate the kind of detail required in such instruction let us quote from a report of research on the budgeting of research and development activity in a business firm. The details of the study and the meaning of the instructions are not relevant here. What is important is the *style* of the instructions. The instructions quoted yield a graph which, when used in combination with others for which instructions are also provided, produces the budget sought. To aid those who will use the instructions in seeing the whole computational procedure the diagram shown in Figure 14.1 is also provided:

(1) From Table 1 select a value of the factor (F) corresponding to current market share.
(2) Select a trial value of Cumulative Product Research Expenditures.
(3) Calculate the product of (1) and (2).

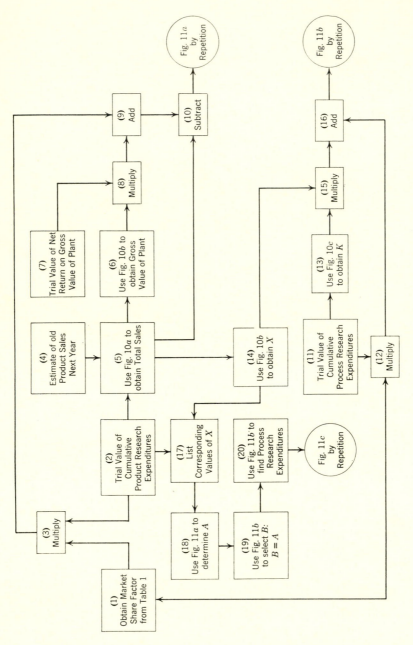

FIGURE 14.1. Schematic diagram of computational procedure, part I.

(4) Prepare an estimate of next year's Old Products Sales.

(5) Using the estimate from (4) and the trial value from (1), determine from Figure 10a the Total Sales.

(6) Using the Total Sales from (5), determine from Figure 10b the Gross Value of Plant.

(7) Select a trial value of net return on Gross Value of Plant from a preselected set of trial values.

(8) Multiply the results of (6) and (7).

(9) Add the results of (3) and (8).

(10) Subtract the result of (9) from that of (5). Call the result A.

Repetition of these ten steps for various trial values of Product Research Expenditures yields Figure 11a.

(11) Select a trial value of Cumulative Process Research Expenditures.

(12) Multiply the value selected from Table 1 in step (2) by the trial value selected in (11).

(13) Using the value of Cumulative Process Research Expenditures selected in (11), determine from Figure 10d the value of the intermediate variable k.

(14) Using the value of Total Sales from (5), determine from Figure 10b the value of the intermediate variable x.

(15) Multiply the value of k obtained in (13) by the value of x obtained in (14): xk.

(16) Add xk (15) to the result of (12). Call this result B.

Repetition of the last six steps for various values of Cumulative Process Research Expenditures, grouping the results by values of x obtained in (14), yields a figure like Figure 11b.

(17) For each trial value of Cumulative Product Research Expenditures used in (1) list the corresponding value of x used in (14).

(18) Using the value of Cumulative Product Research Expenditures from (17), determine from Figure 11a the corresponding value of A.

(19) Let the value of B equal that of A obtained in (18).

(20) Using the values of x and B (derived from A) corresponding to a particular value of Cumulative Product Research Expenditures, determine from Figure 11b the value of Process Research Expenditures.

Repeating steps (17)–(20) for the various values of Cumulative Product Research Expenditures yields one curve for a specified Net Return on Gross Value of Plant as shown in Figure 11c.

Repeating steps (1)–(20) for various values of the Net Return on Gross Value of Plant yields a family of curves such as those shown in Figure 11c. Each curve in the family describes the alternate combinations of required levels of Cumulative Product and Process Research Expenditures.

It will be apparent to many that these instructions are quite similar to many specifications of cost-accounting and data-processing systems (no matter how superficial might have been the background reasoning) and computer programs.

Such instructions should be pretested on members of the population who will use them in order to assure their completeness and lack of ambiguity. The feasibility of the overall implementation plan should also be checked with those who will carry it out. This is best accomplished by involving the operators in the preparation of the plan. We shall consider this aspect of the organization of the research effort in more detail below.

ORGANIZATION OF THE RESEARCH EFFORT

Organization of the research effort involves all the participants in the problem: the decision makers, those who are affected by the actions recommended by the research, and the researchers themselves. Each of these will be discussed in turn.

The nature of the organizational problem obviously depends on the size of the research effort: the number of researchers involved and the duration of the research effort. Since our concern in this discussion is with the relationship between researchers and other participants in the problem, it is most useful to have in mind a relatively small research effort in which each member of the research team is likely to have some direct contact with the other participants. Such a research effort will usually involve from one to eight or nine scientists.

Even in large research efforts some subgroup of the researchers will have access to the other participants, and hence the following discussion can, with minor modifications, be made applicable to such situations.

The Decision Makers

A minute's involvement of the decision maker (and those who carry out the decision) in the research before results are obtained is worth at least an hour of "selling" the results after they are obtained.

There is a strong tendency among researchers to withdraw as much as possible to the isolation of their offices and laboratories to work out a solution. Such a procedure fails to attain the kind of involvement of the decision maker that is required for a high probability of acceptance and successful implementation.

There are other important reasons for the involvement in research of decision makers and those who will carry out the decisions. Continuous review of the research by them serves as a safeguard against errors of omission or oversimplification. There is nothing that can be as frustrating to a researcher as a statement at the end of the project, "The research is fine and very impressive, but unfortunately you forgot to take 'so and so' into account and 'so and so' is very important. Therefore, we can't use your results."

I have found it very desirable to formalize the participation of the decision makers by organizing them into a Research Advisory Committee and meeting with this committee as frequently as is productive, but no less frequently than every other month, to report on progress and plans. Informal meetings with individual decision makers are held as required in the interim. This facilitates a gradual absorption of research findings and promotes understanding. It also produces a sense of participation and involvement that usually removes the need to "sell" results. It also frequently leads to implementation of partial results before the research is completed.

Although the amount of time required of decision makers during the course of research is generally small, it is not always easy to obtain, particularly from executives who are almost always very busy men. In this connection there is an important principle which, if followed, can avoid considerable frustration for the researcher: *never perform research for a decision maker for which he does not pay.* People in responsible positions tend to be suspicious of the motives of anyone who tries to give them something for nothing. In general the amount and the quality of attention they give to an activity are proportional to the cost of that activity *to them.* An individual or group that is not willing to pay for research into a problem is not likely to give serious consideration to results obtained from a study of that problem.

I have had experience working on successive problems for the same decision makers, first at a cost to them and subsequently with the research being paid for by others. Even under these conditions the amount of participation and cooperation provided in the second study was very much reduced.

Motives of sponsors

Not all persons who sponsor research into a problem are primarily motivated by an interest in obtaining a solution to the problem. The research may be used as a device to satisfy some personal motive involving status or prestige. Research, for some, is like an article of clothing worn for the impression which it makes on others rather than for the function it performs for the wearer. Where this is the case, the researcher must try either to avoid involvement or to direct his efforts so that the results are used as they ought to be, despite the sponsor.

In many instances research is solicited for the purpose of "proving" the validity of a conclusion already reached by the decision maker. If the decision maker respects the integrity and standards of the researcher, he is not likely to disclose this motivation until results appear which are at variance with his preconceived notion. For this reason it is important that the researcher probe early the motives of the decision maker as thoroughly as possible and, if necessary, obtain an explicit assertion to the effect that imposition of the preconceived notion will not occur during the research.

In some cases even a well-intentioned decision maker will obstruct progress of the research because of feelings of insecurity which derive from his relationship with others (usually above him) in the organization. This kind of obstacle can frequently be removed once it is understood, and the researcher may be uniquely equipped to remove it. Understanding the nature of the insecurity, however, may require the special skills of the psychologist or sociologist.

Guarding against reorganization

Organizations are subject to almost continuous *reorganization*. Many research projects and their results have been washed down a drain because the person initiating the research is moved to another position and his replacement is either not interested in the inherited research or is so occupied with his new responsibilities that he cannot take time to participate and inform himself about the research. For this reason it is extremely desirable to involve as many persons in the responsible organizational unit as possible. For example, if the work is initiated by the director of a unit, his assistant should also be involved. Then if the director is replaced by his assistant, no hiatus occurs. If he is replaced by someone else and the assistant remains, he can assume a major share of the task of bringing the new director up to date.

Unselling

The tone of the discussion up to this point implies that the decision maker is usually one who must be "sold." Although this is frequently true, it is by no means always the case. In some situations the decision maker may, because of pressures being applied to him, be anxious to grasp any straw the researcher holds out in the wind. The task here may be to "unsell" the decision maker, to convince him that preliminary results are not substantiated enough to take action on. In such cases the decision maker is likely to transmit the pressure applied to him to the researchers. The researchers may be able to relieve the original source of pressure by explaining why time is required to find an adequate solution to the problem and why preliminary results are not to be trusted.

In some cases "unselling" will be required because the decision makers are overenthusiastic even though they are under no pressure. The same kind of irrational enthusiasm which is displayed by many for electronic computers is sometimes displayed toward recently developed and advanced scientific techniques. I have seen decision makers who were more interested in using the output of a scientific technique for its prestige value (e.g., linear programming) than in solving their problems. This kind of attitude toward simulation and gaming, for example, is becoming increasingly prevalent among military and industrial executives.

The possibility of the various kinds of difficulties we have been considering emphasizes the need for effective communication between researchers and decision makers. It is necessary for each to learn a great deal about the other's profession if effective use is to be made of the results of scientific research.

Those affected by decisions

Another common cause for the failure of results to be implemented is contained in a statement by decision makers such as the following: "The results are fine and I'm sure they would help us a great deal, but we do not have the kind of people who can carry out the recommendations," or "The people we have will not change their behavior in the way required by the solution." The safeguard against such remarks is to involve in the research those who will carry out the recommendations and to give them a part in developing the plan for implementation so that the decision maker can be confronted simultaneously with research results and a plan for their implementation developed (at least in part) by those who will carry it out. This also prevents the research from being looked upon by the "operators" as a threat to their security, or as a criticism of their effectiveness. Rather it is likely to be considered as an effort at self-improvement.

I have seen many situations in which cooperation of the operators was considered to be unattainable by the decision maker but was obtained by the researchers as a result of their contact with the operators. Let me briefly recount several such instances, because they may contain some useful guides to the organization and conduct of research.

In a study performed for one of the larger commercial airlines it was found that by changing scheduling procedures additional stewardesses would not be required even though more flights were to be added.

A consequence of the proposed scheduling procedure, however, was an increase in the average number of flying hours per stewardess per month. The increased average was within the limits set by the union contract, but the personnel manager insisted that a large number of stewardesses would quit if their flying was increased by the projected amount. He agreed, however, to let the researchers look into the problem.

First the researchers performed an analysis of available data which showed (a) that a significant percentage of the stewardesses were already flying more than the projected average number of flying hours, and (b) that the senior stewardesses who had first choice of assignments had no inclination to select those with fewer flying hours. Further analysis showed that what the stewardesses did prefer in assignments was as few stopovers away from their home base as possible and regular days off. Discussion with stewardesses and their representatives confirmed the results of the analysis. The scheduling procedures were then modified to give them these desirable characteristics with virtually no loss in efficiency. The final procedure was then acceptable to both management and the stewardesses.

The second case involved sea transport. For many years the managers of steamship lines refused to consider the possibility of automating cargo handling because of what they claimed to be a complete unwillingness on the part of longshoremen to cooperate. The director of a research group in a west coast steamship company persisted in his efforts to bring about automation and finally received permission to set up a joint study with the research group in the longshoremen's union. Their combined effort was directed toward finding ways in which the benefits of automation could be equitably divided among employers and employees. Such ways were found and led to the recent precedent-setting agreement between the companies and longshoremen on the west coast.

In a study directed toward determining how much time salesmen should spend with customers it was necessary to obtain accurate data on how the salesmen were dividing their time between planning visits, traveling, waiting to see customers, talking to customers, and so on. Sales managers were sure that the salesmen would be unwilling to keep such records, since they would be interpreted as spying on them. Again the researchers arranged for a series of meetings with salesmen with no managers present. The reason for and the nature of the study were explained to them, but their reaction was as hostile and suspicious as predicted. At a critical point in the discussion one of the salesmen asked whether, if the proposed data were collected, it would be possible to determine the actual cost of selling each type of product handled and whether this could be used, in turn, to evaluate current company pricing practices. At the mention of this prospect the salesmen became very interested. Their discussion revealed that they believed that they were losing business to their competitors because of improper pricing. In a short time they agreed to keep the desired records if the researchers would use them to examine the pricing practices. The researchers obtained management agreement, and the data were collected as desired and were of even better quality than the researchers had expected.

As indicated earlier, these and similar experiences have a great deal to teach us about how to obtain cooperation between apparently hostile parties. Unfortunately science has been used more extensively to develop strategies of conflict and competition than to study strategies of cooperation. The necessary condition of cooperation displayed in the examples just given is simple to state, but not easy to accomplish in practice: cooperation between parties whose interests are in conflict can be obtained only by finding a set of overriding common interests which can be more effectively served by cooperation. Recognition of these important common interests is seldom the result of insight or intuition. It is the product of a thorough knowledge of the situation produced by sound research methods and techniques and by effective communication between the parties involved, usually through a channel consisting of persons who are not a party to the original conflict. Researchers often are uniquely equipped to provide the channel, as well as the knowledge required to resolve such conflicts, particularly researchers who are not employed by either of the parties involved.

In my research experience I have never encountered a conflict between decision makers and operators which could not be resolved by researchers who had unlimited access to the hostile parties. Since the decision maker usually sponsors the research, he must be "sold" on the desirability of this unlimited access to operators. Such selling requires that the mystery associated with "negotiation" be dispelled. Unfortunately many managers feel that their security is threatened by dispelling this mystery. This, however, is but another conflict that must be resolved, and the same approach is applicable to it.

The Research Team

For reasons which will be discussed below and in the last chapter, research teams—rather than individuals working alone—are being used increasingly for the solution of problems. Most of pure science is still being conducted by individuals working within a scientific discipline, but in the area of application teams of mixed scientific disciplines are more and more common.

The use of research teams—particularly ones involving several scientific disciplines—creates certain organizational problems which, if not solved satisfactorily, can have a detrimental effect on the research. A team of researchers may be either less than or more than the sum of its parts. It will be less than the sum of its parts if friction absorbs a great deal of the energy expended and if the parts simply augment each other's weaknesses. It is important, therefore, to compose a team in such a way as to compliment one man's weakness with another man's strength.

Scientists' personalities in general can be placed into two major categories which correspond to two major philosophies of science: rationalists and empiricists. The rationalist is a formalizer who likes to deal with the abstract and hence proceeds to a model or theory as rapidly as he can. He resorts to data as little as possible, and sometimes not even this much. In the extreme, he is one who likes to find problems which fit his techniques.

The antiformalist or empiricist, on the other hand, insists on knowing *all* the facts before formulating the problem or an approach to it. Since the pit that contains data is usually bottomless, he generally feels that he never knows quite enough to formulate the problem. He tends to deal with the specific and concrete, whereas the rationalist tends to deal with the general and abstract.*

Few scientists are as extreme as the sketches indicate, but tendencies in these directions are usually easily discernable. By combining these types of scientific personality the team is given a more complete personality than any of its parts possesses. The rationalist and empiricist tend to supplement each other. The rationalist presses the empiricist to organize his data into a precise formulation of problem and theory. The empiricist forces the rationalist to relate his abstract generalizations to the problem at hand.

Another dichotomy which affects team performance involves the degree of familiarity with the area in which the problem exists. A person thoroughly familiar with a problem area is usually restricted by many implicit assumptions concerning the area of which he is not

---

* For an illuminating discussion of the difference between the "formalist" and the "realist," see Minas (1956).

aware. He tends to be unable to see alternative solutions or to discard suggestions of new alternatives on the grounds that they have been tried before and failed. A person completely unfamiliar with the area is likely to think of all kinds of alternatives, but he is not likely to be in a very good position to evaluate them realistically. By combining into a team both those who are familiar and those who are unfamiliar with the problem area, assurance is gained that a wide range of alternatives will be considered and that they will be examined in light of the facts of the case.

The interdisciplinary team

There is a natural inclination on the part of those who have a problem to classify it by scientific or technological discipline and therefore set up a research team consisting exclusively of persons in that discipline. A strong countertendency to develop interdisciplinarians and use interdisciplinary teams is presently evident. This recent surge of interdisciplinary activity has its roots in the history of science and the nature of problems being exposed to science.

Contemporary scientists and consumers of science tend to overlook an important and interesting fact about the development of science. Until about the middle of the nineteenth century what we today refer to as science was conducted under the name of "natural philosophy." The inventory of knowledge produced by this pursuit became too full for one man to store in his mind. Specialization was inevitable, and it came about through the separation of science from philosophy, the organization of scientific societies, and the formation of departments of science in universities.

We also have a tendency to think of the division of science into its various branches as corresponding to a natural classification of phenomena. The division of science into disciplines was accomplished by man, not by nature. The disciplines cannot be individuated by a unique set of objects or events which constitute their subject matter, but they are distinguished by the aspects of phenomena to which they direct their attention. Many phenomena may be studied fruitfully by each branch of science, but each will concern itself with different aspects of the phenomena. For example, a communicative act may have physical, chemical, biological, psychological, sociological, and economic aspects.

In the last hundred years it has been necessary to continue to divide our study of phenomena into more and more specialized domains so that progress in depth could be maintained. We began to reach a point, in the second quarter of this century, where the problems most pressing to mankind could no longer be fruitfully treated by specialists. A synthesis of scientific disciplines was required. The effort to create scientific generalists, a much-discussed movement of the thirties, was directed along these lines; but it was doomed to failure because it acquired breadth at the cost of depth. Research by interdisciplinary teams was the only feasible alternative.

The second quarter of our century saw numerous interdisciplinary team efforts. One such movement, philosophical in orientation, was the movement for a unified science. It produced the *International Encyclopedia of Unified Science*. An Institute of Experimental Method was organized at the University of Pennsylvania in the early forties and conducted interdisciplinary research on a variety of problems involving large systems. [See, for example, Churchman *et al.* (1947).] These are but instances of a trend which Kenneth Boulding (1956, pp. 199–200) has described as follows:

> In recent years there has been a . . . development of great interest in the form of "multisexual" interdisciplines. Cybernetics, for instance, comes out of electrical engineering, neurophysiology, physics, biology, with even a dash of economics. . . .
> On the more empirical and practical side the interdisciplinary movement is reflected in the development of interdepartmental institutes of many kinds. . . . Even more important than these visible developments, perhaps, though harder to perceive and identify, is a growing dissatisfaction in many [university] departments, especially at the level of graduate study, with the existing traditional theoretical backgrounds for the empirical studies which form the major part of the output of Ph.D. theses.

The increasing use of interdisciplinary research teams results from the growing recognition of the fact that a large number of problems cannot be solved effectively within the boundaries of any one discipline. In the operation of a system, for example, the aspects of the system which can be manipulated so as to improve its performance are likely to come from many different disciplines. The determination of which of these variables can most effectively be manipulated from a control point of view requires the joint analysis of experts in the areas in which these variables are normally treated. Such joint analysis permits the construction of models in which variables from different disciplines interact.

The interdisciplinary approach to problems does *not* consist of a synthesis of research results obtained by independent *intra*disciplinary studies of the same phenomena. That is, it is not accomplished by first setting up disciplinary teams to study the same problem and then attempting to relate the results that are obtained in this way. Interdisciplinary research does not begin at the end of disciplinary inquiries but at the beginning of the research.

In practice, of course, it is seldom possible to have a wide variety of disciplines represented on a single research team. It is possible, however, to consult with representatives of a wide variety of disciplines and to use people on the team who are aware of the content and methods of other disciplines. It is no accident that so many contemporary scientists and engineers have multidisciplinary educational backgrounds.

Scientific snobbery

Not every scientist works well in an interdisciplinary environment. In my experience the principal obstacle to effective interdisciplinary collaboration is scientific snobbery. Such snobbery is quite pervasive. It is rooted in an assumed hierarchy of disciplines which is defended by invoking such ambiguous criteria as exactness and objectivity. Positions on the scientific totem pole are related, in fact, to the order in which the various disciplines achieved their independence (organizationally) from philosophy: the mathematician and the physical scientist at the top and the social scientist at the bottom.

Effective collaboration between the disciplines must be based on respect, and respect must be based on knowledge and understanding. As in most areas of human relations, prejudice is most firmly rooted in ground well fertilized with ignorance. The younger sciences, alas, lack the dignity of age. Until recently their progress has been retarded by denial of access to their subject matter. They are subject to severe social pressures by the public, particularly the politician. Finally, they must cope with the most perplexing subject of study yet discovered: *man*.

The sciences have a great deal to learn from each other, not only with respect to content, but also with respect to methods and techniques. To mention but one example, biological and behavioral scientists have yet to learn and exploit many mathematical concepts and techniques which have been productive in the hands of physical scientists. On the other hand, the latter have yet to learn and exploit the statistical concepts and techniques which have been so productive in the hands of the biological and behavioral scientists.

Now that most of the obstacles imposed by society on scientific progress have been removed, the principal ones which remain are those imposed by science itself. Ironically, society is now applying pressure to remove these obstacles and will undoubtedly succeed in time.

SCIENTIFIC DEMEANOR

There is an old saying to the effect that a man is judged by what he stands for. There is considerable ambiguity, however, in the meaning of "stands for." On the one hand, it refers to what a man will tolerate, and on the other to what he will not tolerate. The principles of a man are evaluated as much by what he refuses to do as by what he does. These negative acts clearly define his principles in the eyes of the spectator. The amount of compromise of scientific principles which a scientist is expected to make reflects the amount he has demonstrated a willingness to make.

A scientist must be prepared to refuse to perform work under conditions which do not permit him to meet what he considers to be minimal acceptable scientific standards. To the extent that he demands satisfaction of these conditions he will command the respect of the consumers of research.

The ability to stand on principle and to survive depends, of course, on the scientist's ability to perform effectively under the conditions he specifies. Freedom of research action is related to the ability of the researcher. Hence the scientist's best strategy is always to make himself as effective a researcher as possible.

The most powerful weapon a good scientist can have against abuse is the implicit or explicit threat to quit. Such a threat should not be made unless the conditions necessary for his remaining are made explicit and unless he is fully prepared to leave if they are not met. Bluffing is not an effective research strategy.

In effect a scientist should never perform research which he would not be willing to publish in a professional journal at its completion.

A researcher's performance depends on what he knows. Knowledge decays and is replaced. Therefore, keeping up with the developments in a field is an essential part of a scientist's activity. To do so involves extensive reading, conversation, attendance at professional meetings, and so on. Such activities should be a planned part of a scientist's job. Nonscientists who employ scientists are frequently unaware of the importance of such activities. It is necessary in such cases to impress them with the importance of "keeping up." This education of research consumers is the researcher's responsibility.

Dissemination of Research Findings

Such dissemination is an important aspect of science, pure or applied. Military and industrial security has become an increasingly serious barrier to effective scientific communication. The scientist can too easily place responsibility for such a state of affairs on others, but the responsibility is ultimately his. Security regulations can also easily become a screen behind which either poor or mediocre research can be hidden and/or behind which important research findings are withheld from others who can use them effectively. Scientists must increasingly reserve the right to publish at least part of their research findings.

It might be foolish to deny that there is any rational ground for security restrictions on science—but an increasing number of scientists are taking this "foolish" position. However, even granting the reasonableness of security measures some serious thought should be given to how much of research they should apply to. The "hardware" or products produced by research, or a competitive strategy that has been developed, might be reserved for private use. But how can one defend placing research methods and techniques under the "security wrap" except where the difference between method (and technique) and content is hard to define? Good research usually advances research methodology, and this much, as a minimum, should be published.

It is the responsibility of the researcher to educate research sponsors to the distinction between the content and the method of research and to insist on the right to publish at least the latter. I have seen few cases where this right has been denied to the competent scientist who has made a point of it.

Science is a public institution. It could not exist if all scientists were working in complete isolation. Every scientist has the obligation to add to the public pool of knowledge.

Publication, of course, should not be an end in itself. Scientific literature is already overcrowded with trivial and redundant material. On the other hand, restrictions on publication should not be used as a protective cover for poor research or for deprivation of other scientists of findings which would advance their work.

COMMUNICATION

Many books have been written on how to communicate effectively. The intention here is not to summarize this large body of literature. Rather we will consider a few—but, I hope—fundamental observations and principles that apply to the more formalized reporting of research. Some of these remarks will have relevance to day-to-day informal communications between the researcher and other participants in the problem.

It seems to me that individuals are less capable of objective appraisal of their communicative efforts than of almost any other aspect of their behavior. Most individuals, and particularly those with higher education, feel that they do a good—if not excellent—job of speaking and writing. Most don't. Because people are so easily offended when criticized in this area, most of us hesitate to tell them what we really think of their communicative efforts. By doing so we strengthen their illusions. Consequently few adults improve in this respect with practice.

Improvement is possible, of course, but it must begin with an objective appraisal of deficiencies. Such an appraisal can usually be obtained from others. Sincere requests for criticism, particularly before final presentation, are usually rewarded by disturbingly frank comments.

Presentations of the results of research (orally or in writing) should be made by that member of the research team who is the most effective communicator, whether or not he directs the effort. Convention, however, dictates that the senior member of the team do so. If he is not an effective communicator, his vanity may be satisfied by having him make brief opening and closing remarks, but someone else should make the main presentation.

Empathy with the Audience

All the advice and instruction on communication would be unnecessary if each speaker or writer could hear or see his output as his audience does. Empathy with the audience is the most valuable asset a communicator can have; that is, sensitivity to their response to him. Too many of us write and speak to an imaginary audience consisting only of persons identical to ourselves in every respect. To take a common example, how often have you been unable to decipher slides, charts, or writing on a blackboard used by a lecturer? Even the slightest amount of empathy in a speaker would lead him to make sure his visual aids could be seen by all present. But let us consider a more serious manifestation of this insensitivity to an audience.

The great advantage of presenting research results orally is that feedback is possible. Questions can be asked and answered. But unfortunately the questions asked and those answered are frequently not the same. Many a speaker's imagination is a barrier which prevents a question from being heard as it is asked. There are two simple precautions that can be taken to avoid or rectify such misinterpretation. First, the speaker can restate the question and ask the questioner if he has done so correctly. If not, he can modify his statement until it is acceptable to the questioner. Second, the speaker can ask the questioner, after attempting to answer his question, if he has done so satisfactorily. These practices require self-discipline and control, but they can train one to listen to others as well as to oneself.

Organization of Reports

Aristotle once observed that every presentation should have a beginning, a middle, and an end. In the beginning of a report a description of what will be presented in the middle should be provided, and in the last section a description of what was presented should also be provided. Too many speakers and writers try to present technical material in the style of O. Henry, saving the punch for the end. In technical writing surprises should generally appear at the beginning. The listener or reader wants to know what he is in for as quickly as possible, and then he wants to get to and through the point as quickly as possible. The audience prefers to get into details in discussion or appendices, not in the main body of the presentation. The importance of directness, brevity, and conciseness cannot be overemphasized.

This is not to say that the details of research are not important. To the contrary, they are. Every research project should yield a document which makes it possible to duplicate the study in essential detail, since the ultimate test of much research lies in its ability to be duplicated. Certainly the possibility of progress depends on the ability to study past work in great detail.

The Language of Reports

As has been indicated, a necessary condition of effective communication is that the language and mode of expression be those of the audience, not of the speaker if his differ from theirs. Researchers are inclined to defend obscurity on the grounds that the ideas involved are complex, but it is more likely to reflect an unwillingness to take the time to translate ideas into nontechnical language. The researcher should not consider this translation problem as a chore, but as a challenge. He should appreciate the fact that in making such a translation he subjects his work to the most severe critical evaluation of which he is capable. It is very easy to conceal glib assumptions from oneself and others by the use of symbols and technical jargon. As one approaches expression in Basic English, however, self-deception and deception of others become increasingly difficult. Simplicity of expression, like brevity, is the result of extended distillation and evaluation of ideas; it takes a long time and much effort to attain.

It is sometimes helpful for the researcher to imagine he is ghost-writing a report to be delivered by one of his audience. This may help him to get into the appropriate frame of mind for producing a report that is suitable for his audience.

Simulation as Display

One of the major difficulties in communication lies in explaining a model or solution which contains large numbers of variables in complex relationships with one another. Any translation of the symbolic models into ordinary language seems lengthy and too complex. In such cases the use of analogues that can be seen and manipulated can come to our aid. Simulation, in short, is a very effective communication device. It can be used not only to describe, but also to explain a model and solution, and frequently it will succeed in justifying a result in the eyes of the decision maker where other approaches completely fail.

SUMMARY

It has been argued that the researcher is responsible for producing recommendations in applied research and that he must also assume responsibility for and leadership in carrying out these recommendations if they are accepted. This requires detailed planning of the implementation, including programming the action to be taken by each individual involved.

In order to assure the soundness of results and their acceptability, the researcher should involve the decision makers and those who will be affected by the decision in the research process. The more responsibility they can be made to feel for the research outcome, the more likely the acceptance and implementation are.

Where research involves a group effort, the team should be put together with thought given to the mixture of personalities and types of training. Increasing use should be made of interdisciplinary teams because the complexity of most modern problems prevents their successful attack by any one discipline. The principal obstacle to effective interdisciplinary cooperation is scientific snobbery, which in the main is born of ignorance. Mutual respect among disciplines must develop out of an understanding by each disciplinarian of what other scientific disciplines can contribute to research.

If the scientist is to be of maximum use to those who have problems, there are certain scientific operating principles which cannot be compromised in performing services. Minimal requirements for time spent in keeping up with scientific developments, the right to disseminate results, and maintenance of scientific standards are necessary for effective research.

Finally, in communicating the results or the progress of research to the nonscientists the scientist should put himself in the place of his audience and make his presentation in the audience's language. These presentations should be brief and to the point. They should reveal their content at the outset and save details for discussion or appendices, depending on whether the report is oral or written.

An increasing amount of "pure science" involves nonscientists in the role of sponsors or subjects. For such research much of what has been discussed in the context of applied research is applicable. For the laboratory scientist working in isolation from the layman, of course, most of this chapter has no relevance. The problem of communication among "pure" scientists, however, can be approached with the same point of view as has been presented here.

BIBLIOGRAPHY

Ackoff, R. L., "Unsuccessful Case Studies and Why," *Operations Research*, **8** (1960), 259–263.

Boulding, Kenneth, "General Systems Theory," *Management Science*, **2** (1956), 197–208.

Churchman, C. W., R. L. Ackoff, and M. Wax (eds.), *Measurement of Consumer Interest*. Philadelphia: University of Pennsylvania Press, 1947.

Churchman, C. W., and P. Ratoosh, "Innovation in Group Behavior," *Proceedings of the Second International Conference on Operational Research,* English Universities Press, London, 1960, pp. 122–128.

Minas, J. S., "Formalism, Realism, and Management Science," *Management Science,* **3** (1956), 9–14.

Waddington, C. H., *The Scientific Attitudes.* West Drayton: Pelican Books, 2nd ed., 1948.

15

THE IDEALS OF
SCIENCE AND SOCIETY:
AN EPILOGUE

THE IDEALS OF MAN

A problem never exists in isolation; it is surrounded by other problems in space and time. The more of the context of a problem that a scientist can comprehend, the greater are his chances of finding a truly adequate solution. This same principle applies to science itself; it is a part of a sociohistorical continuum. The social and historical significance of science is understood only when we see how science fits into the broader scheme of things.

Scientists continually confront themselves with the question: what is the social role of science? Whatever their answer, it provides an attitudinal background against which research problems are selected and research is conducted; it has a considerable influence on what they do and how they do it.

In turning attention to this question, my intention is to emphasize the importance of the scientist's efforts to answer it self-consciously to both science and society.

Since the dawn of recorded thought philosophers have sought to identify the ideals of mankind; that is, those ultimate objectives to which mankind seeks closer and closer approximations without the expectation of complete attainment. Ancient philosophers identified three such ideals: *truth, goodness,* and *beauty.* Modern philosophers have identified a fourth: *plenty* (i.e., economic abundance).

It is one thing to name these ideals; it is another to define and justify them. Before attempting this difficult task let us move back a step.

Moralists and anthropologists have long argued that there is no single objective that all men have sought. Put another way, it seems that, if all who have lived and do live were granted one wish, there would not be universal agreement in that which was wished. Although wise men may find no universal wish, children do. When they are confronted with the familiar story involving the granting of the three wishes, they frequently observe that if they had the opportunity they would need only one wish. The wish that they would make, of course, is that all their wishes would come true.

In a considerably more sophisticated way, E. A. Singer (1923, p. 109) observed that accompanying every desire is the implicit desire for the power of attainment.

> Now suppose there were something you would have to have whether you wanted to bisect a line, or break a safe, or do anything else in the world; then, whatever you happened to desire, you would have to desire that something . . . the condition of attaining any end in the world is such control of the world's machinery as shall give you power to get what you want.

The desire for the ability to attain objectives is universal. If this ideal were satisfied, all others would be. Now when we analyze what is involved in the pursuit of such an ideal we can find the relevance of the ideals of *plenty, truth, goodness,* and *beauty,* although the connection is by no means obvious.

Men pursue *objectives* (ends or goals) by various *means* (courses of action) which incorporate a variety of conceptual and physical *instruments.* The capability for obtaining any objective presupposes the attainment of four ideals:

(1) *The scientific ideal of perfect knowledge* (i.e., complete attainment of *truth*): the ability of every individual to develop and select instruments and courses of action which are perfectly efficient for the attainment of any end.

(2) *The politico-economic ideal of plenty or abundance*: the availability to every individual of courses of action and the instruments necessary for them which are perfectly efficient for the attainment of any end.

(3) *The ethical-moral ideal of goodness*: (*a*) the absence of contrary and contradictory objectives within each individual (i.e., peace of mind), since no state of plenty or knowledge can make the attainment of such objectives possible; (*b*) the absence of conflicting objectives among people (i.e., peace on earth, good will toward man), since

only in the absence of such conflict can *every* individual attain his objectives.

These three ideals would be vacuously attained if no one wanted anything. The universal wish for the ability to attain any objective itself presupposes that there are desired ends (i.e., unfulfilled objectives) and that they continuously expand. Hence, the last ideal:

(4) *The aesthetic ideal of beauty*: the existence in every individual's environment of stimuli which inspire him to raise his aspirations, to enlarge the scope and meaning of his experience.

That pursuit of these ideals has objective reality and operational significance is apparent from an examination of the way societies are structured and the way they function. Before examining social structure in terms of behavioral institutions it should be observed that the principal differences between societies lie not so much in what ideals they pursue, but rather in the relative importance they assign to the ideals; that is, in the way they allocate their resources to pursuit of these ideals. There are also differences, of course, in what different societies consider to be the best means for pursuing these ideals.

Consider first the politico-economic ideal of plenty. Its pursuit may be broken down as follows:

(*a*) Provision of the instruments (goods and services) necessary for the attainment of objectives, accomplished through the production process. Industry (including agriculture) forms the social institution through which this production is accomplished.

(*b*) Distribution of the available instruments to environments in which they are accessible to individuals. Involved in this function are the various transportation and merchandising institution of society.

(*c*) Creation of awareness among individuals of the availability of these instruments. This function is performed by various institutions involved in the dissemination of information; for example, advertising, news services, and the educational process.

(*d*) Provision of individuals with the means for obtaining the instruments they desire; that is, providing them with purchasing power for the instruments themselves. This may be accomplished by the individual through the sale of his labor or other of his resources (e.g., lending money). Individuals who cannot provide for themselves (such as the young, old, and infirm) are provided for by such private institutions as the family, and certain charitable organizations, or through public welfare institutions; for example, unemployment, old age, and health insurance; and sanitariums, homes, and public hospitals.

(*e*) Protection of the availability of instruments once they are obtained (1) against expropriation from within the social group, by police and judicial institutions, and (2) from forces outside the social unit, by military institutions.

The social institutions enumerated are all directed toward increasing the availability of instruments for the satisfaction of desires, not toward the knowledge of how to use these instruments effectively or how to develop more effective instruments. These latter functions are involved with the scientific pursuit of knowledge or truth.

The function of *instruction* in the use of instruments, physical or conceptual, is performed in society by *educational* institutions. The development of more efficient means and instruments for the attainment of objectives is the function of *applied science,* and the provision of the knowledge necessary for performing this function is the task of *pure science.*

In order for an individual to attain all his objectives there are both personal and social requirements that must be satisfied by the objectives he seeks. On the personal side his objectives must be consistent (that is, logically compatible) if he is to attain all of them; he cannot want contradictory things. Objectives which are practically incompatible are not the same thing as objectives which are logically incompatible. Practical incompatibility (e.g., we cannot afford to buy two things we want, only one) arises out of scarcity of resources and would be removed in a "state of plenty." Objectives which are logically incompatible cannot be simultaneously attained under any conditions; the attainment of one implies the failure to attain the other.

The simultaneous pursuit of contradictory objectives can lead to mental and emotional illness. Hence, the institutions of society devoted to mental health are largely occupied with the removal and prevention of internal conflict, the promotion of peace of mind. Promotion of such a state has long been an important objective of many *religious* institutions and their *ethical* systems.

Conflict of objectives among individuals must be removed before each individual can attain whatever he desires. That is, every individual's objectives must be compatible with everyone else's. In the ideal, progress of any individual toward his objectives would imply progress for everyone else toward his objectives. This would be a state of peace, a completely cooperative society. Morality has had the task of moving society toward such a state. The promotion of *morality* in this sense has been an objective of many ethical and educational institutions.

Man's concept of the ideal state hardly involves a finite number of objectives which he would be able to satisfy with certainty. This would be much too static a utopia. Put another way, man has long recognized that there is a value in the striving as well as in the arriving. Therefore, his ideal involves continuous progress toward an approachable but unattainable state. This process of continuous striving must be energized in some way. Man has found two ways of doing so.

The continuous striving for an objective exhausts man both mentally and physically. In a state of exhaustion man cannot create new means and conceive new ends. It is necessary, therefore, periodically for him to have a change of pace in order to recreate the creator. This is the function of *recreation*. Complex social institutions exist in order to satisfy the recreational requirements of continuous progressive striving.

Recreation is a cathartic which allows man's emotional, mental, and physical forces to be regenerated. But he must also see the next steps and be stimulated to take them. Visions of as-yet-unattained possibilities must be provided if he is to strive continually to progress toward that which he has not yet attained, and he must be inspired. Inspiration has long been recognized as a function of religion, philosophy, and art. Through beauty, art creates what might be thought of as the creative mood. Through art, religion and philosophy paint a picture of what man and his world might yet be.

Thus recreation and inspiration are correlative activities which assure the dynamic properties of man's pursuit of ideals.

What we have done up to this point is argue that there is one desire common to all men, the desire to have the ability to satisfy their desires. This objective, then, is *power;* not power *over* but power *to*. Complete and perfect power in this sense is an ideal. It can be approached continuously but never attained. Pursuit of this ideal requires progress toward other ideal conditions which we have called plenty, truth, the good, and the beautiful. We have tried to make these politico-economic, scientific, ethical-moral, and aesthetic ideals operationally meaningful by indicating the social institutions devoted to their pursuit.

The four ideals and institutions interact strongly. Science, for example, contributes to the pursuit of the politico-economic ideal by developing more efficient means of producing and distributing goods and services, and better ways of protecting these against aggressors.

Science also contributes to the pursuit of the ethical ideal and has been doing so increasingly in the last few decades. It has developed procedures for determining what people desire, what the relative importance to them of these desires is, and how conflicts within and between individuals can be resolved. Science has contributed least to the pursuit of the aesthetic ideal. It has tried to study the art forms which produce an aesthetic response and to gain understanding of the nature of this response. Nevertheless, a science of aesthetics is more a possibility than a reality.

We can turn the coin and consider what might be called the politico-economic, ethical-moral, and aesthetic aspects of science. In doing so I believe we can cast light on some of the more important problems now confronting science as a social institution.

THE POLITICO-ECONOMIC IDEAL OF SCIENCE

To provide every scientist with the physical and conceptual instruments necessary for the efficient pursuit of knowledge.

Physical Instruments

Scientific progress has been closely associated with the development of physical instruments; for example, microscopes, telescopes, micrometers, thermometers, nuclear reactors, and analogue and digital computers. The complexity and hence the cost of equipment required by scientists have been continuously increasing. This has tended to restrict research more and more to large academic, governmental, industrial, and research organizations. The isolated research worker who is tucked away in a small institution or garret has become a rarity in all the sciences.

This centralization of research activities has tended to divide academic institutions into those which concentrate on teaching and those which concentrate on learning (that is, those in which research plays an important role). Such a separation can have serious consequences to teaching, some of which have been recognized and are receiving more and more attention. For example, largely due to the National Science Foundation, there has been a virtual rash of summer (and other types of special) programs for faculty members of smaller colleges and public schools at larger institutions so that they can keep up with recent scientific developments.

There has also been a concentration of industrial research and

hence innovation in large companies. In the United Kingdom associations of smaller companies have been formed to carry on research
which could not be supported by any of the members alone. Only a
relatively few such associations have appeared in the United States.
As a consequence, small businesses find it increasingly difficult to survive here.

To help remedy the academic problem, associations of universities
and colleges have been formed to use large common research facilities;
for example, the Association of Midwest Universities, which is formed
around the facilities of the Atomic Energy Commission's Argonne
National Laboratories. There is no reason why most of the smaller
universities and colleges cannot form such associations and cooperatively develop common facilities for research. Although these involve
increased travel and inconvenience for those participating, they are
certainly preferable to being reduced to a member of an audience
rather than acting as a participant in the scientific venture.

The observer of these developments cannot help but conclude that
in the future a great deal more cooperation between all types of research organizations will be required than there has been in the past.
If cooperative associations do not develop as rapidly as needed, there
will be an ever-deepening chasm worn between science and the liberal
and fine arts, and between teaching and learning. The undesirability
of such a chasm is too obvious to require discussion.

Conceptual Instruments

The availability of conceptual instruments, in contrast to physical
instruments, is more a matter of communication than of economics.
The distribution of conceptual instruments—making their availability
known and providing means for acquiring them—is the problem of
scientific communication. This is a problem which is consuming an
increasing amount of attention and resources. The volume of "material" produced by science has been increasing at a much greater
rate than the ability of the scientist to absorb it or even to obtain
access to it. In order to make progress along these lines a number of
fundamental problems must be more successfully solved than they
have been to date.

Even if a scientist were to devote himself exclusively to keeping
up with his field, he could not do so.* The difficulty is due in part

* For example, it is estimated that, if chemists spend all their reading time in
reading only journals, they could cover only a fraction of 1 per cent of all the
journal articles published [Operations Research Group (1958)].

to two conditions. First, too much time is required to determine what material is relevant; hence more effective filtration of information is required. Second, the information which is relevant is too frequently packaged in such a way that too much time is required to "open it up." There is too much useless redundancy in scientific literature and too many words which convey no information. The problem here is one of "data reduction" and "condensation."

The time required to locate and retrieve useful information has become excessive, and the problems involved in the physical storage and handling of information have become overwhelming. New instruments and means of retrieval are badly needed.

There is some hope in the fact that these problems are receiving increasing amounts of attention from scientists themselves. The recent establishment of the Office of Scientific Information Service in the National Science Foundation and the more recent enlargement of its responsibilities evidence the growing social concern with the problem. [See *Proceedings* (1958) and Brownson (1960).] The problem became a matter of public discussion for the first time when the deficiencies in the current scientific information system in the United States were blamed in part for the superiority of achievement of scientists in the USSR relative to the exploration of space.

Progress in handling these communication problems is not going to come easily. It is clear that good solutions will require scientists and research of high quality. In the past, research in this area has not attracted our most capable scientists, so that the large volume of verbal output contains very little by way of operationally useful results.

A prerequisite for the effective study of an activity, be it scientific communication or industrial production, is good record keeping. Whereas the research scientist is the first to complain about the record keeping of others whom he may study, he is generally the last to observe the inadequacy of the records he keeps on his own activity. Furthermore, he tends to feel that there is something degrading about keeping records.

To a large extent the poor state of scientific communication is due to very meagre knowledge we have of how scientists try to use the literature and the role that literature plays in their work. The scientist is no better at introspection on these matters than the industrial manager is on how he spends his time or uses the information supplied by his subordinates. It is only by an objective accounting of what one does that one can examine the efficiency with which it is done and seek better methods of performance.   [See Operations Research Group (1958 and 1960).]

THE ETHICAL-MORAL IDEAL OF SCIENCE

To remove conflict within scientists, among scientists, and between science and other social institutions.

Conflict within the Scientist

Many scientists desire complete freedom to select their research problems but want no responsibility for the social consequences of the results.   Although fewer and fewer scientists take such a position, many are nevertheless uncomfortable with the internal conflict between their scientific interests and their broader social interests.   This conflict has been most intensive, perhaps, in the increasing body of scientists working on the development of weapons.

It is an old truism that every right brings with it a corresponding responsibility.   Ultimately this is a responsibility to act in the interests of mankind.   The scientist cannot divest himself of this responsibility by claiming inability to judge what is or is not in the interests of mankind.   As an intelligent member of society he is at least as well equipped as most to make such judgments; as a scientist he may be better equipped to do so than is the nonscientist.

The parent who gives his child a loaded gun to play with is clearly responsible for any harm the child does to himself or others.   We say, "He should have known better."   By this we mean that he should have predicted the possibility of a harmful outcome.   Now suppose that the father finds a mysterious mechanism the nature of which is unknown to him.   If he were to give this to his child to play with, he would still be responsible for any harm that resulted.   Unless he is quite sure that an object (virtually) cannot cause harm in the hands of a child, he has no right to give it to him.

Society clearly recognizes the responsibility—if not the obligation —of at least one group of scientists with regard to determining who shall use their output and how; this group consists of medical researchers whose work yields the drug that only they can dispense.

The principle involved in these analogies is that a person who is aware of the possibility of harmful consequences of an instrument in the hands of another has the responsibility of seeing that the instrument does not fall into that person's hands. This principle applies to the scientist and his handling of the results of his research.

Now this principle may not seem to apply when the instrument involved can be used by the recipient to protect himself against unjustified attack by others; that is, when the instrument is more likely to help than to harm the recipient. In this case, then, the critical decision involves weighing the potential harm against the potential help, and this decision must be made by the scientist. To be sure, an individual scientist may not be able to predict the social consequences of releasing the results of his research, but other scientists may, and he is obliged to consult them.

It may seem that such responsibility restricts scientific freedom. This is not so. Since the Renaissance society has increased the scientist's freedom of choice only because it has been willing to assign responsibility for consequences to *him* rather than to representatives of other social institutions such as the Church.

Maturation of the child consists of developing the ability to accept freedom and responsibility and to dissolve internal conflicts which these create. Maturation of science is no different.

Conflict between Sciences

Competition between scientific disciplines for prestige and resource is familiar to all who are acquainted with the institutional aspects of science. Competition for prestige is reflected in the scientific snobbery to which we have already made reference. This snobbery preserves an imbalance in the development of disciplines.

Society reflects the attitudes that prevail within science and hence reinforces the scientific caste system. This fact is illustrated by an examination of the role of sociology in some of the world's dominant scientific powers. I quote from an article I wrote on this subject a decade ago [Ackoff (1952)]:

. . . In the words of the expert on Soviet science, Barrington Moore [1947], "Sociology as such does not exist as a separate discipline in the USSR. Its subject matter is investigated primarily by philosophers and economists." There are no separate departments of sociology in Soviet universities. One sociologist, in a sympathetic presentation of contemporary Soviet sociology, asserts that it "merges with history, economics, law, the work of central statistical offices of the government, the trade unions and the budget and planning authorities" [Kazakevich, 1944]. . . . Sergei Vavilov, President of the Soviet Academy of Sciences, refers to the sciences as "physics and mathematics, psychology, chemistry, biology, medicine, geology, geography" and "agricultural and the technical sciences" [1947]. The titles of the eight sections of the Soviet Academy reflect this omission (i.e., of the social sciences) conspicuously. They are:

1. Physics and mathematics
2. Chemistry
3. Geology and geography
4. Biology
5. Technical (applied)
6. History and philosophy
7. Economics and law
8. Literature and language

From such evidence as this it is clear that sociology and other social sciences, with the possible exception of economics, have lower status than the other sciences. This is reflected in the fact that the Stalin prize in science has not been awarded for work in sociology or related fields, at least not in recent years. . . . (pp. 48–49)

Recognition of the social sciences as a separate discipline in this country is almost complete, but, as in the USSR, these sciences have low status in the scientific community. Our National Academy of Science, like the Soviet Academy of Sciences, has no section devoted to the social sciences. . . .

In other Western nations, the situation is no better and is frequently worse. In England, for example, as in Russia, there are few universities with departments of sociology. There, too, history and economics absorb most social inquiry. Nobel prizes have yet to be awarded for work in the social sciences. (p. 51)

[In the United States] from 1938 to 1948 the estimated total national budget for social science increased from 34 million to 88 million dollars, that is, by a factor of 2.6. During the same period the corresponding budget for the natural sciences increased from 234 million to 1¼ billion dollars, that is, by a factor of 5.3, and hence better than twice as much as the social science budget. (p. 54)

During the last decade we have witnessed some reduction of scientific discrimination in the United States. The outstanding example of this is the recent creation of a division of the National Science Foundation for the behavioral sciences. Heated opposition by scientists prevented the creation of such a division at the time the Foundation was established almost a decade ago. We have also seen the establishment of a Center for the Advanced Study of the Behavioral Sciences. However, suppression of the newer disciplines in the scientific community still takes place. Many physical scientists refuse to recognize sociology and anthropology as sciences and at best consider psychology as an inferior science. These physical scientists obviously believe that progress of their disciplines is independent of progress in the behavioral sciences.

Arguments to the contrary are of two types. The first consists of taking the position that the kind of society that is necessary to provide an environment in which science can continue to exist, let alone thrive, can be maintained only if the behavioral sciences yield knowledge which can be used to attain world peace and democracy. Although I believe that this kind of argument carries a good deal of weight, I prefer a more direct and parochial one, one that asserts that accelerated progress of the physical sciences *requires* the development of the behavioral sciences.

When the role of the observer in the physical sciences was more important than it is today (i.e., before elaborate instrumentation), one could argue that errors due to the observer were always present and that their reduction depended on control of the observer. Such control, it could be argued, depended on increased knowledge that only the behavioral sciences could provide.

Such an argument was very fitting when Bessel discovered that the observer introduced significant error into astronomical observations through his variable response time to visual stimuli. (Bessel's discovery is frequently cited as the beginning of the science of psychology.) Although some reduction of this error was obtained by study of the human observer, the major improvements were achieved by the development of instruments which removed the need for the observer in the operations in which he made his largest contribution to error. This development and many other similar ones seem to indicate that efforts should be made to eliminate the observer through instrumentation rather than to improve him by use of knowledge obtained from the behavioral sciences. But, although the role of the human being in science as an observer may be eventually eliminated, his effect on the instruments which replace him cannot be eliminated.

For example, those who use electronic computers know that errors in computation are all too frequent and that most of them are caused by human operators. Those errors that are due to the "machine" are made generally because some production worker failed to perform his function properly. Somewhere along the line the human being is ever present as a source of error, and the reduction of this effect can be accelerated only by the development of the behavioral sciences.

Moreover, knowledge of the human being and his social envelop is necessary to develop better instruments with which to replace him. For example, research is now going on to replace people as transcribers of information in one form to another that is more suitable for computer input. This involves mechanical reading; that is, character recognition. To develop such machines it has been necessary to learn a great deal more about such recognition by human beings than was previously available.

Perhaps above all we must remember that people are still superior to machines in many of the functions required for the conduct of science, but even where superior they still bring with them that very human quality: fallibility.

Many scientists are discovering that sorties into disciplines other than their own can yield rich rewards. Tools, techniques, and methods developed in one field frequently have applications in others. For example, most of the tools of modern statistical analysis were developed in the biological and behavioral sciences. The theory of sampling was developed in the context of social surveys. Factor, latent attribute, and scalogram analyses, developed in psychology, are finding increasing use in the physical sciences.

Failure to exploit the tools, techniques, methods, and knowledge developed in disciplines other than one's own retards scientific progress. Breaking down the disciplinary barriers, the construction of which seems to have occupied much scientific effort in the past, may well be one of the most important accomplishments of the next generation of scientists. In science, as in society, peace and good will are urgently needed.

Conflict between Science and Other Social Institutions

The social prestige of science has been increasing continuously since the Renaissance. This has been true particularly in the more developed countries, in which the range of problems and questions over which science is considered to be the ultimate authority has been expanding. The "physical" suppression of scientists by religious and political institutions, which characterized science's early history, is virtually removed. There is very little that scientists are warned away from today; and, where transgressions do occur, the consequences to the scientists involved are less damaging than they once were. Today's science is primarily "influenced" by other institutions in the way funds are allocated to different types of research.

Currently there may be more danger in the exaltation of science than in its suppression. Its authority is so widely recognized that manufacturers who are anxious to sell their goods have increasingly introduced *pseudo*-scientific support for the superiority of their products. They have helped start the impression that science can be used to prove anything and that its services are available for such purposes if the proper price is paid. If this trend were to continue, it could well undermine the public's confidence in science.

Science is increasingly being drawn into top-level management decision making in public and private institutions. Such developments as operations research, management science, and systems analysis and engineering have brought science into the domain of important social and economic problem solving. Those who use these services are not always aware of the limitations of current technology. Consequently they frequently use the aid of scientists even where the latter have little more to contribute than judgment. Because most scientists are reasonably intelligent and well educated, their judgment is often sought and treated as are their research skills. Herein lies a danger. It lies not in the scientist's use of his judgment but in his failure to emphasize the difference in results and recommendations based on his research and those based on his judgment. Since his judgment is more likely to be in error than is his research, what error of his judgment is exposed reflects on science, unless the different grounds for his results are kept distinct in the user's mind.

Because of the extensive use of science in managerial problems (in the government, military, and industry) there is a growing fear on the part of managers that science is trying to take over their function. Nothing could be further from the truth.

It is true that a large number of repetitive and routine problems of management can be reduced by scientists to decision rules which can be applied by clerks or computers. This does relieve management of some problems, but it does not put them into the hands of the scientist; it relegates them to less skilled personnel or computers.

This process frees management to devote more of its time to broader and more important problems, particularly long-range planning problems which are generally seriously neglected. Here too science has been making an increasing contribution, and this, perhaps more than anything else, has led to the impression that science will take over management. But this fear is misplaced for two reasons.

First, most complex management problems cannot yet be completely analyzed by science; not all the factors can be handled quantitatively. In almost all broad management problems the solutions offered by science are conditional, and the conditions that pertain must be established by managerial judgment based on long experience with the factors involved.

Second, the fear assumes that the skills and knowledge required of management are fixed and stable, and this is false. The manager of today is much better trained in technical matters than was the manager of yesterday. His knowledge of science and mathematics has expanded. It will continue to do so. The manager of tomorrow will be quite different from the manager of today. He will know at least as much of science and mathematics as did the scientist of yesterday. A major movement has already started in management education to better equip future managers in the skills and knowledge that characterize the scientist. Hence in the domain of management, managers will take over science, rather than scientists take over management. These educational developments will bring management and science closer together than they are now and will increase their collaboration and reduce the mutual distrust which still characterizes many of their associations.

THE AESTHETIC IDEAL OF SCIENCE

> *To enlarge the range and scope of questions and problems to which science can be applied.*

Scientific progress has been defined not only in terms of the increased efficiency of research but also in terms of the scope of scientifically derived knowledge. In each age we can witness arguments against the possibility of applying science to classes of problems which succeeding ages study scientifically as a routine matter. Arguments once prevailed against a science of psychology. The argument still rages on the possibility of social science and a science of values.

History is "on the side of" an expanding domain for science. One by one the curtains separating science from various aspects of reality have been opened. In the ideal one might suspect that all problems will be susceptible to scientific study. At least there is no good reason to suppose a limit to the expansion of the domain of problems to which science can be applied.

This continuous expansion of the scope of science requires both recreational and inspirational activities on the part of scientists. In so far as scientists are human, and they are to a considerable extent, they resort to normal recreational and inspirational activities. They play baseball and listen to classical music, watch television, and expose themselves to comic strips and great paintings. But in addition to these there is a "private" type of recreation and inspiration which is unique to science.

Puzzles and games requiring mental exercise are forms of recreation enjoyed by many besides scientists, but they are forms created in the main by scientists primarily for their own amusement. It is commonplace in research or academic institutions, for example, to find scientists relaxing over new games or variations of existing games which they have invented. Scientists have created many variations of chess which fit well into lunch hours, and they have developed unique ways of gambling to determine who will pay for the refreshments during a coffee break. In general these games are not ones of pure chance but ones in which strategy is relevant and intelligence has a pay-off.

Humor plays as important a recreational role in science as it does in society. For example, Lewis Carroll (Charles Dodgson), who contributed so much to children's literature, also made significant contributions to scientific humor. Articles along these lines appear regularly in professional scientific journals. Three recent efforts come to my mind: an article describing how to become a project leader [Lynn (1956)], a mock research report of a study of the optimal size of a committee [Olds (1946)], and the story of Little Red Riding Hood told in symbolic logic [Rinehart (1959)].

In science itself there are many sources of inspiration. This is manifested, for example, in the response to a particularly elegant proof or argument by the observation, "It is beautiful." The application of the word *beauty* to demonstrations in science is not a loose usage; it reflects the recognition of some of the same properties present in great art. A proof, for example, may have a structure in which beauty is captured. Scientists have long admired the great literary stylists in science. Great teachers of science have inspired their students by inducing in them responses to science itself much like the response we associate with works of art. Just as we can find beauty in natural objects or in commonplace ones that are man-made, we can find beauty in the work of scientists.

CONCLUSION

As we review the history of mankind, it is clear that there has been great progress made relative to economic and scientific ideals. Such progress is not as apparent relative to ethical, moral, and aesthetic ideals. Continuous improvement of the world's standard of living and of the domain of knowledge will continue if civilization survives. Its survival, however, depends critically on ethical and moral progress. The scientist, faced with this situation, cannot just shrug his shoulders and wish for the best. He has a responsibility toward developing a science of ethics and morality; that is, a controlled method of solving ethical and moral problems. To be sure, responsibility for future morality is not the scientist's alone, but perhaps from him can come leadership in the substitution of brain for brawn in settling conflicts between men and between their societies.

BIBLIOGRAPHY

Ackoff, R. L., "Varieties of Unification," *Philosophy of Sciences,* **13** (1946), 287–300.

———, "On a Science of Ethics," *Philosophical and Phenomenological Research,* **9** (1949), 663–672.

———, "Scientific Method and Social Science: East and West," in *Soviet Science,* ed. by R. C. Christman. Washington: American Association for the Advancement of Science, 1952, pp. 48–56.

Brownson, H. L., "Research on Handling Scientific Information," *Science,* **132** 1961), 1922–1931.

Cherry, Colin, *On Human Communication.* New York: John Wiley and Sons, 1957.

Churchman, C. W., and R. L. Ackoff, *Methods of Inquiry.* St. Louis: Educational Publishers, 1950.

Kazakevich, V. D., "Social Sciences in the Soviet Union," *American Sociological Review,* **9** (1944), 312–318.

Lynn, Harvey, Jr., "How to Be a Project Leader—Nine Helpful Hints," *Operations Research,* **4** (1956), 484–488.

Moore, Barrington, Jr., "Recent Developments in the Social Sciences in the Soviet Union," *American Sociological Review,* **12** (1947), 349–351.

Olds, B. S., "On the Mathematics of Committees, Boards and Panels," *Scientific Monthly,* **63** (1946), 484–488.

Operations Research Group, *An Operations Research Study of the Scientific Activity of Chemists.* Cleveland: Case Institute of Technology, November 1958.

———, *An Operations Research Study of the Dissemination and Use of Recorded Scientific Information.* Cleveland: Case Institute of Technology, December 1960.

Proceedings of the International Conference on Scientific Information. Washington: National Science Foundation, 1958.

Rinehart, R. F., "The Modern Approach to LR^2H," *Mathematics Magazine,* **32** (1959), 151–152.

Singer, E. A., Jr., *On the Contented Life.* New York: Henry Holt and Co., 1923.

———, *In Search of a Way of Life.* New York: Columbia University Press, 1948.

Vavilov, S., "Science for the People," *Soviet Russia Today* (September 1947), p. 19.

DERIVATION
OF $\underset{d(y)}{\text{Min}}\ M\{d(y)\}$,
EQUATION (16) IN CHAPTER 8*

To simplify the discussion, without reducing its generality, we will assume that $p(Y)$ is a rectangular distribution between a and b; that is, that any value of Y, where $a \leq Y \leq b$ and $a \neq 0$, is equally likely. This assumption is not necessary for the argument which follows; the argument holds for any other form of $p(Y)$.

In order to obtain the minimizing function $d(y)$, which depends on y alone, we first approximate equation (15) in Chapter 8 by a finite sum. We introduce equidistant mesh points with distances h along the (y, Y)-axis in such a way that

$$a - K = ch$$
$$a = kh$$
$$b = mh$$
$$b + K = nh$$

(1)

as shown in Figure I.1. We further designate the midpoints of intervals of length h by

$$y_i = (i - \tfrac{1}{2})h, \quad i = c + 1, \cdots, n \tag{2}$$

$$Y_j = (j - \tfrac{1}{2})h, \quad j = k + 1, \cdots, m. \tag{3}$$

Writing (15) as a sum of integrations over mesh intervals, we obtain

---

* This derivation is the work of Dr. Fred Hanssmann.

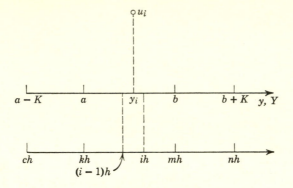

FIGURE I.1.

$$M\{d(y)\} = \sum_{i=c+1}^{n} \sum_{j=k+1}^{m} \int_{(i-1)h}^{ih} \int_{(j-1)h}^{jh} C\{d(y), Y\}p(y\,|\,Y)\,dy\,dY \quad (4)$$

$$= \sum_{i} \sum_{j} G_{ij}$$

with an obvious definition of the abbreviations G_{ij}. Next, we approximate each contribution G_{ij} by the product of the area of the square between the mesh points involved, and the value of the function under the integral taken at the center of the square:

$$G_{ij} \approx h^2 C\{d(y_i), Y_j\}p(y_i\,|\,Y_j). \quad (5)$$

Since $d(y)$ is an unknown function, we introduce the unknown ordinates

$$u_i = d(y_i), \quad i = c + 1, \cdots, n. \quad (6)$$

The function $d(y)$ will be linearly approximated between neighboring points (y_i, u_i); consequently, $d(y)$ will be considered known when the ordinates u_i at all mesh points y_i have been determined. By (5) and (6) we obtain the following approximation of the double integral (4):

$$M\{d(y)\} \approx h^2 \sum_{i=c+1}^{n} \sum_{j=k+1}^{m} C(u_i, Y_j)p(y_i\,|\,Y_j). \quad (7)$$

If we introduce the abbreviation

$$F_i(u_i) = \sum_{j=k+1}^{m} C(u_i, Y_j)p(y_i\,|\,Y_j) \quad (8)$$

or, by (2) and (3),

$$F_i(u_i) = \sum_{j=k+1}^{M} C(u_i, [j - \tfrac{1}{2}]h)p([i - \tfrac{1}{2}]h, [j - \tfrac{1}{2}]h), \quad i = c + 1, \cdots, n$$

(9)

approximation (7) takes the form

$$M\{d(y)\} \approx h^2 \sum_{i=c+1}^{n} F_i(u_i),$$

(10)

where the F_i are known functions. Now (10) is minimized by minimizing each contribution $F_i(u_i)$ individually with respect to u_i. Setting $F_i'(u_i) = 0$ and defining

$$C'(X, Y) = \frac{\partial}{\partial X} C(X, Y),$$

(11)

we obtain the following equation for the minimizing value u_i [from (8)]:

$$\sum_{j=k+1}^{m} C'(u_i, Y_j)p(y_i | Y_j) = 0, \quad i = c + 1, \cdots, n.$$

(12)

The problem has been reduced to the solution of $n - c$ equations each of which contains only one unknown. It can normally be solved by hand. Formula (10) may be used to evaluate the area of reduction associated with the solutions of (12). If we are interested in the expected cost for a given value, Y_j, we can compute it by the approximate formula

$$H(Y_j) = \sum_{i=c+1}^{n} C(u_i, Y_j)p(y_i | Y_j), \quad j = k + 1, \cdots, m.$$

(13)

ANALYTICAL DERIVATION OF DECISION FUNCTIONS FOR A SIMPLE INVENTORY MODEL*

Consider the simple inventory model

$$C(X, Y) = XY + \frac{1}{X} \tag{1}$$

where the estimate y of Y has a rectangular distribution with mean Y and range $2K$. In order to find the optimal bias, we must minimize the following integral:

$$\int_{Y-K}^{Y+K} f(y + \beta, Y) \, dy. \tag{2}$$

Differentiating this expression with respect to β and setting the derivative equal to zero, we obtain

$$f[Y + K + \beta, Y] = f[Y - K + \beta, Y]. \tag{3}$$

With our inventory model

$$f(y + \beta, Y) = \frac{Y}{\sqrt{y + \beta}} + \sqrt{y + \beta}. \tag{4}$$

Therefore, (3) becomes

$$\frac{Y}{\sqrt{Y + K + \beta}} + \sqrt{Y + K + \beta} = \frac{Y}{\sqrt{Y - K + \beta}}$$

$$+ \sqrt{Y - K + \beta} \tag{5}$$

* These derivations are the work of Drs. Shiv K. Gupta and Fred Hanssmann.

$$Y \left[\frac{\sqrt{Y - K + \beta} - \sqrt{Y + K + \beta}}{\sqrt{(Y + \beta)^2 - K^2}} \right] = \sqrt{Y - K + \beta}$$

$$- Y\sqrt{Y + K + \beta}$$

$$\frac{Y}{\sqrt{(Y + \beta)^2 - K^2}} = 1$$

$$Y^2 = (Y + \beta)^2 - K^2$$

$$\sqrt{Y^2 + K^2} = Y + \beta$$

and finally,

$$\beta = \sqrt{Y^2 + K^2} - Y. \tag{6}$$

Considerably more effort goes into finding analytic expressions for the calculus of variation method.   For our inventory problem

$$C(\mu_i, Y_j) = \mu_i Y_j + \frac{1}{\mu_i} \tag{7}$$

$$C(\mu_i, Y_j) p(y_i, Y_j) = \left[\mu_i Y_j + \frac{1}{\mu_i} \right] p(y_i, Y_j).$$

Summing over the j's:

$$F_i(\mu_i) = \mu_i \sum_j Y_j p(y_i, Y_j) + \frac{1}{\mu_i} \sum_j p(y_i, Y_j). \tag{8}$$

For optimal μ_i,

$$\Sigma_j Y_j p(y_i, Y_j) - \frac{1}{\hat{\mu}_i{}^2} \Sigma_j p(y_i, Y_j) = 0$$

$$\mu_i = \sqrt{\frac{\displaystyle\sum_{j=k+1}^{m} p(y_i, Y_j)}{\displaystyle\sum_{j=k+1}^{m} Y_j p(y_i, Y_j)}}. \tag{9}$$

Next we find the values of $\Sigma_j p(y_i, Y_j)$ and $\Sigma_j Y_j p(y_i, Y_j)$.

By examining the sample problem matrix of Table II.1, the following relationships become clear:

For $i = 1, \cdots, 2k + 1$:

$$\Sigma_j p(y_i, Y_j) = \frac{i}{(2k + 1)(m - k)h^2}. \tag{10}$$

For $i = 2k + 1, \cdots, m - k$:

$$\Sigma_j p(y_i, Y_j) = \frac{2k + 1}{(2k + 1)(m - k)h^2}. \tag{11}$$

For $i = m - k, \cdots, h$:

$$\Sigma_j p(y_i, Y_j) = \frac{n - i + 1}{(2k + 1)(m - k)h^2}. \tag{12}$$

With a rectangular distribution of y_i, we know that

$$\sum_{j=k+1}^{m} Y_j p(y_i, Y_j) = \sum_{\substack{j=k+1 \\ |i-j| \leq k}}^{m} (j - \tfrac{1}{2})h \; \frac{1}{(2k + 1)(m - k)h^2}. \tag{13}$$

Let

$$(2k + 1)(m - k) \sum_{j=k+1}^{m} Y_j p(y_i, Y_j) = D_i. \tag{14}$$

Then

$$D_1 = k + \tfrac{1}{2}, \tag{15}$$

and we can establish the following recursive relationship:

For $i = 1, \cdots, 2k + 1$:

$$D_i = D_{i-1} + (i + k - \tfrac{1}{2}). \tag{16}$$

Solving,

$$D_i = k + \tfrac{1}{2} + (i - 1)(k - \tfrac{1}{2}) + \sum_{j=2}^{i} j$$

$$= (k + \tfrac{1}{2}) + (i - 1)(k - \tfrac{1}{2}) + \frac{i(i + 1)}{2} \tag{17}$$

$$= i\left(k + \frac{1}{2} + \frac{i}{2} + \frac{1}{2} - 1\right) = i\left(k + \frac{i}{2}\right).$$

Substituting into (9),

$$\mu_i = \sqrt{\frac{i/(2k + 1)(m - k)h^2}{i\left(k + \dfrac{i}{2}\right)/(2k + 1)(m - k)h}}.$$

Or, for $i = 1, \cdots, 2k + 1$:

$$\mu_i = \sqrt{\frac{1}{h\left(k + \dfrac{i}{2}\right)}}. \tag{18}$$

TABLE II.1. EXAMPLE

$$h = 1, K = 3, F = 14; k = 3, m = 17, n = 20$$

$$j =$$

	$i =$	4	5	6	7	8	9	10	11	12	13	14	15	16	17	(1) *	(2) †
	1	1														1	3.5
	2	1	1													2	8
	3	1	1	1												3	13.5
	4	1	1	1	1											4	20
	5	1	1	1	1	1										5	27.5
	6	1	1	1	1	1	1									6	36
$2k + 1$	7	1	1	1	1	1	1	1								7	45.5
	8		1	1	1	1	1	1	1							7	52.5
	9			1	1	1	1	1	1	1						7	59.5
	10				1	1	1	1	1	1	1					7	66.5
	11					1	1	1	1	1	1	1				7	73.5
	12						1	1	1	1	1	1	1			7	80.5
	13							1	1	1	1	1	1	1		7	87.5
$m - k$	14								1	1	1	1	1	1	1	7	94.5
	15									1	1	1	1	1	1	6	84
	16										1	1	1	1	1	5	72.5
	17											1	1	1	1	4	60
	18												1	1	1	3	46.5
	19													1	1	2	32
	20														1	1	16.5

$$Y_j = (j - \tfrac{1}{2})h$$

* $(1) = (2k + 1)(m - k)h^2 \sum_j p(y_i, Y_j).$

† $(2) = (2k + 1)(m - k)h^2 \sum_j Y_j p(y_i, Y_j).$

To find the recursion relationship for i from $2k + 1$ to $m - k$ we note:

$$D_{2k+1} = (2k + 1)\left(k + \frac{2k + 1}{2}\right)$$

$$= 2k^2 + 2k^2 + k + k + k + \tfrac{1}{2}$$

$$= 4k^2 + 3k + \tfrac{1}{2}. \tag{19}$$

Then, for $i = 2k + 1, \cdots, m - k$:

$$D_i = D_{2k+1} + [i - (2k + 1)](2k + 1)$$

$$= 4k^2 + 3k + \tfrac{1}{2} + 2ik - 4k^2 - 2k + i - 2k - 1$$

$$= i(2k + 1) - (k + \tfrac{1}{2}). \tag{20}$$

Therefore

$$\mu_i = \sqrt{\frac{(2k + 1)/(2k + 1)(m - k)h^2}{[i(2k + 1) - (k + \tfrac{1}{2})]/(2k + 1)(m - k)h}}.$$

Or, for $i = 2k + 1, \cdots, m - k$:

$$\mu_i = \sqrt{\frac{1}{h(i - \tfrac{1}{2})}}. \tag{21}$$

To find D_i for i from $m - k$ to μ, we start with D_n and work backwards:

$$D_n = n - k - \tfrac{1}{2}. \tag{22}$$

For $i = m - k, \cdots, n$:

$$D_i = D_{i+1} + i - k - \tfrac{1}{2} \tag{23}$$

$$\therefore D_i = n - k - \tfrac{1}{2} - (n - i)(k + \tfrac{1}{2}) + \sum_{j=i}^{n-1} j$$

$$= n - k - \tfrac{1}{2} - (n - i)(k + \tfrac{1}{2})$$

$$+ \frac{(n - 1 - i + 1)(n - 1 + i - 1 + 1)}{2}$$

$$= n - k - \tfrac{1}{2} - nk + ik - \frac{n}{2} + \frac{i}{2} + \frac{n^2 + ni - n - ni - i^2 + i}{2}$$

$$= \tfrac{1}{2}[n^2 - i^2 + 2i + 2ik - 2nk - 2k - 1]$$

$$= \tfrac{1}{2}[(n + i)(n - i) + 2i - 1 - 2k(n - i + 1)]$$

$$= \tfrac{1}{2}[(n + i)(n - i + 1) - (n + i) + 2i - 1 - 2k(n - i + 1)]$$

$$= \tfrac{1}{2}[(n + i)(n - i + 1) - (n - i + 1) - 2k(n - i + 1)]. \tag{24}$$

Therefore

$$\mu_i = \sqrt{\frac{2(n - i + 1)/(2k + 1)(m - k)h^2}{(n - i + 1)(n + i - 1 - 2k)/(2k + 1)(m - k)h}}$$

$$= \sqrt{\frac{2}{h(n + i - 2k - 1)}}.$$

Or, for $i = m - k, \cdots, n$:

$$\mu_i = \sqrt{\frac{2}{h(m - k + i - 1)}}. \tag{25}$$

Asymptotic Values of μ as $h \to 0$

Since $y_i = (i - \frac{1}{2})h$, then

$$i = \frac{y_i}{h} + \frac{1}{2}. \tag{26}$$

Now we solve for the asymptotic values of μ_i as h goes to zero by being continually halved.

For $i = 1, \cdots, 2k + 1$:

$$\mu_i = \sqrt{\frac{1}{h\left(k + \dfrac{i}{2}\right)}} = \sqrt{\frac{1}{h\left(\dfrac{K}{h} + \dfrac{y_i}{2h} + \dfrac{1}{4}\right)}} = \sqrt{\frac{1}{K + \dfrac{y_i}{2} + \dfrac{h}{4}}}.$$

Then

$$\mu_i = \sqrt{\frac{1}{K + \dfrac{y_i}{2}}}. \tag{27}$$
$$\scriptstyle h \to 0$$

For $i = 2k + 1, \cdots, m - k$:

$$\mu_i = \sqrt{\frac{1}{h(i - \frac{1}{2})}} = \sqrt{\frac{1}{h\left(\dfrac{y_i}{h} + \dfrac{1}{2}\right)}}.$$

Then

$$\mu_i \underset{h \to 0}{=} \sqrt{\frac{1}{y_i}}. \tag{28}$$

For $i = m - k, \cdots, n$:

$$\mu_i = \sqrt{\frac{2}{h(m - k + i - 1)}} = \sqrt{\frac{2}{h\left(\dfrac{F + K}{h} + \dfrac{1}{2} - \dfrac{K}{h} - \dfrac{1}{2} + \dfrac{y_i}{h} + \dfrac{1}{2}\right)}}.$$

Then

$$\mu_i \underset{h \to 0}{=} \sqrt{\frac{2}{F + y_i}}. \tag{29}$$

The ranges of y as $h \to 0$ are as follows:

For $i = 2k + 1$, $y_i = 2kh + \dfrac{h}{2}$

as $h \to 0$, $y = 2kh = 2K$. $\tag{30}$

For $i = m - k$, $y_i = mh - kh - \dfrac{h}{2}$

as $h \to 0$, $y = mh - kh = F + K - K = F$. $\tag{31}$

Therefore, summarizing,

$$0 \le y \le 2K; \quad \mu = \sqrt{\frac{1}{K + (y/2)}} \tag{32}$$

$$2K \le y \le F; \quad \mu = \sqrt{\frac{1}{y}} \tag{33}$$

$$F \le y \le L; \quad \mu = \sqrt{\frac{2}{F + y}}. \tag{34}$$

AUTHOR INDEX

SUBJECT INDEX